The Road to Black Ned's Forge

EARLY AMERICAN HISTORIES

Douglas Bradburn, John C. Coombs, and S. Max Edelson, Editors

The
Road to
Black
Ned's
Forge

*A Story of Race, Sex, and Trade
on the Colonial American Frontier*

Turk McCleskey

University of Virginia Press Charlottesville and London

University of Virginia Press
© 2014 by the Rector and Visitors of the University of Virginia
All rights reserved
Printed in the United States of America on acid-free paper

First published 2014

9 8 7 6 5 4 3 2 1

LIBRARY OF CONGRESS CATALOGING-IN-PUBLICATION DATA

McCleskey, Turk, 1953–
    The road to Black Ned's forge : a story of race, sex, and trade on the colonial
American frontier / Turk McCleskey.
        pages   cm. — (Early American histories)
    Includes bibliographical references and index.
    ISBN 978-0-8139-3582-9 (cloth : alk. paper) — ISBN 978-0-8139-3583-6 (e-book)
    1. Tarr, Edward, approximately 1711– 2. Shute family. 3. Freedmen—Virginia—
Augusta County—History—18th century. 4. Landowners—Virginia—Augusta
County—History—18th century. 5. Frontier and pioneer life—Virginia—Augusta
County. 6. Augusta County (Va.)—Race relations—History—18th century.
7. Augusta County (Va.)—Commerce—History—18th century. I. Title.
F232.A9M44 2014
305.8009755′916—dc23

                                                                                2013043815

Dedicated to my parents,
Clifton and Jo McCleskey,
  and
  to the memory of my Marine Corps brother,
  Charles Lewis "Dragon Chuck" Armstrong,
  1948–2011

Contents

Illustrations

Figures

Maps

Appendix: Tables

Opportunism and Mobility in Eastern North America
1680–1780

In the autumn of 1761, a hamlet surrounding Augusta County's courthouse officially became Staunton, the westernmost town in colonial Virginia. By contemporary standards, it was a diminutive village in a vast frontier county, and residents faced a long road to any substantial town: 150 miles to Virginia's capital in Williamsburg, 300 miles to Pennsylvania's capital in Philadelphia, over 400 miles to South Carolina's capital in Charleston. For Staunton resident Edward Tarr, however, Philadelphia and Charleston loomed claustrophobically close that fall.

On 6 October, Edward Tarr and a North Carolina white man named Hugh Montgomery stood before two justices of the peace in Staunton. Montgomery complained that he had "purchased a Negro Man Named Edward Tarr" from one Joseph Shute of Charleston, son of the late Thomas Shute, "to whom the said Edward belonged to in the Province of Pensylvania." Tarr denied Montgomery's ownership claim, asserting instead that he had bought himself from Thomas Shute's executor and grandson, William Davis of Philadelphia.

As the magistrates weighed Montgomery's complaint, they reviewed more than a set of documents; they also explicitly considered their first-hand knowledge of Tarr's larger story. Tarr, they noted, "has resided in this County for Ten years last past and is a Freeholder."[1] The magistrates hesitated to enslave someone they had known for a decade as a free and economically independent man.

Throughout colonial Virginia, justices of the peace who considered private complaints outside of a county court session normally left their decisions unreported. Thus, to have a record of Tarr's confrontation with Montgomery is unusual, and for modern historians, the interpretation of that rare type of document poses some contextual challenges. Foremost is the task of understanding how the parties evaluated each other: the narratives on which Tarr's and Montgomery's contemporaries relied for daily orientation—the hundreds if not thousands of individual stories with which they routinely characterized and comprehended each other—today are difficult even to sketch. Additionally, the scarcity of records about out-of-court resolutions of disputes over any sort of property, much less property in people, complicates comparisons of these participants to their contemporaries in other locales. And finally, the careers of everyone involved—Tarr, Montgomery, the magistrates, and the Shutes—transcended colonial boundaries. No single legal framework, unique religion, specialized economy, or common social values applied to all of them simultaneously or to any one of them over his whole lifetime. If anything, their most distinctive shared attribute was their mobility, their repeated traverses of long distances by land or sea.

Therein lies a second challenge. It can be puzzling to track kinetically mobile individuals from one township or county to the next, much less from one of England's North American colonies to another. Part of that difficulty stems from variations in political organization and recordkeeping, but also occasionally individuals ricocheted unpredictably to new careers or places. The study of persons in motion requires observations of change over long periods of time, analyses of patterns that shifted from one generation to the next and the next—or from one socioeconomic context to its successors. Ideally, such observations should draw on an unbroken string of documents, but each additional year in a lengthening study-period increases the likelihood that war, fire, water, rodents, larceny, incompetence, or willful stupidity have prevailed over ink and paper.

The motives and effects of geographic mobility were particularly significant for yeoman families such as that of Thomas Shute, Edward Tarr's last master. Eighteenth-century English satirists like Tobias Smollett routinely depicted geographic mobility as a function of ravenous opportunism endemic to every social class. Characters in Smollett's *The Adventures of Roderick Random,* for example, predatorily prowled the English countryside, London, the European continent, and the high seas in search of new victims or to escape prosecution by previous conquests. Such odysseys appear to have been more than a novelist's device: for many colonial Americans, they amounted to a lifestyle.

Mobility followed momentous choices; that, at least, is the lesson of Thomas Shute and his family. Shute arrived in Pennsylvania around 1680 as a teenager and, despite his servile origins, in time built an enviable yeoman prosperity. From what became a well-appointed home near the falls of the Schuylkill River, a few miles north of Philadelphia, Shute orchestrated far-flung investments in farms, mills, mines, quarries, Philadelphia real estate, and shipping. For decades he prospered, and he owed much of that material success to the labor of his seven children. They in turn seem to have owed something to him: almost all were in varying combinations irreligious, drunken, coercive, philandering, deceitful, conniving, derisive of civil authority, or financially irresponsible.

Probably Thomas Shute did not set out to incubate such a brood. He did, however, act deliberately and consistently in his own economic interest: the family that he and two wives produced eventually comprised the core of a well-integrated set of yeoman enterprises, securing for Shute a prosperous old age. Most of his children saw it in their economic interests to stay close to him in Pennsylvania and vie for portions of his estate. Only the youngest son, Joseph, went abroad.

Joseph Shute apprenticed as a mariner and in 1731 sailed to Charleston, South Carolina, to serve as his father's factor for mundane Pennsylvania products such as bread and beer. Joseph's interests and investments shifted, however, and he ascended through the ranks of those Charleston merchants specializing in the luxurious European goods consumed by South Carolina's planter elite. Eventually he overreached financially and collapsed in bankruptcy. Derisive Charlestonians slapped an ironic label on an island he once owned in their harbor: Shute's Folly.

William Davis, the son of Thomas Shute's eldest daughter, remained in the patriarch's orbit until Shute died. Davis began his career in the ironworks of southeastern Pennsylvania in the mid-1730s, and in time became a business manager at a furnace. His grandfather acknowledged Davis's commercial acumen by naming him executor of Shute's estate in 1748. In the next decade, Davis entered the carting business, first for ironworks, then for soldiers engaged in frontier wars. He followed the latter customers to Virginia's New River Valley and beyond, though he remained a nominal resident of Philadelphia to the end of his life. When conflict abated in the 1760s, Davis became a skinner, hauling leather and fur from the Virginia frontier to Philadelphia.

The last Shute dependent to range far afield was the slave Ned, who bought himself from Thomas Shute's estate. Taking the name Edward Tarr, he moved to Virginia, where a 1754 real estate purchase in Augusta County made him the first black landowner west of the Blue Ridge. Tarr brought to the frontier his blacksmithing trade, a fluency in German, and a white wife with whom he lived conspicuously on the county's busiest road. Additionally, he helped found the still-extant Timber Ridge Presbyterian congregation a few miles north of modern-day Lexington, Virginia. While Tarr and his accomplishments were remarkable racially for his day, his experiences as an immigrant also demonstrated typical challenges, opportunities, strategies, and limitations for people moving out of economic orbits around their parents and into new borderland settlements. His case illuminates interracial dynamics in Virginia's late colonial frontier and would have done so even if Joseph Shute had not sold him to Hugh Montgomery in 1761. But Tarr was not simply acted upon by those forces; his romantic decisions may have influenced the context of race relations in the Valley of Virginia for the rest of the age of slavery. Edward Tarr's saga ended in 1780, a century after Thomas Shute arrived in Pennsylvania.

The narratives of Thomas Shute and two generations of his dependents arc over the terrain of eastern North America, singular trajectories within a larger swarm of thousands of journeys and stories. Collectively, traces of these narratives form two crescents anchored in Pennsylvania and South Carolina. By land, the western crescent stretches from Philadelphia past Lancaster Town into the Great Valley, crossing Maryland into Virginia, ascending the Shenandoah River, fording the James River headwaters, threading through the Blue Ridge at the Roanoke River gap, and rolling over the Carolina piedmont to Charleston. By sea, the eastern crescent descends from Delaware Bay, traverses brown inshore waters between an unforgiving coast and a north-flowing blue Gulf Stream, and bumps over a treacherous sandbar-strewn entrance to Charleston harbor.

Modern maritime scholars have argued convincingly for an historical unity of seafarers such as those who repeatedly plied the eastern crescent. To seamen, mobility defined community. By land, a comparable mobility characterized the western crescent, through which Indians, Europeans, and Africans; carters, farmers, and drovers; peddlers, preachers, and fugitives all traveled routinely. As by sea, so too by land: disparate frontier travelers and frontier residents represented collectively a coherent whole.

Partly by chance and partly by design, intricate social joinery connected frontier inhabitants to each other with an immediacy that transcended distance. Edward Tarr settled among neighbors at Timber Ridge who defined themselves as a Presbyterian congregation some ten miles long and five miles wide. The same neighbors constituted part of a militia company covering roughly twice that area, and the company in turn was one of at least twenty-three in a county some 250 miles long.

For the quarter century before Augusta County's first subdivision, its far-flung settlers consistently acted as if remote events immediately affected them. Edward Tarr's life changed directions as a consequence of Indian raids that began 160 miles from Tarr's house. It seems a great distance, but Tarr's neighbors promptly reacted with an urgency that could hardly have been more feverish if they had heard the first gunshots. Their responses reveal the scale of their mental map: for all its sprawling size, the western crescent had a unified consciousness.

To outsiders, however, Virginia's far western settlements appeared anything but coherent: travelers repeatedly characterized the region as thinly populated and difficult to navigate. Such was the case in the fall of 1753, when a party of Moravian immigrants laboriously escorted a heavily loaded wagon from Pennsylvania along the Valley of Virginia to North Carolina. Still, notwithstanding the travelers' sense of being strangers in a strange land, there were clues in their travel diary pointing to coherent frontier neighborhoods. On 25 October, about thirty miles south of the Augusta County courthouse, the horse of one traveler, Brother Gottlob, threw a shoe. For want of a nail, Gottlob found Edward Tarr:

> Br[other] Gottlob went . . . to a Free Negro, who is the only smith in these
> parts, to have his horse shod. The negro and his wife, who was a Scotch
> woman, were very friendly to Br Gottlob, and told him that they had recently
> come hither from Lancaster [Pennsylvania] and that they had often heard
> Br Nyberg preach, and also the Br[ethre]n in Philadelphia, and that they
> were now reading the "Berliner Reden." They were very glad to see Brethren,
> and happy to serve us. During the night the woman baked bread, invited Br
> Gottlob and Br Nathanael to breakfast, and begged that as they returned they
> would not pass them by but stop and speak to them, for they loved people
> who spoke of the Saviour. The negro understood German well.[2]

Indeed, the Moravians' Negro understood a great deal more than German. As he demonstrated eight years later, Edward Tarr also understood how to fend off Joseph Shute's fraudulent reenslavement.

Travelers' Advisory

The Road to Black Ned's Forge is first a narrative about Edward Tarr, "commonly known as Black Ned." Like Odysseus, however, Tarr appears only briefly in the initial portion of his eponymous book. Instead, part I, "The Yeoman's Dilemma," deals primarily with Tarr's last master and that master's descendants; to understand Tarr's achievements requires understanding his masters' ambitions. These chapters are set in early Pennsylvania and South Carolina and describe three generations of a family striving to achieve disparate American dreams.

Part II, "The Safety Valve," describes the early education of the slave known as Ned and explains how he acquired his freedom, married a Scottish woman, and moved to the Virginia frontier. Ned, now formally called Edward Tarr, purchased a 270-acre farm and opened a blacksmith shop on the Great Wagon Road from Philadelphia to the Carolinas. In his earliest years of freedom, Tarr moved from one accomplishment to another, establishing himself among his Virginia neighbors as a valued craftsman and devout church member. Eventually, however, war disrupted his frontier communities, and Tarr's relationships with his white neighbors began to deteriorate.

Following the decade of frontier warfare from 1755 through 1764, large-scale economic changes further undercut Tarr's earlier high standing. Part III, "Individuals and Social Change," explores the transformation of Virginia's frontier as it affected Tarr. In particular, the settlements in which Tarr initially lived included only a few African Americans, either as slaves or free persons of color. Over time, however, frontier farmers turned increasingly to slavery, and Tarr's status as a free man took on a new layer of racial and social complexity.

The Road to Black Ned's Forge runs past fields long plowed by historians. Readers interested in pausing to converse with those scholars are welcome to start the discussion by referring to the endnotes. The text selectively discusses the works of colleagues but declines the sort of historiographical review that might drown a general reader's interest in the narrative. In the same spirit, portions of the evidence that are most efficiently presented as tables can be found in the book's appendixes. The appendixes also include biographical notes concerning the free and enslaved black pioneers who were Edward Tarr's contemporaries in early Augusta County, as well as synopses of Tarr's lawsuits.

All history has a scholarly context. Most obviously, *The Road to Black Ned's Forge* contributes to the long conversation about American race relations by scrutinizing transitions from slavery to freedom and freedman to freeholder. Historians will recognize other venerable topics en route, including the economic organization of families, the rise and fall of entrepreneurs, the spread of slavery into the continental interior, the role of trauma in transforming societies, and the significance of frontiers in American history. The book closes with a discussion of early American mobility, an essential social phenomenon linking far-flung backcountry settlements.

From the book's inception, I hoped that Edward Tarr's story could draw readers to a more nuanced understanding of ordinary people in the late colonial backcountry. If so, it will be only the latest of his many achievements.

Names, Time, and Money

The roads in this book were trod by diverse people, ran through three calendars, and transected multiple monetary systems. Modern visitors to seventeenth- and eighteenth-century North America can use the following guide to identify some of the travelers, tell time, and count money.

When inhabitants of Britain's North American colonies referred to someone as "Negro" or "mulatto," they meant a person whose appearance indicated either African ancestry or a mixture of European and African antecedents. Neither term has endured in general usage into the twenty-first century, so they sound discordant to modern ears. Students of eighteenth-century race relations will recognize what they signify in this book, however. As I discuss more fully below, most free people of color on the colonial frontier owed their liberty to a white ancestor, usually female. For contemporaries, the terms "mulatto" and "Negro" thus described much more than skin color. Yet the people known then as mulattos could be slaves, and Negroes could be free, so the conditions potentially were ambiguous. Where appropriate, I employ these racial descriptions to convey significant contemporary social nuances about individual people of color.

The language of white ethnicity also reflects a complex American past in which a minor point of contention is worth noting. The majority of initial settlers in that part of colonial Virginia lying west of the Blue Ridge came to America from Northern Ireland. For a variety of reasons, their nineteenth-century descendants took the name "Scotch-Irish." In the late twentieth century, historians began shifting away from that label and toward "Scots-Irish" or "Ulster Scots," terms which also have shortcomings. For simplicity and arguably more accuracy, I employ the name the immigrants most often called themselves: Irish.[3]

Regarding time, in 1752, Britain belatedly switched from the Julian to the Gregorian calendar. The change shifted day one of a new year from 25 March (known as Lady Day) to 1 January. All dates after 14 September 1752 conform to modern usage.

Before September 1752, British subjects followed the Julian calendar but acknowledged the Gregorian alternative with a special notation from 1 January to 24 March. The day after 31 December 1693 thus was written 1 January 1693/4, and the day before 25 March 1749 was written 24 March 1748/9.

Quakers followed the Julian or Gregorian conventions for writing years but rejected pagan month names such as "January." Instead, Quakers numbered months according to precedence in the Julian calendar. March thus was the first month, written "1m"; September remained the seventh month, "7m"; January became the eleventh month, "11m"; and so on. For clarity, dates in the text are usually rendered with conventional English month names and, where appropriate, Julian years that acknowledge Gregorian years.

Like time, money also was counted in ways that varied with context. Coins in many denominations from multiple countries circulated in colonial North America, but only a handful appear in the text. These include the shilling, a silver coin worth twelve pence or pennies, and a penny worth two half-pennies or four farthings.

Gold and silver coins frequently were clipped or chiseled into fragments, so merchants typically kept scales to weigh coin bits. In any form, however, gold and silver coins were rare. In the absence of specie, people typically conducted business by recording credits and debits on various paper instruments denominated in pounds, shillings, and pence. Pounds, symbolized £, contained twenty shillings and were an accounting unit; no pound coin existed. An amount recorded as £2:12:6½ was pronounced "Two pounds, twelve shillings, sixpence, ha'penny."

Amounts of less than one pound were written with other conventions. Shillings alone might be noted as 12/ or 12s; in either case, these amounts were pronounced "twelve shillings." Pence alone were written as 4d, spoken as "four pence." The amount written as 12/4¾ or 12s 4¾d thus was pronounced "twelve shillings, four pence, three farthings."

Each colony managed its own currency, which in turn traded at a discount with British money, known as sterling. At a given time, ten pounds sterling might have equaled seventy pounds South Carolina money, and three pounds Virginia might have been exchanged for four pounds Pennsylvania. Monetary sums mentioned in the text are given in the colonial money of the passage's context unless otherwise noted.

Colonial-era money does not translate smoothly into modern values. For purposes of comparison, on the Virginia frontier from the 1740s to 1775, wages for a day's labor ranged from 1/ to 3/, that is, between one and three shillings. A hot meal in 1750 cost 9d and a quart of Virginia ale to wash it down cost 3¾d.[4] The total bill for food and drink thus was 1/0¾ or 1s ¾d or one shilling and three farthings. At the end of the meal, travelers were expected to pay cash, but local customers simply added the sum to an account that might not be balanced for years.

Upon reading in manuscript form this introduction to English calendars and bookkeeping, my VMI colleague Timothy Dowling exclaimed in exasperation, "How did these people ever run an empire?" The following account of Edward Tarr and his contemporaries is one answer to Tim's question.

Part I

The Yeoman's Dilemma

1

The Yeoman   1666–1732

Young Man in a Young Place—Mines and Quarries—A World of Paper—
Lancaster Aphelion—Thomas Shute's Diversified Dependents—
Gulf Stream Traffic

During most of Thomas Shute's long life, his peers agreed on his identity as a yeoman. By this term they meant, in part, that Shute was a market-oriented farmer who owned land and was not above tilling it himself. Their definition elastically could also cover processors and vendors of agricultural products: some yeomen owned gristmills, chandleries, breweries, tanyards, bakeries, or comparable businesses. Characteristically, the condition of being a yeoman implied a level of affluence well above subsistence farmers and sometimes rivaling lesser gentry. Implicit too was the quality of being a man on the make. Standing in their own fields, yeomen straddled a cultural chasm: independent like landed gentlemen but sweaty, sunburned, and callused like untutored farmhands. Yeomen, as did gentlemen—arguably more so—knew the value of labor. Given enough of it, plus land and luck, some yeomen converted themselves or their sons and grandsons into gentlemen. Across generations, the genteel transformation involved turning wives into mothers, daughters into bargains, and granddaughters into heiresses. Yeomen believed in commodities.

Historians believe yeomen were essential elements of early American society but find them awkward to study. Contemporaries used the label inconsistently, and it has always been difficult to determine when one stopped being a yeoman and started being something else. Although often literate, yeomen wrote fewer surviving letters and journals than the gentry; instead, their lives were documented principally if episodically in religious, governmental, and business records. The latter can be especially revealing: during Pennsylvania's early decades, elite investors sought yeomen partners for a wide range of lucrative projects.

Edward Tarr's last master became a yeoman in Pennsylvania during a propitious era. As Pennsylvania's population, territory, and economy expanded in the late seventeenth and early eighteenth centuries, many and diverse opportunities appeared for yeomen, who in turn profoundly shaped Pennsylvania's culture. The career of Thomas Shute reflects these large-scale trends and more: Shute's life reveals a great deal about both the benefits and pernicious effects of yeoman family fortunes.

Young Man in a Young Place

Thomas Shute left England as a teenager around 1681 when his father, William, emigrated to Pennsylvania. The two initially settled just southwest of modern Philadelphia at the mouth of the Schuylkill River, on the west bank; a census taker found them together there in 1683 and reported the father's age as forty, Thomas's as seventeen.[1] In the same year, William complained that assemblyman Dennis Rotchford wrongfully detained his son, indicating that Thomas had completed a term of bound service to this influential Philadelphia merchant.[2] Once released from his obligation to Rotchford, Thomas probably labored as a farmer, accumulating a payment for land. The deed for his earliest land purchase in 1690 identified him as a husbandman, a farmer of modest means and social rank. At age twenty-four, he entered the propertied class by purchasing one hundred acres in Bristol Township, Philadelphia County (map 1), thereby reaching a milestone of prosperity that his father apparently never attained.[3]

Thomas Shute improved the Bristol Township farm and sold it for over twice his purchase price before the tax assessor visited in 1693. The sale's timing caused Shute to appear landless in Philadelphia County's oldest surviving tax list, but he already had another, familiar farm in view.[4] A few weeks after the sale, on 1 March 1693/4, Shute bought some of his former master's land, two hundred acres at Edgerly Point, just downstream from the falls of the Schuylkill River, on its east bank (figure 1). The late eighteenth-century house known as Laurel Hill, overlooking modern Philadelphia's Fairmount Park, stands on part of Shute's new land. Shute paid Dennis Rotchford's widow £130 silver money of Pennsylvania, a price that suggests the new tract enjoyed better improvements and future prospects than Shute's first land.[5]

The Edgerly Point acquisition also made Shute a more eligible bachelor, and on 9 August 1694, he married Elizabeth Hood. Unfortunately, their life together was brief. After giving birth to a son, William, Elizabeth died on 4 March 1695/6.[6] Thomas Shute's second marriage lasted considerably longer and did much more to improve his fortune. Late in 1696,

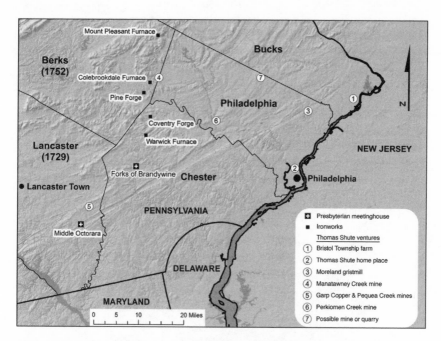

MAP 1. **Pennsylvania landmarks for Thomas Shute and Edward Tarr, 1690–1752.**
Edward Tarr and his last master, Thomas Shute, both ranged widely over southeastern Pennsylvania. (Cartography by James W. Wilson, James Madison University.)

Philadelphia's Arch Street Monthly Meeting approved Shute's union with Elizabeth Powell, daughter of an early Quaker immigrant, the prosperous cooper William Powell.[7] Shute thus entered his thirties having made an advantageous match, and in time, Elizabeth Powell Shute presented her husband with seven children who lived to adulthood.[8] She also appears to have provided him with significant capital and connections.

Shute's farm on the east side of the Schuylkill River remained his home for the rest of his life, a foundation on which he built a considerable landed estate. Beginning on 24 January 1701/2, Shute launched a series of several dozen real estate transactions, the latest in 1743, at the age of seventy-seven. He entered the Pennsylvania land market as demand for property was intensifying; from 1690 to Shute's death in 1748, the colony's population ballooned from 8,800 to about 100,000. Rural and town property alike increased substantially in value as immigrant demand drove up land prices.[9] Shute invested primarily in the farmland of southeastern Pennsylvania and Philadelphia town lots but also ranged as far afield as King and Queen County, Virginia, well over two hundred miles to the south. There he paid

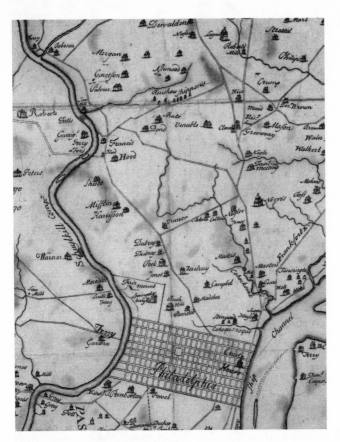

FIGURE I. **Edward Tarr's Philadelphia, 1752.**
Edward Tarr acquired his freedom the year this map was drawn. His earliest known master,
Andrew Robeson, owned a house and mill near the falls of the Schuylkill River, shown here
at top left. When Tarr ran away from Robeson, he probably went to Philadelphia, three and
a half miles to the southeast. Tarr's last master, Thomas Shute, lived downstream from Robe-
son, overlooking the ford on the road from Philadelphia to Lancaster. (Detail from Nicholas
Scull and George Heap, "A map of Philadelphia, and parts adjacent. With a Perspective
View of the State-House." [Philadelphia]: Lawrence Hebert, [1752]. Courtesy of the John
Carter Brown Library at Brown University.)

quitrents—land taxes—on one hundred acres in 1704.[10] Shute transferred
some of these tracts to his children and rented others (table 1).

On reaching middle age, Shute looked beyond farmland and its produce for new investments, shrewdly selecting a variety of productive activities, including milling, mining, and quarrying.[11] In the tract known as
Moreland, about twenty miles north of Philadelphia on Pennypack Creek,
Shute bought a two-hundred-acre mill site in March 1703/4.[12] He built a

gristmill and launched his son-in-law Samson Davis and daughter Christian Shute Davis in the milling business shortly after their 1717 marriage.[13] Shute formally deeded the mill tract to the couple in June 1721, and by 1725, he was active enough in Pennsylvania's expanding flour production to be twice identified in that year as a bolter, a sifter of flour.[14]

The family effort continued, with Davis adding another mill in 1727. When a local road petition referred "to a new Mill of Samson Davis's in the sd Mannor of Moorland," the plat accompanying the request shows the mill in the eastern corner of Davis's two hundred acres.[15] Like other Pennsylvania entrepreneurs, Thomas Shute baked some of his flour into durable biscuit and coopered it for export overseas, shipping at least one such cargo to Barbados in 1729.[16] Perhaps the clearest indication of Shute's ultimate ambition in this field comes from his unsuccessful petition in early 1733 to become the colony's flour inspector, the well-compensated officer charged with protecting the reputation of Pennsylvania flour exports.[17]

Mines and Quarries

Thomas Shute entered his second major industrial venture, mining, by the early 1720s. He and a number of partners agreed in January 1722/3 to open a mine on Manatawney Creek, a tributary of the Schuylkill and home to one of Pennsylvania's earliest ironworks, Rutter Forge. Shute's initial partners included Nicholas Scull (soon to become the provincial surveyor) and James Steel, the provincial receiver-general and Shute's kinsman.[18] In the early 1730s, Steel added Shute to a second mining venture in which they, proprietor Thomas Penn, future provincial attorney-general Andrew Hamilton, provincial secretary James Logan, and land speculator and eventual provincial chief justice William Allen each held one-sixth share of a 250-acre tract known as "the Gap Mine Land in Lancaster County," located on a branch of Octorara Creek.[19] Later in the decade, Shute also helped launch mining operations on Perkiomen Creek, receiving credit and payments in 1736 and 1737 "for Carrying on the Work" at "Perquioman Mine."[20] Clearly Shute had appraised the area's mineral potential even before this service: in 1735, his old mining partner Nicholas Scull, by then the provincial surveyor, delineated a two-hundred-acre tract for Shute adjacent to the "Perkiomy Company"; Shute patented this land two years later.[21]

He also pursued copper mining, though colonial copper production never came close to matching the volume or profitability of iron.[22] Shute's partnership at the Gap Mine in Lancaster County was a copper venture that he bequeathed as "my intrest and Property in the Lancaster Copper mines" in his 1748 will. His heirs subsequently sold Shute's "Moiety of that certain Copper Mine or Mines and of the lands bounding said mines," property still held in company with at least one original partner, Chief Justice William Allen.[23] Additionally, Shute surveyed a four-hundred-acre tract on Manatawney Creek, land identified as the "Copper Mine Tract commonly called Shute's Mine" in a 1742 plat.[24]

Thomas Shute's iron and copper mining necessarily took place far from home, but his third major extractive activity, stone quarrying, was sited literally in his backyard. Quarries at his Edgerly Point home tract in the Northern Liberties steadily provided building stone to Philadelphia Town, about four miles away. Adjoining the Schuylkill River, Shute's "sundry stone quarries, suiting either water or land carriage," served a variety of private and public customers. Projects constructed with Shute stone include the "Bridge over the dock in Walnut Street," Samuel Powel's dwelling and storehouses, and William Parker's home.[25] At least three of Shute's sons used building stone to balance their accounts with local creditors.[26]

Building-stone production probably represented the largest volume of Shute's quarrying enterprises, but he also ventured on several occasions into a more refined market, supplying fine stonework. He participated in Pennsylvania's nascent marble export trade, shipping "2 marble Tables" to Barbados in 1729, and in the following year, he received £13:10:6 "for Putting a Tombstone over the Grave of Samuel Brewster."[27] In seven months spanning 1734 and 1735, a Philadelphia merchant credited Shute with £3:6:0 for "a Marble Hearth and Case" and £6:1:6 for "two Marble Slabs Containing 20 Foot 3 Inches."[28]

A World of Paper

Producing lengths of workable marble was much simpler than producing workable iron. A newly finished iron merchant bar several feet long and twenty-something pounds in weight represented extensive and risky physical exertions. It also signified elaborate financial relationships among ironworks investors as well as the host of merchants, day laborers, artisans, yeomen, and other neighbors who, in one way or another, lived in iron country. In short, furnaces and forges depended on two types of fiscal partnerships: formal ones in which adventurers pooled capital to start an ironworks, and informal ones in which an ironworks generated around itself a magnetic field of economic exchanges.[29]

Details of these formal and informal partnerships are difficult to reconstruct from surviving records, but Shute's activities help illustrate the iron industry's credit complexities. He invested in Pennsylvania's early iron boom of the 1720s and 1730s, purchasing part or all of several mines, both for iron ore and copper. He also was connected to the iron industry through family members working directly for an ironworks or trafficking in iron. His grandson William Davis managed Warwick Furnace, and Shute's daughter Christian and her husband, Samson Davis, received and distributed bar and pig iron from Coventry and Pine forges as well as Mount Pleasant and Colebrookdale furnaces.[30] Another daughter, Rebecca, married blacksmith Anthony Nicholas, to whom Shute sent 2.5 tons of pig iron in 1742/3 and 1745.[31]

Thomas Shute's transactions in iron are especially visible during a period from late 1737 to the summer of 1745 at Pine Forge. His new relationship with the forge's management is indicated by the reassignment of a 1731 debit as well as by the rearrangement of debits previously entered against him in Pine Forge's ledger. In 1731, ironmaster Thomas Potts, Sr., credited one Barnabas Rhodes's account at Colebrookdale Furnace for "a Colt bot for Thos. Shute" for two pounds, ten shillings.[32] Six years later, Potts opened a new account for "Thomas Shute Philadelphia" in a Pine Forge ledger, listing among the earliest entries in November 1737 a debit against Shute for the "Colt bought of Barnabas Rhodes 1731."[33] In other words, Potts shifted the horse's cost from books at Colebrookdale to Pine Forge, signaling the start of a different credit nexus between Potts and Shute.

That new relationship is indicated also by a realignment of Shute's accounts with Pine Forge. In a separate, older ledger, Potts's clerk balanced Shute's accounts with an entry on 2 June 1739 crediting Shute with £4:7:9¼ "By Father Potts's assum[pti]on for you at Rayneer Tyson's wedding."[34] Instead of simply treating Potts's assumption as a cancellation of his debt, however, Shute assigned this credit to a third party who presented the obligation to Potts for payment on 10 March 1740/1, over twenty-one months later.[35] Like the 1731 colt, Potts's assumption had a life of its own, changing hands as it leaped from one ledger to another.

In the case of the colt and possibly in the assumption, Potts treated Shute with a degree of leniency that sometimes implied an existing partnership, and Shute's accounts at Pine Forge for the period from November 1737 to August 1745 share two similarities with contemporary accounts of partners in ironworks. First, most of the entries are debits for pig and bar iron, rather than money. Second, Shute's accounts include no items marked "contra," credits that would have indicated he was purchasing the pig iron rather than receiving a distribution due to partners.[36]

Such partnerships accelerated the exploitation of Pennsylvania's natural resources as yeomen like Thomas Shute combined with gentlemen to convert earth, air, fire, and water into wealth. The documents they generated during those metamorphoses thus amount to artifacts of investor worlds. It was Shute's great fortune to live in Pennsylvania at a time when those worlds were drawn to a yeoman scale: in a colony populated by only tens of thousands of people, yeomen and gentlemen seeking commercial partnerships could find each other easily. Together they created in Philadelphia a center of gravity for their colony's economy, and together they populated increasingly distant orbits around that center.

Lancaster Aphelion

Thomas Shute's mining interests on Pequea Creek and at the Gap were about sixty miles west of his home, an awkward location compared to other parts of colonial Pennsylvania's industrial frontier. The sites lay in Lancaster County, so mine products had to be hauled farther to reach furnaces, forges, navigable rivers, and viable markets. Boggy roads between the Gap and Philadelphia increased both the cost of cartage from the west and the difficulty of supervision from the east.[37] The problem of supervision was especially significant for Shute, who was sixty-four when he bought into the Gap partnership in 1730 and six years older when he purchased his share of the Pequea Creek tract.

Possibly Shute intended for his son Isaac to monitor the investments; as a blacksmith in Lancaster County, Isaac was ideally positioned to keep an eye on his father's mining concerns. In other regards, however, he was less suitable. Most obviously, Isaac lacked his father's fiscal discipline, as evidenced by Lancaster creditors' repeatedly suing him for debts from 1733 to 1737.[38] Perhaps for that reason, Thomas retained his share in the Pequea Creek partnership less than two years before selling it in 1738.[39] Without a reliable family member to oversee the investment, it was too risky to continue.

A cultural concern may also have affected Thomas's decision to pull back from Lancaster County. More than distance separated his home at the falls of the Schuylkill River from the Pequea Creek and Gap mines. Even as early as its formation in 1729, Lancaster County was filling with unfamiliar newcomers. In the county's southern section—a triangle formed by Octorara Creek, Pequea Creek, and the Susquehanna River, with the Gap at its apex—Irish migrants outnumbered earlier English settlers. Much of the remainder of the county was inhabited by recently arrived Germans.[40] Both populations were drawn to Pennsylvania by the colony's permissive religious environment, and to this particular county by the rich land of the Lancaster Plain. Pennsylvania's population thus nearly doubled from 37,000 in 1720 to 73,000 in 1740.[41]

For Thomas Shute and other strategically positioned longtime residents of Pennsylvania, immigrants brought great profits through rapidly expanding demands for land, goods, services, and markets.[42] Other aspects of the boom were less positive, as the surging population transformed the colony in ways that early Quaker settlers deplored.[43] The Pennsylvania alterations most significant for the Shute family, for the slave who became Edward Tarr, and for the Virginia frontier concerned real estate: immigrants debarking in the Delaware River Valley swamped the administrative processes by which Pennsylvania's proprietors converted territory into private ownership.[44] Before the deluge, Shute accumulated fourteen small warrants authorizing the conversion of 120 acres into private property. Shute had the tract surveyed in May 1718 and patented in July, exchanging within weeks a sheaf of papers for a tract of freehold property. By the 1730s, the same administrative process took many years.[45]

For non-Quaker immigrants who explicitly equated independence with land ownership, such delays compounded inexorably, generating frustration, then resentment, then anger, and ultimately emigration.[46] A border dispute between the proprietors of Maryland and Pennsylvania heightened uncertainty over frontier land titles; the competing claims were partially reconciled in 1738 but not completely settled until 1774.[47] As a consequence, Lancaster County residents who failed to acquire land began to be pulled southwest by more favorable real estate markets.

From an institutional perspective, Virginia's attractions are not immediately obvious. The conversion of crown land into private property involved a similarly time-consuming series of administrative steps. Contemporaries characterized the creation of real estate as a slow process, and a comparison of patents to land deeds reveals that it was dominated by residents who already owned land: in Augusta County, Virginia, between 1 January 1736/7 and 31 December 1769, only 576 of the county's 2,405 first-time freeholders (24.0%) patented their initial real estate.[48] Pennsylvania and Virginia thus were comparably inefficient in creating real estate for newcomers.

In one important respect, however, Virginia offered great advantages to potential purchasers: large-scale land speculators sought to sell portions of existing freeholds. It might still take several years to record the deeds from such sales, but the transaction itself was a legally enforceable contract from the date of the signing of the deed. Speculators offered faster access to clear titles at reasonable terms, thereby drawing southeastern Pennsylvanians to the Valley of Virginia in large numbers from the 1730s to the mid-1750s. The relative disarray of Pennsylvania's frontier land market helps account for emigration by Lancaster County inhabitants, some of whom had lived for years in Pennsylvania without formally acquiring real estate.[49]

Beyond faster access to privately owned land, Augusta County also offered a different type of frontier opportunity—local authority. In addition to the difficulties they faced purchasing land in Lancaster County, apparently qualified Irish immigrants achieved only minimal political authority in Pennsylvania. Twelve out of the twenty-three earliest magistrates in Augusta County lived for several years in Lancaster County, but none owned real estate or served as magistrates there (table 2). Virginia thus beckoned not only with relatively more secure land titles but also with superior prospects for leading new communities. By the late 1730s, Augusta County began attracting the initial Lancaster County emigrants. Scores of families followed in the 1740s and early 1750s, as did Edward Tarr.

Thomas Shute's Diversified Dependents

If land was the most essential element of yeoman fortunes, labor ran a close second. Shute's varied real estate interests, agricultural efforts, and industrial operations required a great deal of physical work. The initial familial members of his labor force, Shute's two wives, bore eight children who lived to adulthood: sons William, Thomas, Isaac, Jacob, and Joseph, plus daughters Christian, Martha, and Rebecca.[50] As an adult, eldest son William lived a short distance northeast of Thomas's home on 120 acres that his father formally conveyed to him in 1739 (figure 1).[51] As described above, eldest daughter Christian and her husband, Samson Davis, managed Shute's milling interest for a time, and Davis also participated in iron-related business. The remaining children learned skilled trades: chandler Thomas, Jr.; blacksmith Isaac; cooper Jacob; and ship's master Joseph.[52] At least one of Thomas Shute's grandchildren followed the same tradesman's path; Christian and Samson Davis's son William became "Sub. Clark at Warwick" Furnace by 1743 and manager of the ironworks shortly thereafter. Eventually Shute acknowledged the young man's business skills and sense of responsibility by appointing William executor of his will.[53]

Spread among farms, forests, mills, mines, and quarries, Shute's family enterprises amounted to what modern entrepreneurs might consider a diversified business. At first glance, his assembly of resources and talent appears a triumph of free labor—certainly *he* had risen from humble origins.

But his carts brimming with mine ore, barrels packed with milled flour or baked biscuit, and flatboats riding low in the water from their cargoes of building stone testified that Shute's accomplishments were built on more than just family labor.

Like many of his fellow Pennsylvanians, Shute hired white workers for time-sensitive tasks like making hay, but such laborers could be hardest to find at the moments they were needed most.[54] When a Philadelphian grumbled with frustration in 1737/8 that "Thos Shute still promises me to bring those men," he complained of labor uncertainties facing all Pennsylvania employers in the early eighteenth century.[55] Pennsylvanians who engaged in complex business affairs therefore sometimes turned to slavery.

Shute's slaves are almost invisible to modern historians until the very end of his life, perceptible mostly in the voluminous output of Shute's enterprises. Some, like the boy he apprenticed to a Philadelphia artisan "to be taught the trade of a cooper," were assigned to specialized tasks.[56] Other slaves, like "Stone cutter and quarry man" Samuel and blacksmith Ned, labored as vital artisans but also bent to the many other essential though less-skilled tasks implied by Shute's interests—carting, mining, and stevedoring are obvious examples, as well as "every kind of Country Business."[57] Shute owned six slaves at his death, a relatively large number for Pennsylvania masters.[58]

Shute acquired and held his slaves during a transition in Quaker attitudes toward slavery. Famously, his Palatine neighbors in nearby Germantown renounced slavery in 1688. English Quakers in Pennsylvania abandoned slavery more gradually; masters such as Shute apparently rationalized slavery as a variant of dependent status. He himself seems to have believed firmly in masters governing dependents. The patriarch's attitude toward the control of servants and slaves is revealed sarcastically in his 1721 newspaper advertisement:

> Run away from her Master, Thomas Shute, of the Northern Liberties of the City of Philadelphia, a She Bear, aged about six Months, an Indian born, but understands English a little, of a grim Aspect and ill-humoured: She is one of few Words, but very quarrelsom, having on a fear-nothing Coat, her Neck wore with a Collar, and the inner Side of her fore Paws wore with leaping over her Chain. Whoever takes up the said Bear, and brings her unhurt to her said Master, shall have 10 s Reward.[59]

Unlike the usual newspaper listings for lost livestock, Shute's notice anthropomorphized the animal, and not just because standing or sitting bears resemble humans. In this rare surviving example of the yeoman's unfiltered voice, Shute seems to have been deliberately satirizing newspaper notices for fugitive workers. By describing a bear cub with linguistic conventions normally reserved for human runaways, Shute implicitly derided those masters unable to tame their unruly dependents. In contrast, through all his long career, Shute never had to advertise a truant laborer.

Gulf Stream Traffic

As he reached his early sixties, Shute was poised to launch into overseas trade. Two important trends of the late 1720s whetted his ambitions. Expanding sugar and rice production in the Caribbean and South Carolina required large quantities of finished and semifinished products, especially food, furniture, lumber, and iron, which he and other Pennsylvanians could efficiently produce. Simultaneously, a lull in European conflicts and vigorous Royal Navy patrolling reduced the risk of losing a vessel and cargo to national warships, privateers, or pirates.[60] At home, Shute's family-operated businesses were ready to exploit this conjunction of economic and imperial opportunities. Abroad, Shute's youngest son, Joseph, was nearing his majority and completing his education as a ship's master and seagoing trader—the ultimate link in his father's chain of ventures.[61]

Thomas Shute seems first to have intended to enter the Barbados trade. On 28 February 1728/9, he "apply'd in behalf of his Son Joseph Shute for a Certificate for him to the Monthly Meeting of Friends in Bridgetown Barbados," signaling Thomas's intention that Joseph should reside permanently among the Quakers of Barbados's chief port. The following month, Quaker leaders in Philadelphia approved the request, certifying Joseph's conformity to Quaker doctrine.[62] All seemed in order, but if Joseph actually took his certificate to Barbados, as he could have done that spring with a cargo of his father's bread, he did not stay long: when Thomas shipped additional goods to Barbados in late 1729, he did not consign the freight to his son.[63] Quaker monthly meeting records from Barbados for this period have not survived; in their absence, there is no way to determine whether Joseph even briefly visited the island.

Thomas Shute retained for a while his interest in the Barbados market, but clearly he had to defer his plans for Joseph and overseas trade.[64] In the meantime, something drew his attention to the mainland port of Charleston, South Carolina. Shute apparently recognized just ahead of his potential competitors that by comparison to Barbados, Charleston represented an underdeveloped market for Pennsylvania staples. Shute's otherwise busy and better-known contemporary, Philadelphia merchant Peter Baynton, did not send a trading vessel to South Carolina until late 1731.[65] By that time, Thomas Shute already had installed Joseph in the seaport.

Preparations for the South Carolina venture began in February 1730/1 when Thomas Shute requested a certificate of Joseph's "Conversation & Clearness in Marriage," this time directed "to Friends in South Carolina." Philadelphia's Quaker leadership again complied.[66] As the father surely hoped and the son quickly discovered, Charleston's small Quaker community offered important resources for the new Shute venture. The Friends held their monthly administrative sessions in the home of chair-maker Thomas Kimberley, custodian of the meetinghouse and grounds since the meeting organized in 1718.[67] Soon after arriving in Charleston, Joseph Shute identified Kimberley's stepdaughter Anna as a desirable mate; the couple announced their intention to marry even before Joseph submitted his certificate from Philadelphia.[68]

Joseph's marriage to Anna Gull Arnott offered something for everyone concerned. The young woman regained a measure of respectability lost through her previous wedding to a non-Quaker: Anna had married her short-tenured first husband, John Arnott, on 17 July 1728 and buried him six months later.[69] Her mother and stepfather, whom the Charleston Monthly Meeting "appointed to see their marriage be orderly accomplished," doubtless appreciated the opportunity to report in the fall of 1731 that the marriage between Joseph and Anna was accomplished "according to Form & according to Order."[70] Additionally, the childless Thomas Kimberley gained an energetic step-son-in-law and junior business partner.

Joseph gained most of all. His wife, an only child, stood to inherit a substantial amount of personal property and real estate, and his in-laws were influential. Shortly after the marriage, Kimberley provisionally deeded to his stepdaughter six acres near Charleston, charging her a nominal ten shillings and promising her full title after her mother's death. Kimberley's deed noted that he and Shute "have proposed and agreed to erect some buildings on the sd six acres of land at the joynt cost & charge" to each, and the two men agreed "that all rents whatsoever ariseing from sd buildings shall be [divided] in equall shares between them."[71] Thanks to his new father-in-law, Shute soon became one of the trustees for the Friends' meetinghouse tract and, shortly before his benefactor's 1736 death, assumed the duties of clerk in the Charleston Monthly Meeting.[72]

Kimberley was equally useful in secular affairs, introducing Shute to other significant Charlestonians. Witnesses to Shute's marriage included

Othniel Beale, Stephen Beauchamp, Thomas Bedon, John Blamyer, Thomas Elliott, Thomas Fleming, and John Witter, all merchants or affluent planters. Several were political officeholders as well, and together they represented a formidable endorsement in a commercial environment where personal connections doubled as credit references.[73]

Joseph's marital coup completed Thomas Shute's preparations to enter North Atlantic commerce. During a May 1732 visit to Philadelphia, Joseph registered a small sloop, the *Dove*, and embarked on the family's first voyage to Charleston. He conned the *Dove* on the initial trip, delivering ninety-seven barrels of flour, thirty-two barrels of bread, and six boxes of soap after eleven days at sea.[74] Thereafter he remained in Charleston to act as his father's factor, receiving and dispatching cargoes.

The family-controlled trade that Thomas organized between Philadelphia and Charleston doubtless had its frustrations and anxieties, but on occasion it also must have delivered deep satisfaction. Behind the *Dove* followed one Shute-owned vessel after another, standing down the Delaware River loaded with flour, bread, corn, beer, soap, bar iron, apples, butter, pork, earthenware, and barrel staves (table 3). In South Carolina, Joseph assembled cargoes primarily of naval stores and leather, dispatching his vessels as quickly as possible to ride the Gulf Stream northeast to Philadelphia (table 4).

The key elements of this trade lacked the cachet and profitability of more speculative products like sugar, rice, and tobacco, but arguably a Quaker yeoman-exporter could appreciate a plain trade in familiar commodities with honest profits.[75] Certainly Thomas Shute's commerce illustrates a vital process in colonial America, building economic momentum with each transaction's small profit, repeatedly compounding as goods passed from hand to hand. Shute's signal accomplishment was the collection of so many hands—including Ned, the slave who became Edward Tarr—and the control of so many recurring small exchanges for such a long string of years.

2

The Merchant   1731–1761

Navigating Inefficient Markets—Joseph Shute's Investments—Risks—
Failures—Joseph Shute's Opportunism

When Joseph Shute arrived in Charleston in 1731, the North American economy was languishing in one of its periodic contractions. Within a year or two, however, another cycle of economic growth began and continued until the 1739 outbreak of war between Spain and Britain.[1] In the rising markets of this expansion, smaller merchants like Shute could prosper even though larger rivals dominated certain businesses.

Through the 1730s, South Carolina's major commercial investors paid particular attention to external demand for rice, leather, and naval stores, and to internal markets for finished European goods, labor, real estate, and food and drink. Such a summary gives Carolinian commerce a well-ordered sound, but the colony's business could drag on as interminably as a hazy August afternoon: like their contemporaries elsewhere in colonial America, Charleston's buyers and sellers exchanged commodities, capital, goods, and information via slow and unreliable transportation.[2]

Through the shifting estuaries of South Carolina's inefficient economy prowled enterprising lesser merchants hoping to parlay small gambles into fortunes. In its beginning, this was Joseph Shute's story, and his initial success derived from familiar sources. Like his father before him, Shute married well, invested in land and labor, and sought security through diversification. He differed from his father, however, by emphasizing commercial rather than productive activities. Contemporaries thus identified him as a merchant even as a young man.[3] In that capacity, Shute's successful contribution to his father's diversification strategy required daily awareness of wide-ranging details, but the routine management of his many investments could be—and properly was—assigned to accountable subordinates. Storekeepers, sea captains, and overseers attended their particular responsibilities, leaving Shute free to manage the sum of the parts, the total risk of his ventures.[4]

To Shute, risk had four aspects: where to invest, what types of business to enter, how to limit financial losses, and when to respond to official regulation. For American marketplaces outside of Charleston, Shute chose entrepôt and staple-producing islands and the rural mainland interior; later he tested markets in three European countries. Second, his business selections emphasized retailing, shipping, and commercial real estate. Third, his options for reducing financial hazards included insurance, commercial finance, and what is now called arbitrage. And finally, Shute dealt with official regulation by building an interest with politically powerful men, by minor officeholding, and ultimately by ignoring inconvenient laws.

Joseph Shute was one of many coastal merchants whose reach extended to settlers far inland. As conduits for capital and enablers of territorial expansion, he and merchants like him played essential parts in the growth of frontier communities, despite their great distance from new settlements. Sometimes, however, merchants destroyed as well as built, and when their own fortunes foundered, they clawed at others in order to save themselves. In 1761, Shute grasped across a distance of four hundred miles from Charleston to Augusta County, fraudulently attempting to reenslave Edward Tarr.

Navigating Inefficient Markets

Joseph Shute's initial mercantile sally beyond Charleston was to New Providence, principal port of the Bahamas. In late 1732, he sent a small cargo of Pennsylvania products on the first of many voyages to New Providence (table 5).[5] Returning vessels brought tropical wood, cotton, fresh fruit, and edible turtles (table 6). The relatively low volume of total shipping in New Providence enabled Shute vessels occasionally to seize large portions of that market—most notably, in 1740 a schooner in which Shute was a partner loaded 1,700 pounds of lignum vitae, the entire Bahamian export and Charlestonian import of this valuable wood in that year.[6] Typically, however, Shute vessels enjoyed a more modest share of the trade between Charleston and the Bahamas.

As the colonial American economy continued to accelerate, Shute opened a second retail operation in George Town, South Carolina. Situated about sixty miles northeast of Charleston on Winyah Bay, George Town was ideally located to serve inland customers along the Black, Peedee, and Waccamaw rivers, the bay's major tributaries. Shute first tested these waters in August 1734, when he delivered George Town's only flour and bread imported during the quarter ending on 29 September.[7] The following June, Shute and two local storekeepers formed a seven-year partnership "in order to carry on a store at George Town." Initially each partner contributed goods valued at three thousand pounds South Carolina currency to stock the operation, with Shute also securing partner John Abbot's purchases on credit. In other words, Shute bore two thirds of the risk.[8] The size of their investment suggests that Shute and his partners intended to acquire a major portion of rural trade in the region, and George Town's shipping records hint at their success. In May 1737, a vessel partly owned by Shute carried to London all of George Town's pitch and tar exports for the quarter (table 7).

Perhaps staid profits from a coastal trade in flour and bread or pitch and tar satisfied the aging Thomas Shute back in Philadelphia, but as American appetites for consumer goods awakened, Joseph began investigating more distant Atlantic markets. His debut retail advertisement in the *South Carolina Gazette,* the first of many such notices, offered "A Choice Parcel of good blue and white Cottons, fit for Negro cloathing, strip'd Hollands, cloth colour'd Silks, silk Handkerchiefs, silk Hose"—European manufactures all—before ever mentioning the "Flour, middling and brown Bread" that Thomas Shute had sent from Pennsylvania the previous week.[9]

For all its attractions, the expanded trade was risky. Transatlantic exchanges of American produce for European luxury items entailed much more uncertainty than ventures shuttling among American ports. Ultimately, however, Joseph Shute could not ignore the ways in which successful merchant-gamblers quickly multiplied their stakes. Around the end of December 1734, he entered a partnership with merchant captain Thomas Henning. Shute's new partner was ready to retire from the sea, but as a skillful and experienced mariner, Henning brought to the joint venture both substantial insights into European commerce and a political influence beyond the reach of his Quaker partner.[10]

Changes in the emphasis and phrasing of Joseph Shute's newspaper advertisements hint at his excitement over this significant transition. He continued to offer plain Pennsylvania produce in terse *South Carolina Gazette* announcements: "Just imported and to be sold by Henning and Shute choice new Philadelphia Flour, Bread and Indian Corn, very reasonable."[11] Still, less than a month after this particular entry, Shute struck a much different tone in his lush inventory of newly arrived merchandise from Europe and intermediate Caribbean ports:

A List of sundry Goods to be sold by Henning & Shute. . . . Negro clothing, oznabrigs, 3 qu[arter] & 7 eighth Garlix, bagg- and gulick hollands, all sorts of Plantation tools and Iron ware, mens and womens saddles, mens fine and coarse hatts, pewter of all sorts, cuttlary ware of all sorts, silk and thread hose, earthen & stone ware and glasses of all sorts, Scriptories and chests of drawers, pier glasses and sconces, sheeting linnen, check linnen, duroys, sagathies, allipeens, ballertines, buckram, silver trimmings, velvet of different coulours, black padufoys, printed linnens, Indian trading guns and cutlasses, pistols, mens shoes and pumps, millenary ware of all sorts, brown paper holland, prepared oyl for paint, blacking, white lead ground, fine red paint, fine yellow stone oker ground, Prussian blue, pipes of all sorts, Rhenish wines, Port wines, Iron potts and kettles, gartering, Barbados rum, muscavodo sugar, Limes, fowling pieces, fine stows, bread & flower, horse-bells, and sundry other goods generally imported.[12]

Of all these goods, only horse bells took a lower precedence than Pennsylvania's mundane bread and flour. As Charleston's elite increasingly defined itself by conspicuous consumption, Joseph Shute took his cue and launched a twelve-year campaign of conspicuous advertising.

For all of his obvious relish in enumerating exotic wines like "french claret, french white wine, fronteniack, proniack, high proniack, french mountain wine, old hock, rhenish and old port," Shute did not completely neglect his bread and butter.[13] But increasingly, he invested in cargoes from Europe. His first transatlantic venture by one of his own vessels, a Charleston-to-London round trip of the schooner *Dolphin,* cleared Charleston on 8 November 1734 loaded with rice and braziletto, a valuable tropical wood, and returned 173 days later on 29 April 1735.[14] In 1736, Shute sent the snow *Endeavour* to London with rice and logwood; it returned after 218 days in 1737, and repeated the voyage just a few weeks after reaching Charleston. On the second trip, *Endeavour* cleared from George Town/Winyah with 205 barrels of pitch, 613 barrels of tar, and 23 bags of ginger, the small port's sole pitch and tar exports for the quarter.[15] In 1739 and 1740, Shute's brigantine *Anna* ventured twice to Cowes, opposite Southampton on the Isle of Wight, and from there called at Bilbao, Spain, on the first voyage and the Netherlands on the second before returning home. On the former voyage, *Anna* carried rice, logwood, and sassafras; descriptions of the latter cargo have not survived. The first trip lasted about 239 days, the second about 225 days.[16]

Such lengthy voyages faced the usual maritime hazards of coastal trading plus some additional complications. As the weeks of an Atlantic transit slipped away, an owner's instructions to his vessel's master grew increasingly stale. Talented and lucky masters might successfully execute their owners' careful directives, but major seaports like London and Bilbao represented better-informed, better-capitalized marketplaces than any North American port. European access to current financial intelligence was especially important: in the dog-eat-dog arena of North Atlantic commerce, European merchants generally knew better where to bite. Aspiring American merchants thus might learn to their chagrin that a voyage to Europe could produce only paltry profits.[17] Additionally, European ventures chanced an unexpected outbreak of war—Shute's *Anna* departed Charleston on her second voyage to Cowes within a few days of England's 1739 declaration of hostilities against Spain, news of which doubtless provided the owner with many anxious weeks before *Anna* safely reappeared off the Charleston bar.[18]

When Shute added fashionable merchandise to his inventory, he also began paying closer attention to his address, relocating his retail business several times. He and his father-in-law, Thomas Kimberley, first built a store on the main road into Charleston, just outside the town limits. Shute moved from this property and offered it for rent in the summer of 1733. He remained commercially active during the next two years, but his address for that period is uncertain.[19] By May 1735, Shute based his retail business in Elliott Street, an address in the second tier of Charleston's commercial districts during this period.[20] Built over a serviceable cellar and fitted with "good lodging Rooms over-head," his residence stood in front of separate storehouses.[21] At first Shute rented the entire property—the buildings and their twenty-five-by-ninety-one-foot lot.[22] The Elliott Street house thus became the headquarters of his twenty-six-month partnership with Thomas Henning.[23] According to Charleston customs records, this period marks Shute's most extensive involvement in the import business.[24] When the Henning and Shute partnership concluded on 1 March 1736/7, Shute was ready to expand still farther, and by December 1737, he employed a storekeeper at Elliott Street, a sure indicator of his increasingly voluminous affairs.[25] He purchased the Elliott Street tract outright on 4 May 1748.[26]

Joseph Shute's Investments

Shute's most notable ventures other than retailing were his investments in shipping. In all, he owned part or all of at least twelve different small- to midsized vessels over the course of about sixteen years. His first, the *Dove*, was rated at ten tons displacement, and his largest, the *Endeavour* and the *Anna,* were rated at fifty tons each (table 8). The lower startup costs for these vessels seemingly appealed to middling merchants like Shute. His sloops, snow, schooners, and brigantine were less elaborate to rig and equip, and they could be crewed by fewer hands than full-rigged ships: only six men took the sloop *Dolphin* to Britain in 1734.[27] Smaller, cheaper vessels probably also reflected a strategy for risk management, since their loss dealt owners a less-severe blow.

Even relatively modest investments in shipping apparently strained the resources of middling merchants: Shute held shares in eight vessels but owned only four outright. He embarked on most of these ventures sequentially, never joining more than two partnerships at a time, and never wholly owning two vessels at a time. Only once did he purchase a vessel entirely for himself while engaged in a separate partnership, and in that exceptional case, the partner was his father, Thomas. The overall pattern of his vessel ownership thus suggests that Joseph Shute viewed ship-owning as profitable but risky, and that he hedged its dangers in part by never staking too much at one time on this sector of his business.

In addition to his shipping ventures, Shute entered a second type of business connected to retailing by early 1742, operating a wharf at the foot of Elliott Street. His profits derived in part from mooring fees for vessels, which sometimes paid several pounds in wharfage per voyage.[28] Substantial additional revenue came from renting store and workshop space over the water. In 1743, one Charleston merchant reckoned that "his Buildings on his Wharff were worth about [£]300" and rented for about two hundred pounds a year. Another Charleston wharf owner rented "her Stores on her Wharff" for eight hundred pounds annually. Wharf tenants provided a predictable cash flow as well as free promotions for the landlords: merchants Christopher Gadsden, John Moore, partners Lindsay and Dexormandie, John Glegg, William Bard, and Alexander Magee frequently solicited prospective customers to visit their stores on Shute's Wharf (or Shute's Bridge, which was synonymous), so each newspaper advertisement for their businesses mentioned Joseph Shute.[29]

Beyond indicating Shute's increasing importance in Charleston's merchant community, his wharf also suggests an interest in another line of business—real estate (table 9). Some Shute property had no immediate connection to his retail operations but instead marked his participation in the colonial American land boom. Like his father, Shute knew the value of prime real estate in a colony with a rapidly growing population and expanding economy. Between 1734 and 1736, he patented 1,550 acres of land with easy river access to George Town.[30]

Despite these impressive rural holdings, however, Shute's primary interests were unmistakably urban. On his own, he acquired two lots in George Town as part of his venture on Winyah Bay.[31] More importantly, his marriage secured prime lots in and just outside of Charleston: the six-acre tract on which he and his father-in-law first entered business passed to Anna Shute in 1731 for a nominal ten shillings, and the couple sold the same parcel in 1737 for three thousand pounds South Carolina currency.[32] Joseph and Anna Shute liquidated a second portion of her property in 1741, the 2,175-square-foot waterfront Lot Number Ten on the corner of Elliott and East Bay streets, which brought four thousand pounds.[33] Shute expanded his wife's remaining inheritance in 1747, patenting a low-water lot on and under the Cooper River, adjoining the front of her valuable bayside Lot Number Nine.[34]

The addition ran three hundred damp feet to the east, paralleling Shute's Wharf and pointing toward a larger Shute purchase, the island he called Shute's Delight. This included 224 acres bounded on the east and south by the Ashley River, on the west by the Cooper River, and on the north by Hog Island Creek (figure 2). Although described in the deed as marsh land, Shute's Delight in fact included ground firm enough to support heavy masonry structures.[35] The island provided an artist's vantage point for the pre-1739 "Prospect of Charles Town," a visual demonstration that any ships arriving before Charleston could just as easily unload on Shute's Delight. As seen from the island, Charleston offered vast commercial prospects.

Risks

When Shute paced the Charleston waterfront, how sure was his tread? Even in well-documented enterprises, the investments and profits of colonial merchants elude precise calculation, and Shute's ledgers and other personal records have not survived. By several measures, however, his achievements were notable among his contemporaries.

Probably the best comparative estimate of his economic success derives from one of Charleston's worst disasters. In November 1740, fire swept the town from Broad and Church streets down to Granville's Bastion, "which was the most valuable Part of the Town on account of the Buildings and Trade." Over three hundred dwellings burned, "besides Store-houses, Stables, &c. and several Wharfs." Contemporary estimates placed the losses in merchandise alone at £200,000 sterling, and complaints about the

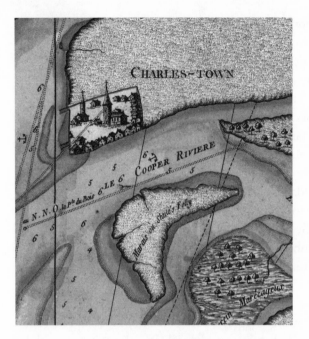

Figure 2. Charleston harbor and Shute's Folly, 1776.
In 1746, Joseph Shute purchased an island that he called Shute's Delight, located across the Cooper River from Charleston. Shute's illegally imported molasses apparently was landed here before port authorities confiscated the contraband. By 1750, Charlestonians called the island Shute's Folly, the name it still bears. North is right. (Detail from "Plan de la barre et du havre de Charles-Town d'après un plan anglois levé en 1776," Library of Congress, Geography and Map Division. Sources: Joseph Shute's 1746 purchase of the island: Conveyance Book, CC:437–443, SCDAH. Earliest designation as Shute's Folly: *South Carolina Gazette*, 11 June 1750, 3.)

devastation eventually moved the British Parliament to grant Charlestonians £20,000 sterling in relief for damages sustained in the blaze. A joint committee drawn from the colonial council and the Commons House of Assembly received petitions for a share of this largesse and eventually assigned each claimant a portion. The claims process closed in June 1742, having heard from 171 individual petitioners; out of these, 32 Charlestonians (18.7%) lost more than the £568 sterling damages claimed by Shute.[36] Of the 32 large claimants, 18 were merchants, of which Charleston had at least 145 between 1738 and 1743.[37] By this admittedly rough standard, Shute had scrambled into the second decile of Charleston's merchants before attaining the age of thirty.

In the winter of 1744–1745, Shute was ready to move the headquarters of his commercial operations down Elliott Street to the waterfront; on

FIGURE 3. "Prospect of Charleston" before 1739.
These buildings on Bay Street overlooked Charleston's waterfront in the 1730s. The gap between buildings on the right-hand side of this detail is the mouth of Elliot Street. The three-story building on the corner of Elliot and Bay stood on a lot inherited by Shute's wife. Whether this building survived the fire of November 1740 is unknown, but Shute's store occupied this space in 1745. The stone curtain line along Bay Street contains a gap, or bridgehead, from which Shute's Wharf stretched into the Bay. (Detail from "View of Charleston, South Carolina," watercolor by Bishop Roberts, Charleston, South Carolina, 1735–1739. The Colonial Williamsburg Foundation. Museum Purchase.)

18 February 1744/5, he announced his relocation "into the Corner-House of Elliott street fronting the Bay."[38] His windows overlooked Shute's Wharf in the foreground and, in the distance, Shute's Delight; he in turn stood in plain sight of Charleston and its mariners. The prominence of "his Store on the Bay" established a new benchmark in Shute's ascent among Charleston's merchants, but he must have understood that his future success depended on more than symbols alone.[39] Given the uncertainties besetting his many ventures, how could he hold on to his gains?

Like other colonial merchants, Shute had available a variety of financial management tools. One was arbitrage, buying and selling money to take advantage of variable exchange rates. "Gold and Silver is now become scarce here," warned the *South Carolina Gazette* in late 1749, "and what little we have likely to be wholly drained from us by the petty Traders from the Northern Colonies, who generally resort here this Time of year with their

Beer, Apples, Chestnuts, &c. picking up all the Gold and Silver they can by giving more for the same than it here at present passes current for."[40] Another tool, insurance, could offset losses at sea, though even Quakers shuffled on the brink of fraud to avoid paying high wartime premiums; alternatively, captured captains might be authorized to ransom their vessels.[41] Quakers usually stopped short of arming their own vessels but could more easily rationalize sailing in guarded convoys.[42]

Peril at sea of course might pale in comparison to trouble by land; the inferno of November 1740, for example, struck Shute a terrible blow. In the wake of disaster, however, properly maintained community connections could help offset a devastating financial loss. Charlestonians learned in the spring of 1741 that Pennsylvania Quakers had subscribed £300 Pennsylvania money "for the Relief of the Sufferers by the late Fire."[43] On reading the news, Shute reached for his pen. The leading Friends of Philadelphia's Arch Street Meeting reported that,

> It appearing by a Letter from Joseph Shute that he hath been a considerable Sufferer by the Fire at Charlestown So Carolina & as he hath had his Education amongst us & professeth to be of our Society, this Meeting considering his distressed Circumstances, directs the Friends that are appointed to receive Friends' Collections for the Relief of the Suffer[er]s there to send Joseph Shute One hundred Pounds out of the said Subscriptions raised by Friends.[44]

Perhaps Thomas Shute encouraged this generous donation; in any event, the gift affirmed the Philadelphia Monthly Meeting's commitment to mitigating disasters that befell one of its own, even far from home.

Ideally such powerful communal ties among Quakers also enabled them to avoid litigation, turning instead to arbitration to resolve disputes. As a practical matter, however, arbitration involving non-Quakers was likely to put Friends at a commercial disadvantage. In a locale occupied by only a few Friends, Joseph Shute could not long have ignored debtors in arrears without losing credibility among the remainder of his clients and his own creditors. What is remarkable, then, is not that he went (or sent his attorney) to court in Charleston, but that he appears so infrequently on the docket. During the expansionary economic cycle that peaked in 1739, Shute appeared in the Court of Common Pleas only six times as plaintiff. In the nine years of war between 1739 and 1748, Shute pursued just five lawsuits against debtors, and in one of those may have been acting solely as an estate executor. Possibly some customers (especially in George Town) were so economically marginal that, if they could not pay Shute, they had nothing worth seizing in compensation. Under the circumstances, though, it is more likely that Shute generally was extending credit prudently, accepting few outright gambles. When necessary he would "trust till Crop" for goods sold in his Charleston store, but not for great sums.[45] The largest debt Shute alone sued for in peacetime was about fifty-seven pounds South Carolina currency, only slightly more than eight pounds sterling (table 10).

In the same way that Shute managed his credit risks and litigation reasonably, he also can be glimpsed at work negotiating with officials. Despite his relative youth, he sought to impress his Charleston associates as a man of intercolonial influence. Shute's only surviving personal letter, a 1734 request for economic advice from his kinsman James Steel, sandwiched a self-focused demand for help between two thin slices of familial duty, revealing both the tactics and the intensity of his effort to become an Atlantic man:

> Uncle Steele
>
> After my wifes and my kind Love to thee and thy family, this is to Desire of thee to be so good As to Send me, a Perticulr Account how Your Currency is made and upon What footing it goes upon for several of our Members, Desired of me to Send to Philadelphia to know upon What footing your money is, and I thought thee would be as propper a Person as any to Give us an Account, so Pray be very Perticuler in it and Send it by the Scooner [Thomas and Joseph Shute's *Dolphin*] when She Returns, and in so doing thee will very much oblige thy Loving Cozen and Please to Remember me to thy family.[46]

Joseph Shute probably intended his request for information bearing on South Carolina's monetary debate to demonstrate to Charleston's political leaders his connection to authorities in Pennsylvania. And, of course, his implied status could be observed by northerners as well: Shute's claim to his uncle that "several of our Members, Desired of me to Send to Philadelphia" appears calculated to impress Pennsylvania's chief financial officer. In this Shute apparently exaggerated, given that detailed studies of South Carolina's currency debates mention neither him nor any advice from Pennsylvania.[47]

Like his father, Shute sought posts of authority within the business community, winning election as a Charleston fire master in 1739 and a wood measurer in 1745 and 1748.[48] He also repeatedly acted as a juror in Charleston's Saint Philip Parish, sitting on grand, petit, or special juries in 1740, 1744, and 1751.[49] As a Quaker in Charleston, however, his political opportunities could never flourish. Beyond his own minor services, Shute carefully tended his connections with other official and unofficial men of power. His business partner Thomas Henning won a Commons House of Assembly seat in 1736, and in the same year Shute rented a Charleston pied-à-terre to assemblyman David Hext.[50] Future assembly member John Seabrook relied on Shute to post an appearance bond for Seabrook in the Court of Common Pleas in 1744.[51] Othniel Beale, a witness at Shute's wedding, eventually took a seat on the colonial council.[52]

A final example of Shute's efforts to maintain ties to influential Charlestonians involves his sponsorship of a relative from Pennsylvania. Like his father, Shute introduced a dependent family member to the seaport's business community, presenting his nephew, Thomas Shute, in 1747. The younger Thomas Shute sailed for Philadelphia in September of that year, taking with him a load of Joseph Shute's sole leather, "one Trunk Sadlery Ware" belonging to Henry Laurens, and detailed instructions from Laurens about purchasing a return cargo.[53] This errand for one of Charleston's leading merchants provided the nephew with valuable experience and the uncle with yet another link to a prominent member of South Carolina society.

Failures

Joseph Shute's early rise in South Carolina benefited enormously by that colony's expanding economy, but even so, the sixteen years between his own arrival and the launching of his nephew's career were fraught with maritime hazards. The shipping business always had posed both natural and economic risks, as Shute experienced firsthand in the spring of 1736. His schooner *Dolphin*, which left Philadelphia for Charleston on 6 March, disappeared and by 15 May was given up as lost at sea with all hands.[54] Shute seems to have weathered his first maritime catastrophe without a visible setback, forming a partnership to purchase the snow *Endeavour* within a few weeks.[55] A far worse loss was the 1742 disappearance at sea of the brigantine *Anna* and her valuable cargo of cocoa, sugar, and lignum vitae.[56]

Beyond natural disasters loomed the threat of war. Once it became clear that the conflict with Spain begun in 1739 would not end soon, Shute was forced to reconsider his shipping tactics. Faced with wartime uncertainties, he placed his freight to and from Charleston in the hands of other merchants for over two years after *Anna* disappeared in late 1742, rather than risk both vessel and cargo.[57] At last, in the summer of 1745, Shute chanced his newly built schooner *Industry* on a quick run from George Town to Virginia. He should have waited longer still: a Spanish privateer immediately pounced on the luckless schooner.[58] After another year, Shute tried again, this time with a guarantee of safe passage. Shute and a partner purchased *Victory* in July 1746, and for its first voyage, the sloop "sail'd for the Havanna with a Flag of Truce and Spanish Prisoners."[59] *Victory* delivered its passengers to Cuba and returned to Charleston in early December 1746.[60] Shute then sent the vessel on four quick roundtrip voyages to New Providence and a longer venture to Antigua before attempting an ill-fated run to Pennsylvania in June 1748.[61] The sloop almost reached Philadelphia, but on 14 June, an enemy privateer in the Delaware Bay drove *Victory* into shoal water, boarded it the next morning, and "carried the Sloop off."[62]

After 1739, Shute's voyages tended to diminish in frequency and increase in risk. The pattern points to the dilemma facing all lesser shippers during wartime, especially after Britain's protracted war with Spain expanded in its fifth year to include France.[63] During peacetime, shippers in small vessels had opportunities to dispose of cargoes faster than their larger competitors, especially in outlying ports. But during hostilities, the advantages of economic scale enjoyed by larger ships were amplified by advantages of self-defense. No sloop with a crew of four could protect itself against a Spanish or French privateer—such vessels did put to sea, but to send them out unescorted was a reckless gamble, not an investment.

Why accept such ruinous odds? Shute may well have lost the schooner *Industry* in an attempt to cover his debts to other Charleston merchants. Between September 1744 and February 1744/5, Thomas Smith and Edmond Cossens sold Shute two pipes of wine and sundries valued at almost £250. When Shute produced only £80:5:0 in payment, his creditors summoned him to the July 1745 session of the Court of Common Pleas. About the same time, Shute ran afoul of the politically active merchant John Crokatt and his business partner, Kenneth Michie. Having purchased from them two hogsheads of sugar on ninety-days' credit, Shute remitted only £93:10:0 in cash and rice when the bill came due—approximately 20 percent of the total charge. In August, one week after *Industry's* capture, the chief justice of the Court of Common Pleas issued a second writ attaching Shute for his appearance at the October session.[64] Somehow he settled the debts, but watchful Charleston creditors would have noted the two lawsuits and the lost vessel as possible signals of Shute's weakening finances.

Perhaps his 1745 difficulties can be traced to the extraordinary expenses of moving into his bayside house and store early that year, but a second voyage, the *Victory's* 1746 retrieval of English prisoners in Havana, points to an additional problem: Shute was interested in trading illegally with foreign clients. Since the war's beginning in 1739, vessels under flag of truce occasionally exchanged captives—first Spanish and then French vessels repeatedly visited Charleston in the same way that *Victory* sailed to Havana. Whatever their nationality, mariners aboard flag-of-truce vessels regarded their protected voyages as lucrative opportunities to trade with their nominal enemies.[65] If caught in South Carolina, Englishmen receiving such shipments forfeited the entire lot of foreign goods, which were divided in equal parts among the king, the governor, and the local customs officer.[66] Smuggling on the flag-of-truce vessels incensed part of the community, including the Charleston grand jurymen who in March 1744/5 denounced "the pernicious Practice and under hand Trade carried on in Charlestown and other Ports in Carolina, by Vessels under the Protection of a Flag of Truce, which Vessels do carry and convey to the King's Enemies at [St.] Augustine [Florida] and the Havanna not only Provisions, but Ammunition, Arms, and Intelligence."[67] In a letter to the *South Carolina Gazette* editor a few weeks later, "A FAIRDEALER" railed against the "clandestine Trade with his Majesty's E[nemie]s," and the editor in turn dutifully published a cautionary story about English smugglers betrayed and imprisoned by their Spanish clients in Florida.[68] Given such institutional and public outcry, smugglers clearly chanced the full penalty of the law.[69]

Whether Shute's *Victory* traded illegally during its 1746 voyage to Havana and back is unknowable, but certainly by 1748, he had accumulated a series of accounting irregularities for some of his cargoes (table 11). These discrepancies apparently eluded prosecution, but official tolerance evaporated in April 1748 when a French flag-of-truce vessel was apprehended off the Charleston bar and charged with illegal trade, incensing patriots and fair-dealers alike.[70] A few weeks later, on 1 June 1748, South Carolina's customs comptroller seized one of Shute's boats and its contraband contents, over 1,000 gallons of molasses. He petitioned the colonial council, protesting that he had been "waiting for proper Time of Tide to convey it to his own Wharf, intending to enter and pay the Country Duties for the same." The council referred his case to the Commons House of Assembly on 16 June, which in turn appointed a committee to interview Shute. Admitting "that he took the said Molasses from a Land before Charles Town and put the same on board his Boat," Shute offered two witnesses—one a longtime commercial partner, the other a deputy customs collector—to confirm that before the fact, he had announced his intention to pay all required duties. The committee was unimpressed by his alibis, however, and recommended the forfeiture stand. After a second reading of the damning report, the rest of the house agreed.[71]

Shute's assertion that a contrary tide prevented his compliance with the law is especially evocative in light of his own fortune's ebb. By now he clearly sensed financial shoals ahead. On 7 June 1748, six days after the molasses seizure, he and his wife, Anna, transferred the town lot for his Elliott Street store to their fifteen-year-old daughter Isabel. The deed identified this transaction as satisfying the girl's £1,500 legacy from her grandmother Isabella Kimberley, of whose estate Shute was executor.[72] The characterization of the transfer as a legacy was true but likely not the whole truth. Probably the merchant sought to place valuable assets beyond the reach of his creditors. Alternatively, Anna Shute may have hoped to put her daughter's inheritance beyond reach of her husband.

Either interpretation is consistent with Shute's mounting economic distress. Over the next few weeks, cash grew ever scarcer: on 28 June, the assembly rejected Shute's claim for over £130 expended in supplying Indians and coastal guard vessels, and on 12 July, Shute had to borrow £340 on short credit.[73] The scramble to protect his assets continued into the fall of 1748, with Shute hastily installing his nephew Thomas and another understudy, Frederick Merkley, as ostensibly independent storekeepers in Shute's bay-front house.[74] Once Merkley and the younger Thomas Shute set up in his store, Joseph never again advertised merchandise or services as available at that address. Behind the scene, however, the Merkley and Thomas Shute partnership silently continued Joseph Shute's retail operations, with the uncle paying duties on two more incoming cargoes before his nephew left town in 1749.[75]

In transferring control of his operations and assets to his dependents, Shute apparently was planning a long delaying action, invoking the English common law's many protections of private property. To succeed, he had to raise enough money to cover his debts before his attorney's last quibbles collapsed. Toward that end, Shute's other preparations for a financial tempest doubtless included overtures to his father for an infusion of capital, but this time the patriarch could not help. Although intellectually Thomas Shute still remained "preserved in Sound and well disposing mind and memory," physically his health had failed in the fall of 1748. He died by early December, and his will must have disappointed Joseph. It offered the Carolina merchant only a little ready cash and no prospect at all for fending off circling creditors.[76]

Joseph probably learned of his father's death by mid-December 1748, around the time that he published a newspaper advertisement listing all the shipping in Charleston harbor. Perhaps he intended the announcement to reassure Carolinians he was still a commercial player.[77] Possibly his wife's illness in the spring of 1749 helped deter Shute's creditors briefly. But in late July, weeks after Anna followed her father-in-law into the grave, her husband declared bankruptcy and was "in the Custody of the Provost-Marshal" as a debtor.[78] Arrested "by Virtue of several Capias's ad Satisfaciendum, and upon Mesne Process"—that is, arrested both for suits he already had lost and for suits still pending against him—Shute faced a formidable array of creditors (table 12). Nevertheless, he declared himself "ready and willing to make Surrender, upon Oath, to one or more of his Creditors, in Trust for the Rest, all and singular his Estate, both real and personal," as listed in his petition of bankruptcy.[79]

In exchange, the Court of Common Pleas summoned his creditors to appear before the court a month hence "to shew Cause, if any they can, why the said Joseph Shute should not be entitled to the Benefit of the [South Carolina bankruptcy] Acts, upon his complying with the Terms therein prescribed."[80] The so-called benefits of those acts were stark: debtors filed in court a complete financial account of all assets and liabilities, swore to have committed no fraud, handed their property over to trustees, and then stood by while their assets were auctioned, retaining only essential bedding, clothes, tools, and, if they owned any, arms for muster. The proceeds of such sales first were applied to the costs of litigation and then proportionally to all creditors willing to settle for part of their due. Creditors accepting this partial payment could prosecute their debtors no further.[81]

As a legal process, Shute's distress was not unusual in Charleston during the late 1740s. Since the 1745 statutory revisions concerning bankruptcy, fifty-eight South Carolinians had accepted the act's requirements and advertised their financial embarrassment in the *South Carolina Gazette*. But while the procedure was common, Shute's occupation was not. He was the first Charleston merchant to declare bankruptcy since the new law was enacted.[82] Nor was this Shute's sole distinction among his fellow bankrupts: initially, he phrased his published announcements identically to the other insolvents, but one week after admitting that his business had capsized, Shute publicly proclaimed that he would not drown without a struggle. Relying on the newspaper as a means of reaching the widest possible genteel audience with a carefully crafted message, Shute repeated the *pro forma* advertisement of his arrest and court order for creditor attendance. Then he added a coda unparalleled in South Carolina among contemporary announcements of bankruptcy:

> The subscriber having (since the exhibition of his petition aforesaid) diligently and carefully examined his affairs, and thereby found himself capable of saving his houses, land and slaves, provided his creditors will allow him two years for recovery of such monies as are due to him, which alone will be more than sufficient to discharge every debt he oweth, with interest thereon to that time,— desires a meeting of his creditors, on Monday the 14th of August, at his lodgings on the green.

Shute's creditors had nothing to lose by their forbearance, he argued. "If there should be any unexpected deficiency," he promised to "oblige himself, immediately on the expiration of the said Term, to sell so much of his estate as shall suffice."[83] It was a remarkable proposition, this unique entreaty that his creditors, despite their legal claims on his property, should for two years bear the risk of Shute's litigation against his own debtors.

Shute's plan was as unrealistic as it was audacious, and his bankruptcy proceedings rumbled on implacably. The business front of Merkley and Shute collapsed, and Joseph Shute's nephew retreated to Philadelphia in the spring of 1749.[84] By April 1750, Shute relinquished his house on the bay to former client Christopher Gadsden, who began retailing there in May.[85] Shute persuaded several of his principal creditors "to accept of an assignment of his estate real and personal," and in June announced his intention of leaving South Carolina if the rest of his creditors would permit. Calling another meeting of creditors for 26 June "in order to see a state of the subscriber's affairs," Shute promised to account fully for "all the book-debts, notes, bonds, and every thing else due to him, and the whole real and personal estate which he is any ways interested in, or intitled unto." At a public vendue two days after that meeting, the provost marshal auctioned Shute's bay-front house and its several outbuildings, the adjacent low-water lot, the remainder of the island Shute's Delight, a long-term lease of "some houses near the Market-Square . . . Several valuable negroes, a pettiaugua [boat], and all his houshold furniture, seized on execution."[86]

The auction laid bare Joseph Shute's financial failure, and derisive Charlestonians soon dubbed his island Shute's Folly, the name it bears to this day.[87] Nevertheless, he clung tenaciously to credibility and old connections in Charleston—for example, in September 1750, he witnessed a codicil to magnate Samuel Wragg's will, signifying Wragg's ongoing acquaintance.[88] But the financial problems endured: creditors continued to file suit and the provost marshal's deputies continued to serve their writs. At last, in the summer of 1751, Shute sailed to Philadelphia after empowering his Charleston attorney to sue old debtors and negotiate with old creditors, a financial rearguard action that continued intensely for the next two years and sporadically for another eight (tables 10 and 12).[89] Twenty-two years after arriving in Charleston, Joseph Shute departed a ruined man.

He returned to his boyhood home to discover his father's estate in the hands of his nephew William Davis. Thomas Shute had named three executors in his will; only Davis was related, and at first only Davis agreed to perform this time-consuming task. The executorship proved a contentious chore, especially after Joseph Shute and Davis disagreed over the disposition of the patriarch's home. Their dispute revolved around Joseph's contract to pay his father £1,000 (Pennsylvania) for that tract and its improvements, a bargain sealed earlier with a 10 percent down payment. But to inherit the land, Joseph needed to pay the balance. If he did not do so, Thomas Shute had instructed the executors to sell his property "with all convenient speed after my decease and my son's refusal," and to disburse the proceeds as legacies to children, grandchildren, and great-grandchildren.[90]

William Davis waited until May 1752 for Joseph Shute to produce nine hundred pounds, but when his uncle still could not pay the balance, Davis and a fellow executor offered the land at public vendue.[91] Davis probably felt that he had allowed Joseph sufficient time, and certainly Davis faced a number of claims against the estate for which he needed cash.[92] Not surprisingly, Shute resisted the sale and forced an ejectment suit.[93] Their legal wrangling concluded in early November 1754, when Philadelphia merchant Abel James paid Thomas Shute's estate four hundred pounds for the tract and its buildings, a bargain price for such a well-developed and strategically located site.[94]

As Joseph Shute apparently saw it, the sale severely threatened his chances of recovering his footing. Part of that threat was financial: the Shute homestead represented the capital improvements of over half a century—120 well-watered acres cleared out of 200 total, with good timber and an orchard on the remainder; a good stone house with separate kitchen, barn, and stables; and the quarries, plus three associated houses nearby. Moreover, Philadelphia merchants were beginning to build ornate summer houses overlooking the Schuylkill River; a fashionable neighborhood was taking shape in the vicinity of Thomas Shute's industrial center.[95]

And, finally, occupying his father's longtime base could reassure Joseph's commercial connections and testify to his financial resurrection.

Shute had every reason to try to recover the estate, but even so, the price he eventually paid seems recklessly high. In late June 1756, owner Abel James accepted one thousand pounds as Shute's payment for the property and handed over title.[96] To quiet his father's executors and legatees, Shute also paid the estate the full one thousand pounds he had originally promised; with this money, executor Joseph Fox disbursed the long-awaited bequests to Thomas Shute's many descendants. Some of those bequests came back immediately to Joseph, so for a net price of over £1,580, he at last took uncontested possession of his father's home.[97]

The new owner immediately put his quarries back into production but to no avail. As happened in Charleston before his collapse, ready money ran short; over a fifty-seven-day span from June to August 1756, Shute tapped a local ironmonger repeatedly for a total of eighteen pounds in unsecured cash.[98] Within two weeks of purchasing his father's place, Shute sold three small parcels of the troubled legacy—tracts of 30, 26, and 12 acres—and mortgaged the remainder for £448.[99] By July 1757, he sold a fourth parcel of about seventy acres to his eighteen-year-old son John, just as he had sold a valuable Charleston lot to his minor daughter Isabel. Within the next four months, Shute took a second mortgage on the much-diminished remainder. The creditor for both loans, ascending Philadelphia gentleman Joseph Galloway, insisted in the second mortgage with palpable exasperation that this time payment was due "without any Fraud or further Delay and without any Defalcation or Abatement to be made for or in respect of any taxes Charges or assessments." In an unusual move underscoring Galloway's suspicion, Shute was required to repay the second mortgage of £155 in "good & lawful Spanish Pistoles each weighing Four penny weight and six grains ... at the Rate of twentyseven Shillings each Pistole."[100] By demanding payment in gold coins, Galloway implied he had no confidence in Shute's paper obligations.

Such foreshadowing of trouble ahead took tangible form when Galloway's lawsuit led to sheriff's vendues in June 1759, February 1760, and May 1760, dragging out the public humiliation even longer than in Charleston.[101] Thomas Shute's longtime Schuylkill River tract, "well known by the Name of Shute's Plantation," thus slipped from the family's control for a second and final time. By then, Joseph had embarked for Charleston in the forlorn hope of collecting long-due debts and selling some rural land, turning his back on the wrecked dream of a Pennsylvania renaissance.[102]

Joseph Shute's Opportunism

Shute began his southern career as a more active Quaker than his father, and certainly he benefited greatly from Friends in both Philadelphia and Charleston, especially in the early days. In the small southern meeting, he quickly received significant responsibilities. Although he had barely reached the age of majority, by February 1731/2 he was chosen as one of three trustees for the parcel of Charleston land on which their meeting-house stood.[103] In 1736, Shute was esteemed enough to be appointed to inspect and certify a departing Friend, and to serve as clerk of the monthly meeting. It was a short-lived office: the handful of Charleston Quakers slumped into inactivity in 1737, and Shute made his last entry as clerk in early August. No additional activity was recorded until February 1750/1.[104]

Despite his religious community's decline, Shute long retained many of the forms of Quaker observance—as late as March 1750/1, he still affirmed, rather than swore to, a legal statement "according to the ritual of his persuasion."[105] He continued to act like a Quaker when it suited him, but a mountain of evidence indicates he had fallen away from his faith, trespassing against Friends as well as against numerous other Americans.

His lesser transgressions were of the sort routinely decried in contemporary minutes of Quaker meetings to the north. Singly they do not appear especially alarming, but taken together, his venial misbehaviors amount to a pattern of expedient self-serving acts that imposed as much on social proprieties as theological ones. His litigation, for example, might be justified as essential when most of his debtors were not Friends; recourse to the law in such cases would not necessarily breach Quaker doctrine. Similarly, his "full Bobb peruke" and his nine-year-old son's "short Brown Bobb" might signal vanity but could also be explained away as mandatory accessories for a merchant beckoning to elite clients wearing comparable wigs.[106] The 1754 marriage of Shute's nineteen-year-old daughter Elizabeth by an Anglican priest could be characterized as the sort of youthful indiscretion that constantly plagued even large, well-established Quaker communities.[107] Indeed, Elizabeth's mother had committed the same breach in her first marriage.

As the calendar of Shute's transgressions grew, however, it became increasingly difficult to preserve his facade as a good Quaker. He embraced smuggling, which Friends denounced, and given the opportunity in 1750, he too was "married by a priest" outside his professed faith.[108] When Shute hastily inventoried the scant property of his intestate brother Isaac, he dated the document in a format rejected by Quakers as pagan, calling it the "7th day of January 1756" rather than "seventh day eleventh month."[109]

Beyond his many encroachments on the form of Quaker faith, he more directly assailed the Quaker community itself. When Charleston's few remaining Friends ceased to meet in 1737, Shute took control of the buildings on the meetinghouse lot. For eleven years, he managed the property for his own profit, until at last, just as Thomas Shute was dying, the handful of other Quakers still in Charleston requested intervention by the Philadelphia Monthly Meeting. Having learned in November 1748 "that the few Friends that live in Charles Town So Carolina are debarr'd from the Use of their Meeting House by Joseph Shute," Philadelphia Quaker leaders appointed a four-man committee to lay the matter before "the Governour & Council" of South Carolina or any other appropriate persons. Neither the governor's official letters nor the council minutes include any mention of the problem, but the Philadelphia committee reported writing to Governor James Glen and to Shute himself.[110]

In addressing Shute, the committee began the difficult task ordered by the Philadelphia Monthly Meeting in 1748:

> In as much as the Conduct of said Joseph Shute is said to be in other Instances very disreputable & unbecoming a Person making Profession [of faith] with us & as he was educated among us in this City the same Friends are likewise desir'd to consider & take some Way to be fully inform'd of his Character & Conduct that this Meeting may afterwards proceed to testify against him if it should appear necessary & that he cannot be reclaim'd.[111]

Shute understandably wished to avoid this investigation and successfully delayed it for almost three years. Eventually, the Philadelphia Monthly Meeting in August 1751 appointed a new committee "to treat with Joseph Shute (he being now in Town) concerning his Conduct, while he lived in South Carolina." First, however, Shute was to settle the question of the meetinghouse lot: "endeavour to persuade him to Consent to the Appointment of new Trustees for [the] Friends Meeting house in Charles Town."[112] On 10 September 1751, the committee extracted from him a written renunciation of any claim to the disputed tract.[113] Even so, it took over three more years to resolve the dispute. Finally, in early December 1754, Shute conveyed to a new set of trustees the Quaker lot "together with the Meeting House Edifice."[114]

His unwillingness to relinquish control of the lot owed much to the special use he made of the tract's dwelling house. When he decamped from

Charleston in 1751 after declaring bankruptcy, Shute left his new second wife, Mary, in rent-free residence on the Quakers' lot, safe from any threat of eviction by Shute's creditors. This economical arrangement eventually ended in August 1753, when the Charleston Monthly Meeting directed Mary Shute to pay for her lodgings, including six months' back rent. On 27 April 1755, having at last received and recorded the property's deeds of lease and release, the meeting's leaders promptly ordered Shute's wife "to remove out of the house at the back end of the Lott."[115]

While Mary made shift in the meetinghouse tract's "much decayed" dwelling, Joseph resided in genteel comfort in the Second Street house of his Philadelphia relative, Rebecca Steel.[116] Indeed, he was a little too comfortable, as leaders of the Philadelphia Monthly Meeting discovered in October 1755, when they were "informed that some scandalous Reports have been spread concerning Joseph Shute of his being too intimate with his Servant, a Maid who is lately gone from his House & said to be with Child."[117]

The Philadelphia Monthly Meeting's earlier 1748 orders to investigate Shute's "Character & Conduct" had languished unheeded after the exhausting struggle over the Charleston land, but now they were once again at issue. The meeting dispatched two Friends "to advise him to take speedy Care to do all in his Power to clear himself" but to no avail. Seventeen weeks and "repeated Admonitions" later, the Philadelphia Monthly Meeting declared Joseph Shute not "worthy of our religious Fellowship & Communion."[118] At first, he fought his expulsion, announcing on 27 April 1756 his intention to appeal. Finally, after the Philadelphia Quarterly Meeting confirmed the decision in October, he let the matter drop.[119] By then he had purchased his father's home and faced pressing financial problems; the consolations of Quaker society could wait.

Did Joseph Shute's female servant consent to their sexual relations? No evidence survives to indicate whether he was persuasive rather than coercive, but Shute certainly resorted to force in numerous other contexts. Perhaps no part of Quaker doctrine is more popularly familiar than its renunciation of violence, yet Shute repeatedly ignored this proscription. He offered weapons—pistols and cutlasses—for sale in 1735, and purchased the armed sloop *Pompey*, carrying three guns, later the same year.[120] After the war with Spain turned Gulf Stream merchantmen into lucrative targets, Shute added six guns to his previously unarmed brigantine *Anna*.[121] Quakers elsewhere increasingly were renouncing slavery, but like his father, Shute enthusiastically embraced it, despite the physical domination on which bondage depended. At least fifty slaves passed through his hands between 1735 and 1752 (table 13).[122]

The final example of Shute's predatory impulses, the fraudulent attempt to send Edward Tarr back into bondage in 1761, illustrates the remarkably long reach of Shute's opportunism. With this last deceit, Joseph Shute slipped out of the written record, vanishing abruptly for a man of his disposition and habits.[123]

3

The Skinner 1736–1771

William Davis, Manager—The Skinner—The Yeoman's Dilemma

When Thomas Shute passed over his own children to select William Davis as his executor, he acknowledged his grandson's accomplishments as another man of business. Broadly speaking, Davis's career resembled his grandfather's, especially in their mutual recognition of frontier opportunities. But the frontier changed a great deal in the eight decades between Shute's first purchase of a farm and Davis's last breath. Part of that was a matter of scale: Lancaster County once had been the outer limit of Shute's economic reach, but Davis routinely passed through Lancaster Town while heading as far southwest as Virginia's New River Valley for business. Davis's repeated journeys between Pennsylvania and Virginia facilitated more than his own profits, however; he and common men like him maintained communications between genteel frontier land speculators and Atlantic seaports.

Most importantly, Davis represented for his parents' generation an alternate course, a way to transcend an essential problem facing colonial families from New England to Georgia. Yeomen like Shute fathered many children as a means to ensure their own economic security in old age, so populations grew faster than real estate. Most of Davis's aunts and uncles chose to stay home in hopes of receiving a portion of the patriarch's shrinking estate. By contrast, Davis ranged abroad in search of commercial opportunities.

William Davis, Manager

William Davis was about eight years younger than Joseph Shute, but while his uncle initially had gone to sea, Davis spent his teenage years working in Pennsylvania's industrial frontier.[1] From 1736 through 1738, Davis's name appears incidentally in the ledgers of Pine Forge and Coventry Forge, mostly in conjunction with the purchase of shoes and small amounts of liquor.[2] By 1739, he was retailing small quantities of goods in exchange for pig iron, and by 1741, he was helping to manage Mount Pleasant Furnace, located in what today is northern Chester County (see map 1).[3] In the spring of 1743, iron impresarios Robert Grace and John Potts hired Davis on an annual contract as subclerk of Warwick Furnace, where he remained for about seven years. Davis's employers subsequently acknowledged his abilities by engaging him as manager, though the timing of this promotion is uncertain.[4]

His managerial duties involved the business of iron, not the making of it. He frequently received cash from and on behalf of his employers, and disbursed money and credit across the vast array of payees involved in the iron trade.[5] In hundreds of transactions from May 1745 to May 1746, Davis's expenditures on behalf of Warwick Furnace totaled over £158, and his receipts amounted to over £137.[6] Beyond the logistics of making, transporting, and selling iron, Davis handled lawsuits for delinquent accounts, traveling to attend courts in Lancaster County, Chester County, and Philadelphia in order to sue debtors in 1745.[7] In exchange for his careful reckonings and far-ranging activities, Davis drew a modest annual salary of fifty pounds in 1746.[8] Early in his managerial career, Davis added silver buckles to his wardrobe and an expensive stallion to his stable, but unlike his uncle Joseph Shute, Davis does not appear to have been much drawn to a higher level of material culture and social status.[9] Ten years later, while settling his grandfather's estate, Davis was identified in a land deed as a yeoman; like Thomas Shute, he never identified himself as a gentleman.[10]

Davis appears to have left his employment in the iron industry when his annual contract as manager expired in May 1750.[11] Probably he then assumed full-time management of Thomas Shute's estate, a task that grew considerably more complicated after Joseph Shute arrived in Philadelphia in 1751. Around this time, Edward Tarr completed his payment of thirty-six pounds, and Davis signed the receipts that under the terms of Thomas Shute's will made Tarr a free man. Possibly Tarr and Davis were in Lancaster on this momentous occasion: Tarr said in 1753 that he had recently come from there, and Davis was identified as a resident of Lancaster County in 1752 and Lancaster Borough in 1754.[12]

Tarr's payments seem not to have improved the overall financial health of Shute's estate, if the subsequent lawsuits against it are any measure. Unfortunately, the records of Philadelphia County's Court of Common Pleas have not survived for this period, but three public vendues for portions of his land signal that the executors could not readily produce enough cash to fend off impatient creditors.[13] As late as July 1756, eight years after Shute's death, one of his executors still was requesting "speedy payment" from debtors.[14]

By then the Seven Years' War was under way, and William Davis had entered the carting business. In December 1757, he began hauling one-ton loads of bar iron from Pine Forge to Philadelphia, and over the next twenty-eight months undertook twenty-six comparable loads. Davis signed receipts for each of these shipments, so he may have driven the wagon himself.[15] He left town sometime between his last bar iron delivery to Philadelphia in late April 1760 and the July advertisement in the *Pennsylvania Gazette* that his unclaimed letters awaited retrieval at the Philadelphia Post Office.[16] Like many Pennsylvanians before him, Davis went to Virginia, where on 19 August 1760, he struck a partnership with Augusta County sheriff William Preston. The two men agreed to provide four wagons drawn by sixteen horses to supply a military expedition against Cherokee Indian towns located in what today is eastern Tennessee.[17] Davis's and Preston's startup expenses amounted to a substantial £247:11:3 Virginia money, and within a month, they added three more horses worth £38 in all.[18]

Virginia's war with the Cherokees in 1760 and 1761 was a small and ultimately inconclusive part of a larger conflict between that tribe and inhabitants of North and South Carolina.[19] Mobilized militiamen for whom Davis and Preston hauled supplies advanced as far as Great Island on Holston River (modern Kingsport, Tennessee), but when Virginia's General Assembly initially funded the expedition, the burgesses directed the effort to cease by 1 December 1760. In the autumn, the troops therefore marched back to eastern Virginia.[20] In the context of the wider war, Virginia's 1760 campaign did little to relieve North and South Carolina, but for inhabitants of Augusta County, the army prevented further Cherokee raids. Of course, the troops also represented a market for local horses, beef, flour, and whiskey, some of which was hauled to the army by wagons belonging to Davis and Preston.[21]

The on-again, off-again campaign resumed in the spring of 1761 with Virginia's army returning to the Holston River, fed in part with food transported as in the previous year by the wagons and teams of the Davis-Preston partnership. Davis's sole known surviving correspondence is his directive of 20 June "To fields the waggoner" written from Looney's Ferry, where the Great Wagon Road crossed the James River: "You are to tack your waggan to John Paxton [in the southern end of the Borden Grant] and Leve it & goo to Mr Christain [in Staunton] and he will inform you woth you [shall do] with it[.] tack care of your Gears & tack them down to the town with you [half a line illegible] to goo to Stantown given under my hand at Loneys farry[.] Wm Davis."[22] He directed his teamster to report to "Mr Christain" in the latter's capacity as a commissary for the expedition, but Israel Christian simultaneously held other offices. Sixteen weeks later, when Hugh Montgomery attempted to reenslave Edward Tarr, Justice of the Peace Christian was one of the magistrates hearing Montgomery's complaint.[23]

Virginia's army returned to southwest Virginia the following spring. As in the previous year, the 1761 expedition proceeded no farther than Great Island, and once again the troops saw no action. Lieutenant Governor Francis Fauquier thought the whole business a waste of money, notwithstanding that, however badly managed, the campaign appeared to have induced the Cherokees to negotiate an end to hostilities and doubtless protected Augusta County from renewed raiding. Moreover, Augusta County's refugees hurried home on the heels of the returning army: the tithable count—that is, the tally of taxable persons—jumped 32.1 percent from June 1760 to June 1761.[24]

As directed by the General Assembly, the army again began to disband in November, and at the end of the month, Davis and Preston concluded their partnership.[25] On 28 November, Davis borrowed six pounds from Preston, and the following day they divided their equipment and twenty horses.[26] By this time, Davis had proved to be a useful connection to the northern colonies for the Augusta County gentleman. In April 1761, for example, Davis paid a Wilmington, Delaware, printer for blank land deeds and postage on behalf of "Mr William Preston of Virginia," and ten months later, Davis repeated the service.[27] Modest northern businessmen like Davis, as well as other Augusta County yeomen traveling on business to the Delaware Valley, helped frontier gentlemen to maintain their connections to Atlantic seaports.[28] In exchange, Davis received an implicit endorsement to a wider circle of acquaintances and business connections in Augusta County.

An instructive example of Davis's diverse associations comes from a list of Augusta County participants in the Conestoga Creek Bridge lottery, as recorded by William Preston in September 1762. Preston, Davis, and four other partners bought fifteen chances costing "four Dollars Each"—that is, Spanish silver dollars—in a Pennsylvania scheme intended to raise 8,100 dollars for a bridge for "the Great Road leading from the City of Philadelphia to the Borough of Lancaster" where it crossed Conestoga Creek. That Davis may have brought the tickets to the other parties is suggested by his recent arrival in Staunton from Pennsylvania and the fact that Preston recorded all of the ticket numbers at the same time as he recorded their price.[29] Preston listed the other lottery partners as John Brown, Charles Lewis, William Crow, and William Cabeen. Of these, Preston, Brown, and Lewis were gentlemen: Preston was a militia colonel, Brown a militia major, and Lewis a militia lieutenant on the cusp of promotion to captain. Brown was a former magistrate, Preston a current one, and Lewis was added to the commission of the peace the following year. Crow was a Staunton storekeeper commissioned as a captain the following year but not named as a magistrate for at least the next eleven years. Cabeen, also a storekeeper, was the least reputable of the lot; in 1757, he assaulted and beat deputy clerk of court Thomas Bowyer in a dispute over gambling at cards. In 1761, Cabeen insinuated himself into the business of supplying the Cherokee expedition.[30]

The six lottery gamblers contributed the round sum of ten Spanish silver dollars each. Since the fifteen tickets could not be divided evenly among them, the men acquired an equal share in the fifteen separate numbers: three gentlemen, two storekeepers, and a yeoman entrepreneur joined in a partnership facilitated by one of its least prestigious members, William Davis. The partnership is interesting because unlike gamblers in other colonial Virginia contexts, these men seem less competitive and more cooperative.[31] As in gaming, so too in business: a year after the lottery partnership, in September 1763, Davis attended Augusta County court as a witness for plaintiffs Charles Lewis and David Robinson. Robinson was Preston's particular friend who had helped arrange a profitable land transaction for Davis earlier that year.[32]

The Skinner

After dissolving the carting partnership in 1761 and returning to Pennsylvania, Davis retained a considerable financial and personal interest in the Virginia frontier, revisiting the county at least six more times before his death in 1771.[33] He identified himself during this period as a skinner, a trafficker in hide and fur; his absence from Indian trade records probably means Davis was a middleman, not a direct trader among Indian towns.[34] As table 14 suggests, it often is easier to identify the skinned animals than their hunters. Some undoubtedly were killed by Augusta County settlers, as indicated by the total of six beaver traps listed in four estate inventories between 1755 and 1759, but Indians hunting among the county's widespread farms also traded with settlers.[35]

Regardless of who skinned the animals, hides flowed through local trade and credit networks and into the regional economy like any other commodity, facilitated by skinners like Davis. The full economic significance of that flow is revealed by two conflicting petitions from the Valley of Virginia in 1759.[36] The first, from merchants north of Augusta County in the town of Winchester, complained "That their Trade is greatly prejudiced by the great Number of Pedlars from Pennsylvania, dealing in Skins and Furs, without being duly authorized, who carry out such Commodities without paying any Duty."[37] The Pennsylvania skinners "import Rum, Wine, and other Commodities, without paying any Duty [and] carry away Skins and Furs in the same Manner." Their unfair trade advantage enabled Pennsylvania chapmen to undersell the Winchester merchants who took hides in trade from retail customers, and consequently the interlopers "carry great Sums of Money in Specie out of the Colony."[38] It was the same Pennsylvania trading device about which South Carolinians complained ten years earlier.[39]

By contrast to their neighbors in the northern valley, "sundry inhabitants of Augusta County" complained in another 1759 petition that expensive peddler licenses, such as the ones advocated by the Winchester merchants, generated "many Inconveniences . . . to the Trade in Skins and Furs," and requested the assembly to set a lower rate.[40] In short, Augusta County residents had quantities of hides and wanted better access to markets for them.[41] Small wonder, then, that the enterprising skinner William Davis shuttled repeatedly between Philadelphia and Augusta County.

If his real estate transactions are any indication, Davis traded widely throughout western Virginia. On 17 May 1762, the county surveyor recorded an entry for "Wm Davis of Phil[a]d[elphi]a 400 acres Joining his Land at the Egale [Eagle] Bottom on the New River," a first step toward acquiring a patent that incidentally indicates the surveyor already associated Davis with a nearby but unidentified tract. Two months later, Davis entered claims for 450 acres, and in 1767 filed for a total of 150 acres more; in all, Davis initiated claims to 1,000 acres along the New River, approximately 400 miles from Philadelphia.[42] The total acreage sounds impressive, but entries were both cheap and tenuous; the land was unimproved, and until surveyed and patented, it lacked the legal protections and durability of real estate.[43] Davis surveyed only a single tract in Augusta County, forty-five acres on Buffalo Creek in the Forks of the James, and patented nothing.[44] His behavior thus suggests that Davis saw the small entry fees more as preemptive wagers than long-term investments.

Davis's four purchases of developed land have a similar short-term character. In every instance, the grantors no longer resided in Augusta County. During the Seven Years' War, one seller had decamped to Pennsylvania and another to South Carolina; the remaining two were the Pennsylvania heirs of deceased Augusta County men. In June 1762, Davis purchased 280 acres on Buffalo Creek and within a few weeks reconveyed it.[45] The following year, Davis bought 400 acres on the New River from a refugee in Pennsylvania for £65 and resold it within months for £120.[46] In 1767, Davis purchased 125 acres on the New River from a Pennsylvania heir for £60 and in three years sold it for double that price.[47] Davis died before he could sell the fourth tract.

The most intriguing of his Augusta County investments were in Staunton, where he undertook complex agreements for purchasing town lots and operating retail stores that his frustrated executor still was trying to untangle two decades after the skinner's death.[48] One such arrangement involved half of County Lot Nine in Staunton.[49] In 1766, former ordinary keeper George Wilson acquired half of the lot, a well-situated tract adjoining the courthouse (map 2).[50] Wilson agreed to convey the lot to William Davis and Matthew Reid, a Staunton merchant.[51] Davis died in 1771 before the deed was recorded; in 1789, Davis's executor, Benjamin Loxley, received thirdhand information "that Wm Davis own'd sundrey Houses & Lotts of Land in Stanton in Virginia which I have never had any accot of or heard of before."[52] Decades after Davis's death, his heir at last completed the transaction in 1791.[53] The unfinished conveyance helps explain why Reid and his partner, Hugh Johnston, long operated in Staunton but never appeared in colonial land records as purchasing a Staunton lot.[54]

In 1748, Thomas Shute recognized William Davis's merits as a yeoman's man of business by selecting Davis as an executor. Shute understood that such men were meticulous accountants with hands tough enough to control a wagon and team, men who, though competent to relate in a range of contexts with everyone from gentlemen to slaves, never mistook themselves for the former. As an ironworks manager, a carter, and a skinner, Davis demonstrated entrepreneurial virtues of which his grandfather approved. He also demonstrated integrity considerably more robust than that of his uncle Joseph Shute. Although Davis was a slaveholder himself both early and late in life, he carefully recorded Edward Tarr's payments and in

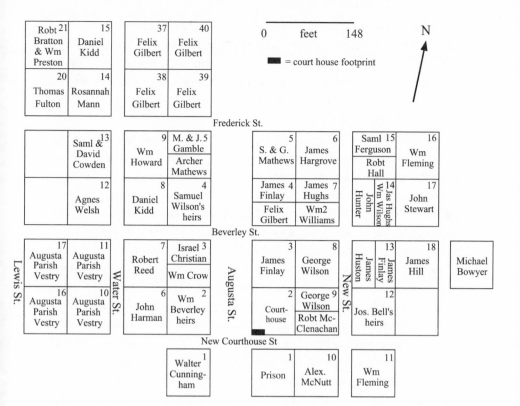

MAP 2. **Staunton, Virginia, 1766.**

Edward Tarr relocated his shop to the edge of Staunton in 1760, when the village consisted mostly of retail stores and ordinaries serving crowds periodically drawn to court sessions. Six years later, William Davis, Staunton merchant Mathew Reid, and frontier entrepreneur George Wilson jointly acquired half of County Lot 9, adjoining the court square. Edward Tarr was a customer of Reid's from at least February 1765 to June 1770. (Plat by author. Sources: Lots conveyed by William Beverley east of Augusta Street are shown as of 1749 in "A Plan of the Town of Staunton, in Augusta County," Augusta DB, 2:410. Lots conveyed by Augusta County trustees west of Augusta Street are described in Augusta DB, 2–27.

1761, appears to have at least tacitly acknowledged the legitimacy of Tarr's freedom.[55]

Davis made his last journey to the Virginia frontier by 4 October 1770, when he sold 125 acres of New River land to Israel Christian's son William. Davis's presence in the valley is indicated by the fact that the grantee and all three witnesses to the deed resided south and west of the upper James River. Davis either departed or died soon after the sale; he did not appear at the mid-November court session to acknowledge the deed.[56] He expired in an unknown location by July 1771, at the approximate age of fifty-three;

given that he drew a will on 1 March 1764, his health may have been declining for some years.[57] Over a ten-month period in 1768 and 1769, Davis consulted a Staunton physician who bled him, prescribed an eye lotion, and repeatedly dosed him with Glauber's salt, a purgative. Considering the primitive state of eighteenth-century medicine, these treatments offer little insight into Davis's ailments.[58]

His widow, Christiana Davis, and his executor, Benjamin Loxley, presented Davis's will and its witnesses on 24 July 1771. Loxley requested an appraisal of the estate, which was produced in court in Philadelphia on 8 August 1771. Local appraisers found £1,396:12:8 in assets: Philadelphia real estate worth £365 (26.1%); household furnishings valued at £103:13:5 (7.4%); and £927:19:3 in bonds, notes, and accounts owed to the estate (66.5%). Left unevaluated were Davis's debts, but fifteen years and an unknown amount of payments later, Loxley tallied Davis's remaining obligations as amounting to £1,578:1:6½. As with his grandfather's, Davis's estate took many years to settle. In 1772, Andrew Lewis, brother of Davis's associate Charles Lewis, collected £151:16:11½ Virginia currency (£189:16:3 Pennsylvania) that was owed to the estate by valley debtors; in April 1777, Andrew Lewis produced another payment of 603⅓ dollars (£226:5:0 Pennsylvania), and in November of the same year added another £500 in Continental currency.[59] In 1789, fourteen years after the widow's death, Loxley continued to plead with Davis's old partner William Preston for assistance in settling some of Davis's uncompleted land transactions.[60]

The Yeoman's Dilemma

American frontier history is partly a tale of unpaid bills. A century after Thomas Shute arrived in the Delaware Valley, the heirs of his grandson still were trying to collect their due. In more than just a metaphorical sense, their difficulties were a legacy from their great-grandfather.

The birth of Thomas Shute's second child in 1697 confronted the thirty-one-year-old Shute with a momentous decision. The issue had for its context the financial ambition of Pennsylvania's proprietor, William Penn, who hoped to profit handsomely from gradually selling pieces of his colony to immigrants. Toward that end, Penn restricted land sales in order to increase demand and elevate prices.[61] As an established landholder, Thomas Shute benefited from the resulting increase in real estate values, but Penn's land policies had serious implications for Shute's two existing children and for the future children he had not yet fathered.

In colonies where real estate was the basis of wealth and where available real estate increased less quickly than population, it was in the best economic interest of maturing offspring for their parents and the parents of their future spouses to produce on average two or fewer children who reached adulthood. This maturation rate would ensure that, again on average, the next generation of mating couples would find available as much land as the reproductive members of their parents' generation. If parents produced more children, however, the amount of land available to newlyweds of the rising generation necessarily would diminish. These circumstances generated a strategic dilemma for yeomen: whose future was more important, the yeoman's or his grandchildren's?

To secure his own future, a yeoman needed reliable, affordable workers. Short- and intermediate-term options ranged from day-labor hirelings to chattel slaves, but the most attractive long-term option was to father as many children as a wife or series of wives could bear. Given chronic shortages of enslaved and contractual labor in early Pennsylvania, Thomas Shute could best protect his future by tying his children's economic prospects to his own.

To secure comparable amounts of land for his grandchildren, however, Shute needed to limit his progeny to two. If a third child reached adulthood, the siblings faced hard choices from among three options. They could remain within the patriarch's orbit in hopes of receiving a reduced portion of land, they could move to less-populous districts and establish their own families on undeveloped tracts, or they could seek their own economic independence via careers not contingent on the ownership of real estate.[62]

The effects of what can be called the Yeoman's Dilemma accelerated geometrically with increasingly rapid growth in eighteenth-century colonial populations. For maturing children of yeomen who chose to remain near their patriarch, economic opportunities inevitably constricted. For their siblings—and the European immigrants with whom they competed—who chose to move to frontier lands in western Pennsylvania, Maryland, Virginia, the Carolinas, and Georgia, the dilemma generated ever more friction with Indians and other colonists over land usage and ownership.[63] And adult children who followed the third option, entering careers not directly linked to land ownership, helped bring forth American capitalism. Each course had its hazards.

All but one of Thomas Shute's children stayed in his vicinity and pursued the occupations the patriarch chose for them. The firstborn, William, eventually received 120 acres as a gift from his father and stepmother in 1739, eighteen years after his marriage, when William was about forty-five years old and already had three daughters of his own.[64] Shute gave a mill tract to his next child, Christian Shute Davis, and her husband in 1721; eleven years later they returned the property to him.[65] In his 1748 will, Shute devised the use of buildings on a Philadelphia town lot to Christian during her lifetime; his will also directed that Christian's son William Davis and Shute's son Isaac split a copper mine tract of one hundred acres in Lancaster County. The considerable remainder of the estate he ordered to be sold (see table 1).[66] Shute's five other adult children received no land from their father in their lifetimes.

Thomas Shute may have left his children only modest legacies out of a sense that their bad behavior deserved nothing better. William fathered several illegitimate children and refused to give satisfaction to the other Quakers in his monthly meeting until he was imprisoned for debt; only then did a jailhouse epiphany belatedly move William to condemn "his scandalous conduct."[67] Younger son Isaac at least twice required his father's financial assistance with outstanding store accounts, was sued repeatedly for unpaid debts, and died owning only a trivial estate.[68] Another son, Jacob, chronically refused to pay at least one financial obligation, relied on his father for help with other debts, was forced like his half-brother William to send "a Paper Condemning his Imprudend Conduct and Behaviour" to the Philadelphia Monthly Meeting, and owned little property when he died.[69] Daughter Christian committed no documented breach of Quaker discipline, but the Philadelphia Monthly Meeting expelled her husband Samson Davis as an unreformable alcoholic.[70]

When Thomas Shute sent his youngest son to South Carolina in 1729, Joseph's ability to cultivate his father's generosity from a distance diminished relative to Joseph's siblings in Pennsylvania. Joseph's decision to trade in European consumer goods therefore represented his best strategy for ensuring his own future; through commerce, Joseph transcended the diminishing freeholds of the Yeoman's Dilemma. It is impossible to tell what Thomas Shute thought of Joseph's coats of many colors, or even if he knew about them, but the patriarch's endorsement of his grandson William Davis demonstrates an appreciation for men of business. In any event, Thomas did not live to see Joseph's financial collapse; for all of the patriarch's life, Joseph contributed to Thomas's financial security by serving as his Charleston factor.

To the extent that Joseph Shute and William Davis labored entrepreneurially in order to look out for themselves, they participated in familial economic strategies that have not been rigorously examined since the early days of quantitative social history. In a widely cited analysis of those strategies, historian James A. Henretta describes how rural families of the eighteenth and early nineteenth centuries increasingly participated in non-subsistence production for the marketplace, an activity that Henretta interprets as protecting the family as a social unit. Henretta does not acknowledge how this kind of activity served fathers well but not necessarily their families or their neighborhoods.[71]

Henretta discusses various tactics in the patriarchal quest for security, the most successful of which were the increased production for markets by women and the shift in productive efforts to include home factories. In any given neighborhood, these economic innovations helped bridge the ever-widening gap between arithmetically increasing family wealth and geometrically increasing family heirs. For the short term at least, these social adaptations succeeded in preserving existing family relationships. Drawing on evidence from a range of times and places, Henretta demonstrates that rural patriarchs widely shared this goal.[72] But behavior found in many places over time did not necessarily endure in one place or even in one family, and in overlooking that distinction, Henretta misses a critical observation.

In the eighteenth century, the most important historical significance of families' economic strategies emerged from the ongoing tension between generations. Consider Thomas Shute's effort to set up his son Joseph as a factor. Henretta's expanded definition of yeoman agricultural activity reasonably makes a place for such activity; factoring is comparable to milling or other processing and handling of rural produce. If Thomas Shute's plans had proceeded as he intended, Joseph still would have been called a merchant, but his function would have remained close to its agricultural roots, vending bread, flour, and beer.

Such a career for the son would have been in Thomas's best interest, though not Joseph's. Far from home, he could not easily compete with his older siblings for his father's affection and largesse. Therein lay an explosive evolutionary potential. Once beyond his father's immediate supervision, Joseph transcended his father's strategy and expanded his marketplace activities to emphasize commerce in consumer goods. Here was a traffic whose rate of growth far outpaced the more modest accretion of agricultural profits; here was an escape from the grim mathematics of yeoman inheritance.

Historians of colonial America have long recognized that to survive in the eighteenth-century marketplace, to prosper as profits from consumer goods outstripped those of agricultural commodities, required increasingly individualistic behavior that paid ever-less attention to restraints and obligations of the rural social order. The Shute experience illustrates that this transformation was driven by family economic choices in favor of the patriarch. Joseph Shute seemingly recognized how barren the future rural social and economic order was. Since his yeoman father had sired more children than could be sustained at the parents' level of wealth, Joseph logically took his chances in the new economy.

He was early, but he was not alone. When land grew scarce locally in rural neighborhoods across colonial and early national America, fathers' attempts to secure their own old age created many Joseph Shutes for every one new yeoman heir. If they remained in place, adult children of initial settlers could only destabilize rural families and neighborhoods with a scramble for limited agricultural inheritances. If they moved deeper into the continent, they deferred the day of reckoning, shifting their own dilemma to the next generation. Increasingly, they turned away from farms, and whether as entrepreneurs or wage laborers, joined and fed the emerging new commercial and industrial economies. Eventually the numbers prevailed: elite Charlestonians mocked Shute's folly, but the social and economic changes that he represented—and hastened—would in the next century destroy their own descendants' worlds.

Part II
The Safety Valve

4

The Slave 1711–1751

A World of Fire—Ned's Literacy and Numeracy–Ned's Social Education—
Ned's Religious Education—Freedom by Installments

Thomas Shute's slave Ned received a more momentous bequest than any of the patriarch's children: an opportunity to buy his own freedom. Having purchased himself, Ned attained a level of prosperity that many of his white contemporaries would have envied. In the process, Ned became Edward Tarr, and by either name, he exemplified an enigma. Ned's career seemed typical for unfree Pennsylvania ironworkers; Tarr's career seemed normal for landowning white artisans of western Virginia. The two conditions were worlds apart, yet Ned vaulted from one identity to the other.

His achievements reflected a remarkable education. At least three of his masters were variously engaged in the iron business, a trade that unintentionally generated learning opportunities in liberal as well as vocational arts. Despite his enslavement, Ned made the most of those chances. The context of Ned's Pennsylvania years thus is essential for understanding his extensive accomplishments later in Virginia. Evidence from these early years is fragmentary but sufficient to discern that his path to a free mind stretched across iron country.

A World of Fire

The infant who became Edward Tarr was born about 1711 to unknown parents in an unknown location. As an adult, Tarr was "commonly known as Black Ned."[1] He was uniformly described as black or Negro rather than mulatto, so if Ned had a white ancestor, she or he likely was a distant relative. Ned's facility with Anglo-American culture may indicate that he was raised within the British colonies rather than imported to them, but that too is unrecorded. The sparse details concerning Ned's early life were typical for his enslaved peers, who often were documented only at narrative inflections devised by their masters as a consequence of sale, flight, probate, or litigation.

A 1732 newspaper listing suggests that Ned initially was trained to be a farmer and "tend a Grist-Mill." The advertisement offered "a Young Negroe Man about 21 Years of Age" and invited potential purchasers to "Enquire of Andrew Robeson near Scuylkil-Falls."[2] Both the seller and his location amount to clues about the anonymous slave. Robeson, the namesake son of a prominent merchant and gentleman, had inherited "the Roxborrow Mill and Beating Mill" located where he lived.[3] His home and mill site on Wissahickon Creek were a short distance up the Schuylkill River from Thomas Shute's home (see figure 1).

The unnamed slave's age also was significant: his implied birth year matched that in a second newspaper notice by Robeson in early 1739. Given the matching ages, Robeson thus may have retained the young man he offered for sale in 1732; Pennsylvania masters rarely owned more than a handful of slaves, and to possess two men of the same age would have been unlikely.[4] In any event, this time Robeson explicitly was describing Ned, the man who became Edward Tarr.

Robeson advertised as a fugitive "a Negro Man, named Ned, about 27 Years of Age." When Ned ran away, he wore "an old leather Jacket and Breeches" over more conventional textile clothing.[5] Laborers in other occupations sometimes wore leather outer garments, but spark-resistant clothing was especially common in descriptions of fugitive ironworkers.[6] Ned was "middle siz'd and well set," which in eighteenth-century usage described a powerfully muscular build, and he was last seen in the company of "Mulatto Will," a free man who drove a cart for iron furnaces. According to Robeson, Ned "Speaks the Dutch [i.e., Deutsch, the German language] very well."[7] Probably Ned returned or was apprehended almost immediately, since Robeson did not repeat his advertisement the following week.

Robeson's high opinion of Ned's fluency was verified later by the Moravian native German speakers who visited Edward Tarr's blacksmith shop in October 1753. They noted that "The negro understood German well."[8] It was an unusual skill among slaves in the middle colonies. By the time Ned ran away in early 1739, masters in Pennsylvania, New Jersey, and Delaware had been publishing announcements about fugitive people of color for almost two decades. Newspaper notices described at least fifty-three runaways as "Negro" or "mulatto" before Ned's flight. None was advertised as speaking German.[9]

Possibly Ned learned the language as a child, but if not, he had good opportunities to do so while working for Robeson. In 1734, Robeson advertised an eighteen-year-old runaway white servant named James Bell, noting that, like Ned, "He speaks good High-Dutch."[10] After Robeson died in 1740, appraisers of his estate enumerated "Two Dutch [Deutsche] men Servants, to serve 2 years Each," valuing them together at sixteen pounds.[11]

At death, Robeson also owned three anonymous slaves, "A Negro man . . . woman . . . [and] boy." These laborers plus the indentured Germans resided "In the Mill," where Robeson's appraisers found "a Bed for the Servants" and "another for the Negroes." None of the five laborers was named, and it cannot be absolutely proved that Ned was the "Negro man," but strong circumstantial evidence suggests that for the time he was owned by Robeson, Ned lived and worked in close quarters with German speakers. The mill containing beds for Robeson's anonymous servants and slaves also held "A Sledge, Iron bars," and "a Smiths vice."[12]

Ned's ironworking career probably started with on-the-job training by a blacksmith, in the tradition of apprenticeships for white youths. Alternatively, Ned might have developed the smith's craft as a subset of furnace- or foundry-man skills. Such expertise was demonstrated "By Negro Caesar," another ironworking slave, in the credit his owner received "for Smith Work" in 1747; normally Caesar labored as a hammer-man in a foundry.[13] Given Ned's absence from ironworks records before the 1740s, however, it seems more likely he learned his trade as an apprentice in a blacksmith shop.

In a transaction for which no documentation survives, Andrew Robeson's executors conveyed Ned to veteran ironworker John Hansen, Ned's second known master. Hansen was an expert forgeman known as a finer, a specialist who converted pig iron into thin marketable bars.[14] The sale had ominous implications, even for an experienced blacksmith, because laborers in furnaces and forges inhabited a world of fire. Other American workers—especially those cooking sap from sugar cane or pine trees—toiled miserably within the same terrible realm, but no other colonial occupation demanded as much proximity to so many deadly forms of combustion and heat as ironworking.

The physical processes in an ironworks were simple but not easy, demanding constant tending and prodigious quantities of natural resources. Charcoal, the essential fuel of ironworking, burned hotter and more evenly than firewood without adding impurities to the iron. Unfortunately, making charcoal was a laborious, filthy, and dangerous process that consumed vast amounts of timber. A single bushel represented over sixty-four cubic feet of firewood, and a single cartload required almost all of the trees in three acres of forest.[15] Charcoal burners, or colliers, risked severe injuries while tending earth-covered mounds of smoldering wood. Charring timber slabs into lumps of pure carbon required approximately two weeks, during which colliers jumped up and down on the mounds in order to settle evenly the burning wood inside. If a collier accidentally broke open the earthen covering, flames roared out of the hole, and if he fell through, he was seared.[16]

Using picks and pry bars, miners dug stone-like ore in open pits and loaded it onto carts for delivery to furnaces. At the furnace top, workers under the direction of an expert furnace master dumped alternating loads of charcoal, iron ore, and limestone into a roaring chimney. As the ore heated, some of its impurities bonded to the limestone flux, though when the ore eventually melted, it still contained unwanted minerals.[17]

Furnaces burned voraciously for months on end. One ironmaster estimated that keeping a single furnace in blast required the ongoing labor of three men to quarry iron ore and twelve colliers to make the eight hundred bushels of charcoal devoured daily by the fire. Blast furnaces also required reliable water streams to power the bellows that injected extra air for hotter combustion and more efficient oxidation of impurities in the iron. Periodically, the furnace master drained molten iron into channels cut into the earthen floor beyond the furnace hearth to create pig iron. Each pig could weigh over one hundred pounds.[18]

Once cooled, pig iron was carted away for further processing in nearby forges. At this stage, expert finers like John Hansen and his slaves set about removing more impurities from the iron. They began by melting two or three pigs into a malleable mass called a loup. Using tongs, Hansen and someone such as Ned shifted the loup to a large anvil and held it under the blows of a water-powered hammer weighing several hundred pounds. The two men repeatedly reheated their work and returned it to the anvil; gradually, the hammer expelled some of the molten impurities from the loup's solid iron. Slowly, the unwieldy mass assumed the characteristic shape of what was called an anchony, a squared thick bar of iron that initially had irregular lumps on each end. Hansen would cut the anchony in half so that either man could hold the square end with tongs while heating and hammering the remaining lump to complete the crude bar. Subsequent heating and hammering pounded the anchonies into smaller merchant bars of half an inch to no more than two inches in thickness. Such bars were thin enough for individual smiths to heat and hammer by hand in small shop fires.[19]

Ned's first day as a helper for John Hansen must have been daunting. Hammer mills were noisy, and finers continually faced the hazards of handling awkward masses of red-hot metal. Anchonies were especially dangerous, given that the unwieldy loup could weigh as much as 250 pounds. In 1736, a Coventry Forge manager billed Hansen's white helper "for curing your Burns," and lesser injuries must have been common.[20]

By the time he bought Ned, Hansen had moved to New Pine Forge (see map 1). Although the exact date of Ned's purchase is unknown, Hansen was credited in 1742 for three days' labor on behalf of the forge by "John Hansons Negroes"; the slaves were unnamed, but in the same ledger and same year, the New Pine Forge manager began an incidental account for "Black Ned."[21] A little over two years later, the manager credited Hansen £1:4:9 "By 9 Days work of Black Nead abt ye Dam &c" on 28 February 1744/5, adding another 13/9 for five days' labor by Hansen's slave York as of the same date. Hansen received further credit from the forge for two days of work by "Black Nead the 11th July 1745."[22]

The credits Hansen received from New Pine Forge for York's and Ned's labor were part of a larger reconciliation of accounts between the finer and the ironworks. The next bookkeeping entry for Hansen after the 11 July 1745 credit was a substantial credit of £154:4:10¼ for "making and Drawing 38 Tunns 12 [hundredweight] 1 [quarter and] 20 [pounds] of Barr Iron from the 4 July 1744 until the 6 of May 1745."[23] In about eleven months of fining, Hansen, York, and Ned jointly hammered out over 7,800 pounds of bar iron per month.

Hansen probably sold Ned in the summer of 1745. The transaction date is unrecorded, but on 16 September, sixty-seven days after Ned's two days of work for New Pine Forge, Ned helped load a ton of pig iron onto a wagon in the yard of Warwick Furnace, the ironworks managed by William Davis. Once the pigs were stacked, Ned goaded his team into motion and rumbled off to a hammer mill belonging to ironmaster William Bird.[24]

From then until Thomas Shute signed his will in October 1748, it is unclear who owned Ned. The simplest possibility is that Hansen sold Ned to Shute in the summer of 1745. Such an arrangement would explain why Ned only appeared in ironworks records on one other occasion, as a carter delivering bar iron about fifteen months later in early 1747. This interpretation is supported by Davis's annotation that the 16 September 1745 shipment of pig iron was sent to "William Bird p[er] Negro Ned," while a second shipment two days later was sent "to William Bird p[er] his Negroe." It seems unlikely that Bird owned Ned; Bird's detailed forge accounts survive but with only the single incidental mention of "Black Nead."[25]

Ned's work "abt ye Dam" and his stints as a carter in 1745 and 1747 serve as reminders that Pennsylvania masters often shifted slaves among a variety of tasks and job sites.[26] Shute's mills and quarry sporadically required semi-skilled labor, but when he purchased Ned, the aging master was engaged in several businesses that might have steadily employed a metalworking slave. Shute's son Isaac was a blacksmith, and on three occasions Shute paid for pig iron sent to his son-in-law Anthony Nicholas.[27] In addition to investments in various ironworks over the years, Shute also owned shares in two copper ventures. One copper mine was in Bucks County and the other, known as the Gap Mine on Pequea Creek, was located in southeastern Lancaster County.[28]

Ned's Literacy and Numeracy

Pennsylvania's laws regarding slavery could be sterner than in colonies more reliant on enslaved labor, but its economy sometimes created significant opportunities for slaves to assert episodic control over a portion of their time.[29] Whether they labored as artisans at highly skilled tasks or as semiskilled laborers at grain and livestock production, Pennsylvania slaves possessed a few advantages relative to their peers in staple-crop colonies. In a variety of ways, enslaved Pennsylvanians seized on occasional opportunities to mitigate their bondage. Ned too appears to have taken such openings when he found them. In the process, he seems to have learned sophisticated lessons about the intersections of law, social hierarchy, and race relations. His invaluable if unintentional education ultimately enabled him to transcend slavery.

One part of Ned's education was comparable to that of white apprentices throughout the colonies: literacy and numeracy. Possibly he could read German, given the Moravian report that he and his wife "were now reading the 'Berliner Reden.'"[30] This collection of sermons was widely available in English translation, however, so Ned's facility with spoken German was not necessarily complemented by literacy in that language.[31] In any event, as Edward Tarr, Ned wrote and signed several surviving English documents and kept detailed business accounts. He appears to have learned these skills in Pennsylvania since he exercised them shortly after arriving in Virginia.[32]

Exactly how Ned learned reading, writing, and bookkeeping is uncertain, but a variety of paths led to literacy for Pennsylvania slaves in this period. In 1722/3, when Ned was about eleven years old, a would-be instructor advertised his readiness to teach "male negroes to read the Holy

Scriptures" in Philadelphia.[33] Other schoolmasters taught at frontier iron-works. One was employed by refiner John Hansen during the period that he owned Ned: Hansen was charged nine shillings "on Accot of the School Master" as of 2 April 1745. This amount presumably was for the schoolmaster's salary; Hansen also owed eight shillings, four pence, "for your part of the Schoolmasters Dayet [diet, or board]" after 22 April 1745. Hansen's schoolmaster accounts thus were bracketed temporally by entries crediting Hansen for "work of Black Nead" on 28 February 1744/5 and 11 July 1745.[34]

These accounts put Ned close to a schoolroom but not all the way inside; Hansen was more likely to have employed a schoolmaster for his own children than for his slaves. For that matter, at thirty-four years of age in 1745, Ned already may have known how to read. If not, however, Hansen's schoolmaster represented an opportunity for Ned in more ways than one. As Frederick Douglass demonstrated a century later, ingenious slaves could persuade white children to unlock the secrets of reading.[35]

Business practices in the world of fire further emphasized the significance of literacy, and wittingly or otherwise, numerous free black business transactions could have formed part of an observant slave's education. Ironworks managers required free black carters to mark receipts for the pig iron they were hauling from rural furnaces to Philadelphia.[36] When iron adventurer Thomas Potts credited "Black Mingo" with five shillings, three pence, in 1732 for "yr Wife's Spinning," both Mingo and his wife had a stake in the documentary record.[37] Each time "Negro James" drew rum, cash, and tobacco against the value of the brooms, mine baskets, and coal baskets he had crafted for Warwick Furnace from May 1755 to June 1756, he had reason to scrutinize the bookkeeping of those exchanges.[38] As with illiterate white laborers, a black person's interest in bookkeeping existed independently of whether that individual could read and write.

Indeed, slaves as well as free blacks could have drawn an ongoing lesson from routine ironworks operations: literacy, including the ability to keep accounts, was vital. Managers' ledgers recorded interactions that slaves could see being documented, and to a limited extent even slaves could audit the records. The rum and cider Ned began drawing in 1742 from a store serving Hopewell and New Pine forges represented an operating expense that arguably his master cared to monitor much more than Ned did, but other accounts hint at his ability to manage a small amount of store credit.

On New Year's Day 1742/3, Ned received one shilling, a pint of rum, and two pints of cider; the following Midsummer's Eve, he received cash and thread valued together at six shillings, seven pence, as well as two thirds of a pint of rum. These expenses were charged against the ironworking company as holiday perquisites granted to Ned. Additionally, Ned earned store credit by work beyond that normally expected of slaves in his position, to include cutting "2 Coard of Wood . . . Helping Wm Gilmore Home w[i]t[h] a Cow . . . Sheaving of Ditto." Ned's credits for cordwood and the cow are unambiguous, but the "Sheaving" entry is less clear. Perhaps Ned worked outside the forge as a barber and shaved William Gilmore; this interpretation is supported by the razor whose two-shilling value was charged to Ned on 20 March 1742/3.[39] A second possibility is that sheaving was harvest work with sheaves of grain.

A document Ned produced in Virginia indicates that he learned the conventions of eighteenth-century accounting before leaving Pennsylvania. As Edward Tarr, Ned recorded extensive blacksmith work performed for Timber Ridge residents George Stevenson and George's son Andrew. The Stevenson accounts are of the sort commonly maintained in typical artisan or merchant day books, a detailed chronological listing of work performed on thirty-four days between 4 April 1752 and 28 December 1756.[40] The Stevenson accounts are written and signed in a single hand, and the signature "Edward tar" matches Tarr's signature on a bond dated 26 April 1754.[41] Taken together, the two documents provide conclusive evidence that Tarr knew how to write his own financial records before arriving in Virginia.

Ned's Social Education

A second part of Ned's Pennsylvania education produced formidable social skills. These emerged from personal and professional contacts with blacks and whites alike during Ned's service with Andrew Robeson, John Hansen, and Thomas Shute. Each master represented a different class within white society and consequently had a different work relationship with Ned. Although they almost certainly did not intend to, each master facilitated Ned's observation and analysis of a portion of white society. They made it possible for Ned to experiment with white social connections in diverse contexts.

Ned's education included opportunities to reflect on free blacks' transacting a range of business far afield. "Negro Mingo" drew on his credit with ironmaster Thomas Potts while trading with white men both in Colebrookdale and Philadelphia.[42] Ned's acquaintance William MacBean, also known as Mulatto Will, was a familiar face on southeastern Pennsylvania roads, hauling ore to furnaces, pig iron to forges, bar iron to Philadelphia, and supplies from town back to ironworks.[43] Equally well-known was John

Herculus, whom Coventry Forge credited in 1732 for "6 Months Wages Carting after the Rate of 20 pound p[er] y[ea]r," plus a monthly twenty-shilling bonus for hauling charcoal.[44] Possibly Herculus demanded the bonus to offset the risk that still-smoldering charcoal might set his cart on fire; alternatively, the premium may have ensured timely delivery of the essential fuel.[45] Beyond providing examples as men of business, carters such as MacBean and Herculus helped rural blacks communicate with their urban counterparts by carrying news as well as passengers. Deliberately or otherwise, black carters also may have encouraged slaves to abscond. When Ned decided on 14 March 1738/9 to run away from Andrew Robeson's service, he departed "with a very lusty Fellow, who goes by the name of Mullato Will"—William MacBean.[46]

The temptation to visit Philadelphia without authorization must have been a constant tug for slaves and indentured servants who lived as close to town as Robeson's mill (see figure 1). Robeson's advertisement of Ned's flight in Philadelphia's leading newspaper tacitly acknowledged the town's allure for runaways and lower-class Pennsylvanians in general. What attracted fugitives like Ned had quite another complexion for colonial leaders, however. Where runaway slaves saw opportunities "to ramble about under pretense of getting work . . . and so go to work at their own wills," the 1725/6 Pennsylvania Assembly saw threats "to the safety and peace."[47]

Such fears were widely shared. In a 1731 "Petition to the Pennsylvania Assembly regarding Fairs," Benjamin Franklin deplored how during periodic markets, "a Concourse of rude People many of them intoxicated with strong Liquors . . . [and] quarrelsome or mischevious . . . tend to corrupt the Morals, and destroy the Innocence of our youth; who are at such Times induc'd to Drinking and Gaming, in mix'd Companies of vicious Servants and Negroes."[48] In 1737, a year and a half before Ned's unauthorized absence, the president of the colonial council, James Logan, informed his fellow councilors that "the insolent Behaviour of the Negroes in and about the city, which has of late been so much taken notice of, requires a strict hand to be kept over them, & shows the Necessity of some further Regulations than our laws have yet provided."[49] Robeson's prompt advertisement, published just two days after Ned departed, hints by its immediacy that blacks in Philadelphia were not routinely stopped and questioned; if within the city there was only casual scrutiny of blacks at large, then masters needed to advertise a runaway as soon as possible.

Nor were slaves alone targets of official suspicion; white authorities thought Pennsylvania's free blacks in particular needed close control. As the 1725/6 "Act for the Better Regulating of Negroes in This Province" noted, "'tis found by experience that free negroes are an idle, slothful people and often prove burdensome to the neighborhood and afford ill examples to other negroes."[50] Whether Ned observed Philadelphia's free blacks first-hand, heard about them from carters, or read about them in newspapers, they and the ongoing public discussion about them offered to perceptive contemporaries important evidence regarding the dynamic intersections of white authority, black enslavement, and interracial tension.

A key lesson for contemporary students of race relations was that white interests and even slave-owner interests were far from monolithic. Additionally, white officials conducting the public debate probably did not recognize that black interests also were diverging. As white officials saw it, problems generated by unsupervised blacks arose in part when masters struck bargains with their slaves, "giv[ing] liberty to their negroes to seek their own employ" in exchange for fixed payments. Officials grappled with the fact that fugitive slaves could hire their own time in a labor market characterized by episodic high demand; despite statutory prohibitions, white employers with time-sensitive work had compelling economic incentives to disregard the property rights of masters who owned runaways.[51]

As an additional complication, some unsupervised slaves were abroad legitimately on their masters' service, far from direct oversight. Ironworks masters especially needed slaves who could travel with accountable autonomy, for while some tasks demanded little more than a strong back, other assignments required individual initiative and a sense of personal responsibility. When Thomas Potts assigned his slave Cudjo to "breaking mine 5 days," he seemingly expected of Cudjo little more than the brute labor required to smash ore into manageable chunks. But after Cudjo's ore had been converted to pig iron, Potts repeatedly assigned him to carting the pigs from Colebrookdale Furnace to Pine Forge.[52] As a teamster, Cudjo had ample opportunities for destructive passive resistance of the sort all too familiar to masters elsewhere in colonial America, but his numerous stints of carting indicate Potts's confidence in Cudjo's sound judgment and continuing good behavior. Of course, it was possible for Cudjo to protect Potts's individual interests and still have ample time to subvert the collective good order that Philadelphia's white authorities craved.

Potts was not the only master and Cudjo not the only skilled slave in a relationship demonstrating an advanced degree of trust and mutual commitment. Numerous white finers, including John Hansen, made anchonies and merchant bars with slaves. This was a dangerous activity in which each worker's safety depended on his partner's good faith.[53] Arguably the hazards of furnace and forge ensured that Hansen and his slaves would cooperate in ways that transcended racial boundaries. For a handful of skilled slaves at least, master-slave relations thus likely were less racist in the world of fire than in the City of Brotherly Love. If so, the "mix'd Companies of vicious Servants and Negroes" denounced by Benjamin Franklin in one sense threatened black artisans even more directly than the multiracial rabble menaced nervous colonial elites. Misbehavior encouraged governmental authorities to respond with sterner racial controls that did not distinguish among varying conditions of enslaved and free blacks.[54]

Ned's Religious Education

Ned's education included extensive religion. A variety of evidence indicates Ned's close study of religious doctrines, and in contemporary Pennsylvania, theology would have been difficult to ignore. Doctrinal arguments reverberated throughout the colony in the 1730s and 1740s, and pervasive activism by rival denominations ensured ongoing popular interest in theological disputes. Ironworking slaves who wished to follow these discussions could do so on the Sabbath and religious holidays.[55]

Ned attended at least two types of religious services, Moravian and Presbyterian. The Moravians were newcomers to Pennsylvania; Hansen's purchase of Ned in the early 1740s coincided with their arrival in force. Moravian immigrants established a major settlement on the Lehigh River in Bethlehem, and from there Moravian ministers and lay leaders fanned out across the colony. Edward Tarr's possession of the Moravian book *Berliner Reden* underscored his interest in the Moravian message. As Tarr told Moravians at his Virginia shop in 1753, he and his wife "had often heard Br Nyberg preach, and also the Br[ethre]n in Philadelphia."[56]

The reference to Nyberg provides an ambiguous but useful clue about Ned's location. Laurentius Thorenson Nyberg initially served in Lancaster County as a Lutheran minister but in the mid-1740s, switched his affiliation to the Moravian Church. Nyberg continued to minister to congregations in Lancaster Borough until he moved to Bethlehem in 1748, the year of Thomas Shute's death. After about two years in Bethlehem, Nyberg embarked for Europe in August 1750.[57] Because Nyberg itinerated widely from both Lancaster Borough and Bethlehem, Ned's claim to have often heard Nyberg cannot by itself indicate a location. In combination with other clues, however, Ned's remark suggests that he attended Nyberg's services in Lancaster County.

One of those supporting clues was Thomas Shute's retention of the Gap Mine at Pequea Creek, in southeastern Lancaster County (see figure 1). The site was about fifteen miles east of Lancaster Borough, close enough for a horseless slave to walk in four hours. By all accounts, the preaching alone would have been worth the trip—Moravian ministers like Nyberg employed vivid imagery that drew large crowds. Beyond the theological content and emotional impact of the service, other attractions also beckoned: sometimes the crowds turned violent. In 1742, German Reformed congregants assailed a Moravian minister in his Philadelphia pulpit. Another crowd threw mud at Moravian Bishop August Gottlieb Spangenberg in Lancaster Borough in 1745. Nyberg, the only minister Tarr singled out by name, was the target of violence in a January 1745/6 riot, shortly after John Hansen sold Ned.[58] Tarr's recollection of Nyberg as distinct from "the Br[ethre]n in Philadelphia" thus amounts to a second hint of Ned's association with the Moravians in Lancaster County rather than Philadelphia.

For all his interest in Moravian doctrine, including his ownership of *Berliner Reden,* Tarr did not claim to be a Moravian, nor did the travelers identify him as such.[59] The book of sermons only signifies Tarr's interest in pietistic religion, not his denomination. His pietism may have produced an impromptu service at Tarr's Virginia shop when his wife served the Moravians a breakfast of freshly baked bread: the meal has overtones of a Moravian love-feast. But Tarr was an active Presbyterian at the time, and this was not an easy identity to establish.[60]

Unlike Moravians, who vigorously proselytized among slaves and free blacks, Presbyterians baptized black congregants, but before the 1750s, few ministers actively sought them out.[61] During the final years of Ned's enslavement, only four black couples married in Philadelphia's First Presbyterian Church, and no identifiably black adults were baptized in that congregation in the same period.[62] Surviving contemporary records offer no clues about how Ned became a Presbyterian. There are, however, circumstantial geographic clues about where he worshipped before moving to Virginia.

Thomas Shute's mine at the Gap was about eight miles from Middle Octorara Presbyterian Meetinghouse, where Reverend Alexander Craighead ministered (see figure 1). Like Tarr, Craighead immigrated to Augusta County, Virginia, by the spring of 1752. The minister and the former slave first appeared in Augusta County records within not more than eight weeks of each other.[63] Craighead occupied land near modern Lexington, a tract that he had agreed to purchase a decade earlier, and Tarr set up his blacksmith shop at Timber Ridge, a few miles away.[64] The hypothesis that

Tarr was part of Craighead's Middle Octorara congregation in Pennsylvania is reinforced circumstantially by the presence of other Pennsylvanian emigrants near Tarr's Virginia forge. Two members of the Timber Ridge congregation, Thomas Paxton and John Patton, had presented to Donegal Presbytery in 1735 the Middle Octorara congregation's call for Craighead to be their minister.[65] Nearby in Virginia, John Paxton was identified as coming from Lancaster County, Pennsylvania, when he purchased land close to Craighead's tract in 1750.[66]

With each of his masters, Ned found opportunities to study pietism at a time when Pennsylvania was saturated with it. His religious studies formed the capstone of a wide-ranging education. After the death of his last master opened a door to freedom, Ned's studious diligence was rewarded.

Freedom by Installments

Ned's opportunity to profit by his education came in late 1748. On 4 October, the aging Thomas Shute felt death approaching and characterized himself as "being much indisposed as to Bodily health." In his will, he directed the futures of six slaves, bequeathing one, ordering the sale of another, manumitting one outright, and providing three with the chance to purchase their freedom. One of these latter three was Ned.[67]

The slave Shute bequeathed was anonymous, described only as "a Molatto Girl the Daughter of a Negro Woman of mine," whom Shute directed "to be held & Enjoyed by my . . . granddaughter from the age of Eighteen Years for & during the Natural Life of her the said Molatto." A terse order directed the sale of a second slave: "I Will my said Excutors shall sell my Negro man John for the best Price that Can be gotten." Shute treated a third with solicitude. "I also for me and my Heirs forever Manumit discharge & declare free my old negro [m]an Samuel," committing "the Children of my Son Jacob Shute and of my Son in law Samson Davis to Supply and assist the said Negro with what necessaries of Life he may Stand in Need of at all times when required."[68]

From Ned's perspective, the most important clause of the will contained conditional terms of freedom for Ned and two other men, to whom Shute offered liberty if purchased in annual installments totaling thirty-six pounds each:

> I hereby for me and my Heirs forever Manumit free & discharge my three
> Negroes Peter, Samuel & Ned at the end of Six years after my decease[,] Each
> of said Negroes paying to my Executors six pounds per Year during the said

six Years[;] but on default of Payment of the said sum[,] which I Will may be paid Quarterly by even Portions[,] by the space of one Year after the first Quart[er']s payment shall become due such Negro or Negroes who makes such default in Payment shall be sold by my said Executors.

Within two months of drawing his will, Shute died.[69]

It is impossible to tell why he offered Peter, Samuel, and Ned the opportunity to purchase their freedom. Shute's disposition of John and the mulatto girl precluded a deathbed acknowledgment that slavery was immoral.[70] Perhaps he was making a financial decision on an actuarial basis: in 1748, Ned was about thirty-seven years old, still fit but no longer a prime hand. Alternatively, for reasons invisible now but obvious then, the thirty-six pounds that Shute stipulated each slave should pay for himself may have been more than the best bid he anticipated from a white purchaser. The price was lower than contemporary evaluations of ironworking slaves but in line with earlier values; Shute may not have been aware of the recent increase in prices paid for adult male ironworkers.[71]

What Shute offered these three men was the possibility of purchasing their freedom, not freedom itself. At least one of them either failed to meet Shute's terms or bound himself as an indentured servant; in 1755, a Chester County resident advertised to recover the runaway he described as "A Negro servant man, named Sam ... formerly belong[ing] to Thomas Shute, who lived near the Falls of Schuykill."[72] But from Ned's perspective, the price was easy to earn: within about three years of Shute's death—half the authorized time—Ned completed his remuneration to executor William Davis. With that transaction, Davis made out a receipt for payment in full.[73] Then Ned turned southwest and, identifying himself as Edward Tarr, took his education to the Virginia frontier. He had not, however, heard the last of the Shutes.

5

The Freeholder   1752–1755

Initial European Settlements in the Upper James River Valley—
A Call for a Minister—Edward Tarr, Freeholder—Frontier Prosperity

When Moravian travelers stumbled upon "a Free Negro" and his Scottish wife in the autumn of 1753, everyone involved seems to have assigned considerable significance to the encounter. Certainly, the couple joyfully embraced an unanticipated spiritual opportunity, and no other strangers the Moravians encountered from Pennsylvania to North Carolina received such an effusive description.

Part of the palpable Moravian sense of *finding* the blacksmith appears to have stemmed from timidity. As their diarist told it, the Moravians arrived at Edward Tarr's smithy in an hour of need when they were strangers in a strange land, surrounded by menacing Irishmen. Repeated diary entries about Irish people speak in the unmistakably nervous tenor of tourists blundering through a bad neighborhood. Their first alarm came just five nights into the five-hundred-mile journey when, "At midnight a drunken Irishman came and laid himself by our fire, but did not disturb us."[1] The word "disturb" in this context requires a little explication; what the diarist actually meant probably was much closer to, "Suddenly, out of the dark, a drunken Irishman abruptly crashed into our startled encampment and fell down snoring by the fire, but thank God he didn't attack anybody."

The following night the Moravians "passed a little town called Carl Isles, [Pennsylvania,] which contains about 60 houses and is chiefly inhabited by Irishmen." Presumably the risk of being disturbed in Carlisle seemed high, because the pilgrims delayed camping until four in the morning in order to go "four miles beyond Carl Isles so as not to be too near the Irish Presbyterians." Three days later, after crossing Conococheague Creek, the diarist twice mentioned the Irish presence, first noting them as inhabitants in the immediate vicinity and then commenting that, "From the

Susquehannah [River] here the residents are chiefly Irish." The day before reaching Tarr's smithy, the Moravians found "This whole section is settled by Irish and English," and as they left Tarr's shop, they traversed yet another district "settled mostly by English and Irish."[2] In the midst of all this potential disturbance materialized an improbable interracial couple with an essential artisan's anvil—a German-speaking, Moravian-loving, bread-baking oasis in a sylvan Irish Sahara.

At one level, the Moravian astonishment resonates with modern intuition that Thomas Shute's ex-slave Ned seems an unlikely latecomer among the overwhelmingly white early immigrants in the Valley of Virginia. Nevertheless, Edward Tarr belonged to a vibrant rural community. Within the context of his Timber Ridge neighborhood, he was a social and economic success. Tarr and his neighbors made integration look easy, which is puzzling. If black men could have so easily joined white settlements, or if white settlers found compelling economic incentives to accept talented black outsiders, surely many more would have done so.

Initial European Settlements in the Upper James River Valley

Edward Tarr became Virginia's first black landowner west of the Blue Ridge on 15 May 1754, when he completed his purchase of 270 acres from Jacob Gray (figure 4).[3] Officials handled the transaction in the usual manner: as the purchaser, Tarr appeared before the Augusta County court bearing the original deed given to him by Gray. The county clerk read the deed aloud, Gray acknowledged it, the court ordered the clerk to record the deed, and the clerk transcribed the document into the county deed book. Almost immediately, one of Tarr's neighbors referred to Tarr's property in another land deed; when James McClung purchased the adjoining two hundred acres on 21 August, McClung's metes and bounds included a course beginning at "two Poplars from one Root Corner to Ned the Black Smith thence with his Line North fifty three Degrees East one hundred and Seventy Eight Poles to his corner in Mr Deans line."[4]

Rural real estate is such a durable artifact that this property line and others for Tarr's land still can be traced on the modern real estate tax map of Rockbridge County.[5] The face of that land has changed considerably, however. Today's U.S. Highway 11, which in this vicinity closely approximates the route of the Great Road, intersects Interstate Highways 64 and 81 in the middle of what once was Tarr's 270 acres. Uphill, just a few hundred yards north of the interchange on Highway 11, the modern version of Timber Ridge Presbyterian Church stands on land conveyed to the congre-

FIGURE 4. **Edward Tarr's land.**
Edward Tarr's land was transected by the Great Wagon Road, shown here as the solid line entering Tarr's tract at Robert Huston's corner. Huston deeded land for the Timber Ridge inhabitants to build a Presbyterian meeting house adjoining the road, so Tarr's forge stood near the geographical center of the congregation. North is left. (Detail from Jacob Peck, "A Map of Ninety two thousand one hundred Acres of Land Granted to Benjamin Borden by Patent The Sixth of November 1739 . . .," *Jacob Peck heirs v. Robert Harvey & wife*, Augusta County Chancery Causes, 1850–027, 427, Local Government Records Collection, LOV. Thanks to Joshua Anderson for locating this document. Thanks especially to John Davis, clerk of Circuit Court, Augusta County, for permission to publish.)

gation's trustees in 1759 by Robert Huston.[6] The year after Tarr's purchase, county magistrates designated his smithy as one end of a segment of the Great Road "from Isaac Taylors to Tarrs Shop."[7]

The earliest farms near the site that became Tarr's smithy belonged to the McDowell family. As Mary McDowell Greenlee recalled it, when she and her relatives arrived in Virginia in the fall of 1737, "This was the first party of white people that ever settled on" the vast tract originally acquired by speculator Benjamin Borden (map 3).[8] The McDowells established themselves near the center of Borden's 92,100-acre patent, about two miles north of Timber Ridge Presbyterian Church's future site.[9] Another nearby

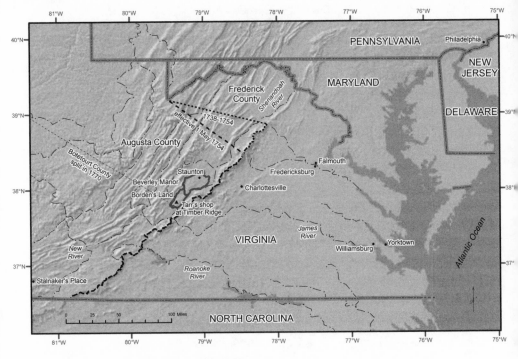

MAP 3. **Landmarks of Edward Tarr's Virginia, 1738–1780.**
In 1752, Edward Tarr established his forge in the tract known as Borden's Land, within the expansively drawn Augusta County. During Tarr's residence, the county borders were re-aligned first in 1754 and next in 1770. (Cartography by James W. Wilson, James Madison University.)

initial settler, John Peter Salley, dated his arrival from Pennsylvania as some time in 1740.[10] In the same year, a neighbor of the McDowells named Francis McCown swore to having imported his wife and two children from Ireland by way of Philadelphia.[11] No systematic immigration records enumerate the subsequent neighbors joining the Greenlees, McCowns, McDowells, and Salleys, but in mid-October 1741, ten fathers in the vicinity sponsored the baptisms of thirteen children, and by July 1742, at least fifty-three other men and their families lived in John McDowell's vicinity on the upper reaches of the James River.[12]

For all their distance from seats of government, these newcomers were not beyond the law. Some two hundred miles lay between their settlements and the capital in Williamsburg; they were Virginia's most remote frontier inhabitants, but they behaved as subjects of multilayered jurisdictions even in their earliest days. Some social regulation derived from or was imposed by external officials, but the neighbors themselves primarily enforced the same social standards that prevailed in English colonies. A powerful confluence of civil, religious, and martial obligations permeated the earliest settlements in the Valley of Virginia.[13]

In late 1739, the council and governor of Virginia acknowledged the growth of new upper James River settlements by appointing two Borden's Land residents as magistrates: John McDowell on the north side of the Maury River and Richard Woods on the south.[14] These earliest magisterial appointments were to the commission of the peace for Orange County, which as of its establishment in 1734 embraced Virginia's meager initial settlements west of the Blue Ridge.[15] By 1739, those western settlements grew sufficiently for the colonial government to plan an initial partition of the Valley of Virginia into Frederick and Augusta counties. The former encompassed all of Lord Fairfax's proprietary land in the northern end of the valley, and from late 1745 through 1769, Augusta County expansively embodied the rest of Virginia's territorial claims from North Carolina to the Great Lakes.[16]

For John McDowell and Richard Woods, appointment as Orange County magistrates represented a degree of official recognition more prestigious than they had attained during several years of residence in Lancaster County, Pennsylvania. Woods had served on Lancaster County's grand inquest once in 1733, and McDowell had served on four petit juries in 1735 and 1736, but these assignments were the incidental duties of ordinary yeomen, far short of the authority vested in gentlemen justices of the peace.[17] Woods's and McDowell's immigration to the edge of Virginia settlement thus brought within two years a social promotion that had not been awarded to them during much longer Pennsylvania sojourns (see table 2).

Historians long have recognized the centrality of magistrates to colonial Virginia society, especially when convened as multimember courts.[18] But the high drama of court days took place at county seats, and by comparison, other magisterial functions performed across local neighborhoods are today much less visible. Magistrates were not required to record the ongoing duties of small claims settled, misbehaviors rebuked, disputes arbitrated, or warrants issued. They kept no systematic records of the minute daily exercises of local authority that encouraged good order throughout colonial Virginia's neighborhoods. At best these minor but essential adjudications and adjustments can be glimpsed only occasionally, as in the declaration by John McDowell's neighbors in 1742 that "he was verre good and usfoll to the poore & Loved to opres all vise."[19]

If Virginia counties needed magistrates like McDowell to promote good order in their neighborhoods, the neighbors in turn relied on county governments for essential protections, especially with regard to property.[20] This fundamental, symbiotic bond between even the earliest settlers and their officials is apparent in the land deeds, wills, and lawsuits of upper James River inhabitants. As real estate changed hands, as persons of property died, as material disagreements arose, settlers expected and the Orange County court delivered key legal protections, albeit from a considerable distance.

Over one hundred miles separated Orange County's courthouse from its most distant settlers in the Forks of the James. Even with good weather, an excellent horse, and unerring navigation, this was a demanding two- or three-day trip. In some contemporary colonial Virginia counties, such vast distances reportedly diluted the effectiveness of county and colonial authority, but as long as magistrates such as McDowell "Loved to opres all vise" in their own neighborhoods, great distance posed an inconvenience, not an insurmountable obstacle.[21] McDowell was sufficiently undeterred by the journey to attend five of the eighteen court sessions for which he was eligible. He also traveled to the Orange County courthouse in August 1742 to swear to his commission as a militia captain.[22]

McDowell's neighbor in the 1739 commission of the peace, Richard Woods, was perhaps not so hardy and thus never swore to his commission. But the distance between upper James River settlements and a county courthouse shortened considerably with the organization of Augusta County in late 1745. From the court's inaugural session on 9 December 1745 until the county's subdivision in 1770, that portion of Virginia lying west of the Blue Ridge and southwest of Massanutten Mountain was governed by Augusta County, with its courthouse at the site of modern Staunton.[23] The initial Augusta County commission of the peace contained two magistrates from the upper James and Roanoke River valleys, including Richard Woods, and by the time the Moravians visited Tarr's shop, that number had grown to three.[24] Woods, who lived a short distance south of modern Lexington, obviously considered the day's ride to court a more reasonable journey. He attended ten of twenty-three sessions (43.5%) for which he was eligible between the inaugural session in December 1745 and August 1753, the last session before the Moravian transit in late October.[25]

Magistrates played an essential role in maintaining society—they were after all justices *of the peace*—but they hardly were the first line of defense against social upheaval. The new county vigorously enforced good order through grand juries, panels of between sixteen and twenty-four freeholders assembled by the sheriff as directed by the court once or twice a year.[26] Grand juries reported individual offenses to the court via presentments based on information from a third party or on personal knowledge of a juror. Either way, the accuser had direct cognizance of the problematic behavior. For example, one grand jury presented a woman for fornication on information from her father, a Timber Ridge resident.[27] Thus, while grand juries were county institutions, individual presentments emerged from highly localized neighborhood censure rather than elite disapproval by distant magistrates or, later, officious meddling by parish churchwardens.[28]

Augusta County's grand jury began handing in presentments at the November 1746 court. From then until November 1753, thirteen grand juries presented thirty-six persons who lived in Tarr's vicinity or past him in the distal southwestern parts of the county. Of these, county magistrates found twenty-one guilty (58.3%) and levied fines ranging from five shillings to six pounds per offender. Additionally, four absconders could not be prosecuted, and a fifth charge was dismissed prejudicially with the defendant paying court costs. If these five cases are scored as guilty also, the conviction rate for grand jury presentment of offenses committed in or beyond Tarr's neighborhood rises to 72.2 percent (table 15).[29]

This evidence of strong local as well as magisterial support for good social order is especially significant because magistrates, grand jurors, and informants alike passed Tarr's business on the Great Road in order to reach the county courthouse. Four weeks after the Moravians visited Tarr and his white wife, Forks of the James magistrate John Mathews sat as a justice of the peace for three days during the November 1753 court session; the road from Mathews's land to the courthouse ran past Tarr's forge. Nor was Mathews the only authority figure in Tarr's vicinity during the Moravian visit: the 21 November 1753 grand jury included Timber Ridge residents Archibald Alexander and William Carruthers, as well as Forks of the James residents Samuel McClure and John Paxton.[30] These were men of rectitude—decades later, Mary Greenlee recalled that Archibald Alexander "was as respectable a man as any I knew"—and they took their official duties seriously.[31] Even had they done otherwise, informants such as David Dryden, the man who reported his own daughter's fornication, lived at Timber Ridge and knew Tarr in 1753.[32]

As table 15 indicates, much early grand jury business involved irreligious behavior: swearing, sexual misconduct, blasphemy, or breach of Sabbath. Another major sector of the grand jury's attention concerned the state of the county's roads, indicating a high level of scrutiny along even second-ary byways. Thus it was impossible for the most senior officials in Augusta County not to have known that at Timber Ridge a black man kept house with a white woman; indeed, as of 24 March 1755, the court designated Tarr's forge as an official landmark on the Great Road.[33] Neighbors and county authorities alike accepted his domestic arrangement without official comment. Their silence implies two facts about the union. Given that Tarr's neighbors as well as senior county officials were observing and *not* tolerat-ing many other banned behaviors, including unmarried cohabitation, their quietude first signifies that they accepted what Tarr told the Moravians: the "Scotch woman" was his wife. Second, county officials also found no reason to prosecute Tarr for an interracial marriage. Despite Virginia's ban on such marriages, no charges were presented.[34]

The Scottish woman and Tarr appear to have been exploiting a legal loophole, as Tarr's statement "that they had recently come hither from Lancaster" helps explain. Under Virginia law, the *act* of interracial mar-riage was punishable for the white partner by a six-month prison sentence without bail and a ten-pound fine; black partners were not punished.[35] By contrast, Pennsylvania's penalties for matrimony across the racial divide were much harsher: convicted white partners drew either a thirty-pound fine or sale as a servant for a term not exceeding seven years. The punish-ment for black partners also was sterner: "if any free negro man or woman shall intermarry with a white woman or man, such negro shall become slave during life, to be sold by order of the justices of the quarter-sessions of the respective county."[36] Both colonies thus punished interracial mar-riage ceremonies, but neither colony nullified the resulting unions. If Tarr and his white wife married in Pennsylvania and emigrated before they were prosecuted, they would have avoided any penalties in the former colony and could not have been punished by a Virginia court for a crime commit-ted in Pennsylvania.

Significantly, Tarr's neighbors declined to contest his illegal marriage. A pragmatic explanation of their lenience might be built on the Moravian characterization of Tarr as "the only smith in these parts." If the Moravians were correct, then arguably Tarr's white neighbors ignored his miscegena-tion in order to retain the services of an essential artisan. In this as in so much else, however, the Moravians reported only what they saw. A more accurate statement would have been that Tarr was the sole blacksmith situ-ated directly on the Great Road between the Augusta courthouse and the North (now Maury) River. Travelers never see the same landscape as inhabitants, however. As local residents could have pointed out, on the day the Moravians came to Tarr's shop, they passed another blacksmith, albeit one located away from the Great Road. Indeed, if customers chose smiths on the basis of distance alone, on 4 April 1752, Tarr's earliest known client would have taken the iron edges for his plow to that alternate craftsman instead of to Tarr.[37]

The acceptance granted to Tarr when he arrived in Virginia thus apparently derived from a conjunction of localized circumstances, not just naked economic expediency. Beyond his utility, a second contextual factor in the apparent permissiveness was the absence of a well-developed culture of slavery in this portion of the settlement frontier. In the early 1750s, the upper Valley of Virginia contained almost no slaves and was populated largely by white newcomers to America who lacked longstanding cultural commitments to slavery.[38] If these new white settlers brought bigotry to Augusta County, the initial near-absence of slavery made prejudice easier to waive for an exceptional individual. One of Tarr's great accomplishments was persuading his new neighbors that he deserved such treatment, and the Moravians provided an essential clue as to how he did it: Tarr and his Scottish wife "loved people who spoke of the Saviour."[39]

A Call for a Minister

The frontier inhabitants whom the Moravians called Irish likely also included emigrants from the north of England and Scotland. Regardless of their origins, most followed some version of Presbyterianism in America. Like their Anglican cousins, Presbyterians required an educated ministry, but because the Irish population in America for many years grew faster than its ministers, pastors were hard to find. One of the central administrative problems for American Presbyterians was the issue of supply ministers, a term they used for itinerants dispatched by presbyteries representing geographically proximal congregations or by synods, the regional assemblies of presbyteries. Presbyteries and synods coordinated supplies of designated itinerants as well as congregational ministers dispatched periodically to untended neighborhoods.[40]

In practice, visits by itinerants often amounted to auditions in which congregations scrutinized their supply ministers and attempted to recruit the ones who seemed suitable. It was a competitive, slow process. Residents of Timber Ridge long struggled to obtain a permanent minister. One supply from Donegal Presbytery, Reverend Alexander McDowell, made such a positive impression on the Presbyterians on "the Head of Shenadoe

&James River" (which included Timber Ridge) that they called him to be their minister on 15 June 1742.[41] McDowell eventually declined but seems to have thought seriously about accepting: at some stage he filed the paperwork and paid the fees for a patent of crown land on South River adjoining the Timber Ridge neighborhood. Virginia patents took a notoriously long time to complete, and this one was no exception, but eventually it issued in 1745, a belated 350-acre testimonial to McDowell's former interest.[42]

Timber Ridge Presbyterians next called Reverend William Dean, pastor of the Brandywine Manor congregation in Chester County, Pennsylvania (see map 1). On 22 January 1747/8, Dean purchased 265 acres adjoining the land that subsequently became Tarr's.[43] A few months later, Augusta County magistrates certified the construction of "a presbyterian Meetinghouse at a place known by the name of Timber Ridge," close by Dean's tract.[44] Unfortunately for all concerned, Dean died in 1748 before he could move to Virginia.[45] In his absence, Timber Ridge residents could only hope for occasional supply ministers, who remained rare.[46]

County magistrates did what they could to make the Timber Ridge congregation more attractive by improving access to the meetinghouse. In May 1751, the court authorized a new road connecting it and the New Providence Meetinghouse; this act probably signaled an intention by residents of the two neighborhoods to call a single minister to serve both congregations. The court also ordered a road to Timber Ridge from a fulling mill on Hays Creek, a few miles north of the meetinghouse.[47]

For frontier Presbyterians, the dearth of ministers was spiritually devastating. As the Timber Ridge congregation described themselves in 1753,

> We [have been] for these many years past in very destitute Circumstances, for want of the Ordinances of the Gospel statedly amongst us, many of us under distressing spiritual Languishments, and multitudes perishing in our sins, for want of the Bread of Life broken amongst us, our sabbaths wasted in melancholy silence at home, or sadly broken and profaned, by the more thoughtless amongst us; our Hearts and Hands discouraged & our Spirits broken with our mournful Condition, and repeated Disappointments of our Expectations of relief in this particular.[48]

Certainly those repeated disappointments included the refusal of Reverend McDowell and the untimely death of Reverend Dean.

Success at last came in 1753. Over a year after Tarr's immigration and a few months before the Moravian passage, the Timber Ridge Presbyterians issued a call to Reverend John Brown, an Augusta County native son and recent graduate of the school that became Princeton College. In what must have been for him an especially satisfying action, Tarr joined his Timber Ridge neighbors in inviting Brown to lead them spiritually.[49]

Acting in partnership with the New Providence congregation adjoining them to the northwest, the Timber Ridge congregation assured Brown that they were "universally well satisfy'd with your ministerial Abilities in general, and the peculiar agreeableness of your Qualifications to us in particular, as a Gospel Minister." In calling him to be their minister, members of the two congregations promised to "receive the word of God from your mouth, attend on your Ministry, Instructions, & Reproofs, in publick & private; and submit to the Discipline which Christ has appointed in his Church administred by you, while requested by the word of God; and agreeable to our Confession of Faith and Directory."[50] In short, the congregants pledged themselves to orderly submission.

One hundred and seventeen congregants at Timber Ridge and New Providence meetinghouses signed Brown's call, which a commissioner from each congregation jointly delivered to the New Castle Presbytery in August 1753. Presbytery minutes do not survive for this period, but fortunately the call itself was preserved. The first page and part of the second are taken up with its text, after which the remainder of the second page and all of the third are filled with the names of the subscribers, arranged in two columns. The right column of the third page includes "Edwd Tarr."[51]

The call to Reverend Brown reveals more about Tarr than just his presence. In colonial American lists of names, ordinal position often conveyed meaning. For example, magistrates attending Augusta County courts were listed according to seniority in two columns at the start of a given day's court order book entry, with the most senior magistrate's name at the top of the left column, and the most junior magistrate's name at the bottom of the right column.[52] In other documents, the order of names can reveal geographic information, such as the path followed by surveyors moving from one tract of land to the next. Brown's call includes comparable information.

The first underlying order in the list of subscribers is the unlabeled grouping of names into the two congregations. The second-page names all belonged to New Providence, and the third-page names all came from Timber Ridge. This division is confirmed by a subscription list for Timber Ridge dated 22 July 1753, in which the same congregants individually pledged varying sums "for the support of the Revd. Mr. John Brown as our Stated Pastor."[53]

But while the names are identical, they do not appear in the same order, which reveals a second internal structure in the call. The pledges for pastoral support appear to have been originally recorded on both sides of two separate pieces of paper, to which the person writing Brown's call subsequently referred while transcribing all of the names onto the call and subscription. The individual segments of the two surviving lists show no internal evidence of geographic order, such as groupings of freeholds in various quadrants of the congregation or linear progression between adjoining tracts. The absence of such an order confirms that, rather than the original paper coming to households, householders came to the paper at Timber Ridge Meetinghouse during a meeting called for that purpose on the day of the document's dateline, Wednesday, 22 July 1753.

Two former magistrates were named at the top of one segment, but otherwise there is no sign of deference to authority; current officeholders were scattered throughout all four segments. The three women named as subscribers were listed in a single segment, but likely not due to discrimination. If anything, they enjoyed a privileged position: their segment was headed by the two former magistrates, so the women appear to have enlisted before their fellow congregants on the other side of the paper. Probably the initial name recorded on the second piece of paper was that of Robert Huston, owner of the tract on which was built the still-extant Timber Ridge Meetinghouse.[54] Huston at that time was a road overseer and previously had served as a processioner, a parish duty involving the confirmation of property lines, whereas the two individuals listed first on the other side of Huston's paper never had held office.[55]

If Huston was the first subscriber on his piece of paper, then Edward Tarr preceded seven men on Huston's side as well as all seventeen on the reverse. The apparently random order of the names suggests that Tarr stood in the midst of an irregular group of men shuffling toward a table in the meetinghouse to pledge their support. Tarr's pledge also stood near the middle statistically: his ten shillings per year for Reverend Brown constituted the mode, the most frequently pledged amount, for which twenty of fifty-nine people (33.9%) enrolled. Overall, the fifty-nine commitments ranged from four to thirty shillings annually (table 16).

The Timber Ridge congregation's call to Brown and their pledge for his support defined Tarr as belonging to the Presbyterian communion, which was no simple feat. To join a Presbyterian congregation, individuals either needed to present a letter of demission certifying that they had departed from a previous congregation in good standing, or they had to be baptized by the congregation's minister.[56] For adults, the second option was rare as indicated by Presbyterian baptismal records for the period October 1740 to September 1749. Out of 847 baptisms performed in Augusta County, all but 8 (0.9%) were infants.[57] However and wherever Tarr became a Presbyterian, his credentials were sufficiently satisfactory to justify his participation in calling John Brown only three months before the Moravians travelers found Tarr reading a book of sermons by Count Nicholas Ludwig von Zinzendorf, the Moravian spiritual leader.

Edward Tarr, Freeholder

Tarr's ownership of 270 acres on Mill Creek raises the question of what his property meant to him and his neighbors. Clearly Augusta County officials thought real estate set Tarr apart. When magistrates reviewed Hugh Montgomery's claim in October 1761 that Tarr was his slave, they noted that Tarr "is a Freeholder."[58] In colonial Virginia as in England, "freeholder" was a significant word. For the magistrates, Tarr's ownership of land amounted to a credential. A white freeholder was an independent adult man, a full political person able to hold office and vote, and while Tarr by Virginia law could do neither, his possession of land nevertheless set him apart from many whites as well as most free blacks. If nothing else, owning the Timber Ridge tract ensured that Tarr never could be prosecuted as an idle person.

His acreage ranked in the second quartile among his Timber Ridge neighbors, slightly lower than the neighborhood median of three hundred acres but still solidly of the middling sort (table 17). Had Tarr been white, his landholding would have qualified him for service as a grand juror or even a deputy sheriff. Timber Ridge residents John McClure and William Carruthers served on a grand jury in 1753; the former owned 200 acres and the latter owned 262. William Lusk, whose 200 acres adjoined Tarr, served as county undersheriff through the early 1750s.[59]

Beyond taking turns in exercising various aspects of local legal authority, freeholders shared in the enforcement of their own property boundaries. Like all land deeds, Tarr's described a set of metes and bounds—the geometry of a real estate polygon—with a combination of compass bearings, descriptions of marked corner trees, and natural features such as Mill Creek. Since written descriptions did not always conform to owner expectations, Virginia law required "That once in every four years the bounds of every person's land shall be processioned, or gone round, and the land marks renewed." Parish vestrymen assigned the neighbors who oversaw the ritual.[60]

The concept was sound, but in practice, ceremonial confirmation of

Augusta County real estate boundaries was widely neglected throughout the colonial period. The county court ordered four rounds of processioning during the eighteen years that Tarr owned land, but only in the winter of 1764–1765 did processioners walk his bounds. In their report to the vestry, processioners Andrew Hall and James Buchanan failed to say whether Tarr attended and showed his lines and corners, but the task required the owner's deed. Hall and Buchanan listed as a witness to their review Tarr's neighbor William Lusk, the former deputy sheriff who owned and lived on the tract across Mill Creek from Tarr.[61] Tarr's inclusion in only one of four possible inspections appears to be part of a pattern of nonprejudicial benign neglect experienced by many of his white neighbors.

The dilatory pace of processioning at Timber Ridge suggests that most resident landowners either agreed on the location of their property lines or agreed that the exact location was unimportant. In the absence of encroachment by neighbors, little else threatened the security of their land. Taxes on it in peacetime were light: quitrents, the annual contributions by freeholders to the crown in lieu of feudal obligations, were set at a low rate of one shilling per fifty acres. For Tarr, that amounted to 5/4¾, equivalent to wages for a couple of days of labor.[62]

Little documentation survives regarding rituals of quitrent collection in Augusta County's colonial period. The chief exception and sole comprehensive record is a register kept by William Preston for his term as sheriff from 21 November 1759 to 18 November 1761.[63] Tarr's acres were listed in the Borden's Land section of Preston's register, and Tarr apparently delivered his quitrents in a timely manner. Fifteen Borden's Land residents (19.9% of Borden's Land acreage) were annotated as insolvent, but Tarr paid as scheduled.[64] Virginians who did not tender their quitrents could be prosecuted by sheriffs, and persons whose quitrents were three years in arrears risked legal action by other citizens to have the lands declared as lapsed and subject to seizure by a tax-paying new owner.[65] During Preston's term as sheriff, the quitrent roll was not marked in such a way to indicate that anyone's land had been declared lapsed. Indeed, Preston recorded a small minority of Augusta County landowners who delayed payments well past the three-year mark.[66] Their deferral seems to have been an indulgence granted by previous sheriffs to well-connected nonresident gentlemen. Tarr and most ordinary resident landowners appear to have paid on time during Preston's tenure.

Beyond quitrents, Virginia landowners also paid special taxes from 1755 through 1767 for the financing of the Seven Years' War and the Cherokee

War; these included additional levies on both land and the taxable persons known as tithables (table 18).[67] As a head of household, Tarr's total tax obligations included the special war levies plus annual levies for the expenses of Augusta County and Augusta Parish, which in both cases were calculated annually on a capitation basis by dividing the total number of tithable persons into the total amount of governmental expense. Even allowing for the wartime charges, the annual totals were relatively low. Tarr's largest total annual tax bill was just over thirty shillings in 1760, an amount he could have earned by shoeing twenty horses.[68]

Frontier Prosperity

Edward Tarr prospered in his early years at Timber Ridge. His productivity can be estimated by multiplying the average annual value of his work for George Stevenson, fourteen shillings, seven pence, times the fifty-eight other households represented in the Timber Ridge congregation's subscription of 1753.[69] By this calculation, Tarr's gross productivity in the year of the Moravian visit amounted to £42:5:10, almost the same as the £42:11:6 that Timber Ridge congregants promised to pay Reverend Brown in his first year as pastor. Brown, of course, had a second income from his New Providence congregation plus fees for supply preaching, baptisms, and burials, but the two men were compensated comparably for the routine duties each performed within the Timber Ridge neighborhood. Tarr's accounts receivable for smith's work apparently made him a good credit risk: between 1752 and 1766, six Augusta County men advanced Tarr credit on at least nine occasions for a total of over eighty pounds.[70] Throughout colonial Virginia, such credit arrangements helped connect neighbors in a social web of mutual obligations, and certainly that was true for Tarr.[71]

Farmers in the eighteenth century needed blacksmiths for a variety of services, as the record of Tarr's work for Stevenson and his son illustrates (table 19). George Stevenson first visited Tarr's smithy in April 1752, and continued to call on Tarr for repairs, maintenance, and farrier work until the end of 1756. Stevenson also set up his son Andrew as a farmer and promised to pay Andrew's blacksmith accounts from September 1754 to June 1756.[72] The jobs Tarr performed for the Stevensons indicate that both father and son were raising more than just a subsistence crop of corn, which required only the simplest tools to produce: an axe and hoe could suffice to clear and till a corn field. By contrast, the Stevensons had between them at least two iron-edged plows drawn by draft horses to which Tarr attached forty-two iron shoes in about four and a half years. The Stevensons' repeated visits to Tarr for repairs, farrier work, and sharpening of tools emphasize that without a blacksmith, the Stevensons could not have felled trees; chopped underbrush; grubbed stumps and roots; weeded vegetables; plowed in preparation for sowing wheat, oats, rye, or flax; cut fodder; or harvested small grains.

The agricultural labors of Timber Ridge farmers required them to deal with Tarr frequently and to come to his smithy to solicit his services. Their many visits to his forge as well as their journeys on other errands along the Great Road across his land thus implicitly reminded them that they and Tarr shared essential features of yeoman identity. From Tarr's perspective, by the winter of 1754–1755, he had achieved a remarkable series of accomplishments. In less than three years, he had moved over 250 miles to a new location, persuaded an overwhelmingly Anglo-Irish neighborhood to accept both him and his interracial marriage, launched a business that drew customers from as far as five miles away, joined a Presbyterian congregation whose fortunes were waxing, and purchased a substantial and well-located tract of land. Tarr's future appeared as bright as that of any other freeholder on the western edge of Virginia's settlements.

6

The Warriors 1733–1761

Frontier Competition—Key Terrain in Southwest Virginia—War Comes to Edward Tarr—Flight versus Fight—Tarr Moves to Staunton

Edward Tarr's forge on the Great Wagon Road had a continental context as well as a local one. Like the rest of Augusta County's early settlers, he dwelt in a landscape that Indians frequently traversed while hunting or traveling to trade, negotiate, or fight. Two major Indian routes intersected in the county southwest of his property, one following the Shenandoah, James, Roanoke, New, and Holston River valleys, the other trending north to south, cutting across the grain of the Appalachian Mountains through the valleys of tributaries to the James and Roanoke or New rivers. The route up the Valley of Virginia—the Indian Road that became the Great Wagon Road—connected the Iroquois Confederacy to the Overhill Cherokee towns and beyond; the route across the Allegheny Plateau linked southern piedmont Indians like the Catawbas and Lower Cherokees to the many tribes of the Ohio Valley, usually called Northern or Northward Indians by Augusta County residents.[1]

The volume of Indian traffic on these routes is impossible to estimate, but as in so many other Indian issues, quality was as important as quantity. One early resident described how Indians "March[ed] in Small Companies from twenty to fifty Sometimes more or less [and] they must be Supply'd at any house they Call at with victuals or they become their own Stuarts [stewards] & Cooks spairing nothing they Chuse to Eat or Drink in the house and Carries with them bread and meat as they please which was troublesome Expensive & sometimes dangerous for they Go all Arm'd for war in their way."[2] Settlers along Indian roads found the traffic burdensome if not frightening for decades.

As early as 1733, residents in a Massanutten Mountain neighborhood that became part of Augusta County complained to the Virginia government that they were "frequently visited by the Indians."[3] Five years later, "the Inhabitants on Sherrando River [i.e., Shenandoah, also in what would become Augusta County] by their petition . . . represented that the Northern Indians frequently passing through their plantations Commit frequent Outrages."[4]

In 1742, about thirty Onondagas and Oneidas journeyed from what now is upstate New York to South Carolina; upon arriving in the upper James River Valley, the men "went to Peoples houses, Scared the women and Children [and] took what they wanted," including at least one hog.[5] In 1746, the Augusta County court certified to the General Assembly the names of eleven people "for Losses Sustained by the Indians."[6] As one visitor noted in 1750, the settlers "would be better able to support Travellors was it not for the great number of Indian Warriors, that frequently take what they want from them."[7] Four years later, Catawba Indians "took up camp" on the Holston River near Samuel Stalnaker's landmark outpost "in order to get some Provisions from the Inhabitants of the Place" (see map 3).[8] These and numerous additional accounts indicate that Indians made settlers nervous even in ostensibly peaceful times.

What Indians thought about settlers can be at least partially discerned from their high-handed demands for provisions. Warriors on the roads were already on an aggressive mission, and they behaved more roughly than did hungry but peaceful travelers arriving in Indian towns. Indian hunters likewise took advantage of their superior numbers, and neither warriors nor hunters could have gotten away with treating other Indians so presumptuously.

As the losses of settler Adam Harman suggest, the river basins of southwestern Virginia sometimes contained significantly more Indians than farmers. Harman, who lived on Toms Creek in the New River Valley, was robbed on three successive days in April 1749 by parties of Indian hunters. On the first day, seven Indians took one elk- and nine deerskins from his house. The unwelcome visitors spread the word of their good fortune, and "the next Day came six indiens & Did Rob the sd house of fourteen Deer Skins & one Elk Skin." These were substantial losses—the elk skins alone could be worth fifteen shillings each—but even so, the warriors had not stripped Harman completely. Instead, they told yet another, larger party about the goods stored at Harman's place, so that "the next Day following there came a number of indiens to the sd house and Did rob, or take out of it seventy three Deer Skins & six Elk Skins & twenty seven Pounds of Leather and Two Buck Skins in Parchment &c."[9] The robbers clearly outnumbered Harman's isolated family, and the incident reveals the presence of many more Indians than just the thieves. To amass almost one hundred deerskins, eight elk hides, and a considerable quantity of dressed leather required greater time for hunting and tanning than one farmer could afford. Harman almost certainly acquired his leather trove by trading actively with Indian hunters in his vicinity.

By their behavior, Indian men demonstrated that they perceived settlements on Augusta County's margins as good places to hunt; frontier farms routinely provided food and trade as well as occasional criminal opportunities. Furthermore, the combination of European agriculture and wolf eradication may have encouraged local increases in deer populations.[10]

Not surprisingly, friction dominates the documentary evidence of Indian-white relations during the county's earliest decades. At best, commerce with Indians had an edgy quality that could degenerate easily into confrontation. At worst, in times of war, Indian tactics emphasized shock, fostering warfare so unpredictably violent that Augusta County ministers identified it as the wrath of God.[11] From each new clash, in peace or war, flowed a stream of correspondence, official records, and bills, all seeming to emphasize a bitter struggle between two cultures. To these contemporary documents, local historians and antiquarians in the nineteenth century added numerous graphic legends and oral histories about "Border Warfare." As with the primary sources, these too focused on violence.[12]

The bias toward violence inherent in documentary records poses a substantial challenge to historians. Warfare was not universal, of course, and accounts of even the most contentious meetings usually refer indirectly to less confrontational if not entirely tranquil alternatives. Taken together, these references suggest multifaceted relationships among Indians and Virginians in which violence was only one option in a wider range of intercultural possibilities. A number of historians have explored nonviolent Indian-white interactions in the eastern woodlands during the eighteenth century, and these analyses offer essential insights.[13] Ironically, however, the dynamics of peace were irrelevant to Edward Tarr. Instead, his life in Augusta County took a new direction because of Indian violence. To understand his situation requires paying less attention to the nuanced modern investigations of peaceful coexistence and giving precedence instead to the strategic causes and social consequences of border warfare.

Between 1754 and 1764, only two years passed with no recorded Indian-on-settler violence in Augusta County. Subsequent accounts distinguish three conflicts in this era—the Seven Years' War from 1755 to 1759, the

Cherokee War of 1760 and 1761, and Pontiac's Rebellion in 1763 and 1764—but the lived experience was endemically violent. The earliest clash famously was triggered by overly ambitious French, Pennsylvanian, Virginian, and British machinations to control trade with Indians in the Ohio River Valley, but Augusta County farmers had no direct involvement in that commerce. Instead, war came to them because southwestern Virginia's settlements lay in the path of Ohio Indian strategy.

Frontier Competition

Augusta County's decade of war was a consequence of the French imperial decision to bar English traders from the northern gateway to the Ohio River Valley. In 1753, French troops and Canadian militiamen began a campaign to fortify the Forks of the Ohio (site of modern Pittsburgh) and the portages leading to it from Canada. Virginia's lieutenant governor, Robert Dinwiddie, responded to their presence, which he considered an incursion into his colony, with an eviction notice to the campaign's French commander. Assigned to serve this writ, the young George Washington threaded his way across the Ohio headwaters, eventually finding French troops on the upper Allegheny River, some five hundred miles from Williamsburg. Dinwiddie's message produced no withdrawal.[14]

News of Washington's unsuccessful mission circulated quickly and was discussed widely among Virginians. Presumably Indian residents of the Ohio Valley paid equally close attention to the implications of Washington's ultimatum and its rejection. Judging from the subsequent behavior of some of their men in Augusta County, Indians in the Ohio towns debated how best to respond during the winter of 1753–1754. The results can be seen in the actions of Indian hunters the following spring: as Augusta County's senior militia officer Colonel James Patton reported, "from the 10th to the 20th of June [1754] our People on the Frontier of this County was visited by Sundry Companies of Norward Indians who charged the People to remove off the Land otherwise it would be worse for them in a little time."[15]

The threat was unmistakable but also puzzling. None of Augusta County's most far-flung farmsteads, from the South Branch of the Potomac River to the upper Holston River, had direct connection to the Ohio River, its Indians, or their trade. Understandably, Patton took the warnings seriously and relayed them to the colonial governor. But Patton and his fellow leaders failed to recognize that, although an ominous message was directed *to* frontier settlers, it was not immediately *about* frontier settlers. Meanwhile, events in the upper Ohio Valley were moving to a crisis; on 28 May

1754, Virginians and Indians commanded by George Washington ambushed and killed a French officer and some of his escort in the Monongahela River Valley. A month later, angry French and Indian forces closed in on Washington's forces and on 3 July at Fort Necessity, compelled Washington to surrender after enduring numerous casualties.[16]

Augusta County's outlying settlers reacted swiftly to the news: "Hearing of the Defeat of our Forces by the French has so intimidated them," Patton informed the governor, "that many of them have moved in to our Thickest [settlements?] with their Families & part of their [live]Stock leaving their Harvest & the rema[inder] of their stock a prey for the Enemy."[17] In this instance, rumor outran fact, demonstrating how jumpy the frontier settlers were. Uncertainty churned the county, and as the summer wore on, "sundry Inhabitants of the upper [i.e., more distant southwestern] Part of the County of Augusta" nervously informed the House of Burgesses "that the Successes of the French in the late Engagement with the Virginia regiment has greatly alarmed and terrified them [and] that several Indians have lately been discovered lurking about, and doing Mischief to the People."[18] Eventually the long-anticipated blow fell: in October, four months after the warnings to the Augusta County settlers, Indians killed three men and seized a fourth on the Holston River.[19] A seasonal lull then followed.

During the winter of 1754–1755, Indians apparently discussed how best to proceed with the Ohio Valley crisis. While they talked, Major General Edward Braddock landed in Virginia and began planning an expedition to seize Fort Duquesne, the newly constructed French defenses at the Forks of the Ohio. With the arrival of spring, British and Indian forces alike left home on the road to war.[20]

Key Terrain in Southwest Virginia

The overall tumult of the next summer obscures the fact that well before Braddock's notorious defeat, a major Northern Indian campaign was unfolding in southwest Augusta County. On 18 June 1755, snapping rifles and thudding hatchets abruptly announced the onset of war at Samuel Stalnaker's house on the Holston River, over 350 miles south of Fort Duquesne (see map 3). Shawnee warriors killed five adults there and captured Stalnaker and another man. The attack immediately triggered a wave of refugees from nearby settlements, one of whom reported that "It was believed that [Stalnaker] would be cruelly tortured, since the Indians hated him."[21]

Certainly he had had a troubled history with Ohio Valley Indians: the colonial government had reimbursed him in the amount of twenty pounds "for Damages done ... by the Northward Indians" in 1751.[22] But the decision to capture Stalnaker, like the decision to attack his house first, reflected Shawnee strategy, not hatred. In particular, the Shawnees appeared concerned about Stalnaker's longstanding connection to Overhill Cherokees.[23]

Stalnaker lived at the western terminus of both a metaphorical and literal road. When Overhill Cherokee diplomats journeyed from what today is eastern Tennessee to the colonial capital at Williamsburg, they entered Virginia at his house. The site as well as the man linked the colony to the Cherokees, whom Virginia officials and Northern Indians alike courted as war approached in the early 1750s. By 1754, Northern Indian diplomacy had apparently failed to win a Cherokee alliance against English colonists; as an experienced trader reported in July of that year, "It is now a general War between this Nation [the Cherokees] and the Northward Indians, especially those belonging to the French."[24]

Diplomacy having failed, the Northern Indians deliberated about their difficult situation over the winter of 1754–1755. Clearly British and French forces, as well as their surrogates, were about to collide. Through the winter, French imperial soldiers and Canadian diplomats and traders emphasized sternly that neutrality was not an option for the Ohio River Valley's Indian towns, which were vulnerable to attacks by French-allied Indians from Canada.[25] If the Ohio towns had to join a war against English colonies, they needed to keep the conflict as far from home as possible. Most obviously, this meant forestalling any attacks from the south by English allies, especially the Cherokees.

Stalnaker's place consequently assumed great strategic importance. Eliminating that outpost triggered the flight of nearby settlers who otherwise could have fed wagon teams and sheltered teamsters. Northern Indians severed Virginia's supply line to the Overhill towns. Cut off from Virginia's trade incentives—including essential ammunition—the Cherokees only tepidly supported Virginia over the next four years.[26]

War Comes to Edward Tarr

On 3 June 1755, Hugh McAden reined his horse onto the Great Wagon Road and began riding from Lancaster, Pennsylvania, to North Carolina. Like the Moravians who preceded him in 1753, McAden often felt as if the road stretched through a wasteland. Sixteen days after departing Lancaster, McAden described himself as making his way up the Shenandoah Valley "alone in the wilderness. Sometimes a house in ten miles, and sometimes not that." Unlike the Moravians, however, he found nothing alarming about Irish Presbyterians: he was one, a minister of New Castle Presbytery.[27]

As he traversed Augusta County, McAden preached first at North Mountain Meetinghouse, then at the courthouse in Staunton. Continuing south, on Tuesday, 8 July, he reached the house of Reverend John Brown, near the north end of Brown's Timber Ridge congregation.[28] The settlers were abuzz with news of a fresh attack: the raid on Stalnaker's place had been followed on 3 July by another in which warriors killed or wounded ten New River settlers and captured twelve more.[29] Although the scene was over eighty miles away, the Indian threat preoccupied the ministers: "I was vehemently desired by Mr Brown to preach in one of his places, having set apart a day of fasting and prayer, on the account of the wars and many murders committed by the savage Indians on the back inhabitants. To this I agreed.... So I tarried, and preached at Timber Ridge on Friday [11 July 1755], which was the day appointed, to a pretty large congregation."[30] It is unknown whether Edward Tarr and his wife attended, but the meetinghouse was within sight of Tarr's land.

McAden's audience doubtless listened intently as he tailored his message to the times. The visiting minister began by identifying the root cause of current Indian hostilities. On that July day, McAden warmed to his work spiritually as well as physically and

> felt some life and earnestness in alarming the people of their dangers on account of sin, the procuring cause of the evils that befal us in this life, or that which is to come; encouraging them to turn to the Lord with all their hearts, to wait upon him for deliverance from all their enemies, the only sure refuge in every time of difficulty; and exciting them to put themselves in the best posture of defence they could, and endeavor, by all possible means in their power, to defend themselves from such barbarous and inhuman enemies.[31]

As historian Ned C. Landsman has pointed out, such "language of martyrdom and resistance" resonated powerfully among frontier Presbyterians, and the "life and earnestness" McAden experienced demonstrated the particular suitability of Presbyterian faith for inspiring frontier settlers.[32]

McAden's message and homiletics had an arresting effect on the Timber Ridge congregation, as was revealed by a sudden fluke of the weather: "Great attention and solemnity appeared throughout the whole assembly; nay, so engaged were they that, though there came up a pretty smart gust, they seemed to mind it no more than if the sun had been shining on them. But in a little time the Lord turned it so about that we were little more disturbed than if we had been in a house." As the turbulent wind revealed, McAden's congregation had gathered outside, but whether because of July heat or because it had outgrown its meetinghouse is impossible to tell. In any event, the minister's words transfixed his Timber Ridge listeners by compounding a sense of their own sin with a reminder of their total dependence on God, through whose help alone they could resist Indian assailants.[33]

And those assailants were poised to descend in force. McAden arrived at Timber Ridge just ahead of shocking news that a small number of French troops, Canadian militia, and Indian warriors had devastated a powerful British and provincial army under Edward Braddock on 9 July. Less than five days after preaching at Timber Ridge, McAden and the North (Maury) River settlers

> received the most melancholy news of the entire defeat of our army by the French at Ohio. . . . This together with the frequent account of fresh murders being daily committed upon the frontiers, struck terror to every heart. A cold shuddering possessed every breast, and paleness covered almost every face. In short, the whole inhabitants were put into an universal confusion. Scarcely any man durst sleep in his own house—but all met in companies with their wives and children, and set about building little fortifications, to defend themselves from such barbarious and inhuman enemies, whom they concluded would be let loose upon them at pleasure.

When he heard the news of Braddock's defeat, McAden was staying near the southern edge of Benjamin Borden's 92,100-acre patent, a couple of miles from the future site of Lexington, Virginia. Clearly it was too dangerous for McAden to visit the Roanoke River settlers, so he hastened to North Carolina by way of piedmont Virginia.[34]

The initial shock he described in the upper James River settlements was merely a prelude to what became for Edward Tarr and other Augusta County settlers a prolonged and ultimately transformative period of conflict. The county lieutenant, James Patton, attempted to rally what few Augusta County inhabitants remained in the New River Valley, but to no avail. On 30 July, Indians killed Patton and three others before carrying off five prisoners from Drapers Meadow, near modern Blacksburg.[35] The Drapers Meadow attack completed the first successful Northern Indian campaign within Augusta County of the Seven Years' War.

Six more campaigns followed, the last against the Kerr's Creek settlement, a few miles from Tarr's forge, in October 1759 (table 20).[36] Like the first campaign, each provided extensive evidence regarding Northern Indian intentions, but throughout the conflict, colonial Virginia's leaders consistently misread the strategy of the Ohio River towns.[37] It was a monumental error and the cause of much suffering on the part of Augusta County settlers. Moreover, the mistake allowed Northern Indians to retain the strategic initiative throughout the course of their war.

On 25 June 1756, a fresh onslaught overran a remote outpost called Vause's Fort in Augusta County's Roanoke River settlements. Spurred by the appalling casualties—nine dead and wounded, twenty captured in a single day—"the Inhabatants on the South Side [of] James River Deserted there pleaces," abandoning years of labor and investment.[38] According to one horrified observer,

> To Describe the Confusian and disorder the Poor People on the South Side [of] James River were in . . . is Impossable. To See the Mothers with a team of helpless Children at their heels stragling through Woods & mountains to escape the fury of these merciless Savages to See Sundry Persons Crawling home with Arows Sticking in Several Parts of their Bodies . . . with the Cries of Widows & Fatherless Children realy is Shocking.[39]

As assiduous hunters, Northern Indian men knew how to start a stampede.[40] The resulting mass evacuation left unguarded the Roanoke River Gap, a gateway through the Blue Ridge into piedmont Virginia and the Carolinas.

Flight versus Fight

For over two years after Braddock's defeat, Tarr stood at his forge, continuing to work as Timber Ridge's blacksmith. Eventually, however, the fear of Indian attack grew unbearable. Augusta County's population shrank convulsively under repeated raids and rumors until the war's worst year, from June 1757 to June 1758, when in twelve months a quarter of the inhabitants fled the county. One of those refugees was Tarr; like almost 1,600 of his fellow tithables during the Seven Years' War—plus an estimated 4,800 more of their dependents—Tarr abandoned the improvements to his land (figure 5).[41]

Many refugees fleeing Augusta County sought shelter in North Carolina, but Tarr headed north, retracing his steps across Pennsylvania to the world of fire.[42] Tarr spent 1758 laboring at the same forge where he and his master John Hansen had worked in the 1740s; New Pine Forge manager William Bird credited an artisan for "Dressing Negro Neds Bellowes" on

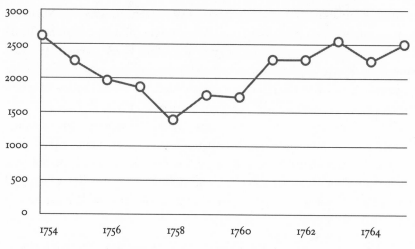

Figure 5. Frontier population change during Indian conflicts, 1754–1765.
(Sources: For 1754–1757, 1760, 1762–1765: Augusta OB, 4:321, 494; 5:244; 6:37, 429; 7:356; 8:327; 9:159; 10:143. For 1758–1759, 1761: Augusta Parish VB, pp. 235, 266, 351. For Virginia's 10 June tithable reporting date, see "An act concerning Tithables," Oct. 1705, Hening, *Statutes at Large*, 3:258–261.)

31 January 1758 and again on 12 December.[43] Tarr's return to Pennsylvania was relatively brief, however. By the end of 1758, the fortunes of war shifted in England's favor and refugees began returning home. These included Tarr, who by the spring of 1759 was back in Virginia.[44] He found at Timber Ridge a much less permissive environment, however. The change reflected differences both in his neighbors and himself.

Most strikingly, Tarr's Timber Ridge neighbors lost patience with his domestic arrangements. In May 1759, a twenty-one-man grand jury, which included at least six Timber Ridge members, presented "Ann Moore for being a Common Disturber [of] the Peace and a Woman of evil fame & Behaviour in he[r] Neighbourhood and harbour'd by Edward Tarr in de-spight of all his Neighbours."[45] For all its brevity, the presentment said a great deal about Moore's relationship with Tarr. In an eighteenth-century context, to harbor someone might mean only to provide them lodging, but in the context of disturbing the peace, harboring took on a strongly nega-tive sense.[46] In this particular case, Tarr's persistence, despite his neighbors' urgings, compounded the situation. Absent from the presentment, however, was any implication of sexual impropriety between Tarr and Moore. Au-gusta County grand juries and churchwardens presented numerous couples for adulterous cohabitation in the colonial period, so the jurors' silence on this point implies that Moore was harbored in a household headed by Tarr but also still including his anonymous white wife, the baker of bread for the Moravians in 1753.[47] It is unlikely that Moore's unhappy neighbors would have missed an opportunity to accuse her of fornication if she had been living alone with Tarr.

The May 1759 presentment also generated an important clue regarding Moore's identity. The grand jury's six Timber Ridge members explicitly named the object of their presentment as Ann Moore, but the county clerk was not so certain. When the clerk wrote out her summons, he twice identified her as Ann Montgomery before scratching out that surname and replacing it with Moore: "Ordered that Anne ~~Montgomerie~~ Moore be summoned to appear at the next Court to answer the presentment of the Grandjury agst her for being a common disturber of the Peace &c." On the reverse of the summons, the clerk repeated the revision: "Sum[mon]s Anne ~~Montgom'y~~ Moore."[48]

The clerk's confusion seems to have arisen from the fact that he previously had dealt with this woman as Ann Montgomery, the widow of James Montgomery, a resident of the lower Cowpasture River Valley who died between March and November 1756.[49] Her husband had left a very small estate worth £12:12:9½, according to an appraisers' report recorded in court on 16 March 1757. Thereafter, official records remain silent regarding Ann until 19 August 1758, when the court noted the widow had left the county with what remained of her late husband's goods.[50] Her exact departure date cannot be determined, but her absence was at least partially congruent with that of Edward Tarr, who spent 1758 in Pennsylvania. The two reappeared in Augusta County records simultaneously in the May 1759 grand jury presentments.[51] How Ann Montgomery became Ann Moore is unknown.

Moore's contentious relationship with her neighbors contrasts sharply to the acceptance enjoyed by Tarr and his white wife during their initial years at Timber Ridge. Their clash may have reflected undocumented doubts about Tarr's relationship with Moore. Possibly, however, her abrasive behavior might be explained as a *consequence* of the chilly reception she and Tarr met on returning home, not a *cause* of that treatment. Such a reception would be typical for populations who persevere through hardships while their less resolute members temporarily abscond. In the case of Timber Ridge, the hardships were more psychological than physical: the neighborhood was not attacked directly during the Seven Years' War, but the flight of settlers living just south of Timber Ridge left the neighborhood's inhabitants vulnerable for several years. Women especially would have felt this oppressive, long-impending threat, given that, unlike men on militia duty, females could take no direct action to relieve their sense of uncertainty in the face of an apparently implacable enemy.[52] And of course women, not men, were more likely to interact with Moore. If they criticized her and her harborer for their flight to a Pennsylvania haven, Moore's sharp retorts quickly could have made her "a Common Disturber [of] the Peace."[53]

Ann Moore and the Timber Ridge inhabitants were not the only people metamorphosed by the Seven Years' War; Tarr behaved differently after the conflict, too. The same May 1759 grand jury that presented Moore for disturbing the peace also presented "Edward Tarr for retailing Strong Beer wit[hout a] Liscence."[54] County officials had no problem with drinking alcohol or vending it wholesale—as senior magistrate James Patton noted approvingly in 1750, there was "whiskey plentey here, maney new stills being Cume into this Countey this fall." But colonial law directed and local social order demanded that retailers sell alcohol by the drink only at ordinaries licensed annually by the county court.[55] Tarr seems to have returned from Pennsylvania and immediately set up an illegal tippling house. That his place may have become a resort for persons of dubious repute is indicated by the county court's August 1759 order to the parish churchwardens that they bind to an appropriate master until age twenty-one an illegitimate child named Joseph Vance "now in possession of Edward Tarr."[56]

For a combination of reasons, prosecution of all the May 1759 presentments proceeded fitfully. Part of the problem derived from county growth. In 1746 and 1747, Augusta County magistrates adjudicated grand jury presentments swiftly at the next court sessions, but as the county's population spread ever farther afield and sheriffs needed more time to serve a summons, cases increasingly took longer to resolve. Service was especially spotty during the tenure of Richard Woods, sheriff from November 1757 to November 1759; with the exception of the summons for Tarr that deputy sheriff William Bowyer annotated as "Ex[ecute]d by me" and returned to county clerk John Madison, Woods and his deputies initially found none of the persons presented by the May 1759 grand jury.[57] A decade later, one of Woods's rivals derided him as inattentive if not incompetent, but his poor overall record for process serving in 1758 and 1759 also could have been a function of defendant flight in wartime, not necessarily the sheriff's neglect.[58]

Eventually, however, the millstones of justice lurched and grated into motion. Tarr's presentment was originally scheduled for the November 1760 court but then was continued. A new sheriff's deputy returned Moore's summons as not executed, so in November 1760, the clerk issued an alias summons returnable to the next court.[59] "Next" turned into three sessions later: in August 1761, the alias summons for Moore again came back unexecuted, so the clerk renewed it. At the same session, the king's attorney declared he would not prosecute Tarr further, whereby that case was discontinued.[60] For a time Moore's summons went dormant, though the magistrates did not dismiss it.[61]

The court dealt with Tarr's and Moore's presentments in different ways, but the net effect was the same. In neither case did the court dismiss the charge; if either party misbehaved in the future, prosecution could resume. This device was well suited for regulating certain types of Augusta County residents, particularly those who knew the rules and generally followed them but on occasion needed to be recalled to compliance. Fining such offenders punished them, but threatening a fine disciplined them.

Tarr Moves to Staunton

Edward Tarr moved to Staunton by the late summer of 1760, when he rented a field near the courthouse hamlet from one Charles Donnelly.[62] A number of factors may have contributed to his decision, beginning with the censure of Ann Moore by the 1759 grand jury. Tarr also may have seen better employment prospects for a blacksmith in Staunton: quarterly court sessions brought numerous potential customers to town for a week at a time, and in May 1760 the vestry agreed to fund a major construction project, an Anglican church on the parish's town lots (see map 2).[63] Additionally, the onset of the Cherokee War in April provided a fresh incentive to live in a more densely settled area.

Little detail survives regarding early fighting in Augusta County during the Cherokee War, but a few specifics were recorded in the antebellum abstract of a no-longer-extant newspaper published on 18 April 1760: "Houses of Malcolm Campbell, J. Mason, J. Neely & J. Bane, on Roanoke [River] in Augusta, attacked by about 80 Cherokees. Indians beaten off. Major [Andrew] Lewis and Capt. Gist on the scout. Consternation of Inhabs. Col [John] Buchanan and others have removed—signs of enemy as far down as Lo[o]ney's Ferry [across James River]."[64] Augusta County freeholders matching the partial names in this note include John Mason, James and John Nealy, and James Bean; they and Malcolm Campbell all owned Roanoke River land. Colonel John Buchanan was a longtime resident at Reed Creek, a tributary of New River.[65] A number of Augusta County residents took part in the 1760 and 1761 campaigns that followed, but no additional attacks on county settlers are documented after April 1760.[66]

For Augusta County residents, the chief consequences of the Cherokee War were two benefits that followed Virginia's mobilization of militia forces to defend the frontier settlements: safety and sales, both due to an influx of troops. The General Assembly authorized recruiting seven hundred men to join three hundred more from Colonel William Byrd's Virginia Regiment in Winchester.[67] It proved impossible to field the full thousand, however, and almost as difficult to feed the ones who did muster. Byrd arrived in Staunton on 3 July at about the same time as several hundred mobilized militiamen.[68]

By 9 July, the troops reached the Roanoke River Valley and Vause's Fort, which Northern Indians had overrun in 1756.[69] Lacking what he considered sufficient supplies for a more aggressive advance, Byrd inched into the New River Valley in August, reaching Alexander Sayer's mill on Reed Creek.[70] From there Byrd dispatched a reconnaissance in force under Major Andrew Lewis to the vicinity of Great Island on the Holston (modern Kingsport, Tennessee), an estimated 140 miles from the Overhill Cherokee towns.[71] Thus when William Davis and William Preston agreed to their carting partnership in August 1760, as discussed in chapter 3, the forward elements of the army were 250 miles southwest of Staunton.

Byrd's army had been directed by the General Assembly to disband as of 1 December, so in the early autumn, he and his troops returned to eastern Virginia.[72] The on-again, off-again campaign resumed in the spring of 1761, lurching southwest with frustratingly unreliable logistical support. When troops from Winchester reached Staunton on 27 May 1761, they found little food on hand.[73] Eventually the situation improved, and the army advanced more rapidly, but they once again saw no action before disbanding in the fall.[74]

For Edward Tarr, the militiamen represented a profitable source of legitimate blacksmith employment in Staunton, and perhaps he profited from the Cherokee campaign in other ways, too. A lawsuit suggests that he may have covertly poured whiskey for bored militiamen loitering around Staunton, waiting for food and weapons to arrive. The suit concerned forty pounds of bacon and beef plus ten gallons of whiskey that Tarr had purchased on account from John Lewis earlier in 1761. When Lewis called on Tarr to settle accounts for two pounds, five shillings, Tarr declined to do so.[75]

Lewis, who at that time was Augusta County's senior magistrate, obtained a summons for Tarr to appear at the autumn 1761 court session, the first day of which was 17 November. When the case eventually was called on the last day, Saturday, 21 November, the court continued it, signaling that Tarr had been present but Lewis was not ready to prosecute the complaint. John Lewis died before the next session, so the February 1762 court dismissed his petition as "abated by death of plaintiff," and his heirs did not revive the action.[76]

The late summer and autumn of 1761 proved to be eventful for Edward Tarr. In August, the county court discontinued the grand jury presentments against him. In September, the rent came due for the field he was using, but he neglected to pay what he owed.[77] In October, Lewis initiated legal action to recover Tarr's overdue payment for beef and whiskey. Soon afterward, the Virginia troops concluded their campaign against the Cherokees, and William Davis and William Preston prepared to disband their wagon-driving partnership.

Most importantly for Tarr, on 6 October 1761, Hugh Montgomery complained to two magistrates in Staunton, James Lockhart and Israel Christian, "that the said Montgomery [had] purchased a Negro Man Named Edward Tarr." According to Montgomery, the seller was "one Joseph Shoot son to Thomas Shoot to whom the said Edward belonged to in the Province of Pensylvania."[78] Hugh Montgomery had come for his slave.

7

The Anomalies 1742–1769

*Credit, Credibility, and the Power of Paper—Other Free People of Color in
Augusta County*

On paper, Charleston seemed a long way from Staunton, but paper also
drew Virginia toward South Carolina. As of 1739, the single road out of
Charleston forked six miles beyond the city. A west branch led to nearby
Georgia, and a northwest alternative ran to "Goos[e] Creek & Virginia."[1]
Carolina's Virginia road carried people, and people carried writs. Between
1746 and 1755, thirteen North and South Carolina plaintiffs launched fifty-
five suits against Augusta County residents.[2] More than four hundred
miles of dirt roads separated Edward Tarr and Joseph Shute in 1761, but a
piece of paper that Shute gave to Hugh Montgomery spanned the distance.

Shute's attempt to reenslave Tarr in Virginia generated the surviving
document that explicitly identified him as Thomas Shute's slave in Pennsylvania.[3] Less obviously but no less deliberately, Joseph Shute's fraud also
linked Tarr to the rest of Augusta County's black population. When Montgomery claimed ownership of Tarr, Montgomery forced Augusta County
magistrates to consider Tarr in light of Virginia slave law and frontier slave
ownership. In challenging Tarr's status as a free black inhabitant, Montgomery implicitly generated suspicions about all frontier free blacks: if a
landowning artisan was lying about his free status, then other, less prosperous black men and women surely deserved closer scrutiny.

Montgomery's claim came at a time of transformation for Augusta
County's labor force. During the first quarter-century of frontier settlement, European immigrants brought or bought few slaves, but in the 1760s,
masters accelerated their acquisition. The resulting demographic and economic changes had significant implications for Edward Tarr, but it is important to recognize also that he himself exerted an enduring influence on
the social meanings of black and white interactions.

Hugh Montgomery was an early resident of Augusta County. In 1753, one of Tarr's neighbors petitioned the county court to recover one pound, nine shillings, that Montgomery owed him for a steer.[4] Like a number of other Augusta County residents, Montgomery departed for the Carolinas in the 1750s; the date of his emigration is uncertain, but the fact that a summons to answer the petition for the steer's value was returned "not executed" may indicate Montgomery had left Augusta County by early 1754.[5]

By 1757, Montgomery was operating an ordinary in Salisbury, North Carolina.[6] As of 1758, his financial credibility had improved to the extent that he could secure a substantial debt in Perquimons County, North Carolina; the following year found Montgomery in Charleston, South Carolina.[7] In March 1759, he purchased goods on credit to the value of £2,079:3:5 (South Carolina currency), and in May he borrowed another £2,604:16:11½ for merchandise and slaves. Like the money Montgomery owed for the Augusta County steer, these much larger debts also went unpaid, so Montgomery's creditor filed suit against him in South Carolina's Court of Common Pleas. The court found for the plaintiff on 30 January 1761, handing down a judgment of £2,679:3:5 against Montgomery.[8] Even after deflating that amount by the exchange rate of £7 South Carolina currency per £1 sterling, it still was a large debt by contemporary standards.[9]

Montgomery's financial difficulties in Charleston likely motivated his return to the Virginia backcountry. In June 1761, he delivered the first of "several Droves of Beef Cattle" to William Byrd's army in Augusta County.[10] On 6 October, he informed two magistrates in Staunton, James Lockhart and Israel Christian, that he had purchased Edward Tarr from Joseph Shute and sought the magistrates' approval for seizing his alleged slave.[11] Montgomery's approach was significant. By complaining to a pair of magistrates between scheduled court sessions, he selected the speediest legal procedure for recovering a fugitive slave.[12] He also likely hoped for something more: to avoid rigorous scrutiny of his claim in an open court.

If so, he was disappointed. Tarr trumped Montgomery's bill of sale with a sheaf of his own documents. He began by citing Thomas Shute's "Last will and Testament dated the 8th month [October] 1748 [which] sett and allowed the said Edward Tarr to be free on his paying six pounds per year for six years to the said Thomas Shoot or his Executors." Tarr next "produce[d] full Receits for the said Thirtysix pounds signed . . . by one William Davis Executor to the aforesaid Thomas Shoot."[13] This was especially significant evidence as Davis at the time was in Augusta County, concluding his carting partnership with William Preston; if necessary, Davis could testify to the validity of Tarr's receipts.[14] Even in Davis's absence, magistrate Israel Christian could have recognized Davis's signature from when he worked for Christian to supply William Byrd's army.[15]

Tarr concluded by handing to the magistrates "abstracts and divers other papers Concerning the freedom of the said Negro Edward." Having reviewed the evidence, Lockhart and Christian ruled in Tarr's favor, although not as definitively as he doubtless would have preferred. As the magistrates saw the issue, "it seems to appear to us that the said Montgomery ought not to carry out of this County as a slave the said Edward until he Can have a Just hearing or until the said Montgomery proves his Right and Claim to the said Negro which he is allowed to do at the next November Court for this County or at the next General Court for this Colony." Lockhart and Christian then directed that "the said Edward is to give Five Hundred pounds security for his appearance at the next Court for this County."[16] This was a very high sum: in Augusta County through 1769, typical bonds for appearance or good behavior by accused criminals were for one hundred pounds or less, and only four bonds were for five hundred pounds or more.[17] By setting Tarr's appearance bond at five hundred pounds, Lockhart and Christian were hedging their decision carefully.

They need not have worried. As Tarr demonstrated at the hearing, he obviously understood the importance of legal documentation and administrative procedures, and failing to present himself in court would have validated Montgomery's claim. Court opened on Tuesday, 17 November, but Montgomery did not appear. Court continued on Wednesday, Thursday, and Friday without his arrival. Saturday, the final day of the session, must have seemed interminable to Tarr, but as the day drew on, it became clear that Montgomery was not going to press his complaint. Tarr apparently perceived in Montgomery's absence an opportunity to add to the stack of documentary evidence supporting his freedom and seized the chance.[18]

On Saturday, when the court had finished almost all of its November business, Tarr addressed the court. Lockhart was presiding, and one of the other four justices of the peace was William Preston. Tarr presented to the magistrates Lockhart's and Christian's written report of the 6 October proceedings. Notwithstanding Lockhart's presence on the bench, Tarr left nothing to chance; the document "was proved by the oath of George Wilson," a sometime Staunton resident, sometime militia captain, and sometime business partner of William Davis who had witnessed the 6 October report by Lockhart and Christian. Then, "on the motion of Edward Tarr," the court directed the county clerk to record the document. The terse order transformed what had been a report of Hugh Montgomery's complaint into "A Certificate from Under the hands of James Lockart and Israel Christian of the freedom of Edward Tarr." Nothing in the document indicates that Lockhart and Christian had intended to certify Tarr's freedom, but Montgomery's absence made possible this legal legerdemain.[19] The court then turned its attention to other business, which included Tarr's attendance in response to John Lewis's petition against him for an unpaid whiskey and meat bill.[20]

By creating an official Augusta County record of his freedom, Tarr prepared for fresh challenges. Montgomery did not resume the assault on Tarr's liberty, however. Instead, he remained quietly for a time in Augusta County, purchasing two tracts of land on Reed Creek in the New River Valley. By 1765, he had returned to Salisbury, North Carolina, which remained his home thereafter.[21] Near the end of his life in 1779, Montgomery owned four slaves, but none of them was Edward Tarr.[22]

An obvious question remains regarding Montgomery's claim to have purchased Tarr as a slave: did Joseph Shute dupe Montgomery, or was Montgomery complicit in the fraud? The surviving South Carolina Court of Common Pleas filings include no litigation by Montgomery against Shute, as might reasonably be expected if Shute had defrauded Montgomery. Nor did Montgomery appear to have exercised the option offered by the magistrates to make his complaint before the General Court in Williamsburg. Virginia General Court records for this period burned in 1865, so it is impossible to know certainly, but if Montgomery ever had complained unsuccessfully to the colony's highest court, it seems likely Tarr would have entered the decision in the Augusta County records, just as he entered his so-called certificate of freedom. Montgomery's reluctance to press the matter in the Augusta County court and the absence from county records of any report of a ruling against Montgomery in the General Court thus suggest his complicity in Shute's fraud.

Hugh Montgomery's attempt to reenslave Edward Tarr also offers some insights into how Augusta County authorities thought about Tarr's legal standing. On the one hand, Lockhart and Christian gave Montgomery a full set of legal options for proving his claim and demanded a high bond for Tarr's appearance at the next Augusta County court. By these actions, the magistrates affirmed their commitment to the law of property, including property in people. But their own account of the 6 October proceedings also hints that Lockhart and Christian saw Tarr as a credible witness on his own behalf.[23] The magistrates consistently identified the alleged slave by his given name and surname, not by the diminutive Ned, and began their report by identifying him as "a Negro Man Named Edward Tarr who has resided in this County for Ten years last past and is a Freeholder."[24] Having known Tarr for a decade, in other words, they were inclined to accept as authentic the documents supporting Tarr's claim. Moreover, they saw him as possessing a particular status; despite his race, they called him a "freeholder," a term that to colonial Virginians powerfully evoked economic independence and complete political personhood. A freeholder was more than just an owner of land—he was a fully realized member of the community.

Other Free People of Color in Augusta County

As a land owner Edward Tarr stood out among his peers, but he was not the only free person of color in Augusta County during its earliest decades. At least fourteen other free black or mulatto adults and twenty-three minors made Augusta County their home during Tarr's residence there (see appendix 2). Some frontier free blacks were not just accepted but demonstrably welcomed by their white neighbors and associates, and in all cases, neither official records nor other documents indicate that their relationships west of the Blue Ridge included discernible racial discrimination.

When William Carr, the mulatto son of an Albemarle County white woman, reached age eighteen, his white stepfather directed him "to go to the fronteer and seek his fortune and never return." Carr arrived in Augusta County in the mid-1750s and stayed for at least two decades, making his living as a commercial hunter. In the 1840s, an elderly white man recalled of Carr that "Notwithstanding his coller he was treated with as much respect as any white man." Carr's success hinged in part on his convivial personality: he was "allways cheerful and the very life of any company he was in." Such an apparently buoyant disposition might be dismissed as nothing more than an external accommodation to the white associates who outnumbered him, except for the fact that Carr provided more than lighthearted entertainment. He also embodied traits that his white contemporaries esteemed: "Few men possessed a more high sence of honor, and true bravery than he did."[25] By the strength of his character as well as his congenial demeanor, Carr established and maintained a respected place in frontier society.

The 1760 estate inventory of Joseph Bell, another Augusta County mulatto, hints that he too may have hunted professionally: at his death he owned a horse, saddle, bridle, rifle, and shot pouch, but no farm implements.[26] In 1756, Bell purchased half a pound of gunpowder and "Lether for mockisons" from Staunton storekeeper George Wilson, the man who witnessed Edward Tarr's so-called certificate of freedom.[27] The ammunition and moccasin leather further suggest that Bell worked as a hunter. This account is a rare documented example of an Augusta County resident wearing anything but European-style shoes or boots.

Bell's precise residence is now unknown, but as of 11 August 1756, when he enlisted in Wilson's militia company, a number of his fellow privates lived along the Cowpasture River.[28] Wilson charged Bell eight pence a day for boarding with his household "when Raising Corn for him Self on my place" for fifty days in May and June 1756. This crop may have been normal for Bell, but it could also reflect that the Seven Years' War had interrupted Bell's regular occupation of hunting. Wilson further charged Bell's estate for hay while Bell was raising corn, for "attending and feeding his hors and Salting him one winter and Sumer" and for "washing one year," accounts demonstrating that, if Bell was not living on Wilson's farm, he at least resided close enough for Wilson's household to cook his meals and launder his clothes. Bell's and Wilson's connection was obvious to at least one of their mutual acquaintances; fellow militia private Valentine Miller handed Bell a shilling on the strength of Bell's statement that Wilson would repay it.[29]

Edward Tarr, William Carr, and Joseph Bell all supported themselves through their own labor, but one of their contemporaries, "Nicholas Smith a free Mulato," seems to have chosen not to work at all. In 1752, the Augusta County court received information that Smith "has removed himself out of this County & left behind him five small Children unprovided for."[30] The magistrates therefore ordered the parish churchwardens to bind Smith's children as the law directed, on the same terms as poor orphans: males until age twenty-one and females until age eighteen, to learn a "suitable trade or employment."[31] Robert Breckinridge, Elijah McClenachan, Robert McClenachan, William Preston, and George Wilson accordingly accepted responsibility for the children. According to a surviving churchwarden contract, Elijah McClenachan agreed to teach four-year-old Peter to read, write, cast accounts, and practice the cooper's trade. Preston contracted to provide the same education to Nicholas, Jr., and to train him as a weaver, and Wilson committed himself to teach Sophia to sew, spin, and read.[32]

The official arrangements held for almost two years, until the absent father reappeared. On 20 May 1754, Smith petitioned the county court, complaining "that his Children were taken from him and bound to Robert McClenachan . . . and others Contrary to Law." Smith's complaint was especially pointed given that McClenachan was sitting on the bench when Smith addressed the court. Despite McClenachan's presence, the magistrates directed that the persons to whom Smith's children were bound be summoned to the next court to respond to his complaint.[33] The court remained dubious of Smith's merits as a father, however; the following day, the same four justices of the peace—still including McClenachan—characterized Smith as "an Idle person" and directed that the churchwardens bind his daughter Esther as the law directed on the grounds that Smith "has no visible way of Educating and bring her up in a Christian like manner."[34]

When Smith's petition was called at the next court session, the defendants' attorney moved for a continuance. By then, Smith had engaged his own attorney, Gabriel Jones, who objected to the continuance and threw the court into disarray: the magistrates could not agree on how to rule on Jones's objection. Jones then moved for trial of the facts, "but the Court being still divided refused further to proceed thereon."[35] The cause of the court's internal division was not recorded, but the split could have reflected varying degrees of acquaintance with and opinions about blacks, whether enslaved or free: senior magistrate James Patton was a slave owner, Peter Schull never possessed a slave, David Stewart eventually owned slaves but apparently did not at the time, and William Williams never owned a slave but was the master of mulatto Joseph Bell, Jr., who was bound by his father to Williams as a youth.[36] The magistrates thus illustrated varying levels of frontier commitment to slavery.

Consensus about how to deal with Smith's complaint was easier to achieve at the following court session on 25 November 1754, when less than half of the magistrates were current or eventual slave owners.[37] Court began with Robert McClenachan on the bench, but he stepped down when Smith's case was called. The court then heard arguments from Jones for the plaintiff and from the defendants "in their proper persons," meaning without an attorney to represent them. Despite Jones's efforts, the magistrates ruled that "Smith is an Idle disolate person and that the Children in the Petn named are bound & Provided for according to Law," whereupon the court dismissed the case. Smith immediately "pray'd an appeal to the General Court" in Williamsburg and provided the necessary security—that is, produced a financially credible backer to cover the costs—so the magistrates allowed his appeal.[38] Once again, destruction of Virginia's General Court records complicates the investigation; no further information survives regarding Smith's possible appeal.

For all of Nicholas Smith's shortcomings as a father, in one significant respect he was a model citizen in Augusta County. At a time when thousands of his white peers fled the war-ravaged frontier, Smith served in the county militia for lengthy periods from 1757 to 1759. On 1 May 1757, Smith and mulatto Joseph Bell enlisted as privates in the militia company of William Preston, master of Smith's bound son Nicholas, Jr.[39] When Preston enrolled two free men of color in his militia company, he broke Virginia law but acknowledged Virginia reality: as he knew all too well, willing soldiers were scarce throughout the colony.[40]

Shortly after the Seven Years' War erupted, Preston had raised a company of rangers that subsequently melted away. Out of forty-two privates he enlisted between 17 July 1755 and 1 January 1756, nine (20.5%) deserted by May 1756.[41] When Preston began assembling a new company in May 1757, none of his 1755 privates reenlisted.[42] Most of Preston's 1757 soldiers also declined further service. He disbanded the company in late November 1757 at the end of the campaign season and reconstituted it again in 1758. Only seven of the sixty-one privates he mustered in 1757 (11.5%) enrolled in the 1758 company and still remained with it by the end of February 1759. Joseph Bell had died of unknown causes by then, but Nicholas Smith was one of the remaining seven.[43]

Despite his steadfast soldierly service, Smith's parental merits remained questionable. On 21 November 1759, the magistrates repeated the now-familiar order for Smith to be summoned "for not keeping his Childeren in a Christian like manner." The summons went unserved and was dismissed after a year.[44] Eventually Smith abandoned his children and in the summer of 1766 departed Augusta County for the last time; in August of that year, the court once again ordered the churchwardens to bind Nicholas, Jr., as well as Betty and Johnny Smith.[45]

It is impossible to tell whether the children were better off being raised by white masters, but of the six known offspring—Nicholas, Jr., Sophia, Peter, Esther, Betty, and John—at least two grew up to head their own households in late colonial western Virginia. John was described as a mulatto head of household in the lower district of the New River Valley in 1771, and Peter was identified as "Melato" and an independent tithable in a 1774 tax list for Big Levels precinct of Greenbrier Valley, in what by then was Botetourt County.[46] In the following year, Peter was listed without racial indicator as an independent tithable in the Two Sinking Creeks precinct of Greenbrier Valley.[47]

Nicholas Smith was the only free person of color to draw official criticism for neglecting his children. He was not, however, the only one to face difficulties in raising a child. Joseph Bell's binding of his son to William Wilson suggests that Bell recognized he could not look after the boy while hunting. Elizabeth Joseph, commonly known as Black Bett, bound her daughter Sarah to John Smiley of Timber Ridge in early 1760 for a period of sixteen years. Smiley agreed to provide "meat, drink, & lodging fit for a servant" and to teach Sarah to read; by Virginia law Smiley was obligated to pay her three pounds, ten shillings, when she completed her service.[48] Sarah Joseph's indenture was one of four surviving churchwarden contracts for the children of free black parents; in each case, the terms of care and education were comparable to those stipulated for white children.[49]

Whether they were minors or adults, most of early Augusta County's free people of color were of mixed race: ten out of fifteen adults and at least twenty-one out of twenty-three children were described as mulatto (see appendix 2). Only "*Edward Tarr*, commonly known as *Black Ned*," can be identified as a manumitted slave.[50] Contemporary distinctions between "Negro" and "mulatto" thus likely indicate that most of Augusta County's free people of color owed their liberty to white mothers or grandmothers, not white masters.[51]

Virginia statute threatened white women who bore children by men of color with heavy fines of fifteen pounds sterling or the loss of liberty for up to five years. Augusta County magistrates enforced this miscegenation ban selectively on the few occasions when it came to their attention.[52] County officials responded with the full weight of the law when white indentured servant Eleonor Road gave birth to a mulatto boy in 1747. Parish churchwardens bound the boy to Road's master until age thirty-one with no provisions for training or schooling, and the court ordered her master not to release the mother "from his Service till She pay her fine or be Sold according to Law for five Years."[53] Jane Scot, also a white servant, met an equally implacable sentence. When her master first reported in 1748 that she had given birth to an illegitimate girl, county magistrates assigned the mother an additional year's service after the expiration of her contract. The sentence was a standard one, routinely passed on any servant woman bearing an illegitimate child. A year later, when the child was identified as a mulatto, the court modified its sentence. Once Scot had served her master the extra twelve months, parish churchwardens would "sell her for the said offence according to Law" for five additional years of bound service.[54]

The heavy penalties drawn by servant women contrast sharply with the desultory prosecution of Jane Knox. She first was summoned to answer the charge of "having a mulato child" in May 1758, but she disregarded that order and its sequel six months later. A summons from the May 1759 court, annotated that she "lives at James Knox's," was likewise returned unsuccessfully: Jane eluded the process-serving deputy sheriff. Following one more futile effort, the magistrates gave up, discontinuing the charge in August 1761. Jane probably evaded the punishments meted out to other women because of her father's status: James Knox was a freeholder, and his daughter was no servant. But even though she escaped official sanctions, Jane may have been stigmatized by the illegitimate birth or the race of her lover, or both. As of April 1769, at least eleven years after the birth, she remained unmarried.[55]

By the end of 1770, mulatto children accounted for six of the eighty-one illegitimate births (7.4%) noticed by officials in Augusta County or Parish.[56] Whatever their relationship to white society, they enjoyed an enormous educational advantage over their enslaved cousins. All but one of the surviving contracts for binding mulatto children of white mothers stipulated that the child be taught reading, writing, or both.[57] Free children of color thus were set apart from slave children by literacy as well as potentially lighter skin tone. Educational distinctions between creole free children of color and slave children emphasize an important nuance of frontier race relations. There was no monolithic black culture on the edge of slavery, just as there was no single white culture.

Indeed, if any unitary culture existed on the Virginia frontier, it was a legal culture emphasizing enforceable contracts. Individuals employed contracts to protect property in all its forms, and in Augusta County, the court upheld contracts for free blacks as well as whites. Some contested property was relatively modest: in 1757, Edward Tarr successfully sued by petition to recover £3:12:7 owed by one of his many white neighbors for blacksmith work.[58] In other property cases, the stakes could not have been higher.

Free people of color in Augusta County repeatedly invoked the law to parry the pretensions of would-be masters. Tarr was one of five colonial-era free blacks who successfully defended or claimed their freedom on the frontier. In May 1761, "Rebeca Roberts a Mulatto" complained "that she was detained as a Servant by John David Wilpart." Upon trial, the court ruled "she be Exempted from any further Servitude for the future."[59] John

Anderson asserted in 1763 "that the Rev'd John Craig detains him as a Slave Contrary to Law," upon which the magistrates summoned the minister to the next court and directed that in the meantime, "Craig [shall] suffer the said Anderson to go to Brunswick County to summon his witness's to make good his Complaint." Anderson returned to court with a deposition "taken before a Majestrate of Brunswick County that the said Anderson is the Son [of] a free white woman" who had been bound until age twenty-one by parish churchwardens. The Augusta County court ruled Anderson "Exempt from any further servitude."[60] The magistrates adjudicated in favor of two more mulattos petitioning against undue detention in 1777 and 1779 (see appendix 2). The Augusta County court thus never denied a petition for liberty from a colonial- or Revolutionary-era person of color.

It is important not to assume that the court's readiness to recognize the legal rights of free people of color was a peculiar product of frontier conditions. Clearly Augusta County's magisterial toleration shared a colonial and in some sense Revolutionary context. On 10 May 1769, Virginia's House of Burgesses received and read "A Petition of the People called Mulattoes and free Negroes, whose Names are thereunto subscribed . . . praying that the Wives and Daughters of the Petitioners may be exempt from the Payment of Levies."[61] Part of the petitioners' objection was financial, but symbolism counted too: free black women were being taxed as if they were slaves. Remarkably, the petition succeeded. In due course, the house passed and the council approved a levy relief act for "all free negro, mulatto, and Indian women, of the age of sixteen years" on the grounds that the old taxes had been "derogatory of the rights of free-born subjects." Free blacks of the late colonial period thus sharpened the distinction between themselves and their enslaved cousins by invoking the same concepts of liberty that preoccupied American politics in the Revolutionary era.[62]

Part III

Individuals and Social Change

8

The Rebels 1742–1763

*The Expanding Frontiers of Virginia Slavery—Economics of Frontier
Slavery—Cultural Origins of Participants in Frontier Slavery—
Scrutiny and Servile Backlash—The Murder of John Harrison*

When Edward Tarr's last master died in 1748 and thereafter through the
American Revolution, slavery was legal in every North American colony.
Slaves were unequally distributed among those colonies, however, so from
Tarr's perspective, perhaps the most important difference between midcen-
tury slavery as practiced in Pennsylvania and Virginia was that his destination as a newly free man had far fewer slaves than his origin. At Pennsylvania furnaces and forges, slaves like Black Ned were commonplace, despite
the fact that slaves represented only a small minority of Pennsylvania's total
population.[1] By contrast, Britain's oldest slaveholding colony embraced a
vast district west of the Blue Ridge in which initially appeared almost no
people of color, enslaved or free. Even as late as 1755, three years after Tarr
came to Virginia, colonial authorities enumerated just forty tithable slaves
in all of Augusta County.[2]

Forty tithable slaves can be put into a frontier perspective in different
ways.[3] The first is the capacity to coerce on which slavery was premised:
the ratio of white to black tithables amounted to a "balance of force" which
in this instance was over fifty-seven to one in favor of white males.[4] Additionally, slave labor was an economic input with a relationship to another
economic input, land. By the end of 1755, Augusta County included 565,583
acres of patented land, or 14,140 taxable acres per tithable slave.[5] Compared both to the overall work force and the total area of real estate to be
improved, slavery initially seems to have been of small importance on the
frontier.

If Tarr deliberately moved away from slavery when he came to Virginia,
though, slavery nevertheless eventually followed him. By 1782, shortly after

Tarr's last documented activities, the upper Valley of Virginia contained 2,010 landowners and 2,315 slaves.[6] From then to 1865, ratios of black to white tithables remained lower than among the long-established counties of Tidewater Virginia but on the same order of magnitude.[7]

The Expanding Frontiers of Virginia Slavery

Unlike in Augusta County, slavery developed quickly in neighboring piedmont settlements just across the Blue Ridge.[8] During the early decades of the eighteenth century, slaves laboring for eastern planters expanded first tobacco and then grain production beyond the Chesapeake counties into the Virginia foothills. Black pioneers—mostly women and children—cleared and fenced fields, tilled crops, and opened roads. This gender imbalance among piedmont fieldhands was new, created by the emergence in Tidewater Virginia of male slave artisans, and it generated unfamiliar opportunities and challenges for the slaves involved. Slavery as experienced by slaves consequently was reshaped in the piedmont frontier, even though slavery as experienced by masters changed much less from its familiar Tidewater contours.[9]

While slave women hacked and grubbed their way inland across red clay piedmont fields, Europeans immigrated through Pennsylvania to the Valley of Virginia and began experimenting with slavery. Chattel slavery therefore developed according to eastern Virginia's legal rules but in a somewhat different cultural framework. The earliest known slaves in Augusta County belonged to Robert King in Beverley Manor and John McDowell at Timber Ridge. King brought an unnamed slave man to Augusta County sometime between 10 June and 28 August 1742, and McDowell owned an unnamed boy and girl when he died in December 1742.[10]

Slavery remained a secondary labor form in Augusta County and its colonial-era subdivisions, augmenting the white indentured and convict servants, bound children, and family dependents who constituted the majority of workers in far western colonial Virginia. In a report based on June 1755 data, Lieutenant Governor Robert Dinwiddie tallied 11.5 percent of Virginia's white tithables and 0.7 percent of Virginia's black tithables as living in the three counties west of the Blue Ridge. Augusta County's 2,273 white tithables constituted the largest white population of any county in Virginia, while its 40 black tithables exceeded the black population of only one other county.[11] Given that white settlement of Augusta County began two decades before Dinwiddie's tithable counts, slavery clearly started slowly on the frontier. But for some ambitious white settlers in the west, slavery offered desirable advantages, and though initially not widely practiced, it came to be widely familiar.

Two issues dominated the racial history of Virginia's late colonial frontier. The first was primarily economic. The relative ability of slaves in various laboring situations to control some aspects of their own lives varied from one context to another, but historians agree in principle that the experience of slavery depended on factors such as the size of an enslaved work unit, the stage of the slave economy, the geographic environment, and the type of work demanded of slaves. In short, the quality of slave life depended on the characteristics of slave tasks.[12] A second issue revolved around the idea that culture defined the limits of possible behavior and that people acted in light of culturally derived standards.[13] In other words, what relevant assumptions and experiences did black and white participants bring to frontier race relations?

The twin influences of economy and culture never were static: they changed over time. Augusta County during its first decades of settlement dampened certain kinds of social change and encouraged others. Like contemporary frontier societies in the piedmont regions of North and South Carolina, Augusta County represented an uneven mixture of prohibitions and possibilities. Not all whites were masters, not all blacks were slaves, and neither black nor white society rested on a single cultural foundation.

Economics of Frontier Slavery

Augusta County justice of the peace William Preston bought sixteen slaves from Maryland merchant John Champe in 1759.[14] Preston may have sold some of them once he returned to Augusta County, but he set others to improving his substantial real estate holdings.[15] When he struck a deal with Champe, Preston owned outright eight widely scattered tracts of Augusta County land totaling some 2,527 acres, and held four surveys giving him first claim on 1,131 acres more.[16] Preston continued accumulating laborers over the next twenty-four years, and died owning forty-one slaves in 1783.[17]

To large freeholders like William Preston, slavery offered a reliable source of labor for the development of land and thus represented a long-term capital investment. As one contemporary observer noted on the nearby Maryland frontier, elite investors preferred slaves to wage laborers because "labouring Men are not to be had always," and those white workers who could be hired "eat up the Profits."[18] Slaves thus made sense as a labor source for some enterprising frontier investors, but even so, large-scale purchases by resident masters such as Preston were rare.[19]

Nor did many outside investors see Augusta County as an attractive place for externally owned quarters, remote farms with resident slave workers. Tidewater planters sometimes established quarters farther northeast down the Great Valley, but only two can be identified in Augusta County.[20] The executors of Fredericksburg merchant Thomas McRedie offered for sale in 1755 a working quarter on the Shenandoah River with ten resident slaves.[21] New Kent County planter Thomas Adams sent slaves to his Calf-pasture River land by 1774, several years before moving to Augusta County himself.[22]

Few of Augusta County's new masters matched Preston's wealth, land-holding, or political clout even in 1759, early in his career. Instead, the majority of known slave owners much more closely resembled a small farmer in Beverley Manor, Samuel McCune. McCune ventured into slave ownership in 1753 and immediately discovered the risks slaveholding posed to would-be masters with no great expertise.[23]

McCune agreed to pay forty-five pounds for an eleven-year-old named Gloster. The seller, a farmer named Joseph Teas, described Gloster as "a Good Sound healthy negro . . . worth six pounds per annum," but Teas lied. The night of the transaction, Gloster arrived at his new home "in a verry bad Condition." Alarmed by the boy's illness, McCune sought to return Gloster for a partial refund, only to have Teas deflect his request by offering to help sell Gloster to someone else. McCune agreed, and, coached by Teas, offered "the sd Slave to sale to sundry persons affirming that he was a good boy and Could work as well as himself at Grubing thrashing or the like." The deception failed to convince anyone, and in six months, shortly after McCune handed over his last installment on the purchase price, Gloster died.[24]

Gloster's case offers economic as well as racial insights about frontier slavery. McCune paid forty-five pounds for a slave advertised as worth six pounds per year. In addition to this annual profit, Gloster's labor presumably would have paid for his food, billed in another case at two pounds, eight shillings, per year, and for his shoes and clothes, worth perhaps two pounds more.[25] Because Teas lied about Gloster's obvious bad health when he reassured McCune that "all negroes was so," Teas also might be suspected of inflating the slave boy's potential profitability. If anything, however, Teas undervalued the future annual income of slave labor, which within fifteen years had increased much faster than the overall inflation rate. In 1769, an Augusta County man committed himself to pay for "the Hire of one Negroe fellow 1 year 1 Hogset of Tobaco which then sold @

20/ pr 100 [pounds]," or ten pounds per annum. Four years later, another master rented his slave man at the rate of eighteen pounds per year.[26]

If Teas had accurately projected Gloster's potential return, then McCune's purchase money would have grossed 13.3 percent annually, a handsome return in an era when legal interest was capped at 5 percent annually.[27] But first McCune had to recoup the purchase price: he had seven full years to wait after making the final payment before Gloster's labor would have produced a profit.

For McCune and small farmers like him, this time frame was arguably too long a maturity for an investment approximately equal to the price of an improved two-hundred-acre farm.[28] Despite Teas's projections, the best reason for small farmers to purchase slaves was not a distant prospect of their eventual profitability. A better clue to McCune's motive may be found in his unsuccessful sales pitch regarding Gloster's talents "at Grubing thrashing or the like." McCune's lie suggests that he and his peers acquired slaves to reduce the brute toil that gentlemen like William Preston never endured: grubbing stumps and roots to prepare fields for plowing, or threshing grain amid choking clouds of dust and chaff. Frontier gentlemen bought slaves for the future, but ordinary farmers bought them for the present.

Small farmers purchased a disproportionately large share of slaves if their acquisition of African children was typical of the overall slave traffic. The purchase of minors is better documented than that of adults because Virginia law required masters to certify in county court the ages of their imported children.[29] As of 1769, sixteen out of seventy-nine first-time registrants of slave children in Augusta County owned no land (20.3%), and another thirty-nine registrants (49.4%) possessed less than Samuel McCune's 406 acres (table 21). Like their counterparts in eastern Virginia, frontier masters of relatively modest means acted as if even a child's labor could improve their lives.[30]

Once potential masters decided to acquire slaves, some purchased their workers from Augusta County storekeepers. Staunton merchant Felix Gilbert reported on 16 July 1761 that "When I was at Fredricksbg last I made a purchase of 21 Slaves."[31] After returning from the Rappahannock River seaport, Gilbert kept one for himself and sold the remainder to his neighbors. His coffle apparently consisted entirely of children: at the August 1761 court a few weeks later, he and eighteen other Augusta County masters, all living an easy horseback ride from Gilbert's store at the county seat, registered twenty-one slave children.[32] Almost certainly these were the same slaves Gilbert reported purchasing in Fredericksburg.

Most of Augusta County's slave pioneers probably labored at tasks typical of grain production throughout eastern North America, as did the slaves of William Preston. In the winter of 1761, Preston contracted to provide two of his white tenants with enslaved assistance during the coming agricultural year. The slaves—"two Negroes Named Swift & Jack"—would help "Plant Corn & sow Oats" in two thirty-acre fields located on Catawba Creek near modern Roanoke, Virginia. Preston committed Swift and Jack to work under the supervision of his renters "untill the Crop be all secured & put up." In addition to the fields of corn and oats, Preston's tenants and slaves would tend a hay meadow, which was "to be carefully mowed & put up in Stacks." Looking ahead, Preston also agreed "to put in a fall Crop of Rie . . . & have two Hands to assist in Reaping & putting it in the following year."[33]

A 1751 appraisal of improvements to two tracts of 254 and 172 acres in the Roanoke River Valley provides additional information about the work performed by slaves for a substantial yeomen, William Carvin. On the larger of Carvin's tracts, appraisers found 15 head of cattle, 2 horses, 2 slaves, "22 Acres Cleared Plan[ted] & fenced," a house 14 feet wide and 17½ feet long, and 114 fruit trees. On the smaller tract were 14 cows, 10 horses, 1 slave, and "Ten Acres of Meadow Ground Cleared & 31 fruit Trees." Notably, the twenty-two-acre field and its crop and fence were assessed at ninety-six pounds, ten shillings, a hefty value created entirely by the labor of Carvin's slaves long before the development of cheap transportation to markets for Augusta County agricultural staples.[34]

Preston and Carvin implied or specified a set of tasks for Swift, Jack, and Carvin's three anonymous slaves. The assignments were typical for those owned by small farmers: felling trees, grubbing stumps, hilling and planting corn, plowing and sowing oats and rye, weeding, mauling rails, fencing, mowing and stacking hay, reaping and threshing oats, pulling corn and cutting the stalks into livestock fodder, tending cattle and horses, and planting and protecting fruit trees. It is unclear how much of that agricultural labor was gender-specific, but slave women went to the fields for some of the same work as men. William Taylor resided with his wife, six children, and a slave woman on a 150-acre farm about one and a half miles down Mill Creek from Edward Tarr's land. Before Taylor died in the winter of 1767–1768, his numerous instructions to his heirs included directions for the employment of his slave: "I also order my negro Wench Lue be kept on the plantation to Rais Bread for the Family."[35]

Eventually Augusta County began growing its first staple crop, hemp, a plant whose long, tough fibers were used for rope, bagging, and sails. County residents produced relatively modest amounts of hemp until 1767; their interest abruptly increased due to the establishment in Winchester of a ropewalk for the manufacture of cordage.[36] Hemp output more than tripled from 101,449 certified pounds in 1766 to 337,480 pounds in 1767.[37] Notably, this surge reflected a major redirection of white rather than slave labor: known slaveholders certified an estimated 18.7 percent of hemp tonnage in 1766 but only 13.4 percent the following year (table 22). The profits from hemp bounties may have helped finance upper Valley slavery: at least 29.6 percent of the 1767 hemp certifiers owned no slaves before that year but subsequently acquired them.[38]

Cultural Origins of Participants in Frontier Slavery

Slavery in colonial Augusta County was shaped by many cultures. The most numerous inhabitants were Irish, though a substantial minority of German-speaking persons also settled in the upper valley. As of the end of 1770, men with Germanic surnames accounted for about 11 percent of all resident male landowners.[39] Additionally, a small minority of white settlers came from eastern Virginia. Except for that handful of easterners, however, masters and nonslaveholders alike were relative newcomers to slavery.[40]

Few records methodically tally the earliest participants in frontier slavery. Elsewhere in colonial Virginia, local tax lists survive to help historians enumerate masters and slaves, but in Augusta County most of these documents vanished long ago.[41] Without them, only crude estimates are possible. The following analysis draws primarily on official registrations of slave children, on probate and sale records, and on incidental mentions of slaves and their owners in both official and personal documents. From those sources, one trend stands out clearly: most slave owners were Irish. Germans were significantly underrepresented among slaveholders: out of 281 German resident men owning county land between 1738 and 1770, only 4 (1.4%) can be shown to have also owned slaves.[42]

Given that almost all Irish settlers immigrated via Pennsylvania, most masters first observed slavery north of their Virginia farms. As the legal background of Edward Tarr's marriage illustrates, such an introduction afforded no advantages to southern slaves: the laws of Pennsylvania bond-

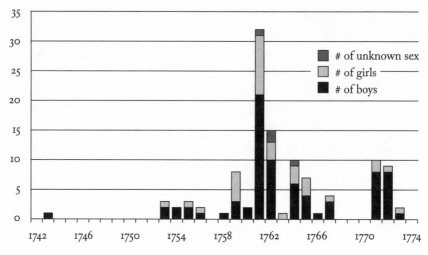

FIGURE 6. Registration of African children, 1742–1774.
Slave registrations from Botetourt County are included with Augusta County totals to provide a comprehensive colonial-era picture for the region. (Sources: For 1753–1767, Augusta OB, 2:356–11:232, 14:220–262, 15:87. For Botetourt County's 1 girl and 3 boys in 1771 and the children in 1772, Botetourt OB, 1770–1771, 362–408, and ibid., 1772–1776, 6–14. Orange OB, 3:349. Thanks to Michael L. Nicholls for assistance identifying genders of names.)

age could be even more severe than Virginia's. Moreover, two key Augusta County officials stood ready to advise on Virginia custom as well as law. The county clerk of court, John Madison, and the king's attorney, Gabriel Jones, were native Virginians.[43]

Like frontier masters, frontier slaves represented a wide range of experience from novice to lifetime veteran. Of all the people involved in western Virginia's slavery, arguably the least experienced were those just arriving from Africa. Some of these newcomers were adults sent in lots directly from their ships to Augusta County masters, as with the "sixteen slaves sold from the True Blue" from the Gold Coast that William Preston purchased in 1759, and "three Negers from the marquis of Rockingham," a vessel that registered its cargo of two hundred slaves from Sierra Leone in the Rappahannock Naval District on 18 August 1760.[44] No records survive that permit calculation of total slave imports into colonial Augusta County, but at least it is possible to tally with some precision one portion of those newcomers, the registered children (figure 6).

Perhaps a few children from other sources were creole—that is, American born—but two key statistics, the date of registration and the age of the child, indicate that most were African. As in the rest of Virginia, Augusta County child registrations crested at the end of each summer, reflecting a seasonal influx of slave ships in June and July.[45] Of equal importance for determining the children's origins, in Augusta County the average registered ages of both boys and girls over time closely matched the average ages of their African counterparts in piedmont Virginia (table 23). Statistical similarities between Augusta County's registered slave children and the African children registered elsewhere in Virginia are reinforced by anecdotal evidence in the case of John Trimble's slave boy Adam, who was twelve when Trimble brought him before the county court in 1761. One of Trimble's descendants who knew Adam recalled in 1843 that "The negro boy Adam was a native African of recent importation, and spoke but little English."[46]

Augusta County acquisitions of African slaves contributed insignificantly to the momentum of the transatlantic slave trade, most of which went to markets outside North America. Within a regional context, however, frontier slavery helped impel a general shuffling of slaves, individually or in small lots, from one colonial location to another. As a boy of about twelve, the slave Will was shipped from his birthplace in the West Indies to Philadelphia and then resold to an Augusta County master in 1762 or 1763.[47] As early as 1764, David Ross, a slave trader from Goochland County, Virginia, was linked to Augusta County storekeeper Alexander Boyd; Boyd probably sold slaves that Ross drew from a variety of sources—Atlantic shipping, mainland colonies, or local sellers in eastern Virginia.[48]

Other slaves moved from the Carolinas to Augusta County as part of a larger traffic along the western crescent from Charleston to Philadelphia. Thomas Fulton brought "from Carolina a Negro Woman and two Horses" in 1765; his expense account included "an old Saddle for the Wench," indicating that the enslaved woman rode with Fulton to the Virginia frontier.[49] The same year, Daniel Smith purchased the twenty-two-year-old slave Tom from a resident of Orange County, in the North Carolina piedmont.[50] Four slaves bought in 1766 by magistrate and militia colonel John Buchanan marched overland from South Carolina to the upper James River Valley in a twenty-five-day trek.[51]

Journeys north to Augusta County and its subdivisions accelerated during the Revolutionary War. Legislation in May 1780 authorized masters evacuating South Carolina and Georgia ahead of British invasions to bring or send their slaves to Virginia.[52] Edward Davis of Georgia thus registered as temporary residents in Augusta County two enslaved men, six boys, five women, and four girls in November 1781; John Twig of Georgia added another four men, five boys, and two women a few weeks later.[53] Glen Drayton of South Carolina sent twenty-five slaves to Botetourt County, where they remained as late as April 1782.[54] These instances of slave relocations away from the theater of war are puzzling. On the one hand, they imply acquaintance, correspondence, or commercial connections among Augusta County residents and Deep South masters. Some such links may have dated back to emigration from Virginia to the Carolinas as early as the 1750s: at least ninety Augusta County landowners moved to the Deep South by 1770.[55] Davis, Twig, and Drayton were not named among the plaintiffs or grantors of Augusta County, however, and how they identified far western Virginia as the best place to secure their slaves remains unclear.

Despite numerous acquisitions in the Carolinas during the colonial period, adult slaves most commonly came to Augusta County from other Virginia locales. Not surprisingly, slave purchasing and redistribution typically followed established patterns of the general retail trade in consumer goods. Storekeepers or merchants like Felix Gilbert and Alexander Boyd, and entrepreneurial gentlemen like William Preston acted as middlemen for many of Augusta County's slave importations. Only a few resident masters are known to have dealt directly with eastern vendors. William Skillern of Beverley Manor arranged to obtain a slave boy from Colonel William Randolph of Tuckahoe in Henrico County shortly before Skillern died in early 1745.[56] Edward Tarr's neighbor Moses Whiteside bought Lucy from two Orange County men in 1766.[57]

Ministerial travel to and from eastern Virginia for semiannual Hanover Presbytery meetings and supply preaching included opportunities to buy or sell slaves as well, and Presbyterian ministers had no inhibitions about human trafficking. Reverend John Craig registered twelve-year-old Dick in 1761 and purchased nineteen-year-old Jack in 1763; Craig died owning five slaves in 1774.[58] Reverend Charles Cummings bought the boy Daniel from a Lancaster County, Virginia, master in 1773, having already registered fourteen-year-old Toby in 1767.[59] Reverend Alexander Craighead owned an adult male slave in 1758; Reverend John Brown brought Phillis, an African girl, to Timber Ridge in 1762; and Reverend Alexander Miller registered eleven-year-old London in 1766.[60] Reverend John Todd of Louisa County, who periodically supplied in Augusta, offered on 5 July 1768 to sell his slave Nell to William Preston.[61]

Anecdotal evidence indicates that most of Augusta County's enslaved pioneers were either African children who arrived knowing little about

American slavery or creole adults who knew everything. The latter were especially important in shaping the course of frontier slavery. For their fellow slaves as well as for Edward Tarr and other free people of color, this was bad news.

Scrutiny and Servile Backlash

By 1763, the slave population of Augusta County expanded to constitute an estimated 5 percent of the county's tithables (table 24). Compared to eastern Virginia standards this was a small proportion, but white residents appear to have scrutinized enslaved newcomers closely for many reasons. Not least of these was boredom: the daily lives of many rural inhabitants remained solitary long after Augusta County's initial settlement, a fact affecting how people behaved when they met one another. As the Moravian ministers recorded about their journey along the Great Wagon Road, all contacts involved an exchange of information. Every passerby, from a next-door neighbor to a complete stranger, had to expect close examination at each encounter. Such inspections did not necessarily equate to hostile interrogations, but implicitly they required outsiders to give plausible accounts of themselves. Strangers might pass each other with little or no acknowledgment on crowded streets in Philadelphia, Charleston, or Williamsburg, but not on the roads of borderland settlements.

Slaves were included in the incessant evaluations of neighborhood members. Such scrutiny is illustrated by the stream of unsolicited advice and commentary about the ill-fated slave boy, Gloster. Before Joseph Teas sold Gloster to Samuel McCune, "one John Cuningham was at [Teas's] house and seeing the boy in verry bad Condition advis'd [Teas] to take Care of him." Another man passing by Teas's farm derisively declined Teas's offer to sell Gloster, remarking that he "would not give three bitts for him." After McCune purchased Gloster, a visitor found the slave "verry disordered" and consequently "advised [McCune] to sell him." McCune attempted to comply with this counsel, and in an effort to minimize the publicity that might inhibit his success, "he desired the people in the house and particularly one of the Witness not to say any thing about the Negro being distempered."[62] McCune's cover-up was almost certainly a complete failure. When he eventually sued Teas to recover damages for Gloster's untimely death, the two men summoned a total of twelve witnesses, some living on adjacent farms, others from six or seven miles away.[63] The number of additional people familiar with Gloster thus would have been much larger than the witness list. Inhabitants of numerous additional farms interspersed among these witnesses could hardly have been ignorant of Gloster's death and the lawsuit that followed.

Nor would these neighbors have ignored Gloster in life. Information concerning slaves inevitably found its way into the public arena, even presumably private details of transactions between buyers and sellers. In 1748, for example, potential purchaser James Given rejected a slave man priced exorbitantly at £102 and fifteen bushels of corn, claiming "that his Neighbours would exclaim at him for giving so much for a Slave newly imported." The would-be vendor "immediately swore in a pretended passion that it should never be said he had made [Given] pay so much for a Negro," but Given's concern over his neighbors' opinions indicates that such secrets were unsustainable.[64] Rural isolation of masters and slaves alike meant that most slaves, whether working on a master's farm or venturing abroad, could expect close surveillance by whites. Given the small size of frontier slaveholdings and the rarity of eastern-style quarters, daily slave life meant daily white supervision.

Routine scrutiny made it difficult for truant workers to remain abroad for long. Behavior by another class of dependent laborers, the indentured and convict white servants, is especially instructive regarding social supervision in frontier settlements. From 1745 to 1769, seventy-one of Augusta County's white servants ran away but subsequently were recaptured. Most of these were taken up quickly; their median absence was fourteen days, and fugitives remained at large for more than two months in only ten of the cases punished (14.1%). The short duration of most servant flights indicates that few escaped permanently from bondage.[65]

For racially distinctive slaves, the chances of passing as free in a region with so few blacks necessarily were even slimmer. Among the larger slave populations of eastern Virginia, as in Pennsylvania, slaves often went abroad on their master's business; legitimate travelers thus provided cover or plausibility for fugitives. West of the Blue Ridge, however, escapees lacked such concealment. The flights of twenty-three fugitive white servants and black slaves are known to have originated in eastern Virginia or North Carolina and ended in Augusta County before 1770 (map 4).[66] Of these, the record for distance and difficulty was set by the slave Sam, who in 1755 eluded his master in New Kent County and dodged every other potential captor in the one hundred miles between his Tidewater home and the Blue Ridge. Sam finally came to grief in Augusta County, where a captor delivered him to the Staunton jail.[67]

The fact that, on average, at least one fugitive per year found his or her

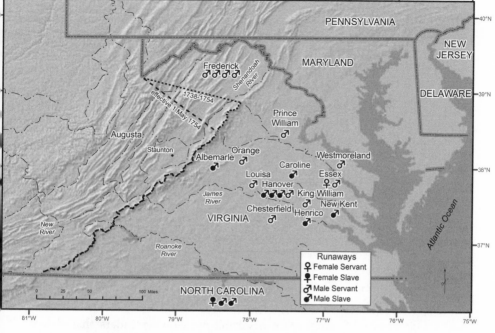

MAP 4. Origins of fugitive laborers captured in Augusta County, 1748–1769.
Runaway laborers from across much of eastern Virginia were captured in Augusta County.
White male indentured servants comprised the majority, and their frequent apprehension
suggests that people of color likewise were closely examined on frontier roads. (Cartography
by James W. Wilson, James Madison University. Sources: Augusta OB, 2:5, 43, 48; 3:196, 241,
473; 4:263, 318, 421, 491, 501; 6:143; *Virginia Gazette* (Rind), 22 Dec. 1768.)

way into colonial Augusta County indicates that occasionally, sufficiently
determined and lucky persons could elude masters, neighbors, and a large
number of casual contacts. Comparable cases of slaves running out of Augusta County reveal something more important than a knack for escape
and evasion, however. When easterners apprehended frontier runaways,
the captives clearly were not seeking a way to escape slavery. Instead, fugitives like the twenty-five-year-old Daniel were running home. Daniel's
master, Edward Hall, understood the power of slave family ties, noting that
because Daniel "was bred in the Northern Neck [between the Potomac
and Rappahannock rivers], it is likely he is gone there." Twelve days after
Hall's newspaper advertisement in May 1766, Daniel was captured in New
Kent County, over 125 miles from his master's Beverley Manor farm.[68] Perhaps Daniel lost his way or Hall misjudged the slave's probable destination,

but it is also possible that Daniel went to the James River deliberately in order to sail to the Northern Neck with one of the Chesapeake Bay's black watermen.

Eastern interceptions of frontier runaways thus point to piedmont or Tidewater origins of some adult slaves. In 1761, Hanover County's jailer released three slaves to the custody of Augusta County's sheriff and largest slave owner, William Preston.[69] A runaway slave belonging to Richard Doggett set the distance record for unsuccessful flight from Augusta County the following year: he was apprehended far down the Rappahannock River in Richmond County, Virginia, over 250 miles from Doggett's farm on New River's Reed Creek.[70] These flights suggest that if slaves sought their families with such determination, then such kinship ties were absent or much diminished in Augusta County.

Beyond flight, unfree workers pushed back against master domination in more menacing ways. These guerilla episodes may have provided temporary satisfaction but likely produced little meaningful improvement of slave circumstances.[71] If anything, two more active forms of slave resistance, talking back and outright violence, generated detrimental changes.

Glimpses of frontier slave insolence provide reminders that sharp tongues were ready weapons—if desperate ones—for lower-class colonial Americans regardless of race.[72] In Augusta County, white laborers snarled at masters with verbal intimidation, accusations of lying, and malicious gossip.[73] As with indentured and convict white servants, so too with slaves: recognizing verbal resistance as a tactic in an ongoing servile struggle helps make sense of the report that the eleven-year-old Gloster allegedly "had no fault but quarrelling."[74] In 1767, a mile or two down the road from Edward Tarr's land, the dying master of the woman Lue instructed that his sole slave continue to labor for the benefit of his family, but "if she proves cross or ill natured I order her to be sold."[75]

Even frontier slaves raised from childhood proved contentious. In 1771, ailing master Paul Whitley tacitly admitted his own failure to instill respectful subservience in a slave child. Whitley had acquired a ten-year-old African boy in 1755, named him Jack, and raised him on Whitley's farm in the Forks of the James River.[76] On his deathbed in 1771, Whitley ordered that Jack and a woman named Lett be retained "for the use of the family . . . [but] if they prove refractory they shall be sold and their price laid out on other Negroes or white servants for the same purpose."[77] Whitley's concern for Jack's and Lett's potentially "refractory" behavior addressed not only the possibility of resistance in the future but also the likelihood of resistance in the past: Jack's indoctrination had begun at age ten, but sixteen years later, Whitley anticipated Jack would make trouble.

Carried to an extreme, such resistance could turn into armed violence. In 1763, slave Tom shot his master with a musket, inflicting "one Mortal Wound in his back."[78] Six years later, another slave, Jacob, allegedly stole a rifle from a white man's house. At his trial Jacob somehow persuaded the magistrates of his partial innocence. The magistrates acquitted Jacob of housebreaking, but because "he is guilty of shooting at the Children of Alexander Moore," a relative of his master, the court sentenced him to thirty-nine lashes.[79] Housebreakers Hannibal and Tom (a different man from Tom the murderer, who by then was dead) separately stole a musket and rifle, respectively, along with other personal property. At the court's command in 1768, the county sheriff gave each thirty-nine stripes and nailed each by the ear to the county whipping post. After leaving them for a time to the torments of the courtyard onlookers, the sheriff cut the slaves loose, leaving severed portions of their ears attached to the post to caution other would-be felons.[80]

Most criminal assaults by slaves in Augusta County involved firearms, a notable trend in light of the fact that only about half their masters owned guns.[81] Slaves throughout colonial Virginia carried firearms, legally and otherwise, so these Augusta County episodes are not unique.[82] One anomalous aspect of frontier slave rebellion gives special weight to the weapons question, though. On a per capita basis, borderland slaves apparently resorted to violence much more commonly than did their peers in Tidewater Virginia. Between 1746 and 1769, Augusta County courts convicted slaves of violent felonies on eight occasions.[83] During an overlapping twenty-four-year period beginning in 1730 and ending in 1754, Richmond County magistrates convicted sixteen slaves of violent crimes.[84] But these eastern criminals came from a much larger slave population—1,235 tithable slaves in 1755, compared to 40 tithable slaves counted that same year in Augusta County.[85] Although the exact number of frontier slaves is unknown for any other year in this period, Augusta County's smaller slave population clearly produced a significantly higher proportion of violent felons than did the much more numerous slaves of long-settled Richmond County.[86]

The relative propensity of frontier slaves to attack their masters seems counterintuitive. In 1755, Augusta County white men outnumbered slaves about fifty-seven to one, and though masters subsequently acquired many more slaves, whites never lost their numerical superiority.[87] Given these odds, slave rebellion in early Augusta County appears suicidal. The story of slave Hampton provides the most vivid illustration of a seemingly irrational, self-destructive impulse. Hampton's downward spiral began in 1756, when his master complained to the Augusta County court that "Hampton frequently absconds from his service." Worse still, the slave "several times attempted to ravish Ann West and other white women." Hampton's owner, Thomas Lewis, proposed to the magistrates that "to prevent the like mischief [Hampton] be dismembered." The court accepted the master's solution, and authorized Lewis to "imploy any such skilfull person as he shall think proper to castrate the sd slave."[88]

Despite his emasculation, Hampton continued to threaten the peace. At different times in 1757 he feloniously broke into a number of Augusta County houses "with force and arms," stealing four shillings from a white woman, a rug and sundry goods from the slaves of his master's brother-in-law, and a jacket, hat, razor, knife, two shirts, and other items of small value from three white men. When arraigned in court for his depredations, Hampton "said he was in no wise thereof guilty," but the four magistrates hearing his case—two of whom had approved his castration the previous year—thought otherwise. The court ordered the sheriff to hang Hampton and recorded his value as forty-three pounds so Lewis could obtain compensation from the colonial government for his loss by the execution.[89]

Arguably the pathology of slavery produced Hampton's apparently irrational behavior; earlier historians attempted to explain slavery and its effects on slaves primarily in these terms.[90] But in the case of Augusta County, to analyze slave crime solely from this perspective is to miss a more revealing characterization. Notwithstanding Hampton's apparent example of irrationally self-destructive violence, assaults on masters were both self-immolating *and* logical, reflecting slave backgrounds as well as frontier conditions.

The first clue to the importance of slave experience and culture comes from comparing slave violence to assaults by white servants. Indentured and convict servants in Augusta County suffered physical coercion similar to that endured by slaves, including beatings. Masters and magistrates alike repeatedly whipped white servants for offenses real and imagined, including the offense of complaining against abusive masters.[91] On two recorded occasions, Augusta County masters fastened iron collars on their white servants, once in 1748 and again in 1751; magistrates and the county clerk treated both cases nonchalantly, implying that masters retained the right to impose such punishments when necessary.[92] Yet despite instances of comparably harsh treatment and essentially the same work regimen as that imposed upon slaves, only 6 out of 225 known white male indentured servants or apprentices violently turned against their masters during the county's first quarter-century.[93] By comparison, 8 out of between 69 and 93 known teenage or adult male slaves rose up.[94] Thus, 2.7 percent of known unfree white males turned violent, compared to between 8.6 and 11.6 percent of known slave men. In this rough estimate, male slaves were at least three times as prone to assault as white male servants.

The background of Augusta County's slaves explains much of their higher tendency toward rebellion. Evidence from other colonies indicates that even just a few Africans could catalyze a revolt, a factor that doubtless contributed to Virginia's frontier unrest.[95] African adults in Augusta County, men such as the "slave newly imported" in 1749, may have crossed the Atlantic Ocean already knowing how to load a musket and lay an ambush.[96] Moreover, it would be a mistake to assume the childish innocence of older African boys registered in colonial Augusta County. In the wake of one master's death at the hands of his slave, the king's attorney for Augusta County indicted another of the decedent's slaves, Farmer, with "aiding helping Comforting and Assisting" the murderer. The charge against Farmer, who probably was not yet eleven years in age, hints that African boyhood in America may have echoed African manhood across the Atlantic.[97] As more slaves arrived in Augusta County, impressionable African boys perhaps found role models for resistance in the fractious men dumped on frontier markets by exasperated eastern planters.

If the origins and journeys of frontier slaves help explain their volatility, other conditions in the new settlements explain their explosions. Rural surveillance and a scarcity of semiautonomous quarters contributed to the stress of daily slave life.[98] Beyond these annoyances, inexperienced masters were less likely than their eastern Virginia contemporaries to temper coercion with cooption or power with persuasion. White frontier society, however briefly acquainted with slavery, supported unreservedly the arbitrary authority of masters, regardless of the servant's race. When John Harrison advised the Augusta County court in 1754 "that his [white] servant man John Stagg had resi[s]ted and offered him Violence," the magistrates backed the master. In addition to twelve more months of service after his indenture expired, Stagg drew "thirty nine Lashes well laid on."[99] Court records reveal no official concern for why Stagg was resisting.

Just as masters felt little legal inhibition on their tempers, so too did angry frontier slaves have little reason for self-restraint. Drawn from diverse origins, Augusta County's enslaved pioneer men initially lacked local families who might otherwise have mitigated their wrath. No loved ones counseled patience, stood at risk for proxy punishment, or offered diversion from a frustrating life. The runaways who scrambled east over the Blue Ridge demonstrated what high value slaves placed on familial connections; without those connections, retribution for an angry man's outbursts could fall on no one about whom he cared. Scattered across a vast landscape, often alone in white households, Augusta County's earliest slaves experienced isolation exponentially greater than that of their masters' families.

Rural solitude magnified every gunshot, scream, and blow, ensuring that when slaves assaulted whites they irretrievably launched their own annihilation. Nor did the damage stop there. The lurid retribution slave criminals brought on themselves had such a powerful effect on white observers of the punishment that in destroying themselves, rebellious slaves also wounded black survivors, both slave and free. To white minds, slave resistance confirmed racial prejudices. Free blacks like Edward Tarr thus could not avoid association with slave criminals, however distinctive the free man's or woman's origins, education, status, wealth, skills, or faith. Given the inevitable consequent reinforcement of white racism, collisions of slave resistance with free black ambitions represent perhaps the most far-reaching negative effect of frontier slave violence.

The Murder of John Harrison

Assaults on masters during the early years of frontier slavery had a larger context of violence. Indian attacks from 1754 through 1764 made masters fearful of slaves in Augusta County.[100] Those perceptions were more influential than accurate; as with Indian hazards, frontier masters had difficulty understanding the true nature of the threats they faced.

Beginning during the Seven Years' War and continuing through the onset of Pontiac's Rebellion in 1763, pervasive white incomprehension of Indian strategy held serious implications for Edward Tarr. When frontier whites failed to identify Indian strategy, they sought other explanations for Indian behavior, characterizing the warriors as "Barbarous & Inhuman."[101] If Indians shared this alien inhumanity with rebellious slaves, then might not the two make common cause? Certainly eastern officials long feared such an alliance: "What a prospect of freedom appears to the slaves and servants on the frontiers?" fretted Lieutenant Governor Robert Dinwiddie in 1754. "It is not to be doubted but they will meet with proper encouragement from the French, whenever they chuse to visit them."[102]

When raiders associated with Pontiac's Rebellion struck Augusta County in July 1763, Doctor William Fleming noted with alarm that "the Indians are saving & Carressing all the Negroes they take," and feared the captures would produce "an Insurrection ... attended with the most serious Consequences."[103] At first glance, Fleming's concerns hardly seem justified: during Pontiac's Rebellion, Indians seized five known slaves in Augusta County, all of whom were recovered by pursuing militiamen.[104] Even if the raiders had reached home with their captives, five slaves did not comprise the strength upon which great insurrections are built. Regardless of its weak factual basis, however, Fleming's fear was important because it explicitly linked slave rebellion to Indian warfare.

His alarm provides essential background for a disturbing Augusta County murder in September 1763. The victim, John Harrison, was a master with a record of physically abusing a white indentured servant.[105] According to family tradition, Harrison's slave Tom shot Harrison in a cornfield. Tom's indictment stated that "Harrison languished the Space of Twelve Hours and then died," which on its face appears to contradict the Harrison family's traditional version that "the body was not discovered for some time, [so] when found, immediate burial was necessary. His grave was prepared by the spot where he fell." The two accounts can be reconciled, however, by presuming the indictment was drawn after Tom was interrogated, in which case Tom could have described Harrison's suffering if Tom stayed with him until he died and then left the body to decompose in the field. This interpretation makes sense of the indictment's blank day: the king's attorney could not tell exactly when Harrison died, so he simply stated that Tom mortally wounded Harrison on "the [blank] day of September last past."[106]

But the king's attorney was certain of the month, which was especially memorable in Augusta County. On September's last day, a sixty-man militia patrol stumbled into an ambush on Jackson River in which Indians killed and scalped twelve white men.[107] The discovery of Harrison's body and subsequent investigation, trial, and sentencing therefore took place during what Augusta County inhabitants experienced as the latest appalling and incomprehensible Indian onslaught. Had Tom hoped the county would assume that Harrison died at the hands of Indians? Harrison's location eight miles north of modern Harrisonburg was far from the scene of Indian alarms, but even if Tom had not intended to mimic a raid, perhaps news of the summer attacks opening Pontiac's war inspired his assault (table 25).[108]

Virginia law directed that capital crimes committed by slaves be tried in a special court. When authorities seized a slave suspected of capital crimes, the sheriff was directed by statute to jail the slave and request from the colonial governor a commission of oyer and terminer.[109] By law, the governor could name "such persons as he shall think fit" in the commission; for Augusta County cases, the fit persons consistently were magistrates already serving in the commission of the peace. Commissioners of oyer and terminer were "impowered and required to cause the offender to be publicly arraigned, and tried, at the courthouse of the said county," which they did in Tom's case on 9 November 1763, six days before the start of the November court session.[110]

Six justices of the peace sitting as commissioners tried Tom. The most senior was James Lockhart and another was Israel Christian, the magistrates who had considered Hugh Montgomery's attempt to reenslave Edward Tarr two years earlier.[111] As the law directed, the commissioners heard the case "without the solemnity of a jury," which meant that, unlike cases tried under an English common-law commission of the peace, the commissioners were finders of both fact and law. Virginia's oyer and terminer courts normally took "for evidence the confession of the offender, the oath of one or more credible witnesses, or such testimony of negroes, mulattoes, or Indians, bond or free, with pregnant circumstances, as to them shall seem convincing," but in this case, the king's attorney presented no witnesses. Instead, "the said Tom was led to the barr under the Custody of" the county sheriff, where Tom "Confessed the fact wherewith he stands Charged and according to the form of the Act of Assembly in Cases of this Nature made and provided did put himself upon the Court."[112]

The commissioners voted unanimously to convict. In light of Tom's confession, they could hardly have done otherwise, which raises the question of whether the magistrates would have convicted Tom without his confession. Perhaps not: as one of Tom's fellow slaves demonstrated, the outcomes of slave prosecutions were not foregone conclusions. In January 1764, a second court of oyer and terminer tried another of Harrison's slaves, the eleven-year-old Farmer, for "feloniously wilfully and of his Malice forethought . . . aiding helping Comforting and Assisting Tom" in murdering Harrison. Farmer denied the fact and "put himself upon the Court and no Witnesses appearing to make good the Charge against him the Court are of Opinion that he be thereof acquitted."[113]

Most official documentation of eighteenth-century slave trials is frustratingly taciturn, and Tom's is no exception.[114] It is impossible to tell whether his confession was coerced, but it need not have been: Tom may have confessed defiantly, as the record hints. Having found Tom guilty, the commissioners "demanded of him if he had anything to say why the Court should not proceed to Judgment and Execution against him [but] he said he had nothing to say but what he had already said." With that, events unfolded inexorably: "It is Considered by Court that he be hanged by the Neck Untill he be dead and it is Ordered that Execution thereof be done on Saturday the Nineteenth Instant [i.e., 19 November]."[115]

The scheduling of Tom's trial and execution is significant. The trial took place on Wednesday, the 9th, during Augusta County's semiannual fair.[116] Like all official proceedings of the county court, it would have been a public spectacle. The execution likewise could be well attended because Virginia law stipulated that under normal circumstances, "when judgment of death shall be passed . . . there shall be ten days, at least, between the time of passing judgment, and the day of execution."[117] The delay of execution allowed time not for an appeal—slaves had none—but for publicizing the hanging, which was intended to provide a gruesome cautionary example. Tom's execution thus was set for the final day of the November court session, when presumably it would be attended by the usual "Clamour, Noise & Nonsense which prevail in the Streets of Staunton."[118]

The greatest possible number of people therefore saw executed the sentence James Lockhart pronounced, including the court's direction to the sheriff that, after Tom was dead, "then his head be Severed from his body and affixed on a Pole." In this the court followed Virginia's customary treatment of slave criminals, which in turn derived from the English practice of quartering bodies of persons executed for treason.[119] What was different—and especially ominous in light of Lockhart's and Israel Christian's presence on the commission of oyer and terminer—was the court's final instruction to the sheriff. The pike impaling Tom's head was to be set "on the Top of the Hill near the Road that Leads from this Court House to Edward Tars."[120]

9

The Concubine

Tom's murder of John Harrison and its judicial aftermath exemplify a difficult challenge with regard to analyzing race relations: when were harsh events involving people of different races motivated by racism? At first glance, race seems inseparable from both Tom's crime and his punishment. White or black, convicted murderers were hanged in colonial Virginia, but after execution only black ones routinely were dismembered and gruesomely displayed. Of all the white capital crimes, piracy and treason alone drew comparable sentences. In that light, an order to impale Tom's head seems unambiguously racist.[1]

Powerful symbolism imbued the episode with ominous implications for Edward Tarr. From atop its pike, Tom's decaying head symbolically shackled a murderous slave to Augusta County's most prosperous free black. The striking sight—not to mention the smell and the squabbling of carrion birds—conveyed multiple messages. In death, Tom reminded white and black unfree laborers to accept their masters' authority. To slaves alone Tom chided that free blacks like Tarr were unique. White masters and slaveless white property owners subliminally heard Tom whisper that they shared responsibility for controlling a growing enslaved population.[2]

Did Tarr hear anything? Arguably the association of Tom's head with Edward Tarr may simply have been a coincidental consequence of Tarr's establishing his new forge beside a busy road just outside Staunton. If the magistrates' sole purpose was to place Tom's head in a prominent location, then their order had nothing to do with Tarr.[3]

There is, however, one important clue that the siting of Tom's head may have been linked to Tarr. The presiding magistrate at Tom's trial, James

Lockhart, handled a subsequent case in a way that indicated careful selection of display sites. In 1772, Lockhart conducted another oyer and terminer proceeding that convicted slaves Jacob and Aaron of murder, sentenced them to death by hanging, and ordered "that one of their heads be affixed on a pole below this Town near the road at the rocks & the other near the road leading from William Mitchells to Staunton."[4] By separating the heads, Lockhart ensured that more people would receive the message, and in naming Mitchell, Lockhart signaled his interest in a specific locale eight miles from town. The road from Mitchell's land near the western edge of Beverley Manor ran past at least ten other farms before it reached the courthouse. Mitchell was a relative newcomer to the area, so the road was not traditionally called after him. Lockhart himself lived about a mile south of Mitchell; some now indiscernible circumstance apparently convinced Lockhart to impale a slave head in Mitchell's vicinity.[5] The specificity of Lockhart's order suggests the depth of his concern.

The question of whether Tom's head was intended to convey a message to Edward Tarr is further complicated by the typical bluntness of county government in colonial Virginia. Few county problems were so nuanced as to require subtle solutions; when justices of the peace needed to caution or intimidate any person, black or white, they normally possessed ample authority to do so. Nevertheless, Tarr's relocation to the vicinity of Staunton may have been unusually perplexing to frontier officials. If Lockhart, Israel Christian, and the other magistrates wanted Tom's head to hint a particular message for Tarr's residence, the hint depended a great deal on who was inside Tarr's house.

Tom's Head and Ann Moore's Body

When James Lockhart sentenced Tom in 1763, he possibly intended to comment on Edward Tarr's ambiguous domestic arrangements. In itself, Tarr's marital miscegenation was unobjectionable: his white wife had been accepted since his original arrival in the county. But a second woman also was associated closely with Tarr: the 1759 grand jury presentment against Ann Moore for disturbing the peace noted in passing that Tarr harbored the contentious woman. When he moved to Staunton, the county court allowed the presentment to go dormant, suggesting strongly that Moore relocated to the county seat with Tarr and his wife. Moore's Timber Ridge neighbors thus rid themselves of a nuisance, and Augusta County officials disregarded a now-irrelevant neighborhood dispute.

In time, however, Moore's residence with Tarr drew fresh criticism. New doubts surfaced about the legitimacy of their relationship. The earliest official suspicion dates to an August 1761 alias summons that unsuccessfully ordered Moore to answer her grand jury presentment for disturbing the peace. County clerk John Madison wittily labeled the writ on its reverse as

A[lias] Summon[s]
Ann Moore
Ned Tars Concubine.[6]

The first two lines were normal endorsements; the third emphatically was not.

Madison's notation should be read as the clerk's private joke with Sheriff William Preston on a document that Moore would not have seen: Preston would have served the writ by leaving a duplicate copy at her residence. Occasionally, Madison provided written guidance to sheriffs about where to find defendants, so at one level, Madison's witticism told Preston that Moore resided with Edward Tarr. Madison's choice of words also indicated that Ann Moore resided with Tarr's wife. In an eighteenth-century context, calling a woman "concubine" invoked Old Testament–style polygamy; she was a subordinate spouse. By smirking with Preston at Moore's junior sexual status, one gentleman to another, Madison revealed that Tarr still was married to the Scottish woman.[7]

Although clerk and sheriff were amused, grand jurors were not. A 16 November 1762 grand jury officially brought Moore's domestic arrangement to the Augusta County court's attention, presenting Moore "for living in adultery & Cohabiting with a negro named Nedd."[8] Significantly, the grand jurors presented only Moore for adultery, not Tarr. By charging her but remaining silent about Tarr, the jury indicated that Tarr's Scottish wife still resided with him. If Tarr had been living alone with Moore, then each would have been presented on a charge of fornication; out of sixteen grand jury indictments for adultery or cohabitation from 1746 to 1763, only two named just one party.[9] With Tarr's uncomplaining wife also residing in the house, however, an adultery charge against Tarr was unsustainable.

Grand jury presentments from November 1762 were prosecuted the following September. At that time, the old presentment against Moore for disturbing the peace was revived, and in both instances she declined to appear when her case was called. Conditional judgments followed accordingly, meaning that unless she attended at the next court, a final judgment against her would be rendered automatically. "Next court" proved to be distant; the magistrates eventually reviewed Moore's cases on 22 June 1764, only to continue them without comment. At last, on 25 May 1765, they fined Moore a nominal five shillings for disturbing the peace. Later the same day, the court took up the 1762 grand jury presentment, now specified more vaguely as "living in adultery and Cohabiting with a Negro." Again Moore forfeited judgment by not appearing, so the magistrates fined her the usual one thousand pounds of tobacco and its cask for the use of Augusta Parish, plus court costs.[10]

In Augusta County at this time officials calculated tobacco's value at a penny per pound, so in cash, Moore's adultery conviction obligated her to pay £4:3:4 plus the cask's value. Apparently she remitted the fine at the appropriate time; detailed sheriff's accounts do not survive for this period, but Virginia law provided that "If the Offender refuses to pay the Fine, or to give Security for the Payment at the laying the next Parish Levy, he or she shall receive 25 Lashes, on his or her bare Back, well laid on."[11] Augusta County's court order books contain no record of whipping Ann Moore, although magistrates previously whipped another couple convicted of "Living in Adultery together" who refused to pay their fines.[12] The only ways for Moore to avoid both fine and scourge would have been to die or leave the county, and perhaps the latter was her prosecutors' intention. If grand jurors hoped to drive her out, however, they were disappointed. She still was on hand in 1767, when a servant woman of hers "agreed to aquit her mistress her freedom Dues" in exchange for Moore's discharging the woman from further service.[13]

Ann Moore complicated Edward Tarr's life far beyond disturbing the peace of his neighbors. Her late husband likely was kin to Hugh Montgomery, who in 1761 had claimed Tarr as a slave only weeks after the county clerk identified Moore as "Ned Tars Concubine." The two magistrates who protected Tarr from reenslavement, James Lockhart and Israel Christian, sat on the 1763 court that conditionally judged her guilty of disturbing the peace and living in adultery with Tarr. Six weeks later, the same two magistrates formed part of the commission of oyer and terminer that ordered Tom's execution for the murder of John Harrison; Lockhart directed that Tom's head be piked on the road to Tarr's shop. The subtlest communication by Tom's head may have been a rebuke to Edward Tarr regarding a widely assumed but unprovable interracial extramarital sexual partnership.

A Quieter Life

Moore's penchant for drawing unwanted attention may have changed Tarr's financial behavior. Once local concern over his ties to Moore was out in the open, Tarr grew more careful about his overdue debts and was sued only twice more for unpaid bills. In the former instance, Andrew Greer, an ordinary keeper and storekeeper in Staunton, initiated a suit against Tarr on 9 November 1762. Greer sought to recover fifteen pounds in damages. A week later, the grand jury presented Moore for living with Tarr, and within six more days Tarr had settled with Greer; on 22 November, the court dismissed the case as agreed.[14]

The final suit against Tarr was initiated by magistrate John Bowyer, who launched a debt action on 4 February 1767 to recover eleven pounds, eleven shillings, plus twenty shillings damages, signifying the debt's principle was half that amount. This too was speedily resolved after the deputy sheriff served Tarr with a summons.[15] A timely county disbursement to Tarr enabled him to repay the overdue obligation: on 19 March 1767, the court ordered the sheriff to "pay Edward Tarr" the sum of £7:17:7½ "for repairs to the prison of this County."[16] Bowyer was present on the bench during the same day as this order, so Tarr had an immediate opportunity to offer him full restitution.[17] On 23 March 1767, his suit was recorded as agreed and dismissed.[18] This was the sole action initiated against Tarr after slave Tom's execution.

As the 1760s wore on, Tarr's activities generated few official records. Occasionally he can be glimpsed while shopping or working, as in the books of Staunton storekeepers Mathew Reid and Hugh Johnston. On 8 February 1765, Reid and Johnston recorded for Tarr a debit for 11/10½ compiled from their daily store journals. This summary form of bookkeeping conceals from modern historians the what and when of Tarr's acquisitions, as does a brief entry three years later for sundries he purchased over a period ending 14 February 1768. Later in 1768, Tarr purchased "5 yds of Cheick [cloth] at 2/9" per yard, but this is the sole entry to identify specific merchandise. Reid and Johnston first entered credits to offset Tarr's purchase on 5 May, over three years after opening Tarr's ledger account. On that date, one credit totaling £1:0:10 was the sum "By yr acct as p[er the daily store] Jourynal." In other words, Tarr probably had performed a variety of work on different occasions, much like what he did for George Stevenson at Timber Ridge in the previous decade. Tarr's second 1768 credit was for fourteen shillings, either by cash he paid or goods or services he delivered to peddler John Smiley upon Reid's or Johnston's order. Hypothetically, for example, Reid might have instructed Tarr to shoe packhorses for Smiley's use. When Tarr settled his store accounts on 27 June 1770, his accumulated credits amounted to a balance of 12/7½, which he accepted in cash.[19]

A handful of other accounts indicate that Tarr remained active as a blacksmith despite his advancing age. The payment he received in early 1767 for repairs to the jail involved a substantial amount of labor, according to an account from the next year indicating Tarr was paid by the weight of metal he shaped. Undersheriff Michael Bowyer's 1768 accounts included an entry of fifteen shillings, four pence, that Augusta County owed Tarr for "working 46 lb Iron for the Goal [jail] @ 4d."[20] If Tarr's work in the previous year was compensated at the same rate of four pence per pound, then Tarr crafted a total of almost 473 pounds of iron for the jail in 1767.

Such labor could help keep an aging blacksmith physically fit, but if he sickened, eighteenth-century medicine offered few restoratives. By 1768, Tarr was about fifty-six years old, and in April of that year he consulted Doctor William Fleming at Staunton. Fleming responded to Tarr's symptoms by opening one of Tarr's veins and draining some blood. For "Blooding Negro Ned," Fleming charged a fee of two shillings, six pence, to the account of Fleming's father-in-law and Tarr's old acquaintance Israel Christian. Fleming's account book thus indicates Tarr's ongoing credit and service relationship with the same justice of the peace who helped protect his freedom in 1761 and participated in Tom's commission of oyer and terminer in 1763.[21] And while Tarr did not consult the doctor again, Fleming's account book also contains one other 1768 entry relevant to Tarr's story. About three weeks before bleeding Tarr, Dr. Fleming provided a purgative—"Two Doses Salts"—to a patient Fleming described as "William Davis of Philadelphia."[22]

Through the 1760s, the narrative trajectories of Edward Tarr and William Davis repeatedly arced near each other in Augusta County. Tarr and Davis stood in the same courtroom and dealt with the same officials. Davis's travels to the New River Valley took him past the site of Tarr's original forge on the Great Wagon Road. When Edward Tarr tucked five yards of check cloth under his arm on 7 June 1768, he was standing in Reid's and Johnston's store, which in turn was standing on William Davis's lot.[23] Despite its ambitious boundaries, Augusta County was smaller than it looked on a map.

Tarr's Land of Opportunities

Living in a land of opportunity had one serious drawback: it was full of opportunists. Schemes abounded in the eighteenth century for converting frontier resources into cash or credit, and local schemers twice were drawn to Edward Tarr's land. Evidence for the first plot is found in a fragment of an account by eastern attorney Edmund Pendleton. In early 1770, Tarr consulted the Caroline County–based lawyer regarding an issue that qualified for trial in the General Court in Williamsburg, Virginia's court of appeals and highest court of record.

A torn document among Pendleton's surviving papers lists lawyer fees owed to Pendleton by various persons bearing surnames of Valley of Virginia land owners. Tarr's entry was a characteristically terse example of Pendleton's legal bookkeeping, which requires some decoding. Under the heading of "1770. April Fee," Pendleton listed surnames of three other persons before entering "v. Tarr 1. .1. .6," followed by identical entries for thirteen more surnames.[24] In Pendleton's notation, the date of April 1770 indicates the biannual General Court session in that month. "Fee" signifies that each named person owed Pendleton a lawyer's fee, so the annotation "v[ersus] Tarr" indicates money Tarr owed to Pendleton, not a lawsuit in which Tarr was defendant. The entry further records that Pendleton charged Tarr £1:1:6, a revealing amount in light of Virginia's statutory stipulation that "lawyers practising in the General Court, may demand and receive, for an opinion, or advice, where no suit is brought, one pound, one shilling six pence."[25]

On what point of law did Tarr consult Pendleton? Over eight years after attempting to reenslave Tarr, had Hugh Montgomery or his assignee at last decided to claim Tarr before Virginia's ultimate judicial authorities? Possibly so, but the more likely issue was a different fraud, one indicated by the account's timing and by the numerous Augusta County surnames appearing before and after Tarr's entry in Pendleton's accounts. At the April 1770 General Court, many Augusta County land owners faced a large-scale attempt to seize land for which patents had not been granted or for which quitrents were overdue. Pendleton was involved in fending off those efforts, and his account fragment indicates that Tarr was one intended victim in an ultimately unsuccessful land grab.[26]

A second opportunistic scheme focused directly on Tarr's land. Other keen-eyed men of business saw great potential in the 270-acre tract and its series of lynns, or waterfalls, down which Mill Creek tumbled along the southwestern edge of the property. The lynns were mentioned in the original 1751 deed for what became Tarr's land, as well as in the original 1765 deed to his neighbor William Lusk and in a deed by Lusk's executors in 1772.[27] The latter transaction is particularly relevant: when Lusk died, his executors soon sold his Mill Creek land to Thomas Stuart, an Augusta County merchant.[28]

Stuart's purchase appears to have been part of a larger family plan for flour production. Mill Creek's mechanical advantages were apparent since at least 1741 when the eponymous watercourse first appears in land records, and for many years Augusta County farmers had produced large wheat surpluses. In 1761, for example, Israel Christian hauled over thirty-one short tons of flour to Fort Burd on the Monongahela River in southwest Pennsylvania.[29] Further expansion of intercoastal and overseas grain markets made Mill Creek's advantages even more alluring by the early 1770s.[30] Stuart and his brother Alexander recognized that a burgeoning wheat economy demanded more processing capacity and so began quietly acquiring valuable mill sites. Their conspiratorial approach masked their intentions and thus kept potential grantors from asking higher prices for stream banks with good potential for milling.

Around 1772, Alexander Stuart approached an Augusta County resident about serving as an intermediary in acquiring Edward Tarr's land. Since Stuart's brother had just bought the adjacent land from the executors of Tarr's former neighbor William Lusk, it probably seemed to Stuart that Tarr would charge more if he knew the Stuarts were amassing property along this stretch of Mill Creek. Stuart thus privately requested that the horse trader Samuel McChesney purchase the tract "adjoining the land of William Lusk, deceased, the property of which was at that time in *Edward Tarr*, commonly known by the name of *Black Ned.*"[31]

The deception successfully concealed Stuart's intentions. Tarr agreed to sell his 270 acres to McChesney for £45, a nominal 25 percent markdown from the £60 Tarr paid for the land in 1754.[32] After accounting for inflation over the eighteen years of his ownership, Tarr realized a loss of almost half his original purchase price.[33] Unlike his white neighbors, Tarr did not profit from rising real estate values in Borden's Land.[34] Whatever else land ownership did for him, Tarr lost money as a freeholder.

It is impossible to know what Tarr thought as he stood before the justices of the peace on 19 August 1772 to acknowledge his deed to McChesney.[35] Possibly Tarr reflected on the changing faces of both court and county. None of the four magistrates on the bench had been justices of the peace when Tarr recorded his land purchase in 1754, in the days when almost no slaves lived in Augusta County.[36] Magistrate Daniel Smith owned at least one slave, and just months earlier, magistrate Michael Bowyer's slaves had murdered a white man.[37] Perhaps Tarr recalled how five years earlier, then-deputy sheriff Michael Bowyer served a writ on Tarr to initiate a suit for money he owed but had not paid.[38] Given his own history of defaulting on payments for the same land, Tarr may have worried that McChesney likewise would do unto him.

As events unfolded, McChesney indeed proved unreliable, though he probably paid Tarr as agreed.[39] But McChesney did not promptly reconvey the land to Stuart. Temporarily oblivious to McChesney's impending bad faith, Stuart pursued his plans by purchasing a third Mill Creek tract containing an existing mill upstream from Tarr's land in 1773.[40] Then Stuart "proceeded to build a saw mill and grist mill" on what once was Tarr's property. McChesney refused to hand over the title, however, and Stuart was forced to sue the balky horse trader. The litigation ground forward until four years later when McChesney finally conveyed the land.[41]

The Artilleryman and the Woman

For eight years after acknowledging his deed to Samuel McChesney, Edward Tarr lived so quietly that his location and activities are a mystery. Like many of his white associates, Tarr repeatedly demonstrated that frontier inhabitants roamed widely, but his absence from documentary records does not necessarily mean he left the Valley of Virginia. Tarr may have continued living in plain sight on the edge of Staunton without generating any surviving written records. A 1780 epilogue to Tarr's saga is ambiguous regarding his location in that year.

Tarr's final documented activities involved the so-called Convention Army, those British and German troops interned during the American Revolution at Saratoga, New York, in October 1777. The convention was a battlefield agreement proposed by British General John Burgoyne and too-hastily accepted by the American commander. Under its terms, Burgoyne's troops were to have marched to Boston and embarked for Europe, never to return to America. The agreement proved so favorable to British interests that Congress reneged and refused to send the troops back across the Atlantic Ocean. For the remainder of the Revolutionary War, Congress shunted the Convention Army from state to state. Motives for relocating the detainees included episodic threats that British forces might liberate a reservoir of reinforcements, sporadic difficulties in feeding and sheltering so many people, and the perennial self-interest of American congressmen.[42]

In 1778, Congressman John Harvie of Virginia induced his fellow solons to direct the Convention Army's march from Massachusetts to Harvie's land outside Charlottesville, the seat of Albemarle County, just east across the Blue Ridge from Augusta County. It was a shrewd move for Harvie, who benefited by the troops' clearing the woods and brush from his future fields. For common soldiers, however, Harvie's site was a disappointment. They marched from Massachusetts in November 1778 and arrived at Harvie's land in January 1779 after a miserable trip.[43] There they found "a few log huts were just begun to be built, the most part not covered over, and all of them full of snow."[44]

The Convention troops did what good soldiers do and made the best of a bad situation. How well they succeeded depended on how closely one scrutinized their condition. In lush vernal Virginia, the encampment's initially frigid vista bore a much-improved aspect to an anonymous senior German officer reporting in June 1779: "The barracks . . . which must have aroused pity in your compassionate heart, now resemble the City of Ninevah as it may have been in its glory. The English Soldiers have built covered walks in front of their barracks and all their streets look like the Jungfernsteig at Brunswick."[45]

Junior officers like Royal Army Lieutenant Thomas Anburey saw the encampment differently. According to him, "the barracks swarm with rats of an enormous size. . . . They are very troublesome, and [even] with every precaution, they are continually destroying the men's cloaths and bedding during the night; it is no very uncommon thing to see them running six or seven, one after the other, in the interstices of the logs with which the huts are constructed."[46]

Although "the Barracks became a little town," not all the soldiers remained within its capacious bounds (figure 7).[47] Officers traveled widely under parole, and enlisted soldiers also received permission to leave camp. Many came or were sent to Augusta County, which since early in the war had secured British troops: long before the arrival of the Convention Army, Virginia's governor sent two prisoners of war "to the Town of Staunton in Augusta County there being a good & sufficient Jail at that place."[48]

German and English soldiers thus passed part of their internment in Augusta County. The most senior of these was Brigadier General Johann Friederich Specht, a likely candidate for authorship of the anonymous barracks description quoted above.[49] Reverend Doctor John August Leonhard

Figure 7. Convention Army barracks near Charlottesville, 1780.
In April 1780, Edward Tarr received permission to search this encampment of detained British and German combatants; he hoped to retrieve his stolen cash and property and to bring the thieves before a Virginia magistrate. (Anburey, *Travels in America*, 2:443.)

Kohly, chaplain of Specht's regiment, ministered to Lutherans in the portion of old Augusta County now known as Rockingham County.[50] Governor Thomas Jefferson authorized Mr. McNiell, a British prisoner, to visit the Warm Springs for McNiell's health.[51]

Beyond the officers, the number of enlisted troops in Augusta County was not recorded, but incidental references to them suggest it was more than a handful. Some were detained in the jail, but the majority appear to have been dispersed around the county.[52] James Chapman, for example, had sufficient liberty to meet Susanna Call and, with permission from his officers, marry her.[53] The logistical task of feeding detained soldiers west of the Blue Ridge was complex enough for Virginia to appoint James Culbertson "as issuing Commissary for the prisoners Stationed at Staunton of Burgoyne's army."[54]

Despite their noncombatant status, some of the Convention Army troops continued to be targets. One Augusta County resident stole a senior officer's horse.[55] Other county men seized two German soldiers and held them until they paid a ransom.[56] The Convention troops responded to such depredations in kind, including an incident involving Edward Tarr.

On 17 April 1780, during the Convention Army's second spring in Virginia, the commander of the American guard detachment wrote formally to the senior officer of royal forces:

Sir, The Bearer Edward Tarr (who is a free man) has lately been Robbed of a Considerable Sum of Money in paper and Specie by a woman who lived with him. he Suspects one Richardson of the Royal Artillery to be an Accomplice. he has obtained a Warrant from a Civil Magistrate to Search for his money, and Other Effects which were taken at the Same time, and to Apprehend the Culprits. you will be Pleased to Direct that no Insult be Offered to the Constable while in the Execution of his Office and that Richardson be Delivered to him to be Examined by the Magistrate.[57]

Despite continued problems with women, Tarr at least still understood how to invoke the law.

He also still had plenty of nerve. Whether he was robbed in Augusta or Albemarle County, clearly he believed the thief had returned to the barracks. Tarr and his constable therefore intended to patrol the streets of "Ninevah as it may have been in its glory" in search of Richardson of the Royal Artillery, the woman, the cash, and Tarr's unnamed other effects.

It was an audacious proposition. The number of troops in the barracks had declined by April 1780—partly by posting them to other locales, partly by escapes across country to rejoin royal forces in New York—but even so, there likely still were as many as a thousand British men on hand and well over a thousand more Germans.[58] For the soldiers, the spectacle of an American constable attempting to arrest one of their own upon the complaint of an elderly black man would have been a tremendous gift of irresistible entertainment. Under the circumstances, it would have been impossible to guarantee "that no Insult be Offered to the Constable while in the Execution of his Office."[59]

Despite the manifest hazards of extricating Richardson for examination by a magistrate, did Tarr succeed? Lieutenant Anburey, ever a keen observer, was silent on the matter in a letter from Charlottesville dated the day after the order on Tarr's behalf.[60] Nor do official records help: as usual in Virginia, the out-of-court activities of individual magistrates went unrecorded. If Tarr was robbed in Augusta County, court orders include no record that Richardson was prosecuted there, and if Tarr was robbed in Albemarle County, relevant court orders burned during a British raid on Charlottesville in 1781. Possibly Tarr successfully recovered his money, in which event there would have been no prosecution in either venue. One thing at least appears likely: Richardson did not use the money to escape from Virginia. Muster and pay rolls of the Convention Army's Royal Artillery companies included two Richardsons, but neither appears to have deserted.[61]

But Richardson was only an accomplice. What about the woman, the thief? Her larceny contrasts to the generosity of the anonymous Scottish bread-baker with whom Tarr joyfully greeted the Moravian travelers in October 1753, over twenty-six years earlier. Her character recalls Ann Moore's "evil fame & Behaviour in he[r] Neighbourhood," despite which Tarr continued to shelter Moore. Perhaps the same woman snarled at her Timber Ridge neighbors and conspired with an enemy soldier, or perhaps these episodes involved different women. Certainly the last one's financial wound to Tarr was a mere scratch beside the slash of her betrayal. Could Tarr's multifaceted Christianity have sufficed to forgive her?

10

The Travelers

Accelerating Mobility—Integral Characteristics of Mobility—
Social Consequences of Mobility—Racial Attitudes in Motion

Edward Tarr's actions after his brush with the Convention Army in April 1780 are unknown. Like his antagonist Joseph Shute, Tarr disappeared from view without leaving a forwarding address. The absence of documentation about him does not necessarily indicate a departure, of course, and in any event Tarr was not soon forgotten. Indeed, memories of Tarr persisted long after his final exit.

A map based on 1804 surveys depicted what its draftsmen believed to be the original grantees in Benjamin Borden's 92,100-acre grant (see figure 4). The surveyors appear to have consulted inhabitants about tract lines and former owners; the surveyors' informants identified Edward Tarr as the first settler on his Mill Creek land.[1] In their minds, Tarr, not the initial grantee Isaac Gray nor the second owner Jacob Gray, stood out as a pioneer. Tarr's identification as an original settler is all the more remarkable for coming over four decades after he moved from Timber Ridge to Staunton.

Probably Tarr did not die in Augusta County, since the deaths of independent adult males typically generated documents that were well preserved in that locale. If he died after making a will, his heir or executor normally would have presented it in court for proof. If he died without a will, county magistrates should have followed English common-law practice for the administration of intestates' property, just as they did in 1759 for "Jos[eph] Bell the Mallato" and for numerous white men who died without wills.[2] No such documents exist, however. Perhaps Tarr died in Albemarle County after obtaining his 17 April 1780 search warrant and before June 1781, when British raiders burned the county court records. If so, records of his death are irretrievably lost. But if he moved from the Valley of Virginia after April 1780, additional records of his life or death may yet turn up in what would be just one more in a long string of far-flung destinations.

Tarr and most recurring figures in this book left few examples of their own words, but their travels by land or sea demonstrated both individual goals and collective trends. The Atlantic voyages of Thomas and Joseph Shute, wide-ranging wagon trips of William Davis, and remarkable journeys of Edward Tarr between Pennsylvania and Virginia all illustrate a vast but routine scale of travel in colonial North America. Ordinary people in peacetime as well as diverse belligerents in war traversed roads hundreds of miles in length. A skein of personal trajectories along a western crescent of trails and settlements bound together thousands of individuals and hundreds of extended families from Philadelphia through Virginia to Charleston.

Early American mobility's origins, characteristics, and consequences are venerable issues in United States historiography. Novelists since James Fenimore Cooper, commentators since Alexis de Tocqueville, and historians since Frederick Jackson Turner have linked mobility to restiveness and economic ambition.[3] For these nineteenth-century observers, mobility amounted to a self-fueling insatiable addiction; for some modern historians, the trait had an addiction's deleterious antisocial effects.[4] Only recently have historians argued that eighteenth-century mobility helped keep communities connected.[5]

For Edward Tarr, mobility at various times facilitated an interracial marriage, channeled a lucrative stream of customers, and expedited an escape from imminent Indian threat. Close scrutiny of the careers of Tarr and some of his contemporaries also suggests that mobility initially fostered frontier toleration of free black men. Over time, mobility introduced Tarr to a wide range of travelers in western Virginia, a familiarity that generated historically significant social consequences.

Accelerating Mobility

From Pennsylvania's earliest days, immigrants such as Thomas Shute were drawn inland by economic self-interest. Arriving in the Delaware River Valley as a teenager around 1681, Shute entered upon a capacious landscape replete with resources. He and like-minded peers learned to range ever farther afield in search of opportunities that, though neither free nor unregulated, nevertheless were accessible when approached with the right combination of labor, capital, and political influence.

As business partners, yeomen like Shute joined gentlemen in claiming land and the lucrative natural resources upon and under it. The more they grasped, the farther they reached. Shute first sent building stone to Philadelphia, then fine marble to Barbados. His son-in-law's mill a dozen miles from his house ground flour that he shipped six hundred miles to his son in Charleston. Shute's career demonstrates that a culture of mobility existed in Pennsylvania even before immigration to the colony surged during the four decades leading to 1755.[6] Established merchants, gentlemen, and yeomen already were accustomed to investing, trading, and traveling over great distances by land as well as sea.

Routes leading inland from the Delaware River Valley began as Indian roads and expanded to accommodate new forms of traffic: wagons and carts, herds of livestock, packhorse trains, immigrant families. As the latter arrived, they brought comparable notions about mobility. German-speaking and Irish immigrants alike included European sojourners who perceived emigration in routine rather than epic terms.[7] People representing both ethnicities readily relocated or traded far inland, discovering quickly that in Pennsylvania and Virginia, courts and the common law facilitated mobility by sustaining creditor rights even among remote settlements.[8] Nuances of that legal regime might have felt new, but the core concept of enforceable contracts was as obvious as it was essential. Joseph Shute's attempt to reenslave Edward Tarr in one sense amounted to a typical demonstration of paper's power to invoke official attention across long distances.

Immigrating settlers expected more than merely reliable access to courthouses, however. They also expected to sit on magisterial benches. When Pennsylvania authorities in the 1730s failed to elevate immigrants to positions of authority as swiftly as those immigrants wished, the newcomers moved south. In the upper Valley of Virginia, they quickly received key appointments as militia officers, magistrates, and surveyors. Most of the population and thus most of the newly made officials were Irish, but in Augusta County's German-speaking neighborhoods, colonial officials and the new magistrates also appointed Germans to exercise local authority.[9]

For almost a generation, immigrant and Indian mobility coexisted in Virginia frontier settlements, generating occasional friction without igniting a war. For Indians, the road past Black Ned's forge amounted to more than a path between destinations: frontier farmers contributed to Indian mobility by providing food and shelter. Moreover, the persistent presence of Indian commercial hunters in the vicinity of southwest Virginia settlements strongly suggests that Indians saw the New River Valley settlers as contributing to an advantageous hunting district. Unfortunately for most southwestern Virginia farmers, their settlements lay along the packhorse road to Overhill Cherokee towns. Individual farms like Samuel Stalnaker's place on the Upper Holston River consequently assumed great strategic significance thanks to the mobility of traders and Indians alike. During the Seven Years' War and Pontiac's Rebellion, Northern Indians from the Ohio River Valley raided southwest Virginia in a successful effort to limit colonial communication with the Cherokees. By destroying farms that could feed draft horses, Shawnee and other raiders impeded an alliance between Cherokees and Virginians. The attacks were motivated by Northern Indian concern over white mobility, not an economic competition between farmers and hunters.

Integral Characteristics of Mobility

Depending on context, contemporaries attached a variety of meanings to mobility. A gentleman's jaunt resembled vagrancy when practiced by a common man. Numerous colonial Americans therefore paid close attention to the characteristics distinguishing one traveler from another. Members of all classes knew what it was to travel long distances. Throughout the colonial period, an overwhelming majority of Augusta County's adults were born in a different colony or on a different continent. From the perspective of mobile yeomen and gentlemen, this widespread base of experience posed a problem: how could dependents be kept close to home?

Establishing or challenging constraints for dependents became a defining tension of American mobility. Not everyone was permitted to exercise independent judgment about traveling. While Thomas Shute moved from venture to venture and site to site, the dependents he supervised remained relatively sedentary. His son William farmed, son-in-law Sampson Davis ground grain, Thomas, Jr., rendered tallow into soap and candles, son Isaac hammered in his smithy, and Jacob assembled barrels in his cooperage. Only Shute's youngest, Joseph, originally was put to a mobile calling at sea.

A variety of mechanisms helped yeomen and gentlemen limit their dependents' movements. Masters could physically punish runaway servants and slaves, and the relatively short two-week median absence for absent servants in Augusta County indicates that even on the frontier, vigilant neighbors stopped fugitives. Other incentives applied to family members. Prospective heirs hoping for a larger slice of a parental estate had powerful economic reasons to stay where their patriarchs put them; only a handful like Joseph Shute and William Davis were permitted to venture abroad. Their example is a reminder that for dependents in longer-settled coastal communities, mobility might be more commonly perceived than practiced, visible but often impermissible.

To the extent that most recorded long-distance travelers were male, mobility also was gendered. Within frontier neighborhoods, however, women moved extensively over shorter distances, as indicated by three female heads of household who signed the call for Reverend John Brown at the Timber Ridge Meetinghouse in 1753. Ann Moore's troubled relationship with her neighbors surely reflected widespread contact. Women appeared as witnesses and garnishees in routine civil trials conducted in Staunton, and the presence of women's saddles in estate inventories and documents concerning indebtedness testifies to a number of women traveling on horseback.[10]

Conducting business over long distances required trustworthy couriers, people whose reliable performance in turn rapidly expanded the frontier social web. For example, William Davis's carting business necessarily required some client trust in the beginning; after Davis transmitted letters of instruction from his carting partner, frontier gentleman William Preston, to a Delaware printer and returned to Virginia with an order of goods, Davis enhanced his reputation among Preston's acquaintances as a reliable agent. Edward Tarr benefited from Davis's good reputation when Hugh Montgomery attempted to reenslave Tarr: Davis, a man known to the Augusta County magistrates who heard Montgomery's petition, had signed receipts that Tarr presented in evidence of his freedom.

Tarr also presented the magistrates with certified documents recording his own freedom, sealed instruments that conveyed through their appearance as well as their content an official confirmation of Tarr's assertions. Such documents were rarely used for conducting ordinary business at a distance; instead, letters, verbal messages, and standing orders were far more typical for routine commerce. In a distinctive exception, however, conveyances of land by distant owners required a sealed power of attorney such as the one that Philadelphia shoemaker William Young sent to Augusta County's clerk of court, John Madison, in order to convey Young's New River land to William Davis. Four men witnessed Young's signature in Pennsylvania; two swore to the mayor of Philadelphia that they were present and saw Young sign the document, and the mayor in turn certified their oaths to Madison. The other two witnesses appeared in Staunton and confirmed their signatures seven months later.[11] Only then was the land conveyance complete.

The mayor of Philadelphia's contribution to Davis's 1763 purchase of land in the New River Valley illustrates how transactions among officials compressed vast distances. Frontier magistrates accepted without further proof the mayor's certification of two signatures, just as they accepted without further proof all commissions from Virginia's governor appointing senior militia officers. Such documents possessed a self-evident legitimacy thanks to their familiar formats and official seals.

A related concept enabled private parties to conduct litigation over long distances. In the same way that official documents from governmental executives were accepted at face value, so too were the assertions of lawyers that they represented parties in lawsuits. The parties themselves, the actual plaintiffs or defendants, did not have to be on hand, and lawyers did not have to prove that they were authorized to speak for parties. Having been admitted to practice in a county court, lawyers needed no power of attorney to litigate. When Forks of the James resident Joshua Mathews wished to recover from Edward Tarr a debt of thirty pounds, Mathews directed attorney Gabriel Jones to launch the lawsuit in Staunton that motivated Tarr to repay his obligation speedily.[12] When Jones said he represented Mathews or any other plaintiff, no one in the courtroom contradicted him. For yeomen and gentlemen wishing to enforce contracts over great distances, lawyers like Jones were essential surrogates.

A final important attribute of frontier mobility concerns the process by which its adjunct skills were communicated. Old hands and novices alike acted as if travel accounts contained essential protocol lessons for frontier cultures. For example, the travels of one of Tarr's neighbors, John Peter Salley, drew repeated scrutiny by elite Virginians. In early 1742, Salley and some partners journeyed down the New River to the Ohio and down the Ohio to the Mississippi River. After being captured by French authorities and sent to New Orleans, they languished in prison for over two years. Salley eventually escaped and made his way by land to Charleston, which he reached in April 1745. Following an abortive attempt to sail to Virginia, Salley set out overland to the Forks of the James, arriving home over three years after starting down the New River. Salley calculated he had traveled 4,606 miles.[13]

After the fact, Salley wrote a journal of his travels but never published it. Nevertheless, the odyssey circulated widely. John Buchanan, a prominent land speculator in early Augusta County, transcribed Salley's manuscript during a six-day visit with him in October 1745.[14] Joshua Fry also copied it and used information from it in his map of Virginia, which depicted the location of Salley's residence in the Forks of the James.[15] Fry apparently passed word of Salley's travels to his friend Reverend Robert Rose, an Anglican minister who made a point of visiting Salley during a 1751 trip to Augusta County.[16] In 1756, William Fleming, a frontier physician educated at the University of Edinburgh, borrowed the journal from Augusta County magistrate William Preston and returned it with the comment that part of the work had been of use to him.[17]

Commoners too listened to travelers' tales. Such performances are easier to imagine than document: it is impossible, for example, to know whether mulatto William Carr, "the very life of any company he was in," entertained white listeners by describing his travels among "the forts and stations" of western Virginia.[18] A handful of ordinary people, however, can be glimpsed telling their travel stories in exchange for food and shelter from sympathetic Augusta County residents. New River Valley resident Katherine Bingaman "lost all she had when carried into Captivity" by Shawnee raiders in 1755.[19] Jane Midley was captured by "Northward Indians" when Ephraim Vause's fort was overrun on 25 June 1756; eventually, she returned to Augusta County and a decade after her capture informed the parish churchwardens that she "has latley been Reduced to beg[ging] Relief from House to House."[20] Mary Ingles was captured in the same raid and also ended up "supported entirely by the charitable Contributions of the Well disposed."[21] As they were hurried into captivity, all three women trod the first part of John Peter Salley's path, the Indian route along the New River. By begging, they heightened their audience's awareness of long roads leading to Indian towns that Salley never saw.

Social Consequences of Mobility

From Pennsylvania through the backcountry of Virginia and the Carolinas, a distinctive regional culture emerged in the eighteenth century. Previous historians labored to explain that distinctiveness in terms of ethnic or national origins.[22] In essential respects, however, the widely shared cultural attribute of mobility played a more important role than specific ethnic characteristics in shaping frontier social evolution. Landholding patterns, sociopolitical identity, and the spread of slavery reflected this key feature of frontier life.

Most obviously, mobility transformed the American real estate market. If immigrants generally were concerned with legal protections for property, then mobility had special significance for a particular class of property, real estate.[23] Migration within the western crescent of backcountry settlements ensured ongoing demand for frontier real estate on both sides of the Blue Ridge. In districts with poor transportation links for bulky crops, mobility generated demand for what otherwise might have seemed to be unlikely real estate. As in the valley, planters in piedmont counties like Lunenburg could not at first cheaply ship tobacco or grain to Tidewater Virginia ports.[24] Nevertheless, immigrants kept buying farms at rising prices, so settlers profited more from the next grantee than the next crop. When that grantee arrived, grantors emigrated to repeat the process elsewhere.[25]

Transactions in frontier land created two important social effects. First, they allowed immigrants to avoid for a generation the problem confronting Thomas Shute's heirs, the Yeoman's Dilemma of whether to wait for a diminishing share of patriarchal property. In Augusta County's most remote precinct, the New River Valley, settlers paid more for unimproved land than was currently charged in the vicinity of Staunton. The higher price reflected their desire for enough land to settle extended rather than nuclear families.[26] Second, frontier land transactions bound grantees and grantors alike much more strongly to their county governments than some historians have recognized. Grantees needed county courts to record their deeds, and grantors needed the same courts to help collect overdue debts.[27] The high degree of real estate turnover in Virginia backcountry counties from 1740 to 1770 thus helped stabilize frontier societies by giving settlers compelling reasons to accept and support magisterial authority.[28]

The mobility of frontier inhabitants facilitated friendships and alignments of self-interest, which strengthened personal bonds across class lines. Business partnerships between gentlemen like William Preston and wide-ranging yeomen like William Davis could also include camaraderie, as when Davis enabled Preston and others to gamble in the Conestoga lottery. Such relationships expanded: Preston's close friend, David Robinson, witnessed a document on behalf of Davis while on a 1763 trip to Pennsylvania. Seven months later, in Staunton, Davis in turn attended a trial as a witness for Robinson.[29] Virginia-style social hierarchies depended on precisely such relationships, as did Virginia-style politics.[30]

A third historically significant aspect of mobility was its correlation with the spread of slavery. In eastern Virginia, slaveholders moved slaves into unsettled piedmont districts to clear land for commercial cultivation.[31] By contrast, settlers west of the Blue Ridge came from locales where slavery was rare or nonexistent; the great majority of immigrants neither brought nor bought slaves for at least a quarter century. Augusta County's earliest slaveholders tended to be mobile men—gentlemen, Presbyterian ministers, and yeomen serving in offices such as constable that required frequent absence from their farms.

Racial Attitudes in Motion

Slavery was present in Augusta County by at least 1742, and from slavery's inception, a handful of gentlemen and yeomen masters had a strong interest in curtailing slave mobility. County court records indicate that these early adapters relied on vigilant neighbors to apprehend fugitives. Intriguingly, however, white suspicions about black movement appear to have been racial but not racist. Free mulattos William Carr and Joseph Bell made a living as commercial hunters, one of the most mobile occupations on the colonial frontier. No evidence survives to suggest that they or Edward Tarr or any other free blacks faced restrictions on mobility within colonial Augusta County. Free black liberty and slave constraint initially existed simultaneously.

Several factors contributed to the ease with which free blacks moved through Augusta County, not least of which was white familiarity with all blacks, enslaved or otherwise. The early enslaved population was so small—only forty adults as late as June 1755—that it was possible for mobile white residents to know every slave in the county. Tarr's forge on the Great Wagon Road and close by Staunton made him a familiar face for white travelers. Complexion also facilitated movement; most freedmen had lighter skin than newly imported Africans (see appendix 2). Additionally, most free people of color possessed personal property that set them apart from slaves: astride a horse, carrying a rifle, and leading a packhorse loaded with deer skins, William Carr or Joseph Bell simply did not look like fugitives.

Beyond these uniquely personal connections, the racial toleration shown to Augusta County free blacks had a more general colonial context. In the 1760s, the Virginia General Assembly enacted several protections and improvements for free blacks. A 1765 law stiffened the penalties on persons fraudulently selling as slaves any mulattoes who were bound to serve for a term of years. Offenders were compelled to repay the purchase price along with a fifty-pound penalty. Informers received twenty pounds from the offender, and any person convicted twice for the crime would forfeit the time remaining on the mulatto's indenture. If offenders could not pay the penalties, county magistrates were authorized to bind them to the would-be purchaser for "the full time of service that would have been due by law from such a servant." Most significantly, the law drastically shortened the period of mandatory service for mixed-race illegitimate children, who previously were compelled to serve to age thirty-one. The new terms conformed to the standards for white illegitimate children: age eighteen for girls and twenty-one for boys.[32] Other positive developments followed: in 1769, the General Assembly revised its longstanding requirement for free women of color to pay public, county, and parish levies. Unlike white women, women of color aged sixteen or above previously had been tithable, regardless of whether they were enslaved, bound, or free.[33]

These redefinitions of free black rights emerged from the increasingly heated debate over the political rights of American colonists. The 1765 "Act to Prevent the Practice of Selling Persons as Slaves That Are Not So" was prepared by Revolutionary firebrand Richard Henry Lee and passed by the House of Burgesses just eleven days before that body approved the Virginia Resolves denouncing the Stamp Act.[34] The 1769 levy relief act, which explicitly described levies on free women of color as "derogatory of the rights of free-born subjects," similarly had its genesis in the midst of legislative protests over the Townshend Acts.[35]

More than just a white struggle over imperial policy produced these major changes. The House of Burgesses drafted its levy relief act after "A Petition of the People called Mulattoes and free Negroes, whose Names are thereunto subscribed, was presented to the House, and read, praying that the Wives and Daughters of the Petitioners may be exempt from the Payment of Levies."[36] This free black petition was presented on 10 May and referred to the Committee of Propositions and Grievances, which reported the following day that the petition was reasonable. The full House agreed and ordered the committee to prepare a bill, but the measure died when the governor dissolved the assembly on 17 May.[37] The following November, the free black petition again was presented and approved in the House of Burgesses. The council made minor amendments, the measure was enacted, and royal assent was proclaimed on 3 April 1771.[38]

Free blacks in the 1760s perceived the time was right for asserting at least partial equality with whites, and elite burgesses agreed with that perception on two notable occasions. Throughout late colonial Virginia, a more tolerant attitude toward free blacks apparently existed than some historians have recognized.[39] Most of the evidence for this relative toleration is found in scholarship focusing on peripheral portions of Virginia, but even in Tidewater counties, contemporaries would not necessarily have considered Edward Tarr's experience in Augusta County to be unique.

In the Southside counties of Amelia, Brunswick, Charlotte, Halifax, Lunenburg, Mecklenburg, Pittsylvania, and Prince Edward, colonial- and Revolutionary-era free people of color repeatedly and successfully asserted their rights in court.[40] In the Eastern Shore counties of Accomack and Northampton, multiple generations of free black families owned land like that of their ordinary rural white neighbors.[41] Individually the Valley, Southside, and Eastern Shore counties were relatively less politically influential than those of the Tidewater and Piedmont, but collectively their population constituted a hefty minority. As of June 1755, they included 27.5 percent of Virginia's white tithables and 11 percent of black tithables.[42] Detailed studies of the Tidewater region indicate that there, too, local conditions were less restrictive than those subsequently imposed on free blacks of the antebellum period.[43] If so, the wave of Revolutionary-era manumissions that transformed Virginia's free black population reflected longstanding local conditions as well as a more recent ideological commitment to liberty.

Seen in its colonial context, white toleration of frontier free blacks acquires a large interpretive significance. One distinctive aspect of free black acceptance was that it did not correlate to a particular level of white numerical superiority. Edward Tarr was not the exotic product of an overwhelmingly white county: people of color successfully protected their freedom in court even in counties where black tithables outnumbered white ones.[44] Tarr therefore represented an upper level of black achievement that could be found in other Virginia counties, and some characteristics of his career can be taken as typical for a small but influential population. Such individuals were rare in any county but present in many. Mobile white contemporaries thus may have perceived independent free blacks as possessing a distinctive collective identity that eluded subsequent social historians examining a single county's records. Free black contemporaries certainly demonstrated a collective identity by signing the levy relief petition that was presented to the House of Burgesses in 1769.

The successes of independent free blacks like Tarr derived from multiple sources. Like his antecedents, the people whom historian Ira Berlin called Atlantic creoles, Tarr and his fellow free black Virginians demonstrated a great deal of perception, ingenuity, and adaptability.[45] Beyond imagination and innovation, successful free blacks also acted in ways that elicited white approval. As one elderly white man recalled, "Few men possessed a more high sence of honor, and true bravery than" Tarr's frontier contemporary, William Carr.[46] Similarly, Joseph Bell and Nicholas Smith volunteered for militia service defending Augusta County at a time when most of their white peers had fled. Other successful free black strategies involved more peaceable values, as Edward Tarr demonstrated. He blended familiar socioeconomic elements (blacksmithing and land ownership) with familiar religious elements (doctrinal conformity as a Presbyterian and a keen interest in pietism). Properly calibrated, an amalgam of reassuringly familiar attributes could even sustain illegal behavior such as Tarr's interracial marriage.

When anomalous individuals like Tarr succeeded, as he did for years at Timber Ridge, they expanded the scope of viable interracial social relationships. By owning land, Tarr unintentionally validated landless free black hunters like Joseph Bell and William Carr. By laboring as an artisan long past middle age, Tarr embodied a skilled identity for free blacks. If Tarr had toiled in an isolated mountain hollow, his example would have passed unnoticed, but instead he lived on one of Virginia's busiest roads. His example derived its force from frontier mobility: he was readily observed, both in Timber Ridge and in the vicinity of Staunton, by travelers on the roads past his forge. High mobility added great momentum to Virginia's small mass of free black men.

People who met Tarr remembered him vividly. The Moravian diarist of 1753 wrote a longer description of him than any other person encountered on that five-hundred-mile journey. In 1804, four decades after leaving Timber Ridge, Tarr still stood out in local memories. Unfortunately, not all those memories were positive. His harboring of the contentious white woman Ann Moore first drew official attention in 1759 and remained sufficiently irritating to draw official condemnation as late as 1765. His robbery "by a woman who lived with him" in 1780 indicates that even as he approached the age of seventy, Tarr continued to harbor problematic women.[47] That he still did so perhaps made him even more memorable. Therein lies a profound historical implication.

Historians long have recognized that, although Anglo-American racism included a preoccupation with preventing interracial sex, social boundaries could be flexible in some circumstances.[48] Tarr's marriage to a white woman seemingly was acceptable because he also was a taxpayer, landowner, and pious church member. Historian Winthrop D. Jordan similarly describes a comparable 1731 case in which free men of color migrated from Virginia to South Carolina with their white wives and were accepted by that colony's governor after receiving a positive review of the newcomers from "a person who has lived in Virginia."[49] The fact that the marriages in question were not performed in the destination colonies removed a legal bar to their toleration, and the fact that the governor consulted a former Virginian emphasized the link between mobility and reputation in distant places.

Over time, miscegenation exceptions had the potential to reach locally significant totals. Additionally, mobility magnified the social effects of those exceptions by extending an awareness of tolerated miscegenation far beyond neighborhood boundaries. The stream of traffic along the road to Black Ned's forge potentially gave his bread-baking white wife an interregional significance.

Ultimately, however, neither Virginia nor the states to which Virginians often emigrated retained this higher degree of late colonial tolerance for free blacks. Nineteenth-century restraints increased in part because of a reenergized southern economic commitment to slave labor.[50] The profits of slavery explain only part of the tighter constraints on free blacks, however, because slavery and toleration had long coincided in the colonial era. Changes in American racism also eroded antebellum free black status. Unfortunately, some of these changes were rooted in the behavior of colonial-era free blacks, including Edward Tarr.

In the 1750s and 1760s, personal decisions by free men of color like Tarr and his Augusta County contemporary Nicholas Smith undermined the prospects for an enduring toleration of free blacks west of the Blue Ridge. On the one hand, both men demonstrated virtues prized by their neighbors. Yet both men violated cultural and legal strictures that their yeoman peers enforced against all encroachers, white and black. Smith repeatedly was denounced as an apathetic parent, as were numerous white men in Augusta County. Tarr sheltered an alleged white concubine, a second and subordinate white wife; bigamy too was prosecuted by county officials, regardless of race. Their shortcomings were unequal, however, because unlike Smith, Tarr was a landowning artisan. Contemporary whites likely conceived of Smith's lapses as typical for poor people of any race, but long after Tarr sold his land for a low price, he still possessed "a Considerable Sum of Money in paper and Specie."[51] By the standards of his day, Tarr's transgression was worse because his status was better. Smith's lapse merely added trivially to a pernicious stereotype of black irresponsibility, but Tarr and his affinity for a second white woman eroded the monumental example of his social and economic success.

Whites in the early national era redefined the nuances of free black social status. From a promising position on the eve of the American Revolution, that status slipped substantially. Many factors contributed to the decline, but it is important to recognize how the transition involved individual as well as collective decisions by blacks and whites alike. Any failure of a prominent free black role model was observed by a wide and influential audience, many hundreds of whom ultimately settled far from Augusta

County. If Tarr had remained an unmistakably monogamous husband, his achievements and perhaps even his marriage could have been remembered as glowingly as the heroic merits of bachelor William Carr. Thanks to endemic frontier mobility, however, the negative consequences of Tarr's decision to harbor Ann Moore may have rippled across the southern backcountry.

Appendix 1

Tables

TABLE 1 Thomas Shute's real estate transactions

Acres	Location	ACQUISITION		DISPENSATION	
		Date	*£ Penn.*	*Date*	*£ Penn.*
100	Bristol Township, Philadelphia County	8-25-1690	£25.5	12-20-1693	£60
200	Edgerly Point, Northern Liberties, Philadelphia County	3-1-1693/4	130		
	Payment to additional claimant	9-7-1707	0.25		
	Conveyance by executors			11-2-1754	
300	Plymouth Township, Philadelphia County	1-24-1701/2			
	Conveyed 200 acres			1-6-1703/4	70
	Conveyed 100 acres			8-4-1721	
Lot	Second Street and Jones Alley, Philadelphia†	1-16-1702/3	6.5		
	Sublet quarter of above†			4-1-1706	5
	Sublet quarter of above†			4-1710	1.5
	Extinguished sublets	4-1-1724	142.5		
	Mortgaged half to secure £200 loan			6-11-1741	
	Conveyed mortgaged portion and annual ground rent			10-11-1743	250
	Bequest of remainder, life estate to daughter Christian Davis			12-10-1748	
600	Moreland Manor, Philadelphia County (undivided half of 1,200–acre partnership)	4-20-1704	180		
	Payment to additional claimant	11-16-1709	22.5		
	Conveyed 200 acres to Christian and Sampson Davis			6-20-1721	5
	Repurchased same 200 acres	3-22-1731/2	400		
	Conveyed 150 acres			8-17-1736	205
1,000	On line of Bucks and Philadelphia County (undivided fifth of 5,000 acres)	9-10-1707	20		
	Patent of same as 309- and 821-acre tracts	11-9-1711			
130	Additional acres included in above patent		12		
	Conveyed 149.5 acres			11-1-1720	250.5
	Payment to additional claimant	5-16-1727	0.25		
	Conveyed 147 acres			11-23-1728	52.5
	Conveyed another 147 acres			12-3-1728	52.5
120	Northern Liberties, Philadelphia Co.				

Table I (continued)

Acres	Location	ACQUISITION		DISPENSATION	
		Date	£ Penn.	Date	£ Penn.
	Surveyed from 14 warrants	5-1718			
	Patent	7-10-1718			
	Conveyance to eldest son William Shute			6-10-1739	0.25
500	Philadelphia Co. (undivided half of 1,000-acre partnership)	12-18-1718			
	Requested survey	12-31-1718			
	Survey	4-26-1720			
	Conveyed 75 acres (150 acres total for partners)			5-18-1720	45
	Conveyed 75 acres (150 acres total for partners)			5-18-1720	45
Lot	Sixth, Mulberry, Seventh, and Sassafras Streets, Philadelphia				
	21-year lease†	3-1-1719/20	1		
Lot	Chestnut St., Philadelphia†	3-25-1720	5		
	Extinguished rent after this date	8-8-1720			
	Conveyance			11-24-1733	110
8	Northern Liberties, Philadelphia County	10-4-1723	8	9-22-1726	10
Lot	Ninth, Pine, and Tenth Streets, Philadelphia	2-21-1723/4	32.5	9-16-1726	40
400	Warminster Township, Bucks County				
	Warrant to survey	3-25-1724			
	Survey returned	4-30-1724			
200	Philadelphia County				
	Survey	8-4-1724			
500	Manatawney Creek, Philadelphia County				
	Warrant to survey	3-24-1724/5	65		
	Surveyed 300 acres	12-2-1725			
	Conveyed above 300 acres			12-21-1725	100
216	Warminster Township, Bucks County				
	Warrant to survey	5-17-1725			
	Survey	6-1725			
40.6	Northern Liberties, Philadelphia County (in 2 tracts: 24 acres and 16.56 acres)				
	Survey (includes 5 separate rights)	3-5-1733/4			

TABLE I   (continued)

Acres	Location	ACQUISITION		DISPENSATION	
		Date	£ Penn.	Date	£ Penn.
	Patent	12-2-1742			
	Conveyed 21.03 acres			8-20-1743	83
	Conveyed 19.53 acres and 4 acres "lately purchased"			8-21-1743	90.55
18.5	Bristol Township, Northern Liberties, Philadelphia County (in 2 tracts: 6.3 acres and 12.23 acres)				
	Survey (6.3 acres only)	4-4-1734			
	Acquisition confirmed (both lots)	3-19-1736/7			
	Conveyance (both lots)			3-24-1736/7	50
Lot	Second Street, Philadelphia				
	Annual rent	11-7-1735	6.55		
	Conveyance			2-1-1737	60
100	Pequea Creek, Lancaster County, undivided seventh share	8-14-1736	2.7		
	Conveyance			6-17-1738	
	Reconveyed by heirs			4-6 and 5-10-1755	
200	Salford Township, Philadelphia County				
	Warrant	6-10-1733			
	Survey	5-15-1735			
	Patent	5-17-1737	31		
	Conveyance			5-18-1737	60

† Annual rent (silver).

Note: Thomas Shute dealt actively in real estate until late in life. Thanks to the rising Pennsylvania land market, his investments guaranteed the economic security of his declining years. Original source documents for some of the transactions shown here have disappeared, but subsequent transactions provide partial details. For simplicity of tabulation, conveyances by deeds of lease and release transacted on consecutive days are shown here with only the release date.

Sources: Bucks County DB, 22:511–514, 23:175; Philadelphia County Exemplification Books, 5:191, 7:441–444, 8:87–90; Lancaster County DB, 2:652–656; Philadelphia County DB, D7:450; E3–6:188, 208, 225; E4:247; F2:194, 414–415; F3:514; F7:255, 264–267, 300, 304, 306; F9:112, 114; F10:82; G1:297; G9:344; G11:61; H1:280; H3:288–290; H4:349–351; H10:388–393, 399–402; H14:305; H19:507, 512; H20:198; I2:121; EF10:9; EF15:40; Patent Book, A5:354, A6:57, A8:396, A11:139; Patent Register, 1701–1728, 40; Patent Register, 1732–1741, 24, 39; Survey Book, B23:204; D88:163, 188; D89:54; Original Purchases Register, 1682–1762, 127, all PHMC. Thanks to Camille Wells for research assistance in compiling Thomas Shute's real estate records at PHMC.

TABLE 2   Lancaster County, Pennsylvania, origins of early Augusta County, Virginia, magistrates, 1739–1745

		Public service in Lancaster County, 1729–1742	Freehold acres in Lancaster County by 1745	Freehold acres in Augusta County in year appointed as magistrate
Magistrates in the Augusta district of Orange County (with date of commission)	John Lewis (1 November 1739)			2,071
	Samuel Givens (1 November 1739)	Member of grand inquest, 1734/5	0	311
	John McDowell (1 November 1739)	Petit juror, 1735–36	0	0
	Richard Woods (1 November 1739)	Member of grand inquest, 1733	0	0
	James Patton (3 November 1741)			474
	John Buchanan (3 November 1741)			784
	George Robinson (6 May 1743)			892
	Peter Shull (6 May 1743)			0
Magistrates in Augusta County's initial commission of the peace (rank order per 30 October 1745 commission)	James Patton			2,773
	John Lewis			1,866
	John Buchanan			927
	George Robinson			1,083
	Peter Shull			0
	James Bell			800
	Robert Campbell	Gave evidence, 1732	0	350
	John Brown			380
	Robert Poage	Member of grand inquest, 1734; petit juror, 1736	0	0
	John Pickens	Member of grand inquest, 1734	0	764
	Thomas Lewis			740
	Hugh Thompson	Member of grand inquest, 1732	0	400
	Robert Cunningham			482
	John Finlay	Gave evidence, 1738	0	483
	Richard Woods	Member of grand inquest, 1733	0	570
	John Christian			538
	Robert Craven			800
	James Kerr	Member of grand inquest, 1737–40	0	473
	Adam Dickenson	Gave evidence, 1738	0	0

TABLE 2 (continued)

	Public service in Lancaster County, 1729–1742	Freehold acres in Lancaster County by 1745	Freehold acres in Augusta County in year appointed as magistrate
Andrew Pickens	Gave evidence, 1737; road viewer 1740	0	400
John Anderson	Road viewer 1734; member of grand inquest, 1740	0	1,017

Note: Many of Augusta County's initial magistrates spent several years in Lancaster County, Pennsylvania, before deciding that Virginia offered better opportunities for leadership as well as landholding. Moving to Virginia's settlement frontier was especially advantageous for men who became junior magistrates. From 1739 to 1745, the district that became Augusta County was governed by magistrates included in the Orange County commission of the peace.

Sources: Orange County OB, 2:106; 3:51, 461, LOV; Augusta OB, 1:1; *EJC,* 5:191; Hening, ed., *Statutes,* 5:78–80; Hawbaker, ed., *Lancaster County, Pennsylvania, Quarter Sessions Abstracts;* Mayhill, comp., *Lancaster County, Pennsylvania Deed Abstracts.* For Augusta landholding, see McCleskey, "Rich Land, Poor Prospects," 449n2.

TABLE 3 Imports to Charleston from Philadelphia in Shute-owned vessels, 1732–1738

Voyage No.	Vessel Year (quarter)	Flour Shute barrels	% of total	% from Penn.	Bread Shute barrels	% of total	% from Penn.	Corn Shute barrels	% of total	% from Penn.
	Dove									
1	1732 (2)	97	18.0	20.0	32	25.5	40.0	0		
2	(3)	94	6.7	45.2	14	3.2	6.7	50	100.0	100.0
3	(4)	86	15.8	15.8	48	37.8	38.7	0		
	Dolphin									
4	1734 (2)	308	31.2	34.1	125	27.2	33.3	48	20.3	75.0
5	(3)	176	8.5	10.2	173	24.5	25.4	186	22.2	56.6
6	(4)	361	18.5	23.5	108	10.5	14.2	0		
7	1735 (2)	144	13.5	27.0	100	21.6	34.4	275	31.4	31.4
8	1736 (1)	338	21.6	27.7	116	14.1	18.7	0		
	Endeavour									
9	1736 (3)	509	35.3	53.8	200	45.2	76.1	0		
	Carolina Paquet									
10	1737 (2)	63	7.4	16.6	45	24.6	59.4	80	5.9	11.3
11	(3)	40	4.3	5.7	91	15.0	20.2	18	1.3	6.3
	Anna									
12	1738 (3)	242	14.1	23.7	322	46.1	61.3	0		
13	(4)	100	6.6	9.5	94	12.0	17.9	0		

Additional cargo per voyage (by number):
1. 6 boxes soap
2. 12 boxes soap
3. 14 boxes soap, 18 firkins butter, 2 casks earthenware, 5 bushels apples
4. 6 barrels beer, 10 boxes soap, 24 iron bars
5. 6 barrels beer, 16 boxes soap, 19 iron bars, 500 staves
6. 19 barrels beer, 47 firkins butter
7. 1,000 staves
8. 28 barrels beer, 2 barrels apples, 45 firkins butter
9. 5 barrels bacon, 21 firkins butter, 20 boxes soap, 57 barrels beer
10. 4 barrels bacon, 34 barrels beer, 96 iron bars, 5 boxes soap
11. 3 tons brazilwood, 26 barrels beer, 3 barrels pork, 3 chests clothing
12. 2⅔ barrels oats, 3 hogsheads buckwheat, 41 barrels ham, 18 barrels beer, 17 kegs butter
13. 3 barrels oil, 10 barrels apples, 32 kegs butter, 1 butt beer

Note: Detailed shipping records survive for thirteen known voyages from Philadelphia to Charleston by Shute-owned vessels. The records are organized by traditional English quarters ending on 25 March (1), 24 June (2), 29 September (3), and 25 December (4).

Source: Vessels Entered In, SC Shipping Returns, CO 5/509, 5/510, BNA.

Table 4   Exports from Charleston to Philadelphia in Shute-owned vessels, 1732–1738

Voyage No.	Vessel Year (quarter)	RICE			PITCH			TAR		
		Shute barrels	% of total	% to Penn.	Shute barrels	% of total	% to Penn.	Shute barrels	% of total	% to Penn.
	DOVE									
1	1732 (3)	8	0.3	6.0	12	0.3	6.0	0		
2	(3)	5	0.2	3.8	42	1.1	22.1	58	10.8%	46.0%
	DOLPHIN									
3	1734 (2)	20	0.2	29.0	250	2.4	55.9	47	1.5	88.7
4	1735 (2)	30	0.5	75.0	0			0		
5	(3)	7	0.3	100.0	0			0		
6	1736 (1)	52	0.3	54.7	0			0		
	CAROLINA PAQUET									
7	1737 (1)	9	0.1	50.0	124	3.9	62.0	50	3.7	100.0
	ANNA									
8	1738 (3)	0			0			0		
9	(4)	22	0.9	100.0	136	69.7	100.0	0		

Voyage No.	Vessel Year (quarter)	TURPENTINE		
		Shute barrels	% of total	% to Penn.
	DOVE			
1	1732 (3)	80	36.4	36.4
2	(3)	10	4.5	4.5
	DOLPHIN			
3	1734 (2)	34	4.0	13.5
4	1735 (2)	0		
5	(3)	200	7.5	78.7
6	1736 (1)	217	32.2	95.6
	CAROLINA PAQUET			
7	1737 (1)	0		
	ANNA			
8	1738 (3)	37	21.4	21.4
9	(4)	0	0	0

Additional cargo per voyage (by number):
1. 130 deerskins, 131 tanned hides
2. 2 barrels pimentos, 3,000 pounds tanned leather
3. Parcel of skins, 250 tanned hides, 203 grindstones
4. None
5. Osnaburg (coarse, inexpensive cloth), 1 keg china, 4 kegs old iron and copper
6. 125 tanned hides, 3 barrels potatoes, European sundries
7. European goods
8. 12 slaves, 1 barrel cocoa, 60 sides sole leather, sundry dry goods
9. 195 barrels potatoes, 28 barrels gunpowder, 2 bales osnaburg

Note: No shipping returns survive for Philadelphia during the Shute period, but detailed shipping records do survive for nine voyages from Charleston to Philadelphia by Shute-owned vessels. The records are organized by traditional quarters ending on 25 March (1), 24 June (2), 29 September (3), and 25 December (4). South Carolina's shipping records for the period 29 September 1739 to 15 November 1752 do not survive, but shipping notices in the *South Carolina Gazette* and *Pennsylvania Gazette* identify three other Charleston-to-Philadelphia voyages by Shute vessels during that period.

Source: Vessels Entered Out, SC Shipping Returns, CO 5/509, 5/510, BNA.

TABLE 5 Cargoes delivered by Shute-owned vessels to New Providence, Bahamas, 1732–1741

Voyage No.	Vessel Year (quarter)	Beef or pork Shute barrels	% of Bahamas volume from South Carolina	Flour Shute barrels	% of Bahamas volume from South Carolina	Corn Shute barrels	% of Bahamas volume from South Carolina
	DOVE						
1	1732 (4)	2	3.9	29	11.3	2	1.5
	RELIEF						
2	1734 (1)	0		0		13	16.7
3	(1)	0		0		0	
4	(2)	5	29.4	0		0	
5	(2)	4	23.5	0		0	
	CAROLINA PAQUET						
6	1737 (2)	2	1.4	10	7.8	0	
7	1738 (1)	42	23.9	8	21.6	0	
	TWO SISTERS						
8	1740 (4)	0		0		0	
9	1741 (1)	0		4	80.0	0	
	MARY						
10	1741 (4)	0		0		0	

Additional cargo per voyage (by number):
1. 8 firkins butter, 10 boxes soap
2. 12 barrels madeira, 2 boxes pipes, 1 barrel turnips
3. In ballast
4. 2 casks bread, 6 crates earthenware, 6 chairs, European goods worth £15
5. None
6. 2 barrels beer, 20 dozen bottles port wine, 2 dozen British hats, 1 case "Stationary Ware," 1 piece osnaburg, 10 pieces checked linen, sundry haberdashery, 1 piece paduasoy (a silk fabric), 1 piece taffeta
7. 4 barrels rum, 1,200 feet boards, 3,000 shingles, 5 barrels bread, 25 pairs shoes, 1 barrel and 1 bag nails, 1 set Chinaware, 12 pounds tea, 17 hatchets, 1 piece diaper, 3 pieces Russian linen, 4 pieces osnaburg, 2 pieces checked linen
8. 6 slaves
9. None
10. In ballast from Antigua

Note: Joseph Shute's vessels carried modest amounts of provisions and a variety of general cargo on their outbound voyages to the Bahamas. Detailed shipping records survive for ten known voyages by Shute vessels to New Providence, Bahamas; all except the *Mary* (1741) entered from Charleston. The records are organized by traditional quarters ending on 25 March (1), 24 June (2), 29 September (3), and 25 December (4). South Carolina's shipping records for the period 29 September 1739 to 15 November 1752 do not survive; Bahamas records for the Shute era have numerous gaps.

Sources: South Carolina Gazette; Vessels Entered Out, SC Shipping Returns, CO 5/509, 5/510, BNA; Vessels Entered In, Bahamas Shipping Returns, CO 27/12, BNA.

Table 6 Exports from New Providence, Bahamas, in Shute-owned vessels, 1734–1747

Voyage No.	Vessel Year (quarter)	Braziletto (for dye) Shute tons	Bahamas Volume % of total	% to South Carolina	Lignum Vitae (for joinery) Shute tons	Bahamas Volume % of total	% to South Carolina	Madera (for joinery) Shute board feet	Bahamas Volume % of total	% to South Carolina
	RELIEF									
1	1734 (1)	4.0	5.4	11.8	4.0	40.0	40.0	400	2.4	100.0
2	(2)	6.0	7.7	12.8	0			0		
	POMPEY									
3	1735 (4)	25.25	38.5	38.5	0			1,200	77.7	77.7
	CAROLINA PAQUET									
4	1737 (3)	2.5	2.0	2.8	10.0	41.7	100.0	660	2.4	4.6
5	1738 (1)	20.1	15.5	17.7	0			302	2.4	2.6
	TWO SISTERS									
6	1740 (4)	16.0	9.0	9.8	4.0	26.7	100.0	3,200	30.7	35.6
7	1741 (1)	21.0	11.8	11.8	0			0		
	MARY									
8	1741 (4)	26.0	15.8	17.0	0			2,350	6.1	29.9
	VICTORY									
9	1747 (3)	0			0			0		

Additional cargo per voyage (by number):

1. 100 pounds cotton wool, beer, fruit, yams
2. 495 pounds cotton wool, fruit, pineapples
3. 400 pounds sweet wood bark, fruit
4. 12 dozen bottles port wine
5. 1,000 oranges, 50 turtles, 1 ton turners wood, 4 baskets bark
6. 300 pounds logwood (dye wood), 1 ton cortex eleuthera (medicinal wood), 41 pounds cotton roping, 3 barrels lime juice, 20,000 limes and oranges
7. 300 pounds cortex eleuthera, 50,000 oranges
8. 22,000 limes
9. Limes, muscovado sugar

Note: Detailed shipping records survive for nine known voyages by Shute vessels from New Providence, Bahamas. The *Carolina Paquet* sailed directly to Philadelphia in 1737; all others returned to Charleston. The records are organized by traditional quarters ending on 25 March (1), 24 June (2), 29 September (3), and 25 December (4). South Carolina's shipping records for the period 29 September 1739 to 15 November 1752 do not survive; Bahamas records for the Shute era have numerous gaps.

Sources: Vessels Entered Out, SC Shipping Returns, CO 5/509, 510, BNA; Vessels Entered In, Bahamas Shipping Returns, CO 27/12, BNA; *South Carolina Gazette.*

TABLE 7   Imports and exports by Shute-owned vessels at George Town/Winyah, 1734–1737

IMPORTS TO GEORGE TOWN/WINYAH

Voyage No.	VESSEL Year (Quarter)	FLOUR		BREAD		CORN	
		Shute barrels	% of imports to George Town	Shute barrels	% of imports to George Town	Shute barrels	% of imports to George Town
I	DOLPHIN 1734 (3)	35	100.0	2	100.0	54	100.0

EXPORTS FROM GEORGE TOWN/WINYAH

Voyage No.	VESSEL Year (Quarter)	PITCH		TAR		TURPENTINE	
		Shute barrels	% of exports from George Town	Shute barrels	% of exports from George Town	Shute barrels	% of exports from George Town
2	DOLPHIN 1734 (3)	22	2.1	0		315	26.5
3	ENDEAVOUR 1737 (3)	205	100.0	613	100.0	0	

Additional cargo per voyage (by number):
   1. 1 barrel pork, 4 hogsheads rum, 1 pipe madeira, 4 barrels brown sugar, 1 hogshead loaf sugar, 1 hogshead molasses
   2. None
   3. 23 bags ginger

Note: Joseph Shute invested substantially in a George Town store in 1735, but so few shipping returns survive for George Town that his operations there can be glimpsed only infrequently. In the eleven quarters with extant records between 24 June 1733 and 25 December 1737, two Shute-owned vessels are recorded as calling at George Town.

Source: SC Shipping Returns, CO 5/509, 510, BNA.

TABLE 8 Joseph Shute's merchant vessels

Vessel name (Joseph Shute's share)	Type/number of crew	Tonnage	Built where and when	Registered where and when	Disposition	Partners (if any)
Dove (whole)	sloop/6	10	Plantation* 1724	Philadelphia 5-22-1732	No record	
Relief (half)	sloop/3	5	New Providence 1728	Charleston 10-1-1733	Sold 1734	Clement Hudson
Dolphin (half)	sloop/4	20	Plantation 1734	Philadelphia 4-22-1734	Lost 1736	Thomas Shute
Pompey (whole)	sloop/6	25	Rhode Island 1735	New Providence 8-5-1735	Sold 1736	
Endeavour (quarter)	snow/9	50	Philadelphia, 1736	Philadelphia 7-4-1736	No record	Anthony Morris, Joseph Wragg†
Carolina Packet (half)	sloop/5	15	Pennsylvania 1735	Charlestown 2-2-1736/7	Sold 1738	Thomas Burges
Anna (whole)	brigantine/4	50	Charlestown 1738	Charlestown 6-28-1738, Jamaica 1741	re-registered 1741, lost/captured 1742	
Two Sisters (whole‡)	schooner/4	20	South Carolina 1740	Charlestown 8-12-1740	No record	
Mary (third)	sloop/4	25	Connecticut 1740	New Providence 6-16-1741	Sold 1741/2	William and Thomas Randall
Industry (half)	schooner	10	South Carolina 1744	Charlestown 7-17-1745	Captured 1745	Thomas Lyol Brumley
Victory (half)	sloop	25	Rhode Island 1744	Charlestown 7-1-1746	Captured 1748	John McKenzie
Dolphin (half)	sloop	40	New York 1744	Charlestown 10-16-1747	Sold 1748	Amos Messervey

* The notation "plantation" in contemporary customs records indicates a vessel built in an unspecified British colonial location.

† As of 16 July 1737, Shute and Joseph Wragg alone were listed as partners.

‡ Initially registered in partnership with Jonathan Scott and William Hare, who together owned one moiety, the *Two Sisters* was re-registered as Joseph Shute's alone before completing its first voyage.

Sources: SC Shipping Returns, CO 5/509, 510, BNA; Bahamas Shipping Returns, CO 27/12, BNA; Kingston, Jamaica, Shipping Returns, CO 142/15, BNA; "Ship Registers for the Port of Philadelphia," 381; South Carolina Secretary of State, Ship Registers, 1734–1783, 13–4, 21, 285, 294, 329, SCDAH.

TABLE 9 Joseph Shute's South Carolina real estate transactions

Acres	Location	ACQUISITION		DISPENSATION	
		Date	£ S.C.	Date	£ S.C.
6	St. Philips Parish near Charleston	11-19-1731	0.5	5-16-1737	£3,000
1,050	Craven County, George Town Creek				
	Surveyed	6-29-1734			
	Granted	5-21-1735			
	Conveyed			5-14-1742	£700
430	Craven County, south side Little River, and 2 George Town lots				
	Mortgaged to Shute to secure £3,000 loan	7-26-1735			
	Conveyed to Shute (late conveyance)	7-7-1739	£900		
	Conveyed by Shute			3-2-1738/9	£4,000
	Conveyance confirmed by Shute			12-29-1759	£250
500	Craven County, east side Waccamaw River				
	Surveyed	12-23-1735			
	Granted	4-22-1736			
Lot No. 9	Charleston, on the bay				
	Bequest to Anna Shute	11-10-1740			
	Conveyed part			9-10-1748	£100
	Conveyed remainder			6-28-1750	
Lot No. 10	Charleston, Callibeuf Lane (now Elliott Street)				
	Bequest to Anna Shute	11-10-1740			
	Conveyed			6-3-1741	£4,000
100	Berkeley County, northeast side Ashley River	ca. 1745		5-13-1747	£500
224	Berkeley County, Cooper River island	5-8-1746	£300		
	Conveyed undivided half			5-9-1747	£150
	Conveyed other half			6-28-1750	
lot	Charleston, low-water lot fronting Lot No. 9				
	Grant	1-22-1746/7		6-28-1750	
lot	Charleston, Elliott Street	5-4-1748	£1,700	6-7-1748	5s
170	Colleton County, west side Ashepoo River				
	Grant	5-24-1752		11-12-1759	£600

Note: Like his father, Joseph Shute invested in rural real estate at a time of rapid colonial growth. His marriage to Anna Gull Arnott brought him a set of especially valuable Charleston properties, including the six acres purchased in partnership with her stepfather in 1731 and two Charleston waterfront lots.

Sources: Conveyance Books, I:535; P:49–51; R:189–193; S:388–390; V:87–90, 364–366; X:5–19; CC:427–429; DD:275–287; EE:160–161; WW:35–40, 238–240, SCDAH; South Carolina Plat Book, 3:62, 83, SCDAH; South Carolina Royal Grants Class 1, 1:448, 2:302, 4:601, 43:307, SCDAH; *South Carolina Gazette,* 11 June 1750, 3.

TABLE 10   Joseph Shute, plaintiff, South Carolina Court of Common Pleas, 1735–1760

Date initiated*	Original debt (£ S.C.)	Litigants	Judgment (if known)	CCP cite (Box, item #)
3-3-1734/5	57:7:6	Shute v. John Show		22a, #59A
11-9-1736	100:0:0	Thomas Henning and Shute v. John August, planter	For plaintiff	22B, #20A
2-8-1736/7	30:0:0	Shute v. John August, planter		22B, #17A
2-8-1736/7	40:0:0†	Thomas Henning and Shute v. Thomas Barton, planter		22B, #24A
5-13-1738	41:14:0	Shute, John Abbot, and Stephen Beauchamp v. William Snow		23B, #45A
5-13-1738	49:3:1	Shute, Henning, and Beauchamp v. James Stewart, planter	For plaintiff	23B, #47A
[1743]	403:0:0	Shute v. John Dexter, saddler, Winyaw	For plaintiff	33A, #110A
7-3-1744	52:2:6	Shute v. Francis Turner, Winyaw	For plaintiff	26B, #13A
4-2-1745	81:0:0	Shute, admin. of Thos. Henning, dec'd., v. Justinius Stoll, blacksmith		29A, #23A
8-1746	117:0:0	Shute v. John Fawkner, surgeon		30A, #58A
[1747]	unknown	Shute v. John Jelsey, [shipwright]	For plaintiff	none
10-2-1750	88:8:9	Shute v. Stephen Dubose, vintner/tavernkeeper	For plaintiff	47B, #37A
1-4-1752	152:16:0	Shute, admin. of Thos. Henning, dec'd., v. John Dexter		33A, #111A
11-11-1752	439:17:3	Shute v. John Dexter		33A, #110A
7-7-1752	170:2:3	Shute v. executor of Robert Brown, planter alias doctor, dec'd.		34B, #12A
1-2-1753	733:14:0	Shute, admin. of Thos. Henning, dec'd., v. John Conner, tavern-keeper		34B, #59A
1-2-1753	607:10:0	Shute v. Edward Wilkinson and Thomas Rose, cooper	For plaintiff	35A, #130A
10-2-1753	280:5:6	Shute v. John Garot, carpenter	For plaintiff	40A, #78A
5-7-1756	8,429:1:0	Shute v. executor of John Seabrook, dec'd.		43A, #205A
10-7-1760	220:16:3	Shute v. executor of William Lewis, planter, dec'd.		53A, #155A

* Date of first writ if available; otherwise, earliest dated action by the court or its officers.
† Debt not recorded; this amount is half of damages claimed, per English common-law practice for penal bills.

Sources: Judgment Rolls (CCP), 1703–1790, SCDAH; South Carolina Gazette, 11 Jan. 1747/8.

TABLE II   Joseph Shute's importation irregularities, 1735–1748

Shute vessel and master	Date entered Charleston	Administrative discrepancies at Charleston (values in £ S.C.)
Pompey Ebenezer Wyatt	12-16-1735	Per shipping return, entered Charleston with 23 tons braziletto, 1,200 feet madera plank, 400 lbs. sweet wood bark, fruit. *Paid no duties.*
Carolina Paquet James Cowie	4-13-1738	Per shipping return, entered Charleston with 20.1 tons logwood, 1 ton turner's wood, 302 feet madera plank, 1,000 oranges, 50 turtles, 4 baskets bark. *Operating with two sets of registration papers. Paid no duties*
Two Sisters Henry Tisdale	1-1-1740/1	Per shipping return, cleared New Providence for Charleston with 16 tons braziletto, 3 hundredweight logwood, 17 hundredweight lignum vitae, 2,000 lbs. cortex eleuthera, 3,200 feet madera plank, 3 barrels lime juice, cotton roping, 20,000 limes. Per *South Carolina Gazette,* this date, entered Charleston from New Providence in the past week. Only one importer, Jonathan Scott, paid duties of £2:18:0, which would not have covered the lime juice alone.
Two Sisters James Barrett	3-1-1740/1	Per shipping return, cleared New Providence with 21 tons braziletto, 3 hundredweight cortex eleuthera, 50,000 oranges. *Paid no duties.*
Mary David Marshall	6-25-1741	Per *South Carolina Gazette,* this date, recently entered Charleston from New Providence. *Paid no duties.*
	12-21-1741	Per shipping return, cleared New Providence with 26 tons braziletto, 2,350 feet madera plank, 22,000 limes. *Part-owner William Randall paid £4:17:6, the sole duties collected.*
Victory Peter Bostock	5-4-1747	Per *South Carolina Gazette,* this date, recently entered Charleston from New Providence. *Paid no duties.*
[foreign]	6-1-1748	Comptroller of duties Robert Austin seized Joseph Shute's boat and 32 barrels illegal molasses.

Note: On seven occasions, vessels owned partly or wholly by Shute brought cargoes to Charleston without paying duties on the full cargo, and in an eighth incident, a foreign hull did so.

Sources: For vessel cargoes cleared out and entered in, see SC Shipping Returns, CO 5/509, 510, and Bahamas Shipping Returns, CO 27/12, both BNA. For additional vessel arrivals, see *South Carolina Gazette.* For vessel owners and registries, see South Carolina Secretary of State, Ship Registers, 1734–1783, SCDAH. For duties paid, see Journal A, 1735–1748, Journal B, 1748–1765, Records of the Public Treasurer of South Carolina, 1725–1776, SCDAH. For Shute's illicit molasses, see Easterby and Green, eds., *Journal of the Commons House of Assembly, 1748,* 323–24.

TABLE 12   Joseph Shute, defendant, South Carolina Court of Common Pleas, 1738–1760

Date initiated*	Original debt (£ S.C.)	Plaintiffs against Shute	Judgment (if known)	CCP cite (Box, item #)
3-1-1737/8	483:10:0	William Laserre, merchant	For plaintiff	23B, #53A
3-1-1737/8	525:0:0	William Laserre, merchant		23B, #56A
2-13-1738/9	201:4:5	John Johnston, merchant		23B, #46A
10-4-1743	872:0:0	Peter Bard, assignee of provost marshal		26B, #7A
2-25-1743/4	1,290:13:4	James Crockatt, merchant		26B, #5A
5-19-1744	79:18:0	John Colcock and William Cattell, Jr., merchants		27A, #87A
7-3-1744	822:0:0	Benjamin Dedcock, assignee of provost marshal		27A, #100A
6-1-1745	169:5:0	Thomas Smith and Edmond Cossens, merchants		29A, #14A
8-13-1745	362:11:0	John Crokatt and Kenneth Michie, merchants		29A, #4A
1748	Unknown	William Bissett, tailor, et ux.		
1748	Unknown	John Wilson		
1748	Unknown	William Miles		
1748	Unknown	Benjamin Mazyck		
1748	Unknown	Thomas Lamboll and Isaac Bradwell, assignees of provost marshal		
1748	Unknown	William Donnem		
1748	Unknown	Nickleson and Shubrick, merchants		
1748	Unknown	Elias Ball		
1-1-1750/1	174:5:2	Morton Brailsford and Samuel Brailsford		32A, #62A
4-7-1752	49:7:6	Alexander McCauley, wigmaker,		32B, #18A
7-7-1752	46:14:0	Jonathan Scott, merchant	For plaintiff	36A, #150A
7-1-1760	250:0:0	Thomas Wright, esq.		51A, #212A

* Date of writ if available; otherwise, earliest dated action by the court or its officers.

Sources: Judgment Rolls (CCP), 1703–1790, SCDAH. For 1748 cases, see South Carolina Gazette, 24 July 1749, 3.

TABLE 13   Joseph Shute and slavery, 1735–1752

Source date	Number of slaves	Action
4-26-1735	4	Shute imported to Charleston from Antigua via *Charming Betty*, Thomas Crosthwaite, master. Duty was rebated, indicating Shute declared the imported slaves were for his personal use.
[1735–1736]	1	Shute imported to Charleston from Oporto, Spain, via John Ball's vessel. Duty was rebated, indicating Shute declared the imported slave was for his personal use.
7-7-1738	12	Shute exported from Charleston to Philadelphia via *Anna* (a Shute-owned vessel), Henry Tisdale, master.
11-22-1740	6	Shute exported from Charleston to New Providence via *Two Sisters* (a Shute-owned vessel), Henry Tisdale, master.
2-14-1742/3	1	Runaway advertisement in *South Carolina Gazette* for Tom, "who formerly had belonged to Mr. Shute."
6-25-1746	1	Boy Carolina, belonging to Joseph Shute, bound by Thomas Shute as apprentice to a Philadelphia cooper.
3-27-1747	15	Shute sold to Charleston merchant Mathew Roche. Thirteen slaves were identified individually: Peter, Rose, Carolina and her child, Sambo, Rhina, Cudjoe, Lancashire, Bess, Hannah, Cesar, and an old man and his wife. The price of £2,500 (South Carolina) included sundry livestock.
7-8-1747	3	Shute sold "fellow" Cupid, "wench" Pheaba, and one other slave to Georgetown resident Edmund Robinson. The price of £500 (South Carolina) included one horse.
6-15-1748	2	Shute sold "Mustee wench named Tulop and her child Mannewell" to George Snow for £350 (South Carolina).
6-11-1750	several	Joseph Shute offered "Several valuable negroes" for sale.
4-14-1752	1	Shute and a partner sold man Shadwell to shipwright David Linn for £300.

Sources: "Cash Dr to Accō Duty on Negroes Imported," 25 Sept. 1745–25 March 1746, Journal A, 1735–1748, Records of the Public Treasurer of South Carolina, 1725–1776, SCDAH; "List of Vessels Clearing Out," 25 June–25 Sept. 1738, SC Shipping Returns, CO 5/510, BNA; *Pennsylvania Gazette*, 27 July 1738; Bahamas Shipping Returns, 29 Sept.–25 Dec. 1740, CO 27/12, BNA; *South Carolina Gazette*, 14 Feb. 1742/3, 4; "Account of Servants," entry dated 25 June 1746, 32:88; Joseph Shute bill of sale, 25 March 1747, South Carolina Miscellaneous Records (hereafter SCMR), GG:142, SCDAH; Joseph Shute bill of sale, 8 July 1747, SCMR, GG:177, SCDAH; Joseph Shute bill of sale, 15 June 1748, SCMR, HH:191, SCDAH; *South Carolina Gazette*, 11 June 1750, 3; Joseph Shute and John McKenzie bill of sale, 14 April 1752, SCMR, II:171–172, SCDAH.

TABLE 14 Leather and fur exports from Augusta County

Type of skin	Quantity, 1745	Quantity, 1762
Bear	4	0
Beaver (in pounds)	79	0
Deer (total)	570	184
Dressed	60	52
Undressed	478	132
Undifferentiated	32	0
Fox and wildcat	77	245
Fox	76	0
Wildcat	1	0
Mink	0	11
Otter	13	0
Raccoon	100	288

Note: James Patton was sworn in as Augusta County's first collector of duties on fur and skin on 23 February 1744 and held the office until his death at the hands of Indians in 1755. The above entries reflect Patton's collection of duties for leather and fur exported by five men in 1745: William Bunting, Patrick Crawford, James Gallt (of Pennsylvania), Henry Martin, and Thomas Tosh (of Augusta County). Patton's nephew William Preston recorded fees paid by five men for leather and fur between 22 March and 13 September 1762. The men—James Crawford, Bryan McDonald, Ben Polson, John Walker, and John Shields—were complying with Virginia's recently revised duties on fur and leather exported from the colony. Paying the duties does not necessarily indicate these men were hunters.

Both years likely are incomplete tallies of duties collected, much less the real number of animals skinned. Even so, the two sets of figures reveal something of Augusta County's ecological evolution. Bears were vulnerable to hunting with dogs and, as of 1762, may have been locally extinct except in rough terrain. Beavers and otters were easily trapped along the county's many waterways; they too may have been hunted out by 1762. The 1762 minks probably were taken in more inaccessible upland habitats where fewer hunters had ventured in 1745. Omnivorous foxes and raccoons thrived in the ecological changes accompanying Augusta County–style agriculture, especially the proliferation of orchards, and so were taken in increasingly large numbers.

Sources: Orange County OB, 4:49, LOV; "A Register Book of the De[u]ty of Skins for Augusta Countey," Preston Family Papers, 1727–1896, VHS; William Preston Memorandum Book, William and John Preston Papers, Perkins Library. For a 1 June 1747 memorandum of duties paid but not noted by Patton, see James Chamberlain's promissory note to John Buchanan, ibid. For ecological changes due to commercial hunting by Europeans, see Silver, *A New Face on the Countryside*, 90–101.

Offender and offense Adjudication date and judgment		Order book vol.:page
INITIAL GRAND JURY, 11-20-1746		
James Burk, swearing 2-19-1746/7	Dismissed	1:134, 156
John Hayes, swearing 2-19-1746/7	Fined 5s for swearing 1 oath	1:134, 158
David Bryan, vagrancy and woods burning 2-19-1746/7	Fined £6 for killing 6 deer out of season	1:134, 156
Israel Robinson, vagrancy and woods burning 2-19-1746/7	Fined £5 for killing 5 deer out of season	1:134, 157
James Bullock, vagrancy and woods burning 2-19-1746/7	Fined £5 for killing 5 deer out of season	1:134, 157
James Huston, vagrancy and woods burning 2-19-1746/7	Fined £5 for killing 5 deer out of season	1:134, 157
Humberston Lyon, cohabitation and adultery 2-20-1746/7	Made £20 recognizance for child	1:134, 166
SECOND GRAND JURY, 5-21-1747		
James Campbell, road overseer 8-22-1747	Fined 15s	1:199, 268
Mark Evans, road overseer 8-22-1747	Fined 15s	1:199, 269
James Kerr, disturbing peace and Sabbath breach 8-22-1747	Fined £5 for former, 5s for latter, and costs	1:199, 268
James Burk, swearing 6-19-1747	Fined 20s for swearing 4 oaths	1:200, 235
THIRD GRAND JURY, 11-20-1747		
George Campbell, breach of peace 3-16-1747/8	Fined 5s	1:331, 359
John Allison, breach of peace 3-16-1747/8	Fined 5s	1:331, 359
Joseph Milligan, cohabitation and adultery		1:332
Forks of the James River road overseers, failure to maintain road		1:332
FOURTH GRAND JURY, 5-21-1748		
Joseph Love, concealing felony 12-3-1751	Dismissed on Love's motion with costs	2:33, 3:233
Samuel Stalnaker, breach of peace 12-2-1749	Fined 5s and costs	2:33, 304
Jacob Harman, Jr., breach of peace 12-2-1749	Fined 5s and costs	2:33, 305
FIFTH GRAND JURY, 5-17-1749		
Andrew McCord, blasphemy 8-25-1749	Fined 5s and costs	2:118, 267
Eleanor Crocket, blasphemy 9-3-1750	Not found in bailiwick, dismissed	2:118, 480
Andrew Fitzpatrick, blasphemy 12-2-1749	Pled guilty, fined 10s and costs	2:118, 305

TABLE 15   (continued)

Offender and offense Adjudication date and judgment		Order book vol.:page
Eleanor Shannon, fornication 8-25-1749	Fined 500 lbs. tobacco and casks, and costs	2:118, 267
Charles Boyle, Sabbath breach 12-2-1749	Fined 5s and costs	2:118, 305
Eleanor Dryden, fornication 8-25-1749	Fined 500 lbs. tobacco and casks, and costs	2:119, 268
SIXTH GRAND JURY, 11-29-1749		
Andrew McNabb, Sabbath breach 5-26-1750	Fined 5s	2:293, 403
NINTH GRAND JURY, 5-28-1751		
John Robinson, road overseer 6-19-1752	Excuse heard, discon- tinued	2:568, 3:279
Isaac Taylor, obstructing road 12-3-1751	Excuse heard, discon- tinued	2:568, 3:233
TENTH GRAND JURY, 11-27-1751		
Mary Kinman, illegitimate child 6-20-1752	Not found in county, dismissed	3:206, 3:303
ELEVENTH GRAND JURY, 11-16-1752		
James Young, taking toll twice as miller 8-17-1753	Fined 15s and costs	3:369, 4:18
William Gerrott, road overseer 5-22-1753	Summoned twice with- out appearing	3:369
William Calhoun, constable refuses service 5-22-1753	Acquitted	3:369, 3:497
TWELFTH GRAND JURY, 5-16-1753		
Catherine Agin, illegitimate child 8-17-1753	Summoned twice with- out appearing	3:437
Richard Woods, breach of peace 5-17-1753	Acquitted	3:437, 3:448
THIRTEENTH GRAND JURY, 11-21-1753		
Rebecca Holliday, illegitimate child 8-27-1754	Not found in county, dismissed	4:64, 316
John Dunbar, adultery 8-27-1754	Not found, dismissed	4:65, 316
John Ramsey, detaining grain at his mill 8-27-1754	Writ not executed, dis- missed	4:65, 316

Sources: Augusta OB, 1:134, 156–158, 166, 199–200, 235, 268–269, 331–332, 359; 2:33, 118–119, 233, 267–268, 293, 304–305, 403, 480, 568; 3:206, 233, 279, 303, 369, 437, 448, 497; 4:18, 64–65, 316.

TABLE 16 Pledges by Timber Ridge subscribers for Reverend John Brown's salary, 1753

0 4 = 4 shillings (n = 1)	0 *4* 0 **5** 0 66 0 0 0
1 0 = 10 shillings (n = 20)	1 **0000**00000000000000000 1 1 222222 1 1 1 555555555 1 1 1 8 1
2 0 = 20 shillings (n = 13)	2 000000000000 2 1 2 2 2 2 555 2 2 2 2
3 0 = 30 shillings (n = 2)	3 00

Key:
Landowning men roman (n = 51)
Nonlandowning men **bold** (n = 5)
Women *italic* (n = 3)

N = 59
Minimum: 4 shillings (*Agnes Martin*)
Mode: 10 shillings (including Edward Tarr)
Median: 12 shillings
Mean: 14.6 shillings
Standard deviation = 5.9
Maximum: 30 shillings (*Magdalene Borden* and Matthew Lyle)

Note: In 1753, Timber Ridge residents pledged £43:1:6 annually for Rev. John Brown's salary. This leaf-and-stem graph shows the distribution of those pledges while also distinguishing donors by sex as well as landowning status. Edward Tarr's ten-shilling pledge was the most common amount subscribed. James Greenlee's pledge of £1:0:6 is plotted as 21 shillings.

Source: Timber Ridge Congregation subscription list, 22 July 1753, Preston Family Papers, 1727–1896, VHS. This source is a typescript copy of a no-longer-extant original.

TABLE 17   Three perspectives on land ownership in the Timber Ridge neighborhood, 1754

TIMBER RIDGE ACREAGE COHORTS

Acreage owned	Land- owners in cohort	% of all land- owners	Cumulative % of all landowners	Acres held by this cohort	% of total acreage	Cumulative % of total acreage
1–100	2	3.6	3.6	200	1.1	1.1
101–200	15	27.3	30.9	2,589	13.8	14.8
201–300	14	25.5	56.4	3,680.5	19.6	34.4
301–400	10	18.2	74.5	3,661	19.5	53.9
401–500	4	7.3	81.8	1,757	9.4	63.3
501–600	5	9.1	90.9	2,709	14.4	77.7
601–700	0	0	90.9	0	0	77.7
701–800	2	3.6	94.5	1,445	7.7	85.4
≥851	3	5.5	100.0	2,741	14.6	100.0
Total	55			18,782.5		

TIMBER RIDGE ACREAGE SPREAD
Minimum acreage: 100
Maximum: 980
Median: 300
Mode (6 tracts):   200
Mean: 341.5
Standard deviation: 201.9
Outliers (3 tracts > 745.3 acres):   851, 910, 980 acres

TIMBER RIDGE ACREAGE BY QUARTILE
1st quartile (Q1):   200 acres
Median: 300 acres
3d quartile (Q3):   407.5 acres
Interquartile range (Q3–Q1):   207.5 acres
Outliers (4 tracts > 718.75 acres):   734, 851, 910, 980 acres

Note: In the year of his purchase, Edward Tarr's 270 acres fell just below the median freehold size for his Timber Ridge neighborhood. Twenty-four of his fifty-four white neighbors (44.4%) owned less land than he did. Cumulative proportions vary due to rounding.

Sources: Augusta DB, 1:173, 200, 203, 205, 207, 209, 211, 265, 267, 269, 272, 365, 369, 412, 434, 436, 461, 463, 493, 497, 505, 509, 525, 527, 532; 2:120, 129, 132, 200, 204, 290, 304, 307, 389, 699, 702, 774, 842; 3:43, 169, 175, 179, 183, 233, 321, 329, 365, 396, 400, 404, 405; 4:48, 264, 354; 5:255, 502, 505, 783; 6:126, 212, 244, 295, 391, 394, 397, 400, 406, 413; 12:336; 13:43; 21:416; Augusta WB, 1:513, 2:36; Chester County WB, C:49, HSP; Orange County DB, 6:321; 7:118, 131, 258, 310, 364, 372; 8:24, 41, 129, 133, 137, 198, 202, LOV.

Table 18   Edward Tarr's tax obligations, 1752–1772 (shillings)

Year	Parish levies	County levies	Colonial levies	Quitrents on 270 acres	Virginia poll taxes	Virginia land taxes	Tarr's totals
1752		1.44	0	0	0	0	
1753	2.0	2.19	0.46	0	0	0	4.65
1754	2.0	2.5	0	5.37	0	0	9.87
1755	2.0	1.75	0.54	5.37	5	0	14.66
1756	2.0	2.0	0	5.37	0	3.38	12.75
1757	1.83	1.5	1.67	5.37	1	3.38	14.75
1758	3.33	1.75	0	5.37	4	6.08	20.53
1759	1.83	2.0	1.0	5.37	4	6.08	20.28
1760	7.25	1.25	0	5.37	4	6.08	23.95
1761	5.0	0.68	1.0	5.37	4	5.37	21.42
1762	3.25	2.5	1.17	5.37	4	5.37	21.66
1763	2.5	1.0	0	5.37	4	5.37	18.24
1764	3.0	3.0	7.67	5.37	6	5.37	30.41
1765	1.58	3.17	0	5.37	5	5.37	20.49
1766	1.83	2.0	1.0	5.37	5	5.37	20.57
1767	2.5	1.75	0	5.37	5	5.37	19.99
1768	1.67	4.0	0	5.37	0	0	11.04
1769	2.0	2.5	1.13	5.37	0	0	11.00
1770			0	5.37	0	0	
1771	2.5	2.5	0	5.37	0	0	10.37
1772	2.17	2.33	0.75	5.37	0	0	10.62

Note: Edward Tarr's tax payments reflected the amount of land he owned and the number of tithables in his household. His annual tax burden was typical for any artisan owning a modest freehold and not controlling the labor of any other tithable person. Parish levies were not recorded in 1752 and 1770; the county levy was not calculated in 1770.

Sources: Augusta OB, 3:365, 4:69, 322, 494; 5:245; 6:85, 209, 314, 430; 7:106, 356; 8:327; 9:159; 10:143, 425; 11:484; 12:469, 508; 13:70; 14:60, 178, 307, 468; Augusta Parish VB, 235, 266, 322, 351, 357, 373, 377, 401, 415, 426, 452, 463, 483, 491; Hening, ed., *Statutes,* 1:228; 6:374, 436, 462–463, 498–499, 522; 7:9–10, 28–29, 77–78, 139, 165–166, 174, 258, 349, 359, 497.

TABLE 19   Blacksmith work performed by Edward Tarr for George Stevenson

Task	Frequency of task	Charge per task (shillings/pence)
Repairs and maintenance		
Axe		
Steeling	4	1/3
Upsetting	2	0/4
Bell		
Buckle for	1	0/4½
Clapper for	1	0/6
Grubbing hoe		
Laying*	2	
Mending	1	0/8
Steeling	1	1/0
Upsetting	1	0/4
Hoe		
Laying*	2	
Mending	1	1/1½
Lock, lock nail for	1	0/10
Pan, mending	1	0/8½
Plow blades		
Coulter only, sharpening	8	0/3
Coulter, laying*	6	
Shear and coulter, sharpening	10	0/4½
Shear only, sharpening	4	0/1½
Scythe, rodding	1	1/2
Farrier		
Removing shoes	23	0/2½
Attaching shoes	42	0/4½
Manufacturing		
Anvil	1	0/8
Bell	1	1/6
Clevis pin	1	0/4
Grubbing hoe	1	4/0
Hoe, small	1	1/6
Hoops, pair	1	0/3
Shear	1	5/3½
Wipers, pair	1	2/6

* Cost depended on amount of iron used.

Source: Complainant's account, *Edward Tarr v. George Stevenson,* Judgment Files, Augusta CCC.

TABLE 20   Indian campaigns in Augusta County during the Seven Years' War

Duration	River valleys raided by Indians	Killed	Captured	Wounded
1755				
Spring/summer	Holston and New	21	20	5
Late summer	Greenbrier and Upper Potomac	12	10	0
1756				
Winter	New	9	1	0
Summer	Roanoke	5	20	4
Late summer	Jackson	14	29	3
1757				
Late winter	Potomac and headwaters of James	0	8	0
Spring	Jackson, Cowpasture, and South Branch of Potomac	8	8	0
Summer/fall	Jackson, Cowpasture, and Upper James	7	15	4
Late fall	Brocks Gap	3	2	0
1758				
Winter	Brocks Gap	1	0	0
Winter	Roanoke, Jackson, and Cowpasture	4	6	0
Winter/spring	Upper Potomac	44	39	2
1759				
Fall	Kerr's Creek (North River, now Maury)	12	14	2
	Totals:	140	172	20

Note: Indians campaigning in Augusta County during the Seven Years' War launched their earliest attacks on the Holston River before Edward Braddock's defeat, signaling their objective of severing Virginia's logistical and diplomatic communications with the Cherokees. The winter 1756 raid in the New River Valley probably was a spoiling attack to deter the Sandy Creek Expedition, a militia expedition that set out from Augusta County to attack Ohio River Indian towns but turned back due to bad weather and food shortages. The fall 1757 and winter 1758 raids near Brocks Gap are anomalous in their location, deep inside Augusta County settlements; given that Indian raiders typically attacked the margins of settlements, these parties may have been guided by white Indians, prisoners who were adopted by their captors. Alternatively, the raiders may have traveled extensively in Augusta County before hostilities began. In the October 1758 Treaty of Easton, Indians from some Ohio River towns agreed to quit fighting in exchange for Pennsylvania and Virginia promises to restrain settlement expansion. The 1759 raiders on Kerr's Creek, therefore, may have represented towns or tribes that did not accept the Easton accords.

Sources: Preston Register, Draper Mss., 1QQ 83; Jennings, *Empire of Fortune*, 274–280, 342–348, 396–403; Ward, *Breaking the Backcountry*, 104–106.

TABLE 21   Landholding by first-time registrants of slave children, Augusta County, Virginia, 1753–1769

Acreage	Number of registrants	% of all registrants	Cumulative % of registrants
0	16	20.3	20.3
1–100 (incl. Staunton lots)	3	3.8	24.1
101–200 (Q1 = 120 acres)	9	11.4	35.4
201–300 (median = 283 acres)	13	16.5	51.9
301–400	14	17.7	69.6
401–500	3	3.8	73.4
501–600	1	1.3	74.7
601–700 (Q3 = 607 acres)	2	2.5	77.2
701–800	4	5.1	82.3
801–900	5	6.3	88.6
901–1,000	1	1.3	89.9
1,001–1,100	0	0	89.9
1,101–1,200	1	1.3	91.1
1,201–1,300	1	1.3	92.4
Outliers			
1,532	1	1.3	93.7
1,672	1	1.3	94.9
1,775	1	1.3	96.2
1,971	1	1.3	97.5
2,562	1	1.3	98.7
4,499	1	1.3	100.0
Total (N)	79		

Interquartile range (Q3–Q1): 487 acres
Outliers = acreages greater than $(1.5 \times IQR) + Q3 = (1.5 \times 487) + 607 = 1,337.5$

Mean acres: 475.0
Standard deviation: 671.3
Outliers = acreages greater than $((2 \times stdev) + mean) = (2 \times 671.3) + 475 = 1,817.6$
Cumulative proportions vary due to rounding.

Sources: For first-time registrants of slave children, see Augusta OB, 2:151, 356; 3:444; 4:70, 109, 262, 379, 424; 5:177, 187, 189, 369; 6:210, 292, 295, 314, 316, 387; 7:2, 50, 52 (second page of this number), 54–57, 64, 69, 71, 105, 109, 114, 156, 163, 208–209, 212, 219, 295, 463 (second page of this number); 8:33, 388, 469–470, 489, 497; 9:67, 72, 141, 162–163, 231, 233, 311, 323, 341, 442; 10:29, 225; 11:64, 111, 232. For their landholding, see Augusta DB, vols. 1–17; Augusta WB, vols. 1–4; Orange County DB, vols. 3–9, LOV; Virginia Land Office Patents and Grants, vols. 16–42, LOV.

TABLE 22   Estimated hemp production by Augusta County slave owners, 1766–1769

	1766	1767	1768	1769
Total pounds of all hemp certificates	101,449	337,480	315,180	320,122
Minimum pounds	135	162	110	117
Maximum pounds	12,721	9,070	9,264	9,172
Number of certificates	75	278	243	231
Average pounds per certificate	1,352.7	1,214.0	1,297.0	1,385.8
Standard deviation	1,722.4	1,083.6	1,112.5	1,248.9
Hemp certifiers who owned slave(s)				
In this year	3	5	2	2
With same name before and after year	6	3	4	5
In previous year, this year unknown	1	0	1	1
With different name before and after	17	13	14	13
In following year	0	0	1	1
Total estimated slaveholders	27	21	22	22
Total pounds certified by slaveholders	18,934	45,208	45,235	37,483
Slaveholder pounds as % of total claim	18.7	13.4	14.4	11.7
Minimum slaveholder pounds	799	203	258	214
Maximum slaveholder pounds	6,113	5,633	4,772	6,676
Average pounds per slaveholder	2,103.8	1,458.3	1,809.4	1,703.8
Standard deviation	1,709.3	1,067.5	1,320.2	1,493.9

Sources: Hemp: Augusta OB, 10:151, 153, 191, 193–196, 198, 200–204, 206, 212–213, 232, 236, 294, 317, 334–335, 337–342, 345–346, 349, 351, 358, 364, 423, 459, 463, 465–470, 473, 481–482, 486–487, 489, 498; 11:59–63, 67–69, 83–85, 90, 98–99, 202, 211–214, 222–223, 232–233, 238–239, 248, 312–313, 337–338, 342–343, 346–347, 350–351, 366, 374, 489–495, 500–502, 507, 512, 520; 12:2, 93, 103, 137–140, 146–148, 156–157, 166, 173, 251–252, 274, 311–313, 317–319, 327, 333, 342, 352, 431, 470–471, 477, 493, 506–507; 13:34, 76–77, 79–82, 86–87, 101, 108–109, 170, 197–198, 202, 205–206, 214, 218, 222–223, 236, 317, 319–320, 324–325; 14:17, 20, 22, 32, 60. Slaveholders: Augusta DB, 12:484; 13:526; 14:22, 100, 103, 112, 115, 229, 312; 15:247, 481; 17:9, 101, 175; Augusta OB, 10:225, 523; 11:64, 111, 232, 488; 12:134, 321, 328; 13:73, 333; 14:59, 220, 249, 250, 262; Augusta WB, 3:472–473, 509; 4:18, 39, 43, 101, 106, 126, 160, 257–259, 267, 277, 332, 344, 354, 401, 483; Botetourt County OB, 1770–1771, 12, 117, 238,362, 371, 408, LOV; Botetourt County Tithables, 1770–1782, 29, 32, 33, 35, 36, LOV; Botetourt County WB A, 12–13, LOV; Thomas Fulton Relinquishment of Property, 4 July 1763, Preston Family Papers, 1727–1896, VHS; John Buchanan, "Notebook of Accounts," April 1766, ibid.; William Thompson, Taxable Property, n.d. but filed in 30 June 1768 folder, ibid.; Andrew Boyd, Bill of Sale, 30 May 1770, ibid.; Judgment Files, Augusta CCC; *Virginia Gazette* (Purdie and Dixon), 2 May 1766, 3; 23 May 1766, 3; Bill of Sale, 7 Nov. 1766, Archibald Stuart Collection, Alderman Library.

TABLE 23   Average age (in years) of slave children registered in Augusta County and piedmont Virginia, 1750–1774

Years	AUGUSTA COUNTY Boy	Girl	CENTRAL PIEDMONT Boy	Girl	SOUTHSIDE PIEDMONT Boy	Girl	NORTHERN PIEDMONT Boy	Girl
1750–1759	11.9	12.5	10.6	11.1	10.7	10.9	11.6	11.2
1760–1769	10.3	11.5	10.3	10.7	10.2	10.7	9.7	11.5
1770–1774*	9.5	8.5	10.3	10.0	10.4	10.8	10.7	10.9

Overall (N = 114)		
n†:	77	33
Mean:	10.4	11.4
Standard deviation:	2.4	2.6
Minimum:	5	6
Maximum:	16	15
Median:	10	12
Mode:	12	14

* Includes two girls and eleven boys registered in 1771 and 1772 in Botetourt County (see figure 8.1), which split from Augusta County in 1770. No children were registered in Augusta or Botetourt counties in 1774.

† Augusta County masters registered four additional children of unknown sex in the 1760s; their ages were eight (2), ten, and fifteen years.

Sources: For piedmont, Morgan and Nicholls, "Slaves in Piedmont Virginia, 1720–1790," 223. For Augusta, Botetourt, and Orange Counties, Augusta OB, 2:356–11:232, 14:220–262, 15:87; Botetourt County OB, 1770–1771, 362–408; ibid., 1772–1776, 6–14; Orange County OB, 3:349, all LOV. Thanks to Michael L. Nicholls for assistance identifying genders of names.

TABLE 24   Estimate of tithable unfree persons of color in Augusta County, 1763

Individual slaves identified in 1763	17
Individual slaves not identified in 1762–1764 but bracketed both earlier and later	64
Individual slaves identified in 1762 but not 1763 or 1764	23
Individual slaves identified in 1764 but not 1762 or 1763	30
Individual bound mulattos identified in 1763	2
Total estimated unfree tithable persons of color in 1763	136

Note: Augusta County included 2,562 tithables in 1763. Augusta Parish VB, 373, 19 Nov. 1763. The 136 unfree persons of color estimated as living in the county in that year thus would have constituted 5.3 percent of all tithables.

Sources: No systematic enumeration of slaves exists for colonial Augusta County. The above estimate is based on incidental mentions of slaves in court records and the personal papers of county residents. These include the sources cited in appendix 3, end notes for chapter 8, and tables 21, 22, and 23.

TABLE 25 Indian campaigns in Augusta County during Pontiac's Rebellion, 1763–1764

	Killed	Captured	Wounded
1763 campaign no. 1: Summer	28	14	3
July Greenbrier River settlements attacked[a]			
17 July Kerr's Creek settlements attacked[b]			
20 July Indian raiders reportedly at Drapers Meadow, New Riverc			
July Roanoke River settlements attacked[d]			
24 July Calfpasture River settlements attacked[e]			
1763 campaign no. 2: Autumn	17	1	3
Sept. Captain Ingles's detachment overtook raiders in New River Valley.[f]			
30 Sept. Captains Moffet's and Philips's detachment ambushed on Jackson's River.[g]			
5 Oct. Colonel A. Lewis's detachment overtook raiders.[h]			
13 Oct. Captain Christian's detachment overtook raiders on New River.[i]			
1764 campaign no. 1: Spring	8	11	4
20 March James River settlements attacked.[j]			
21 March Militia detachment overtook raiders at Johns Creek on James River.[k]			
7 April Warm Springs settlement attacked.[l]			
April–June Jackson, Calfpasture, and Cowpasture River settlements attacked.[m]			
April–June Augusta County militia repeatedly fought raiders.[n]			
1764 campaign no. 2: Late summer	6	8	0
13 Sept. Middle Shenandoah River settlements attacked.[o]			
Total documented casualties	59	34	10

Note: Italicized dates are approximate.

Sources: (a) "Prisoners Delivered by Shawnees," 5 Jan. 1765, Bouquet, *Papers of Henry Bouquet,* 6:753–754. (b) Ibid.; Petition of Hugh Cunningham, 19 Jan. 1764, *JHB, 1761–1765,* 215. (c) Bethabara Diary, 27 July 1763, *Records of the Moravians in North Carolina,* 1:273. (d) Ibid. (e) *Pennsylvania Gazette,* 4 Aug. 1763, 3. (f) William Ingles to William Preston, 13 Sept. 1763, Draper Mss., 2QQ 43; *Pennsylvania Gazette,* 29 Sept. 1763, 2. (g) Ibid., 20 Oct. 1763, 2; John Blair to Thomas Gage, 22 Oct. 1763, Thomas Gage Papers, Clements Library, University of Michigan. (h) Blair to Gage, 22 Oct. 1763, ibid. (i) "Extract of a Letter from Captain William Christian, Dated Roanoke, October 19, 1763," *Pennsylvania Gazette,* 8 Dec. 1763, 2. (j) *Pennsylvania Gazette,* 3 May 1764, 2. (k) *David Cloyd v. James Montgomery,* 23 Aug. 1766, Augusta OB, 10:237. (l) *Pennsylvania Gazette,* 26 April 1764, 1. (m) Ibid., 3 May 1764, 2, and 14 June 1764, 2; Waddell, *Annals of Augusta County,* 184; John Brown to William Preston, [late spring] 1764, Draper Mss., 2QQ 50. (n) *Pennsylvania Gazette,* 21 June 1764, 3, and 5 July 1764, 3; *JHB, 1761–1765,* 249, 253, 254; Kegley, *Kegley's Virginia Frontier,* 288–289; John Brown to William Preston, 8 [June?] 1764, Draper Mss., 2QQ 49. (o) Deposition of Benjamin Estill, 20 March 1765, Chalkley, *Chronicles,* 1:454; Waddell, *Annals of Augusta County,* 191, 193–198; *Pennsylvania Gazette,* 15 Nov. 1764, 3.

Free People of Color in Early Augusta County

Edward Tarr's life illustrates how free people of color developed and depended upon far-flung connections. If their relationships transcended county borders, then the first step in identifying regional social networks is to compile a prosopography—a collective biography—of people who may have been undercounted because of their mobility. The following appendix contributes to that goal.[1]

At least fifteen free black or mulatto adults and twenty-three minors made early Augusta County their home. As was the case elsewhere in Virginia, county recordkeepers did not necessarily distinguish free people of color by race every time they appeared in the records. The following people thus were not always consistently identified as persons of color. The list of adults includes two individuals for whom only a single source indicates they may have been free people of color; these two were not counted in cumulative statistical computations discussed in the text but are included here to facilitate their future racial identification.

HENRY ANDERSON: Bound for two years by an indenture assigned to Thomas Brown from Thomas Hugart. On Anderson's 1779 complaint, the court's opinion was that Anderson was free.[2] Augusta County's personal property tax list for 1782 includes an entry for "Harry a free Negroe 1 Tithable self."[3]

JOHN ANDERSON: Bound by churchwardens of St. Andrew's Parish, Brunswick County, Virginia, to the age of twenty-one; white mother. In early 1763, he complained to the Augusta County court of unlawful detention as a slave by Presbyterian minister Reverend John Craig, so he probably was born by 1741. The court exempted Anderson from further servitude on 22 June 1763.[4]

JAMES ARMSTRONG: May have been white, since sole mention—as "Black James Armstrong" in a 1748 road order—could have been the nickname for a white man.[5]

MICHAEL BARNET/BORNET: Identified as a mulatto minor; the Augusta County court ordered parish churchwardens to bind him to Peter Hogg in 1766.[6]

JOSEPH BELL: Identified as a mulatto; died before 18 May 1759. Bell was survived by an illegitimate son, also named Joseph, whose mother was a white woman. His estate was administered by William Wilson, a creditor, who had Joseph, Jr., bound to him. Bell's personal property suggests he was a commercial hunter; in any case, he owned no agricultural tools at his death. Bell's personal property was sold, and the proceeds were applied to his debts for a net credit of three pounds, four pence.[7]

JOSEPH BELL, JR.: Illegitimate son of free mulatto Joseph Bell and an unknown white woman. He was a minor in 1759, bound to William Wilson, who administered the father's estate during the son's minority.[8]

WILL BLEUFORD: Born before 1765. Initially described without a surname as a mulatto to be freed at age thirty-one. In 1782, he was appraised at thirty-five pounds as part of the estate of Anglican minister John Hinds, and in the same year was categorized as a slave in the personal property tax list.[9] In 1788, he sued William Hinds for his liberty as William Bleuford; the court determined he should serve until age thirty-one.[10]

MULATTO BUTLER: Listed as a tithable person living on Samuel Woods's land in Botetourt County in 1772.[11]

WILLIAM CARR: Born to a white mother in Albemarle County, Virginia, ca. 1735; described as "a dark mulatto." Reportedly, he was given some formal schooling before his white stepfather sent him to the frontier at age eighteen. He made a living in southwestern Virginia as a commercial hunter and apparently never married.[12] A 1771 tithable list from Botetourt County names Carr as a head of household but does not indicate his racial status.[13]

[UNKNOWN GIVEN NAME] CATHER/CAUTHER: Mulatto illegitimate son of Jane Cauther, born ca. 1771. On 12 February 1772, the Botetourt County court ordered Botetourt Parish churchwardens to bind him according to law to James Robertson.[14]

Betty Cather/Cauther: Mulatto illegitimate daughter of Jane Cauther, born ca. 1772. Per an Augusta County court order of 19 May 1772, she was bound by churchwardens until age eighteen to Jacob Miller to be taught to read, spin, knit, and sew, and to receive customary freedom dues.[15]

Rose Cather/Cauther: Mulatto illegitimate daughter of Jane Cauther. The Augusta County court ordered parish churchwardens to bind her to John Campbell on 17 May 1768. Jacob Miller maintained the child for a year, for which the parish allowed him six pounds on 18 November 1768.[16]

Sarah Cather/Cauther: Mulatto illegitimate child, born ca. 1770. Per an Augusta County court order of 19 May 1772, she was bound until age eighteen to Stephen Hansberger to be taught to read, spin, knit, and sew, and to receive customary freedom dues. Valued after Hansberger's death in 1777 at sixteen pounds, ten shillings.[17]

Edward [Edmund?] Fredley: Botetourt County mulatto. He agreed in 1775 that in exchange for release from indenture one and a half years early, he would not require his master, George Skillern, to teach him to read, as called for by the indenture.[18]

Hannah Hurley: Born ca. 1750. She was described as a mulatto when parish churchwardens bound her to William Bethel until age thirty-one. The 1753 contract required Bethel to teach her to read the Bible and pay her the legal freedom dues. In 1777, a "Black Hannah" was listed as a tithable in the Borden Grant in the household of one Robert Sturet.[19]

Joe: Mentioned in June 1765 as a new member of the Smith Creek/Linville Creek Baptist Meeting, described as "a Negro Man called Joe."[20]

Elizabeth Joseph: Commonly known as Black Bett. She bound her daughter Sarah to Timber Ridge resident John Smiley in early 1760. Judging from the location of land belonging to Smiley and to the witnesses to this contract, Elizabeth probably lived within the Timber Ridge congregation's boundaries in the vicinity of South River, a tributary of the Maury. She could not sign her name.[21]

Sarah Joseph: Bound by her mother, Elizabeth Joseph, to John Smiley as of 12 March 1760, for a period of sixteen years. The contract included the usual provisions for "meat, drink, & lodging fit for a servant," plus teaching her to read. The Augusta County court subsequently ordered parish churchwardens to bind the child, but parish records contain no mention of such an action.[22]

[UNKNOWN GIVEN NAME] KNOX: Illegitimate mulatto child of Jane Knox. Churchwardens first complained about the case on 20 May 1758, and the court summoned the mother to the next session. She did not respond and was summoned again in November 1758. The sheriff returned the summons annotated "not found," and she was summoned a third time in May 1759. This latest summons included the note that Jane "lives at James Knox's," but it too was returned not found. The court discontinued the grand jury's presentment in August 1761. James Knox's will eight years later names two possible mothers—he had both a wife and a daughter named Jane—but given that he left his daughter only a token single shilling as a legacy, she is the more likely mother.[23]

GEORGE LUNDY: Illegitimate mulatto child of Mary Lundy. The court ordered the churchwardens to bind him to Benjamin Jones in 1775.[24]

MOSES: Described as Negro when he purchased a pair of shoe buckles at the estate vendue of Robert Andrews in 1766. He was not explicitly described as free, but no slaves named Moses appear in Augusta County records until 1771. The 1771 Moses was a boy, as was the next documented Moses in 1777. No identifiable slaves bought anything at Augusta County vendues during the colonial period.[25]

NATT: Described as a mulatto boy in 1763 when valued at thirty-five pounds in the estate appraisal of James Greenlee.[26] He was described as a mulatto or Indian boy in 1777 when he petitioned for freedom from James's widow, Mary Greenlee, whom the court found to be using Natt inhumanely.[27] The court ordered his release from servitude in 1778.[28]

WILLIAM PARR: Illegitimate mulatto child of white servant woman Anne Parr. In 1754, the court ordered an unnamed child to serve the mother's master, Archibald Stuart, "according to Law." Stuart bequeathed "Melatto Will" to his wife, Janet, in his will, written in 1759 and proved in 1761. Will was not named in Stuart's probate records, but appraisers of Stuart's estate valued "one Melatos time" at thirty-five pounds. William Parr appears as a free adult in Augusta County personal property tax records, 1800–1804.[29]

ANDREW PENMAN: Described as a mulatto child in 1769 when the court ordered churchwardens to bind him to George Elliot.[30]

CHRISTOPHER ROARREY/ROARKY: Illegitimate mulatto son of white servant woman Eleoner Road, born just before the September 1747 Augusta County court session. The court ordered parish churchwardens to bind him to Thomas Milsap until age thirty-one, which they did in 1749. The contract called for customary food, laundry, and lodging. He was not mentioned in Milsap's 1759 will or 1760 appraisal.[31]

MATHEW ROBERTS: Described as a Negro when he paid fifteen shillings to the estate of Robert Finlay in 1765; the purpose of the payment is not listed. He was not explicitly described as free but shared a surname with free mulatto Rebecca Roberts.[32] He also shared a surname with a York County free mulatto, _____ Roberts.[33]

REBECCA ROBERTS: Described as a mulatto; detained unlawfully as a servant by John David Wilpert in 1761. Upon her petition, the Augusta County court exempted her from future service on 20 May 1761.[34]

[UNKNOWN GIVEN NAME] SCOT: Illegitimate child of Jane Scot, a white servant woman. Probably a girl: in 1748, before notification that the child was a mulatto, the county court ordered the child bound to its mother's master, James Beard, until age eighteen, the usual age for girls. A year later, the court described the child as a mulatto and ordered the parish churchwardens to sell the mother in accordance with the law (a five-year term). The vestry book contains no reference to her case.[35]

MOLLY SIMPSON: Described as "a Mullato Child" when the Augusta County court ordered parish churchwardens to bind her to James Patterson in 1772. The vestry book contains no reference to her case.[36]

BETTY SMITH: Daughter of free mulatto Nicholas Smith. The Augusta County court ordered parish churchwardens to bind her in 1766, but the vestry book contains no reference to her case.[37]

ESTHER SMITH: Daughter of free mulatto Nicholas Smith. The Augusta County court ordered parish churchwardens to bind her in 1754, but the vestry book contains no reference to her case.[38]

JOHN SMITH: Son of free mulatto Nicholas Smith. The Augusta County court ordered parish churchwardens to bind him in 1766, but the vestry book contains no reference to his case. A Botetourt County tithable taker listed "John Smith Malato" as a head of household in the New River Valley in 1771.[39]

NICHOLAS SMITH: Described as a free mulatto in 1752. He moved out of Augusta County and abandoned five children in that year, launching a controversy over their control that spanned fifteen years. He served as a private in Captain William Preston's militia company in 1757 and January 1759. He was listed as a runaway (a term used also for white tax evaders) from Colonel William Preston's precinct in 1767. Children Nicholas, Jr., Sophia, Peter, and Esther were all named in Augusta County during the 1750s; Betty, Nicholas, and Johnny in 1766.[40]

NICHOLAS SMITH, JR.: Son of free mulatto Nicholas Smith. He was bound by churchwardens in 1752 to William Preston until age twenty-one. The contract specified he was to be taught to read, write, cast accounts, and weave. His father's efforts in 1750s to recover his children from legal guardians may have been successful, since in 1766 the county court again ordered parish churchwardens to bind Nicholas, Jr.[41]

PETER SMITH: Son of free mulatto Nicholas Smith; born ca. 1748. He was bound by churchwardens in 1752 to Elijah McClenachan until age twenty-one to be taught to read, write, and cast accounts, and to cooper or some other trade. He was to receive legal freedom dues.[42] He was identified as "Melato" and as an independent tithable in the 1774 tithable list for Big Levels precinct of Greenbrier Valley, Botetourt County.[43] In the following year, he was listed without racial indicator as an independent tithable in the Two Sinking Creeks precinct of Greenbrier Valley, Botetourt County.[44]

SOPHIA SMITH: Daughter of free mulatto Nicholas Smith. She was bound by churchwardens in 1752 to George Wilson until age eighteen. The contract specified she was to be taught to sew, spin, and read.[45]

[UNKNOWN GIVEN NAME] STRAND: Illegitimate mulatto child of servant woman Katherine Strand, who in 1774 was ordered to serve her master, Henry Hall, an extra twelve months for his expenses due to the child.[46]

EDWARD TARR: Born ca. 1711. He lived as a slave in Pennsylvania until after the death of his last master in 1748. He was permitted by the master's will to purchase his freedom, and moved to Augusta County, Virginia, ca. early 1752. He purchased land there in 1754. He last appears in Augusta County official records in 1772, when he acknowledged the sale of his land.

JAMES YOUNG: Illegitimate son of slave Ludwick Young and white Jane Colligen; born 24 February 1755. The Augusta County court ordered parish churchwardens to bind him, but no record of such action appears in the parish vestry book.[47]

[UNKNOWN]: Fifteen slaves and "Mulatto Servants to 31 years of age" were advertised to be sold at Staunton in June 1770. The advertiser, John Sutton, was an active eastern Virginia slave trader, so these anonymous persons may have included newcomers to Augusta County.[48]

The Frontier Forty

Enslaved Pioneers in Augusta County

The early Virginia settlements in Augusta County included a small number of slaves. In a report drawing on data as of 10 June 1755, Virginia Lieutenant Governor Robert Dinwiddie stated that the county contained forty black tithables. Virginia law stipulated that male and female slaves alike were tithable—that is, accountable for tax purposes—as "of the age of sixteen years and upwards."[1] Dinwiddie's figure also would have included free blacks Edward Tarr, Nicholas Smith, and probably William Carr and Joseph Bell.

Twenty-one Augusta County slaves who were of tithable age or could have reached it by 1755 can be identified by name before Dinwiddie's data were collected. Another twenty-three possibilities are identified anonymously, for a total of between twenty-one and forty-four potentially tithable slaves incidentally mentioned in early Augusta County before the deadline for Dinwiddie's report. Collectively, these fragmentary glimpses may account for every enslaved pioneer in Augusta County tallied by Dinwiddie.

As with the free people of color mentioned in appendix 2, the entries below include contemporary descriptions of skin color (Negro and mulatto) as well as age (wench, indicating a female of child-bearing age) to facilitate modern identification.

Twenty-One Named Slaves Who Potentially Were Tithable on 10 June 1755

ADAM: Tobias Smith and Samuel Gay sold "Negro Adam" to James Trimble before May 1749. Adam was sickly, and Trimble sued on a writ of trespass on the case to recover damages (presumed to be part or all of the purchase price) and court costs. The suit first was called on 22 May 1749, and after an attempt to negotiate a settlement, it was tried on 23 May 1750. A jury found Smith and Gay guilty of deceit and fraud in the manner and form declared by the plaintiff and said the plaintiff sustained damages of twenty pounds sterling plus court costs. The defendants' attorney filed errors in arrest of judgment, which when argued on 25 August 1752 were judged by the court not to be errors; the court therefore confirmed its original judgment.[2] The assessment of damages is consistent with the appraised value of a contemporary man, Lewis (see below).

BETTY: Worked on "A Plantation in Augusta County, on Shenandoe River, containing 300 Acres more or less, 100 of which are extraordinary rich low Grounds." (The term "plantation" denoted staple crop agriculture but implied nothing about the quality of dwellings on the tract.) Betty and the plantation were advertised for sale in February 1755 along with nine other "choice working Slaves, with Hogs, Horses, and Cattle." The late owner, Thomas McRedie, had been a merchant in Fredericksburg, Virginia. Appraisers found Betty on the plantation in the late summer of 1755 and described her as a Negro woman worth thirty-six pounds.[3]

BILLY: Worked on the same plantation as Betty, above, and advertised for sale in February 1755. Appraisers described him as a Negro man worth forty-six pounds.[4]

CHARLES: Appraised as a Negro man worth forty pounds in the estate of Benjamin Borden, Jr. Borden died in the spring of 1753; the appraisal was dated 6 February 1754.[5]

CHURCH: Added to the Augusta County tithable list on 19 October 1748, on the motion of his master, James Beard.[6]

CUFFY: Worked on the same plantation as Betty, above, and advertised for sale in February 1755. Appraisers described him as a Negro man worth forty-six pounds.[7]

DOVER: Age certified as thirteen years old on 22 May 1750 by his master, William Brown. Possibly it was Dover to whom the county court referred on 19 February 1752 while certifying to the General Assembly that Samuel Campbell had "tak[en] up a negro man slave belonging to William Brown of this County."[8] Brown paid taxes on an unnamed male slave in 1782; if this was Dover, he then would have been forty-five years old.[9]

HANNAH: Added to the tithable list on 19 September 1746 on motion of Benjamin Borden, Jr.[10] Borden did not mention Hannah in his will dated 30 March 1753, nor was she included in Borden's appraisal dated 6 February 1754.[11] The next mention of an adult slave Hannah was in James Patton's will dated 1 September 1750; Patton bequeathed to his daughter Mary Thompson a life estate in Hannah and Hannah's children Cooper, Lucy, and Jack.[12] The name does not appear again before the June 1755 accounting deadline; in the absence of evidence to the contrary, Borden's Hannah and Patton's Hannah are tallied here as the same individual.

HARRY: George Bowman deeded slave Harry, age between twenty-two and twenty-three years, to George's mother, Ann Bowman, on 16 August 1749. No value was mentioned.[13]

JANE: On 10 August 1753, Margaret Love (alias Bryan) mortgaged slaves Jane and Roger plus horses and cattle to indemnify James Mitchell against an adverse judgment in Augusta County court. Mitchell was identified as posting special bail for Love's husband, Joseph.[14]

JENN: Appraised as a Negro woman worth twenty pounds in the estate of John Hays on 25 May 1751. Hays left his widow, Rebecca, a life interest in Jenn and directed that the slave be sold after the widow's death; their three sons were to divide the price.[15]

JUDY: Age certified as eleven on 22 May 1750 by her master, William Brown.[16]

LEWIS: Appraised as a Negro man in the estate of James Coburn; worth twenty pounds on 19 April 1749.[17]

MOLL: Identified as a "Negro wench Named Moll" who had not yet born a child in the will of Benjamin Borden, Jr., dated 30 March 1753. Borden bequeathed Moll to his wife, Magdalene McDowell Borden. Moll was appraised on 6 February 1754 as "a woman Named Mill" worth thirty-two pounds in Borden's estate.[18]

NED: Joseph Love complained that his "Negro Man slave" named Ned had stolen "Sundry store goods" and given them to William Carvin (see his anonymous slaves, below) to conceal. On Love's complaint, Carvin appeared in court on 29 November 1750; when Love did not appear to prosecute, Carvin was acquitted of receiving stolen property from a slave.[19] About the same time Love initiated his complaint (most likely at the September 1750 court session), James Patton wrote a will dated 1 September

1750 in which Patton bequeathed a Negro named Ned to his daughter Mary, wife of William Thompson.[20] In the absence of evidence to the contrary, the masters Love and Patton are tallied as owning a single Ned.

PETER: In accordance with a commission directing them to form a court of oyer and terminer dated 30 March 1750, Augusta County magistrates met on 7 April to try "Peter a Negro Man slave belonging to Silas Hart Gent[lema]n" for theft. Peter was accused of having stolen a horse, saddle, and bridle belonging to John Anderson and a falling ax belonging to John Wallace. The crime allegedly occurred on 4 March 1749/50. Peter "said he was in no wise guilty and . . . put himself Upon the Court." After swearing and examining witnesses and after Peter "was fully heard in his own defence," the court found the proof insufficient and acquitted him.[21]

ROGER NO. 1: Appraised as a Negro man worth forty pounds in the estate of Benjamin Borden, Jr., in an appraisal dated 6 February 1754; Borden died in the spring of 1753.[22]

ROGER NO. 2: A financially distressed storekeeper named Joseph Love gave his wife, Margaret, a power of attorney to mortgage his property. On 10 August 1753, Margaret Love (alias Bryan) mortgaged slaves Roger and Jane plus horses and cattle to indemnify one James Mitchell against an adverse judgment in Augusta County court. Mitchell was identified as posting special bail for Love's husband, Joseph. The amount of the mortgage was £128:7:3, with interest from 1 March 1753 until paid, and payment was due by 15 September 1753. The Loves repaid some but not all of the debt, defaulting on £15:10:0, so Mitchell took possession of Roger to satisfy the debt, claiming to own Roger by right of the mortgage. Roger worked for Mitchell for twenty-two months. On 20 August 1757, one John Hopkins also sued Joseph Love's estate, obtaining a writ of attachment directed to county sheriff James Lockhart and executed by deputy sheriff Sampson Mathews. Lockhart and Mathews assumed that Roger still belonged to Love's estate and seized him. Roger escaped and returned to Mitchell. Lockhart and Mathews again seized Roger; a jury later found that the court officers "did take the said Negro out of the Field of the sd Plaintif Mitchell . . . without the Consent of the said Mitchell." This time, "the said Negro Roger died in the Possession" of the authorities. When Mitchell sued Lockhart and Mathews, a jury valued Roger's twenty-two months of labor for Mitchell at three pounds, a very low value unless the jury meant it as a monthly rate.[23]

SILVIA: Age certified as eleven years on 23 May 1750 by her master, yeoman John Craig.[24]

WILL: Worked on the same plantation as Betty, above, and advertised for sale in February 1755. Appraisers described him as a Negro man worth forty pounds.[25]

LUDWICK YOUNG: On 17 August 1757, the Augusta County court "Ordered that James Young a Mulato Child" born 24 February 1755 be bound by the churchwardens according to law, which then was to age thirty-one. According to the court, James was "begotten by Ludwick Young a Negro Slave on the body of Jane Colligen" in 1754.[26]

Twenty-Two Anonymous Adult Slaves Who Potentially Were Tithable on 10 June 1755

ANDREW BIRD'S HEIRS' MALE: Evaluated at twenty-five pounds as a Negro man in Bird's estate appraisal on 20 April 1751.[27]

JOSEPH BLOODWORTH'S FEMALE: Evaluated at thirty pounds as a Negro wench in Bloodworth's estate appraisal on 7 March 1743/4.[28]

WILLIAM CARVIN'S THREE SLAVES: Appraised on 28 May 1751 as part of the evaluation of improvements to two tracts he patented in the Roanoke River Valley in 1748.[29]

JAMES COBURN'S FEMALE: According to Coburn's estate appraisal dated 19 April 1749, Coburn's brother Jonathan received thirty-three pounds "for a Negro Woman" that belonged to the late James Coburn before the appraisal.[30]

JAMES GIVENS'S MALE: According to Givens's petition in a chancery suit against John Stewart, a Staunton tailor, and Thomas Fulton, a Staunton storekeeper, Givens was drunk in Staunton in December 1748. Stewart plied Givens with liquor, making him drunker, and offered to sell to Givens a "Negro Man" (also described as "Stewart's Neg'o fellow" and "a Slave newly imported") for £102 plus 15 bushels of Indian corn. Conspiring with Fulton, Stewart escalated the price to £115, to which Givens drunkenly agreed. Eventually the conspirators propped Givens on his horse, put the slave up behind Givens, and pointed the horse toward Givens's home. Once sober, Givens refused to pay his bond and sued Stewart and Fulton in chancery to "absolve him from the Bargain." The suit in chancery was agreed and dismissed fifteen years after the fact on 24 September 1763.[31]

Rebecca Hays's female: Bequeathed to her by her husband, John Hays, in his will drawn on 25 December 1750; described as a Negro wench.[32]

Adam Looney's female: Described as a slave wench sold by Patrick Downey to Looney on 18 March 1754.[33]

Joseph Love's female: The Augusta County sheriff reported on 17 May 1754 that he had seized an extensive amount of Love's property in the course of a lawsuit brought by John Mills, including a Negro woman. The sheriff sold some of that property in partial satisfaction of Love's debt to Mills, but not the woman.[34]

John McDowell's heirs' female: Evaluated at twenty pounds as a Negro girl in McDowell's estate appraisal on 20 April 1743; McDowell was killed in December 1742.[35]

John McDowell's heirs' male: Evaluated at twenty pounds as a Negro boy in McDowell's estate appraisal on 20 April 1743.[36] He committed unspecified damages to Thomas McSpaden, a Timber Ridge resident, and ran away repeatedly. McDowell's executors sold him by 1749 for £34:9:2.[37]

Thomas McRedie's six anonymous slaves: McRedie, a merchant in Fredericksburg, Virginia, died by 28 February 1755, when agents for his heirs advertised for sale "A Plantation in Augusta County, on Shenandoe River, containing 300 Acres more or less, 100 of which are extraordinary rich low Grounds; as also Ten choice working Slaves, with Hogs, Horses, and Cattle." In late summer of 1755, four of the ten slaves were named by appraisers evaluating the plantation; these included Betty, Billy, Cuffy, and Will, enumerated above. No record survives regarding the remaining six; the tract sold in 1768 without mention of them.[38]

James Patton's female: In his will dated 1 September 1750, Patton bequeathed to his daughter Margaret Buchanan a Negro woman that Patton identified as presently in Margaret's possession. Patton was killed in the summer of 1755; this slave woman was not mentioned in his probate records.[39]

Samuel Scott's heirs' female: Bequeathed by Samuel Scott to daughters Mary and Jean in a will drawn on 16 March 1748/9. Her name was either Bet or Judea. She was described as a Negro wench and evaluated at thirty-five pounds on 4 July 1749.[40]

Joseph Teas's two slaves: In a will dated 4 December 1753, Teas directed that his sons William and Charles "have the two Negros at my wife['s] Death." On 25 March 1754, a witness in a lawsuit in which Teas was a defendant testified that he had seen Teas and his slaves "in the field at work." Teas's appraisal, dated 19 May 1756, included "two Neagros" valued together at forty-five pounds.[41]

WILLIAM WILLIAMS'S SLAVE: A transcript entitled "Delinquents" lists tithable persons who had not paid the levy for 1748. These include "Wm. Williams and his negro, not found."[42]

An Adult Slave Who Died before 10 June 1755

VALENTINE SEVIER'S ADULT MALE: At a called court held on 5 September 1754, magistrates examined Murty Waters "on suspition of his murdering a negro man slave bellonging to Valentine Sevier." A county coroner held an inquisition, and "it seems to the Court that the sd Waters was Guilty of the supposed Felony but no Witness appearing, it is Order'd that the sd Waters be remanded" to jail. The court directed that Waters be reexamined on 14 September and ordered that two servants, another man, and Sevier be summoned to testify against Waters. The court convened again on 13 September and acquitted him.[43]

Appendix 4

Edward Tarr's Lawsuits

From the founding of Augusta County in late 1745 to its initial subdivision in 1769, hundreds of litigants launched thousands of lawsuits. Parties to those suits included Edward Tarr, who appeared repeatedly between 1756 and 1763: nine times as a defendant and once as a plaintiff.

Taken together, Tarr's litigation offers an instructive series of vignettes about frontier legal culture and free black navigation of credit relationships. At one level, each case is a miniature narrative of obligation. When obligations went unmet, English common law as practiced in Augusta County usually afforded timely, effective remedies for creditors. Despite overwhelmingly pro-plaintiff outcomes of civil litigation, Tarr seems for a while to have experimented—perhaps even gambled—with the law of financial obligations. At another level, the cases demonstrate a widely shared consensus that Tarr deserved to be treated just like other frontier artisans and landowners.

Joshua Mathews, assignee of Jacob Gray, v. Edward Tarr and Joseph Kennedy (in debt)

On 26 April 1752, shortly after Tarr arrived in Augusta County, Timber Ridge resident Jacob Gray extended fifteen pounds in credit to Tarr and a Borden's Land magistrate named Joseph Kennedy. Surviving documents do not say so but this transaction probably was part of Tarr's purchase of 270 acres from Gray; the amount comprised one quarter of the sixty-pound price Tarr paid Gray for his tract on Mill Creek, and the suit is the first of four by persons to whom Gray assigned debts owed him by Tarr. Kennedy was identified as codefendant because he signed and sealed the original debt instrument as a security for Tarr's payment.[1]

The document Tarr and Kennedy signed was a penal bond, an instrument that secured an original debt with a formulaic promise to pay a penalty of double the principle if the obligation was not repaid on time. Tarr and Kennedy agreed to repay Gray "whenever afterwards they should be thereunto required," but rather than collect from them, Gray chose to assign the debt to Joshua Mathews, a nearby resident of the Forks of the James.[2]

Complaining that "altho' often required ... [Tarr and Kennedy] have refused & still do refuse" payment, Mathews initiated suit during the November 1755 court by obtaining from the county clerk a capias, a command to Augusta County sheriff James Lockhart to compel Tarr's and Kennedy's appearance at the next court. As in all suits upon a writ of debt, defendants had the option of either awaiting trial while confined in jail or finding securities for their appearance at the appointed court date.[3]

Given a choice of jail or bail, both Tarr and Kennedy located securities that were deemed sufficient by the sheriff. The bail, or guarantor, for Tarr's appearance was Samuel Gray, kinsman of Tarr's original creditor, Jacob Gray; Samuel owned 241 acres at Timber Ridge, had pledged the below-average amount of twelve shillings annually for the support of Reverend John Brown, and as yet had held no Augusta County office.[4] The three bails for Kennedy's appearance included John Buchanan, a magistrate, vestryman, militia colonel, and land speculator; John Handly, who owned 257 acres in Borden's Land and had never held office; and one-term road overseer James McCown, who owned 370 acres in Borden's Land and another 380 acres on Catawba Creek, a tributary of the upper James River.[5]

The fact that the sheriff accepted a single bail for Tarr's appearance—and one of relatively modest means at that—but required three for Kennedy can be interpreted in two ways. On the one hand, for reasons having to do either with race or economics or both, the sheriff might have assumed Tarr's unreliability and thus sought to ensure that Kennedy, the white debtor, could be held accountable for the debt. On the other hand, the sheriff may have recognized Tarr as a man who was certain to appear when summoned and considered Kennedy to be much more problematic.[6]

Ultimately, however, no appearance in court was necessary. As Joshua Mathews doubtless intended, the November 1755 capias stimulated Tarr to repay the debt; some time during the winter of 1755–1756, Mathews reported to the county clerk that he had received satisfaction, so at the next court session in March 1756, the clerk reported the suit as agreed and dismissed.[7] In a broader context, such agreements were commonplace for debt actions in Augusta County in this period; out of 1,083 debt cases initiated by May 1755, 250 (23.1%) were agreed immediately by the next court session after process was served.[8]

William Reed, assignee of John Robinson, v. Edward Tarr (in debt)

On 6 May 1755, Edward Tarr committed himself to pay three pounds to John Robinson (also spelled Robison, Robson, or Robertson) by 1 August 1755. The debt instrument was another penal bond that Tarr signed in the presence of his Timber Ridge neighbor Andrew Fitzpatrick, who made his mark in lieu of a signature.[9] Robinson's identity is unclear, given that there were three landowners with variants of that name in 1755. The geographically closest was the one owning 160 acres on the South River, on the eastern edge of Borden's Land within the bounds of the Timber Ridge congregation.[10]

Like Jacob Gray in Tarr's first case, Robinson assigned Tarr's obligation to a third party, William Reed, whose location is uncertain because he died intestate in 1760 having never owned land in Augusta County and having never held a location-specific office such as constable or road overseer.[11] But Reed understood legal proceedings in the county court, having successfully petitioned to recover a small debt in 1754 and served as a petit juror on four occasions in 1754 and 1755.[12] After unsuccessfully seeking payment from Tarr, Reed hired Gabriel Jones, one of the few lawyers licensed to practice in Augusta County, and on 20 May 1756 obtained a summons for Tarr from county clerk John Madison.[13]

Deputy sheriff Sampson Mathews executed the capias and again Tarr chose to find a security rather than await trial in jail. This time Tarr's bail was Baptist McNabb, a longtime Timber Ridge resident and minor authority figure within the neighborhood. McNabb was a militia ensign, and Tarr and other local residents had maintained their portion of the Great Wagon Road under McNabb's direction since 1754.[14]

Tarr appeared in court on 19 August 1756 for a hearing that began with an important formality: "Mathew Patton undertook for the Def[endant] that in case he should be cast in this suit he [Tarr] would pay the condemnation of the court or surrender his body to prison in execution for the same or that the said Mathew Patton would do it for him." Patton's action is similar to that of Tarr's securities for his appearance but with an important distinction: where McNabb in this case and Samuel Gray previously had guaranteed to the sheriff that Tarr would appear in court for trial, Patton now guaranteed to the court that if Tarr lost, either Tarr or Patton would be accountable for the judgment.[15]

Patton's guarantee, known as special bail, was frequently requested by plaintiffs. Reed's lawyer had filed similar demands on numerous other occasions, so Tarr did not appear to have been singled out in a racist way by this motion.[16] Patton, who resided in the upper Potomac River Valley but may have been related to Timber Ridge resident John Patton, seemingly was a bystander at court who was making a gesture widely recognized by colonial Virginians as signifying the security's elevated social standing.[17] This and other signals seem to have favorably impressed the magistrates; they recommended Patton in 1758 as a person suitable for addition to the commission of the peace.[18] As far as the documentary record indicates, Patton was not otherwise directly associated with Tarr.

After special bail was set, the proceedings were brief: Tarr "could not gainsay but that he was Indebted to the plaintiff as [Reed] hath set forth in his declaration in the sum of six pounds." The court therefore ruled that Reed recover from Tarr the six pounds plus costs, which included a fee for the plaintiff's attorney. As Virginia law required, the court then specified that, except for costs, the judgment "is to be discharged on the paiment of Three pounds with Interest thereon at the rate of five per Centum per annum ... computed from the first day of August 1755 until paid."[19] In other words, the judgment of the court was that Tarr should pay Reed all of Reed's costs for the suit, the principle of three pounds Tarr had originally borrowed from Robinson, and legal interest from the date the loan became overdue. Separately, Tarr also was obligated to pay clerk and sheriff fees. Apparently Tarr paid without further delays, since Reed never sued Tarr's special bail, Mathew Patton.

William Todd, assignee of Jacob Gray, v. Edward Tarr and Joseph Kennedy (in debt)

On 26 April 1754, Jacob Gray extended another fifteen pounds in credit to Tarr and Kennedy. Like Tarr's 1752 debt to Gray, this obligation probably was connected to Tarr's purchase of Gray's land on Mill Creek; the agreement was struck less than a month before Gray deeded the 270-acre tract to Tarr for sixty pounds. Tarr and Kennedy both signed and sealed a penal bond to remit fifteen pounds by 1 October 1755.[20] In an undated endorsement on the reverse of the bond, Jacob Gray assigned the obligation to William Todd, a freeholder living in the nearby Forks of the James who never held office in Augusta County.[21]

Todd initiated legal proceedings to recover the debt on 1 June 1756, when the Augusta County clerk issued a capias for Tarr and Kennedy. Deputy sheriff Sampson Mathews returned a copy of the capias to the county clerk endorsed "Executed on tar[r,] Alexander McCorkle Bail."[22] Tarr's bail for appearance again was a neighbor of modest means: McCorkle resided on the North (Maury) River, where he was part of a road gang in 1754 and purchased three hundred acres in 1761. McCorkle held no offices during Augusta County's first quarter century.[23] There is no endorsement regarding service upon Kennedy on Tarr's capias, but court records refer repeatedly to the defendants as plural so Kennedy apparently also was summoned. Plaintiff and defendants alike were represented by lawyers when they initially met in court on 21 August 1756. Appearing for Todd was attorney John Semple, a relative newcomer to Augusta County's bar. Tarr's and Kennedy's lawyer was not named in extant documents.[24]

As in the 1756 debt suit by William Reed, the plaintiff asked that the court order Tarr and Kennedy to provide special bail. The court granted Todd's request; this time the two men who stood for Tarr and Kennedy were relatively minor figures even by Augusta County's frontier standards. David Moore, a two-hundred-acre freeholder in Borden's Land since 1754, had never held public office, and Patrick Porter never bought or patented land and never held office in Augusta County. Porter apparently resided in the Forks of the James, where parish land processioners found him in 1760. Moore served once on a petit jury during the county's first decade of civil litigation, signifying a total personal wealth of at least fifty pounds, but Porter never served as a juror.[25] In short, neither represented an especially strong candidate for service as special bail, so the plaintiff appears to have been relatively confident that Tarr could satisfy a judgment.

Having settled the question of special bail, the attorneys commenced the legal minuet of a debt suit. Where in his previous case Tarr had immediately conceded the plaintiff's action as legitimate, his attorney now helped Tarr and Kennedy defer the day of reckoning. The delaying tactics began when the "Defendants by their attorney prayed Oyer of the Writing in the Declaration mentioned," an official reading of the debt instrument. As usual the court granted the request and provided a routine continuance to the next court in course, thereby concluding the suit's proceedings for the August 1756 session.[26]

The parties returned to court the following session in November 1756, at which time "The Def[endan]ts by their Attorney said that they had paid the Debt in the Declaration mentioned and of this they put themself upon the Country." As usual after receiving the defendant's plea, the magistrates gave time to "the Plaintif until the next Court to Consider the Plea." In

March 1757, Todd's attorney informed the court that the plaintiff joined the action, meaning that he rejected the defendant's plea, thereby accepting a trial of the facts at the next court.[27]

On 20 June 1757, "the Parties by their attornies" appeared in court, but "the Defendant relinquishing his former plea says nothing in barr or Preclusion of the Plaintifs Action." In other words, Tarr's attorney announced that Tarr was retracting his plea of payment and acknowledging that the debt remained unpaid. The magistrates therefore delivered judgment for the plaintiff, to be executed by payment of the fifteen pounds principle, interest from 1 October 1755 until paid, court costs of 209 pounds of tobacco, and the usual fifteen-shilling fee for the winner's attorney.[28] A year and nineteen days elapsed between issuance of the capias and judgment, an expensive delay. If Tarr had paid Todd before Todd initiated the suit, Tarr would have saved 30/ for attorneys, court costs amounting to 17/5, and 15/ as a year's interest on £15. The total cost of his failure to pay promptly was £3:2:5.[29]

Edward Tarr v. George Stevenson (on petition)

Tarr performed blacksmith work valued at £3:12:7 for George Stevenson and his son Andrew from April 1752 through December 1756. On 7 May 1757, Tarr filed a petition with county clerk John Madison to recover that account. Acting in the king's name as required by Virginia law, Madison directed the county sheriff to summon Stevenson to the next court.[30] The summons to answer Tarr's petition reflected a streamlined process "for the more speedy recovery of small debts," by which Virginians meant "any debt or demand, due by judgment, obligation or account" valued between twenty-five shillings and five pounds. Unlike the writs of debt upon which Tarr was sued in 1756 and 1757, plaintiffs simply filed a petition in the county clerk's office, and the clerk issued a summons returnable at the next court. At that court, magistrates "instantly proceed to hear and determine the cause in a summary way . . . without regard to form, or want of form, in the process, petition, or course of proceeding." All the law required was that "sufficient matter be set forth, whereupon the court may give judgment according to the very right of the cause." Following judgment, the losing party paid court costs.[31]

For Virginians in general, petitions offered a way to collect book debts quickly and inexpensively. For Tarr, however, a petition was more than just a cheap way to compel payment: it was the easiest way. No black—even if free—could deliver sworn testimony in court, but though the petition was a legal process, it did not require such testimony. All Tarr had to do was attend court at the appointed time and present to the magistrates his account of work performed for Stevenson. If Stevenson appeared to contest the account, the court would hear both sides and decide the case. If Stevenson received the summons but did not appear, then judgment automatically followed for Tarr.[32]

In the eyes of the law, Stevenson did receive the summons, though not in person. Deputy sheriff Sampson Mathews endorsed the reverse side of the original summons with the annotation "A copey Left," meaning that Mathews could not find Stevenson so he officially delivered the summons, Tarr's petition, and a certified copy of Tarr's account to Stevenson's house.[33] When the case was called on 21 June 1757, Stevenson did not attend, so the court ruled for Tarr: "The Defendant being sumoned and not appearing the Plaintif proved his Account against him for Three pounds twelve shillings and sevenpence[.] Judgment is therefore Granted the Plaintif against the said Defendant for the same together with Cost."[34] Stevenson's absence was common for a peacetime debtor who had no defense; defendants defaulted comparably in 653 of the 1,355 petitions (48.2%) filed by Augusta County plaintiffs before the outbreak of the Seven Years' War.[35]

Did officials handling Tarr's case demonstrate any degree of prejudice? In terms of civil procedure, John Madison seems to have been evenhanded: given the wide discretion exercised by county clerks, he probably could have found a way to avoid accepting Tarr's petition and issuing a summons, but issue it he did. Madison also set the court's docket. Tarr's petition was heard on the last day of what proved to be a weeklong session. The summons for Stevenson had directed him to appear on 15 June, the first day of court, but Tarr's case was not called until 21 June, the last day of the session. On that day, the court addressed fifty-nine other petitions before Tarr's and eight after it, and seems to have handled Tarr's case no differently than any others.

In one key respect the court leaned toward Tarr by giving him judgment for accounts more than eighteen months old; Stevenson had accrued the majority of his debt over a year and a half before Tarr's petition. If this had been book debt such as retail merchants recorded for individual customers, Virginia law would have exempted it from collection, but the Augusta County magistrates chose not to apply this rule to Tarr's petition. In keeping with the statutory guidelines for petitions, the gentlemen hearing Tarr's case followed an equitable standard to resolve a local small claim. Virginia law directed the magistrates considering Tarr's petition "to give judgment according to the very right of the cause," and they did.[36]

Having obtained judgment, Tarr had two options for collecting what Stevenson owed him. Under English common law, sheriffs executed a court's judgment by seizing enough of the defendant's property to satisfy the debt; after auctioning the property, sheriffs paid the amount of the judgment to the plaintiff and remitted any remaining balance to the defendant. Alternatively, Tarr could have assigned the judgment in his case to a third party for either credit or cash, albeit probably at a discount. Sheriff records for executions do not survive for this period so there is no way to know how Tarr proceeded.[37]

William Todd, assignee of Jacob Gray, v. Edward Tarr and Joseph Kennedy (two suits; in debt)

As with previous suits brought by assignees of Jacob Gray, these two cases likely concern overdue partial payments for the 270 acres Tarr purchased from Gray in 1754. Todd initiated these suits before the August 1758 court; on 19 August, William Holdman and Thomas Paxton agreed to serve as special bails for Tarr and Kennedy. The suits were dismissed as agreed at the 17 November session, indicating that Tarr paid the debts and probably Todd's costs.[38]

John Lewis v. Edward Tarr (on petition)

As described more fully in chapter 6, Tarr failed to pay for meat and whiskey that he purchased from John Lewis in 1761. Lewis, who was the most senior magistrate in Augusta County, summoned Tarr to the November 1761 court session but did not appear to prosecute the case. Lewis died before the next court session, and his heirs did not renew the suit.[39]

Charles Donnelly v. Edward Tarr (on petition)

Edward Tarr rented a field from Staunton storekeeper Charles Donnelly in 1760, and as of 2 September 1761, owed Donnelly three pounds for one year's rent. During the same period, Tarr purchased 35 pounds of beef valued at 2 pence per pound, butter worth 1/2, and "whisky at sundry times" amounting to 1/10½. In all, Tarr was indebted to Donnelly for £3:8:10½. After Donnelly obtained a capias in July 1762, Tarr settled the account; on 25 August, the two men appeared in court and agreed that Tarr would pay Donnelly's costs, which amounted to sixty-five pounds of tobacco.[40]

Andrew Greer v. Edward Tarr (trespass on case)

As discussed in more detail in chapter 9, Greer sought to recover seven pounds, ten shillings. The writ of trespass on case indicates this was book debt rather than a penal bond. Tarr settled swiftly, and the court dismissed Greer's suit on 22 November 1762.[41]

John Bowyer v. Edward Tarr (in debt)

Tarr owed magistrate John Bowyer £5:15:6. Bowyer initiated the suit on 4 February 1767, to which Tarr responded with payment in full. Accordingly, the court dismissed Bowyer's suit on 23 March 1767. See chapter 9 for details of Tarr's repayment.[42]

Acknowledgments

I am grateful for generous institutional and personal support for the researching and writing of this book.

At Oakland University, where I first imagined Edward Tarr's story could provide the narrative spine of a book, a Faculty Research Fellowship made possible some of my earliest research in Pennsylvania. My Oakland history colleagues Jim Graham and Roy Kotynek generously rearranged their leave schedules so I could accept a resident fellowship at the Virginia Foundation for the Humanities and Public Policy, and mathematician Jack Nachman wrote custom computer programs that allowed me to map the Timber Ridge neighborhood long before the advent of user-friendly geographic information systems.

As a scholar in residence at the Pennsylvania Historical and Museum Commission, I was shown how to navigate the rich land and business records of that archives. The National Endowment for the Humanities provided a travel-to-collections grant that funded a critical visit to the South Carolina Department of Archives and History. A Michael Kraus Research Grant in History from the American Historical Association supported the mapping of Edward Tarr's neighborhood at Timber Ridge. Thanks also to the Rockbridge Historical Society, the Sons of the American Revolution, and the Society of the Cincinnati in the State of Virginia for supporting research on early Augusta County.

I am much indebted to the staffs of the Library of Virginia, especially Brent Tartar; the Virginia Historical Society, especially Francis Pollard; and the John D. Rockefeller, Jr., Library, Colonial Williamsburg Foundation, especially Marianne Martin.

I owe a special thanks to the Honorable John B. Davis, clerk of Augusta County Circuit Court, who has facilitated my research in the court's colonial records for almost three decades.

A resident fellowship at the Virginia Foundation for the Humanities and Public Policy enabled me to reconstruct the narrative of Edward Tarr's last master and to consult other fellows about the many meanings of Tarr's activities.

Thanks also to Dick Holway, Raennah Mitchell, and Morgan Myers at the University of Virginia Press for patient help bringing the project to term. Margaret A. Hogan's keen editorial eye was invaluable.

Numerous fellow travelers generously guided me on the road to Edward Tarr's forge including Katherine Brown, the late Katherine G. Bushman, Reginald Butler, Robert Calhoon, David Crass, Ellen Eslinger, the late Emory Evans, the late John Hemphill, Warren Hofstra, Mary B. Kegley, Susan Kern, Nelson Lankford, Joanna Miller Lewis, Carl Lounsbury, Holly Mayer, Philip Morgan, Michael Nicholls, Nancy Sorrells, Lucinda Stanton, Lee Taylor, Gail Terry, Fredrika Teute, Albert Tillson, Robert Vaughn, Mary Gwaltney Vaz, and James Whittenburg. Additionally, I am much indebted to Philip Schwarz and the many graduate students attending his Stratford Seminar on Slavery; their questions and comments pushed me to recognize critical nuances of Edward Tarr's social skills.

In Lexington, the staffs of the Virginia Military Institute's J. T. L. Preston Library and Washington and Lee's James Graham Leyburn Library patiently supported me and this project for years. A number of VMI cadets assisted with research including Joshua Anderson, Heidi Beemer, Christopher Bowers, Wayne Graham, Joel Harding, Thomas Hart, Colin Mahle, Jessie Rende, Jonathan Safrit, Ryan Schelske, Kenneth Stein, and Bache Whitlock. Also at VMI, four grants in aid of research and a Wachtmeister Faculty Development Leave were essential assistance that I greatly appreciate.

My VMI colleagues—the friends with whom I am so fortunate to work—scrutinized a draft of the book, chapter by chapter, in a process as valuable as it was excruciating. I am grateful to David Coffey, Tom Davis, Willard Hays, Geoffrey Jensen, Clifford Kiracofe, Ken Koons, Malcolm Muir, Megan Newman, Eric Osborne, Adam Trusner, and especially Mark Wilkinson and Timothy Dowling for what can best be described as a blacksmith's approach to shaping the manuscript: repetitive heating, hammering, and rasping. Thank you.

Notes

ABBREVIATIONS

DB   Deed Book
MB   Minute Book
OB   Order Book
VB   Vestry Book
WB   Will Book

EJC   H. R. McIlwaine et al., eds., *Executive Journals of the Council of Colonial*
            Virginia
JCV   H. R. McIlwaine et al., eds., *Journals of the Council of the State of Virginia*
JHB   H. R. McIlwaine et al., eds., *Journals of the House of Burgesses of Virginia*

Alderman Library   Alderman Library, University of Virginia
APS   American Philosophical Society
Augusta CCC   Augusta County Clerk of Circuit Court
Augusta DB   Augusta County Deed Book, microfilm, Library of Virginia
Augusta OB   Augusta County Order Book, microfilm, Library of Virginia
Augusta Parish VB   Augusta Parish Vestry Book, photocopy, University of Virginia
Augusta WB   Augusta County Will Book, microfilm, Library of Virginia
BHS   Virginia Baptist Historical Society
BNA   British National Archives (formerly British Public Record
                    Office)
CCP   Court of Common Pleas, South Carolina Department of
                    Archives and History
Draper Mss.   Lyman Copeland Draper Manuscript Collection, Wisconsin
                    Historical Society
FHL   Friends Historical Library, Swarthmore College
HMWV   History Museum of Western Virginia
HSP   Historical Society of Pennsylvania
LCHS   Lancaster County Historical Society
Leyburn Library   James G. Leyburn Library, Washington and Lee University

LOC	Library of Congress
LOV	Library of Virginia
PCA	Philadelphia City Archives
Perkins Library	William R. Perkins Library, Duke University
PHMC	Pennsylvania Historical and Museum Commission Archives
PHS	Presbyterian Historical Society
PRWA	Philadelphia Register of Wills Archive
SCDAH	South Carolina Department of Archives and History
Swem Library	Earl G. Swem Library, College of William and Mary
UPS	Union Presbyterian Seminary
VHS	Virginia Historical Society
Walker Papers	Thomas Walker Papers, Library of Congress
Winterthur	Winterthur Museum Library

INTRODUCTION

1. Augusta County WB, 3:227.

2. Fries, transl. and ed., "Diary of a Journey of Moravians," 338–39. For an alternate translation from the original German, see Hinke and Kemper, eds., "Moravian Diaries of Travels through Virginia," 147–49. Tarr's possession of *Berliner Reden* is discussed in chapter 4.

3. Leyburn, *The Scotch-Irish;* Griffin, *The People with No Name;* Miller, "'Scotch-Irish' Myths and 'Irish' Identities," 77; Miller, "Ulster Presbyterians and the 'Two Traditions',' 257; Taylor, *The Civil War of 1812*, 81.

4. Augusta OB, 2:351, 3 March 1750. For additional monetary details, see McCusker, *Money and Exchange Rates.*

1. THE YEOMAN

1. The earliest mention of Thomas Shute's father is for his service as a juror for a Chester County court held at Upland on 14 March 1681/2. Lapp, ed., *Records of the Courts of Chester County*, 2:15–16. The census was ordered on 14 April 1683 by Philadelphia County magistrates in response to a directive from William Penn. The actual enumeration dates from sometime after the county order. Soderlund, ed., *William Penn and the Founding of Pennsylvania*, 212–13, 216n.

2. Entry dated 8 Sept. 1683, Hazard, ed., *Minutes of the Provincial Council of Pennsylvania*, 1:80. Rotchford was elected to the 1683 colonial assembly as a member for Chester County and sat on the committee to amend the charter of liberties. Soderlund, ed., *William Penn and the Founding of Pennsylvania*, 230, 255. For Rotchford's occupation and residence, see note 5, below.

3. Samuel Carpenter to Thomas Shute, 25 Aug. 1690, Philadelphia County Exemplification Book, 7:441–42, PHMC.

4. Thomas Shute to John Lucken, 20 Dec. 1693, ibid., 7:442–44. Lucken paid sixty pounds, so Shute recouped his 1690 purchase price of twenty-five pounds, ten shillings, plus thirty-four pounds, ten shillings. "The First Tax List for Philadelphia County," 98. The 1693 tax rolls of Bristol Township tally assessments of one penny per pound of value held in real or personal estate. Shute had no value recorded in the real or personal

estate columns and paid six shillings in tax, the standard payment for all freemen out of service for six months.

5. Mary Rotchford to Thomas Shute, 1 March 1693/4, Philadelphia County Exemplification Book, 7:442–44, PHMC. Dennis and Mary Rotchford's son confirmed this transaction over eleven years later for a nominal price of five shillings. Herriot Rocheford to Thomas Shute, 7 Sept. 1707, Philadelphia County DB, E-3, 6:243, PHMC.

6. Genealogical Data, Sadler–Smylie, Collections of the Genealogical Society of Pennsylvania, HSP.

7. Thomas Shute and Elizabeth Powell first declared their intention to marry on 30 Oct. 1696, and their union was approved on 27 Nov. 1696. Philadelphia Monthly Meeting (Arch Street) Women's Minutes, 1:14, FHL.

8. Hinshaw, *Encyclopedia of American Quaker Genealogy*, 2:420.

9. James T. Lemon reported that by 1750, the population of southeast Pennsylvania was about 108,000, and typical land prices in Lancaster County doubled between the 1730s and the 1740s. *Best Poor Man's Country*, 23, 69. See also Wright, "Ground Rents against Populist Historiography."

10. "Virginia Quitrent Roles, 1704," 154. Early real estate records of King and Queen County do not survive, so it is impossible to know more about Shute's investments in land there. At first glance, the county's distance from Philadelphia might justify some skepticism about whether the name represented the same individual, but because Shute had another commercial interaction with a King and Queen County resident, it is likely the same man. Shute's other connection developed in this way: William Penn gave one James Claypole a warrant for one thousand acres. Claypole sold the warrant to William Smith, a shipwright of Middlesex County, Virginia, in 1683. Smith in turn sold the claim to William Chadwick of St. Stephen Parish, King and Queen County, in 1714. Chadwick relinquished the warrant to William Allen and Thomas Shute, both of Philadelphia, by deeds of lease and release dated 29 and 30 Dec. 1718. These transactions are enumerated in Thomas Shute and James Steel, deed to Adam Van Fossen, 18 May 1720, Philadelphia County DB, H-14:305, PHMC.

11. James A. Henretta has argued persuasively that milling and other processing activities did not signal incipient industrialization but rather represented one aspect of yeoman agricultural activity. "Families and Farms," 10–11.

12. For a price of £180, William Sluby conveyed 1,200 acres to Thomas Shute and Nicholas Waln on 22 March 1703/4. Philadelphia County DB, F-7:255, PHMC.

13. Samson Davis and Christian Shute publicly declared their intention to marry on 28 June 1717 when they appeared before the Arch Street women's monthly meeting to request certification of their clearness, or spiritual fitness. Later that day, accompanied by the two female examiners, the couple repeated their publication before the men's monthly meeting, which appointed two male inspectors. A month later both sets of investigators reported "that they know nothing to obstruct their proceedings," and so on 26 July 1717, with the agreement of the family members, the men's monthly meeting approved the marriage and authorized the couple to proceed. Entries dated 28 June, 26 July 1717, Philadelphia Monthly Meeting (Arch Street) Women's Minutes, 1:105, FHL; entries dated 28 June, 26 July 1717, Philadelphia Monthly Meeting (Arch Street) Minutes, 1715–1744, 29, 30, FHL. For Shute's conveyance to Samson and Chris-

tian Davis, see Philadelphia County DB, F-7:300, PHMC. In July 1718, Samson and Christian Davis announced their intentions to move to Moreland, completing the move by December. The couple signaled their plans to move by requesting that the Arch Street women's and men's meetings certify their spiritual clearness to their prospective neighbors in the Abington Monthly Meeting. Entry dated 29 Aug. 1718, Philadelphia Monthly Meeting (Arch Street) Women's Minutes, 1:112, FHL; entry dated 26 Sept. 1718, Philadelphia Monthly Meeting (Arch Street) Minutes, 1715–1744, 46, FHL. The Abington Monthly Meeting read the certificate and accepted the newcomers on 29 Dec. 1718. Abington Monthly Meeting Minutes, 1682–1746, FHL.

14. Thomas Shute and wife Elizabeth to Sampson Davis and wife Christian, 20 June 1721, Philadelphia County DB, F-7:300, PHMC; Society of Free Traders to Thomas Shute, 24 March 1724/5, ibid., F3:514; Thomas Shute and wife Elizabeth to James Lewis, 20 Dec. 1725, ibid., F2:414. For the expansion of Pennsylvania's flour trade during this period, see Jensen, *Maritime Commerce*, 7–8, 292.

15. Petition of Inhabitants of Horsham Township and Moreland Manor, 5 June 1727, Philadelphia County Court of Quarter Sessions, 43–44, PHMC.

16. Peter Baynton to "Messrs Ben: Faneuil, Gooch, and Tottiell," 24 May 1729, Peter Baynton Letterbook, 3 April–10 Nov. 1729, PHMC.

17. *Pennsylvania Archives*, 8th ser., 3:2171.

18. Like most partnerships in the capital-starved iron industry, this one evolved rapidly. Shute's initial five partners were Marcus Hulings (provider of the land), Jonathan Robeson, William Branson (an ironmaster and merchant), Nicholas Scull, and James Steel. A few weeks after their initial agreement, the partners added John Warder, Barnabas Roades, John Ball, John Scull, and William Shute, Thomas's son. "Articles of Agreement," 14 Jan. 1722/3, amended 19 March 1722/3. As the Manatawney Valley iron industry took off, this mine was conveniently positioned to provide ore to Pool Forge (1725), Pine Forge (1725), McCall's, or Glasgow, Forge (1725), and Spring Forge (1729). Bining, *Pennsylvania Iron Manufacture*, 171. Thomas Shute's son William married Steel's daughter Elizabeth in 1721. Genealogical Data, Sadler–Smylie, Collections of the Genealogical Society of Pennsylvania, HSP.

19. Steel alone received the original survey, which makes no mention of mineral potential. Survey dated 9 Nov. 1730, Survey Book, D81:82, PHMC. A second tidier plat, which cites the same survey, is labeled "The Draft of the Gap Mine Land, in Lancaster County Belonging One 6th part to the Honble Proprietary Thos Penn, one 6th Part to Andrew Hamilton, one 6th part to James Logan or assigns, one 6th part to Wm Allen; one 6th part to Thos Shute or assigns, & one 6th part to James Steel." The second draft's date is unknown; Thomas Penn arrived in Pennsylvania in 1732, so this document does not necessarily indicate that Penn knew Shute or felt personally linked to him as a partner.

20. Entries dated 1 Oct. 1736, 1 July 1737, Peter Baynton Journal, Ledger E, 1734–1743, 145, 175, PHMC.

21. Survey plat, 15 May 1735, Survey Book, C182:130, PHMC; patent, 17 May 1737, recorded 19 June 1738, Patent Book, A8:396, PHMC.

22. Bining, *Pennsylvania Iron Manufacture*, 17, 171. It is possible that Shute's Perkiomen mining operations produced copper ore, not iron; a copper works is mentioned as

a nearby landmark in the records of Mount Pleasant ironworks from the early 1740s. Mount Pleasant Furnace Ledger, 1740–1744, 201, Potts Mss., HSP. For a detailed analysis of copper mining, see Bodle, "'Such a Noise in the World.'"

23. Shute left "one half Moiety" of the Lancaster mining interest to his son Isaac, a blacksmith, and the other half to his grandson William Davis, manager of Warwick Furnace in Chester County. Thomas Shute will, drawn 4 Oct. 1748, presented 10 Dec. 1748, Philadelphia County WB, I:5, HSP. Davis sold his share in 1755. William Davis to Benjamin Koster, 6 April 1755, Lancaster County DB, II:652–54, PHMC. Isaac Shute's heir sold the other half of Thomas Shute's Lancaster County copper mine interest a few weeks later; the deed mentions the Gap Mine on Pequea Creek. William Shute and wife Elizabeth to Benjamin Koster, 10 May 1755, ibid., II:654–56. A subsequent conveyance by the Koster heirs mentions the Gap Mine on Pequea Creek; its courses match William Allen's 1736 sale to Thomas Shute. Ibid., EE:567; Allen to Shute, 14 Aug. 1736, Philadelphia County DB, H-19:507, PMHC. These courses do not describe the same tract as James Steel's 1730 Gap Mine survey, indicating that the Gap mining district encompassed a larger area, and that Thomas Shute's bequest included both his 100-acre freehold purchased of William Allen and his undivided one-sixth of the 250-acre partnership surveyed for James Steel in 1730.

24. Partition of George McCall estate, 24 Nov. 1742, Philadelphia County Orphans Court Record Book, 3:15–20, HSP. Shute's tract is shown on p. 17.

25. *Pennsylvania Gazette,* 14 May 1752, 3; entries dated 5 June 1737, 10 Jan. 1738, Samuel Powel, Jr., Daybook, 1735–1739, Winterthur. Gillingham, ed., "Bridge over Dock Street," 266, includes Thomas Shute accounts for loads of stone not located in Powel's Daybook.

26. Thomas Shute's eldest son, William, sold stones as early as 1725 and as late as 1755. Account dated 5 Sept. 1725 in William Shute bill to Richard Hill estate, Logan Papers, 1664–1871, 18:98, HSP; *William Shute v. William Parsons's executor,* George M. Conarroe Papers, 1:34, HSP. Son Jacob received credit for two loads of stones in May 1739. Solomon Fussell Account Book, 84, LOC. The last Shute to operate the home place quarries, son Joseph, set a local artisan "To Mending 5 Stone Gads," or quarrying tools, on 12 June 1756 and to "Sharpning 5 Gads & mending the heads" one week later. Shute bought a new gad on 24 July 1756. Stephen Paschall Account Book, 1735–1756, Paschall Family Papers, HSP.

27. One piece Shute sent to Barbados was described as a "Small Side board" valued at two pounds, fifteen shillings, the other as an oval sideboard worth four pounds. Entry dated 27 Dec. 1729, New Bristol Hope Account Book, 1729–1732, 43, Chalkley Family Papers, HSP. For the tombstone, see entry dated 10 Dec. 1730, ibid. For an early advertisement of country marble produced in the colony, see *Pennsylvania Gazette,* 21 May 1741, 2.

28. Entries dated 3 Oct. 1734, 2 May 1735, Peter Baynton Journal, Ledger E, 1734–1743, 10, 41, PHMC.

29. For descriptions and analyses of the iron industry's larger business environment, see Bining, *Pennsylvania Iron Manufacture,* 151–62, and Bezís-Selfa, *Forging America,* 16–19, 126–29.

30. William Davis was identified as "William Davis manager" in Warwick Furnace Ledger D, 1748–1749, 183, Potts Mss., HSP. Ironmaker William Branson was charged

for "the Carrage of 3 Tun of pig from Samson Davis" during the period 9 March 1728/9 to 9 Sept. 1729. Coventry Forge Account Book, 1727–1733, 82, Potts Mss., HSP. Ironmaker Thomas Potts, Sr., was debited for a ton of pig iron "sent to Samson Daviss for the use of Mathew Baker." Entry dated 20 Sept. 1740, Mount Pleasant Furnace Ledger, 1740–1744, 29, Potts Mss., HSP. John Hollowell was debited for "4 hund[red-weight] Barr Iron from Sampson Davis's house." Entry dated not later than 5 May 1739, Pine Forge Ledger, 1735–1742, 243, Potts Mss., HSP. Henry Deeringer was credited for "haulling 1 Tunn piggs to Christian Davis." Entry dated 16 Feb. 1743/4, Colebrookdale Ledger, 1740–1750, 25, Potts Mss., HSP. See chapter 3 for William Davis's career.

31. For pig iron, see "Thomas Shute Philadelphia" entries dated 31 Jan. 1742/3 (one ton), 1 Feb. 1742/3 (half a ton), and 12 Aug. 1745 (one ton), Pine Forge Ledger, 1735–1742, 174, Potts Mss., HSP. For Rebecca Shute's marriage to Anthony Nicholas in the Philadelphia Monthly Meeting, see Hinshaw, *Encyclopedia of American Quaker Genealogy*, 2:651.

32. Entry dated 1731, Colebrookdale Ledger C, 1730–1733, 124, Potts Mss., HSP. Rhodes's position at this time is not indicated, but in 1744 he was manager of Poole Forge. Entry dated 18 May 1744, Colebrookdale Furnace Account Book, 1744–1751, 22, Potts Mss., HSP.

33. Entry dated 10 Nov. 1737, Pine Forge Ledger, 1735–1742, 174, Potts Mss., HSP.

34. Pine Forge Ledger, 1732–1740, 178, Potts Mss., HSP.

35. Ibid., 174.

36. For the blank "Contra" side of Shute's ledger entry, see ibid. For comparable examples of iron delivered to partners, see "Thos Potts senior Dr to Barr Iron," entries dated 21 May 1742–1 March 1742/3, and "Dr John Potts to Barr Iron," entry dated 2 May 1743, William Bird Ledger, 1741–1747, 156, 183, Potts Mss., HSP.

37. Wood, *Conestoga Crossroads*, 109–10.

38. Isaac Shute was named as defendant in a series of lawsuits between 1733 and 1737/8 in the Lancaster County Court of Common Pleas. Entries dated 1 May, 7 Aug., 6 Nov. 1733, 5 Feb. 1733/4, 6 Aug. 1734, 5 Aug. 1735, 2 Aug. 1737, Lancaster County Court of Common Pleas, Appearance Dockets, 1731–1732, 1733–1734, 1737–1738, LCHS. In 1748, Thomas Shute bequeathed to Isaac "the one half Moiety or part of my intrest and Property in ye Lancaster Copper Mines." Thomas Shute will, Philadelphia County WB, I:5, HSP.

39. Thomas and Elizabeth Shute to Anthony Morris, 17 June 1738, Philadelphia County DB, H-19:512, PHMC.

40. Figure 12, "Approximate Extent of Settlement by National Groups, 1730," Lemon, *Best Poor Man's Country*, 49.

41. Table 7, "Rates of Population Growth by Decade, Southeastern Pennsylvania," ibid., 23.

42. For land prices, see table 13, "Land Values per Acre, Lancaster County (Mostly from the Lancaster Plain)," ibid., 69. For fertility of the Lancaster Plain, see ibid., 38–40.

43. For William Penn's dismay shortly before his death in 1718, see ibid., 220–21.

44. For an overview of settlement and land issues, see ibid., 42–70. An essential

guide to Pennsylvania's land policy, administration, and records is Munger, *Pennsylvania Land Records;* for particular problems of recordkeeping in the 1730s, see pp. 58–59.

45. "Thomas Shute's [Northern] Lib[erties] Land," [May 1718], Copied Surveys, Book D89, 54; Thomas Shute patent, 10 July 1718, Patent Register, 1701–1728, 39; Thomas Shute patent, 2 Dec. 1742, Patent Book, A11:189; Thomas Shute surveys, 5 March 1733/4, 4 April 1734, Miscellaneous Papers of the Philadelphia Company, 94, all PHMC.

46. Lemon stated that despite delays turning warrants into deeds, "warrants provided certainty of tenure for settlers and so order in the society." *Best Poor Man's Country,* 55. Emigration to Virginia seems to indicate that not all would-be freeholders agreed. For the collapse of proprietary attempts to create orderly dense settlements, see ibid., 41–61. According to Lemon, "Thomas Penn said that 130,000 of 400,000 acres taken up between 1732 and 1740 had not been warranted by the latter date," much less patented. Ibid., 57, citing Thomas Sergeant, *View of the Land Laws of Pennsylvania with Notices of Its Early History and Legislation* (Philadelphia and Pittsburgh: James Kay, Jr., and Brother and John I. Kay, 1838), 137.

47. Ibid., 58.

48. McCleskey, "Rich Land, Poor Prospects," 460–67.

49. For positive aspects of large landholders in western Virginia, see Mitchell, *Commercialism and Frontier,* 80–81. For Frederick County in the lower valley, see Hofstra, "Land, Ethnicity, and Community at the Opequon Settlement." For Augusta County details, see McCleskey, "Rich Land, Poor Prospects" and "Shadow Land."

50. William, Isaac, Jacob, Joseph, and Christian survived their father. Thomas Shute will, Philadelphia County WB, I:5, HSP.

51. A 1742 advertisement describes William Shute's location as "4 miles from Philadelphia." *Pennsylvania Gazette,* 2 Dec. 1742, 3; the site is shown in figure 1. William Shute was about forty-five years old when his father conveyed the land to him.

52. Thomas Shute, Jr., is identified as a tallow chandler in his account with Pine Forge and in his widow's bond to administer his estate. Pine Forge Ledger, 1735–1742, 36, Potts Mss., HSP; Widow Mary Shute's bond, Thomas Shute Estate Administration, 1739, no. 56, PRWA. Isaac Shute performed blacksmith work in 1728 and was identified as a Philadelphia blacksmith after his death in 1749. Isaac Shute's account, Richard Hill estate, Logan Papers, 1664–1871, 18:89, HSP; Joseph Shute's bond, Isaac Shute Estate Administration, 1755, no. 70, PRWA; for his death year, see Hinshaw, *Encyclopedia of American Quaker Genealogy,* 2:420. A Philadelphia grand jury presented Jacob Shute and fifteen other coopers for creating fire hazards on 3 Jan. 1744/5. Franklin, *Papers of Benjamin Franklin,* 3:11–12. Joseph Shute, master and owner, registered the sloop *Dove* in Philadelphia on 22 May 1732. South Carolina Shipping Returns, Dec. 1721–Dec. 1735, 5/509, 116, BNA (hereafter cited as SC Shipping Returns, CO 5/).

53. Entry dated 28 May 1743, Coventry Forge Ledger, 1742–1748, 167, Potts Mss., HSP. Shute's grandson first recorded himself as "William Davis manager" in his own books in 1749, but cash accounts elsewhere make it clear that he was running the financial aspects of Warwick Furnace by 1744. Entry dated 15 Aug. 1749, Warwick Furnace Ledger D, 1748–1749, 183; Colebrookdale Furnace Account Book, 1744–1751, 4–5, both Potts Mss., HSP.

54. In the fall of 1734, Thomas Shute rented a pasture and took from it grass cut by two mowers, each of whom was paid three shillings for one day's work. Entry dated 11 Jan. 1735, Samuel Powel, Jr., Daybook, 1735–1739, Winterthur.

55. John Armitt to Elizabeth Hill, 23 March 1737/8, Colden, *Letters and Papers*, 2:189–90. For a detailed analysis of labor practices during a slightly later period, see Clemens and Simler, "Rural Labor and the Farm Household in Chester County, Pennsylvania."

56. Shute was acting by power of attorney on behalf of his son Joseph. The contract stipulated that the artisan, John Garrigues, would not provide the slave's clothes, which suggests that Thomas Shute retained a measure of responsibility for—and control over—the slave. Entry dated 25 June 1746, "Account of Servants," 32:88.

57. *Pennsylvania Gazette*, 24 July 1755, 3; 2 Dec. 1742, 3.

58. Shute died in possession of an unnamed mulatto girl plus slave men Peter, Samuel, Ned, old Samuel, and John. Thomas Shute will, Philadelphia County WB, I:5, HSP. According to Gary B. Nash, by 1767, "most slaveowners in Philadelphia held only one or two adult slaves." "Slaves and Slaveowners in Colonial Philadelphia," 244.

59. *American Weekly Mercury*, 17–24 Jan. 1720/1, 2.

60. For relevant economic developments in the Shute period, see Lydon, "Philadelphia's Commercial Expansion, 1720–1739," and McCusker and Menard, *Economy of British America*, 51–70, 189–208. For pertinent studies focusing on slightly later periods, see also Egnal, "Changing Structure of Philadelphia's Trade with the British West Indies," and Doerflinger, *Vigorous Spirit of Enterprise*. For the waning pirate threat, see Rediker, "'Under the Banner of King Death.'"

61. Joseph Shute's maritime education is implied by his position as master of the sloop *Dove* in 1732. Every seafaring job in the age of sail required extensive experience and training. Rediker, *Between the Devil and the Deep Blue Sea*, passim, especially 86–96.

62. Entries dated 28 Feb. 1728/9, 28 March 1729, Philadelphia Monthly Meeting (Arch Street) Minutes, 1715–1744, 169, FHL.

63. For Thomas Shute's 1729 shipment of bread via a Peter Baynton vessel, see note 16, above. In the same year, Shute consigned furniture mentioned in note 27, above, to sea captain Thomas Chalkley and requested that Chalkley bring back rum or molasses as a return cargo. Entry dated 27 Dec. 1729, New Bristol Hope Account Book, 1729–1732, 23, Chalkley Family Papers, HSP. Both the consignment and the return order indicate Shute employed no factor in Barbados.

64. Shute owed six shillings, eight pence, for Barbados freight delivered in Philadelphia on 30 May 1730. By comparison, Shute paid seven shillings, six pence, to ship two sideboards to Barbados on the same vessel a few months earlier. Ibid., 43, 57.

65. Peter Baynton Bills of Lading, 1730–1732, PHMC. Arthur L. Jensen assessed the Carolinas as a relatively less attractive market for Philadelphia merchants, but his evidence is drawn chiefly from the second half of the eighteenth century. *Maritime Commerce*, 79–82.

66. Entries dated 26 Feb. 1730/1, 26 March 1731, Philadelphia Monthly Meeting (Arch Street) Minutes, 1715–1744, 197–98, FHL.

67. Entry dated 22 Oct. 1718, Charleston, South Carolina, Monthly Meeting Minutes and Records, 1718–1786, 5, FHL (hereafter cited as Charleston MM Minutes). For Kimberley's occupation, see his will, Charleston WB, 4:24–25, SCDAH.

68. Entry dated 23 Sept. 1731, ibid., 4:28.

69. Salley, ed., *Register of St. Philip's Parish*, 159, 234.

70. The first quotation is from an entry dated 10 Oct 1731; the subsequent entry date is illegible but the context is the next monthly meeting. Charleston MM Minutes, 29.

71. Conveyance Book, I:535, SCDAH. Kimberley confirmed his deed to Anna Shute in his will, drawn 12 Nov. 1736, recorded 2 May 1737, Charleston WB, 4:24–25, SCDAH.

72. Thomas Kimberley, deeds of lease and release to John Witter, Joseph Shute, and Thomas Fleming, 16, 17 Feb. 1731/2, Conveyance Book, I:661–66, SCDAH; entry dated 2 March 1736, Charleston MM Minutes, 31. Thomas Kimberley died on 30 Nov. 1736. Hinshaw, *Encyclopedia of American Quaker Genealogy*, 1:1075.

73. Thomas Elliott was named as a planter and Thomas Fleming and John Witter were named as Charleston merchants in local deeds. Conveyance Book, I:661, DD:275, SCDAH. Elliott, Fleming (who was also identified as a planter), and merchant Othniel Beale served in the Commons House of Assembly. Côté and Williams, eds., *Dictionary of South Carolina Biography*, 1:19, 116. For Shute's later partnership with storekeeper Stephen Beauchamp, see *South Carolina Gazette*, 10 April 1742, 2.

74. According to a Charleston port entry record dated 19 June 1732, Shute registered the *Dove* in Philadelphia on 22 May 1732. The *Dove* was built in the American colonies in 1724 and was registered as a ten-ton vessel. SC Shipping Returns, CO 5/509, 116, BNA.

75. Joseph Shute's leather exports were relatively modest; he was not among the 176 merchants who paid a total of more than one hundred pounds worth of duties on outbound leather. Moore, "Largest Exporters of Deerskins from Charles Town." For the argument that Quaker meetings valued plain dealing above morally dubious profits and supervised merchant behavior toward that end, see Tolles, *Meeting House and Counting House*, 73–79.

2. The Merchant

1. Table D-1, "Periods of Expansion and Contraction in the Economy of Early America, 1701–1838," McCusker, "How Much Is That in Real Money?" 360.

2. Coclanis, *Shadow of a Dream*, 48–110.

3. Shute was named as a Charleston merchant in a deed dated 16 Feb. 1731/2, Conveyance Book, I:661–62, SCDAH.

4. My interpretation dissents from Jacob M. Price's conclusion that management of credit was the premier responsibility of eighteenth-century merchants. "What Did Merchants Do?" 278.

5. The *Dove* departed Charleston on 19 Dec. 1732, per entry of this date in SC Shipping Returns, CO 5/509, BNA. Other movements and cargoes of Shute vessels discussed in this chapter are found in SC Shipping Returns, CO 5/509, 510; Bahamas Shipping Returns, CO 27/12, both BNA. (Pagination of shipping returns often is illegible; vessel movements were recorded chronologically as either entering or departing the port, so the date can be used to locate specific voyages in the absence of legible page numbers.) See also *South Carolina Gazette*, 1734–1737; *Pennsylvania Gazette*, 1739–1748; *American Weekly Mercury* (Philadelphia), 1732–1748.

6. When Shute's *Two Sisters* cleared from New Providence for Charleston on 12 De-

cember 1740, its cargo included 16 tons of braziletto, 3 hundredweight of logwood, 17 hundredweight of lignum vitae, 2,000 pounds of cortex eleuthera, 3,200 feet of madera plank, 3 barrels of lime juice, cotton roping, and 20,000 limes and oranges. Bahamas Shipping Returns, CO 27/12; SC Shipping Returns, CO 5/510, both BNA.

7. Like most customs records, South Carolina's shipping accounts were recorded by quarters beginning on Lady Day (25 March), Midsummer's Day (24 June), Michaelmas (29 September), and Christmas (25 December). On 5 August 1734, the *Dolphin* entered George Town from Charleston to deliver thirty-five barrels of flour and two more of bread, plus fifty-four barrels of corn, one of pork, four of sugar, one of molasses, and four hogsheads (twice a barrel's volume) of rum. SC Shipping Returns, CO 5/509, BNA; see also entry dated 10 August 1734.

8. Conveyance Book, P:49–51, SCDAH. The partnership settled its accounts and dissolved in 1742. *South Carolina Gazette,* 10 April 1742, 2. For an essential introduction to merchant credit in South Carolina, see Menard, "Financing the Lowcountry Export Boom."

9. *South Carolina Gazette,* 16 Dec. 1732, 4; repeated in next two issues. For the *Dove* entry on 4 Dec. 1732 and details of its flour and bread freight, see voyage number three in table 3.

10. For the first advertisement of the new partnership, see *South Carolina Gazette,* 4 Jan. 1734/5, 3. For some of Henning's prior transatlantic voyages, see SC Shipping Returns, CO 5/509, 80, 91, 106, 109, 113, BNA. Just before his partnership with Shute, Henning brought the ship *Success* to Charleston "in 30 days from Calais," shaving at least a couple of weeks off the typical voyage. *South Carolina Gazette,* 26 Oct. 1734, 2. By land Henning claimed membership in the Berkeley County commission of the peace, and he served from 1736 to 1739 as a delegate for the parish of Prince Frederic Winyah in the colonial Commons House of Assembly. Edgar and Bailey, eds., *Biographical Directory of the South Carolina House of Representatives,* s.v. "Thomas Henning"; Easterby, ed., *Journal of the Commons House of Assembly, 1736–1739,* 729.

11. *South Carolina Gazette,* 11 Oct. 1735, 3; repeated 18 Oct. 1735, 4.

12. Ibid., 8 Nov. 1735, 2; repeated 15 Nov. 1735, 3; 22 Nov. 1735, 4.

13. Ibid., 9 Oct. 1736, 3.

14. The *Dolphin* cleared for London with a rice cargo of 203 barrels, 30 half barrels, and 14 quarter casks, plus 5.5 tons of braziletto. Entry dated 8 Nov. 1734, SC Shipping Returns, CO 5/509, 137, BNA. On 31 Dec. 1734, the *Dolphin* entered St. Ives, on the far western coast of Cornwall, as bound for London. *Daily Journal* (London), 2 Jan. 1734/5, 1; *South Carolina Gazette,* 3 May 1735, 2.

15. The *Endeavour* cleared from Charleston for London with 339 barrels of rice, 318 barrels of pitch, and 6.25 tons of logwood, a dye wood. Entry dated 25 Sept. 1736, SC Shipping Returns, CO 5/510, BNA. Shute's exports equaled 5.4 percent of rice, 10.1 percent of pitch, and 12.2 percent of logwood shipped from Charleston for the quarter from 24 June to 29 Sept 1736. For the snow's return from London, see *South Carolina Gazette,* 30 April 1737, 2. The *Endeavour* cleared on its second European voyage from George Town/Winyah on 21 May 1737. SC Shipping Returns, CO 5/510, BNA.

16. The *Anna* cleared from Charleston for Cowes with 325 barrels of rice, an illegible quantity of logwood and braziletto, and 2 tons of sassafras. Entry dated 30 Dec. 1738,

ibid. The *Anna*'s return to Charleston from Bilbao and her prompt departure for Cowes both were reported in the *South Carolina Gazette,* 25 Aug. 1739, 2. For her subsequent entry from the Netherlands, see ibid., 31 May 1740, 2.

17. For example, Philadelphia merchant Joseph Shippen netted only £30:1:1 (Pennsylvania currency) for a voyage to London and back. Entry dated 12 Feb. 1749/50, Joseph Shippen Waste Book, 1749–1750, APS.

18. *South Carolina Gazette,* 13 Oct. 1739, 2; 31 May 1740, 2.

19. For Shute's and Kimberley's agreement "to erect some buildings" on the six-acre tract dated 19 Nov. 1731, see Conveyance Book, I:535, SCDAH. Shute advertised for rental "a very good Dwelling-House, with two Summer Houses, two Cellars under them, a Kitchen, Store House, large Garden, other Conveniences" in the *South Carolina Gazette,* 16 June 1733, 4; his notice repeated in the next two issues. As of early 1736, future assemblyman David Hext resided on the property. Ibid., 28 Feb. 1735/6, 3. Although Shute's location during this period is uncertain, his commercial affairs grew sufficiently complex and profitable for him to employ his first known storekeeper, George Head. Ibid., 22 June 1734, 4. Head's subordinate status is confirmed by his absence from newspaper advertisements and from accounts of import and export duties collected. Calhoun et al., "Geographic Spread of Charleston's Mercantile Community"; Journal A, 1735–1748, Records of the Public Treasurer of South Carolina, 1725–1776, SCDAH.

20. Shute's occupancy of the Elliott Street store is first mentioned in the *South Carolina Gazette,* 31 May 1735, 3. In newspaper advertisements from 1732 to 1735, 9.4 percent of Charleston's business community listed an Elliot Street address. Waterfront addresses (50.1%) and Broad Street locations (20.0%) were more common. Calhoun et al., "Geographic Spread of Charleston's Mercantile Community," 188.

21. *South Carolina Gazette,* 29 June 1747, 3.

22. Conveyance Book, DD:275–81, SCDAH; *South Carolina Gazette,* 3 Sept. 1737, 3.

23. The first advertisement for "Henning & Shute at their Store, in Elliot's Street" appeared ten months after the partnership's initial announcement. Ibid., 4 Jan. 1734/5, 3; 8 Nov. 1735, 2.

24. The partnership of Henning and Shute paid import duties on eleven cargoes in 1735 and 1736, of which seven payments were for fifty pounds South Carolina money or more. From 1737 through 1753, Shute paid duties on fifty-eight more cargoes; in only a single instance did he pay more than fifty pounds, inflation adjusted. Journal A, 1735–1748, Journal B, 1748–1765, Records of the Public Treasurer of South Carolina, 1725–1776, SCDAH.

25. For the conclusion of the Henning and Shute partnership, see *South Carolina Gazette,* 5 March 1736/7, 3. For storekeeper Francis Richardson's advertisements to sell goods and book freight or passages "at the House of Jos: Shute Merchant in Elliot street," see ibid., 1 Dec. 1737, 3 (repeated in the two subsequent issues); 6 April 1738, 3; 11 May 1738, 2 (repeated three times); and 21 Sept. 1738, 3 (repeated twice). The latter offered goods imported from Philadelphia in Joseph Shute's brigantine *Anna.*

26. Deeds of lease and release, 4, 5 May 1748, Conveyance Book, DD:275–81, SCDAH. The Elliott property included houses described as "Brick Tenements."

27. SC Shipping Returns, CO 5/509, 137, BNA.

28. The earliest mention of Shute's Wharf is in February 1741/2; the structure reached

water deep enough for full-rigged ships to moor, at least at high tide. *South Carolina Gazette*, 13 Feb. 1741/2, 2; 18 Dec. 1749, 2. Wharfage rates depended on duration and varied from port to port as well as from one wharf to another, but for purposes of estimation, merchant Peter Baynton recorded wharfage of eight shillings Pennsylvania currency per week for his brigantine *Mary* in Philadelphia. Entry dated 5 March 1730/1, Peter Baynton Ledger C, PHMC. Baynton's sloop *St. Augustine* paid a combined wharfage and porterage bill of three pounds (Pennsylvania) during a 1742 voyage to Charleston. Peter Baynton Journal, Ledger E, loose single page at p. 168 of microfilm, PHMC. In Philadelphia, William Fishbourn received £3:5:4 for mooring the ship *John & Anna*. John Reynell Daybook, 1 July 1731–19 Dec. 1732, 11, APS.

29. For store values, see *South Carolina Gazette*, 16 May 1743, 1–2. For advertisements by merchants with stores on Shute's Wharf or Bridge, see ibid., 13 Feb. 1741/2 supplement, 2 (repeated twice); 27 Dec. 1742, 3 (repeated once); 7 Feb. 1742/3, 3 (repeated three times); 4 July 1743 supplement, 3; 10 Oct. 1743, 2 (repeated once); 10 June 1745, 3; 1 Feb. 1745/6, 2 (repeated twice); 23 Jan. 1748/9, 2; 17 April 1749, 2 (repeated once); 18 Dec. 1749, 2 (repeated twice). Sailmaker Jonn Irons likewise rented a workshop on Shute's Bridge. Ibid., 7 Dec. 1748, 3.

30. Plat dated 29 June 1734, South Carolina Plat Book, 3:62, SCDAH; plat dated 23 Dec. 1735, ibid., 83; grant dated 21 May 1735, Colonial Land Grants (Copy Series), 1:448, SCDAH; grant dated 22 May 1736, ibid., 2:302.

31. Conveyance Book, V:87–90, SCDAH.

32. Ibid., I:535; R:189–93, 319.

33. Ibid., V:364–66; Bates and Leland, eds., *Abstracts of the Records of the Surveyor General*, 3:118.

34. Colonial Land Grants (Copy Series), 43:307, SCDAH.

35. Conveyance Book, CC:437–43, SCDAH. Perhaps as a bonus Shute enjoyed the island's plentiful oysters: in 1780, Sir Henry Clinton remarked that the island's oyster "bed extends above 200 yards." Clinton, "Sir Henry Clinton's 'Journal of the Siege of Charleston, 1780,'" 153. Today the massive ruins of nineteenth-century Fort Pinkney demonstrate the island's load-bearing capacity.

36. *South Carolina Gazette*, 20 Nov. 1740, 2–3; 7 Nov. 1741, 2; Scott, "Sufferers in the Charleston Fire of 1740." See also Mulcahy, "The 'Great Fire' of 1740 and the Politics of Disaster Relief." Reckoned in South Carolina currency, Shute lost £3,977:10:0; he eventually received almost £188 sterling from the relief fund, an amount equal to over £1,300 South Carolina currency. Entry dated 4 June 1742, "Journal of the Proceedings of the Upper House of Assembly," 18 May 1742–18 Feb. 1742/3, 49, Records of the States of the United States, LOC.

37. Calhoun et al., "Geographic Spread of Charleston's Mercantile Community," 186.

38. *South Carolina Gazette*, 18 Feb. 1744/5, 2.

39. Ibid., 10 Feb. 1745/6, 3.

40. Ibid., 11 Dec. 1749, 1.

41. Thayer, *Israel Pemberton*, 19. Daniel Rees, master of the *Globe*, was authorized to spend up to "one thousand heavy p[iece]s of Eight" to retrieve his brigantine. Pemberton to Rees, 7 March 1744/5, Israel Pemberton Letterbook D, APS.

42. Thayer, *Israel Pemberton*, 18.

43. *South Carolina Gazette*, 14 May 1741, 2.

44. Entry dated 31 July 1741, Philadelphia Monthly Meeting (Arch Street) Minutes, 1715–1744, 330, FHL.

45. *South Carolina Gazette*, 27 July 1734, 3. Additional circumstantial evidence of Shute's legal sagacity comes from his complete absence in chancery proceedings. Gregorie, ed., *Records of the Court of Chancery of South Carolina.*

46. Joseph Shute to [James] Steel, 24 May 1734, Pennsylvania Provincial Council Records, HSP. Shute wrote the letter the day before the *Dolphin* departed Charleston for Philadelphia. Entry dated 25 May 1734, SC Shipping Returns, CO 5/509, 131, BNA. Based on his father's request for certification to Barbados in 1729, Joseph Shute would have been no more than twenty-five years old in 1734.

47. Sirmans, "South Carolina Royal Council," 381–85; Jellison, "Antecedents of the South Carolina Currency Acts of 1736 and 1746"; Jellison, "Paper Currency in Colonial South Carolina."

48. *South Carolina Gazette*, 26 April 1739, 2; 22 April 1745, 2; 18 April 1748, 2. Shute typically was listed last or near last of the fire masters, ordinal positions that suggest a lower social status.

49. Warren, ed., *South Carolina Jury Lists, 1718 through 1783*, 109.

50. Easterby, ed., *Journal of the Commons House of Assembly, 1736–1739*, 729–30; *South Carolina Gazette*, 28 Feb. 1735/6, 3.

51. Shute made bond for Seabrook's appearance at the Court of Common Pleas to be held the first Tuesday in July 1744. *Benjamin Dedcott v. Joseph Shute*, Judgment Rolls (CCP), Box 27A, item 100A, SCDAH. For Seabrook's election in 1745, see Easterby, ed., *Journal of the Commons House of Assembly, 1745–1746*, 258.

52. Beale, a merchant immigrant from Massachusetts, won a seat in the South Carolina Commons House of Assembly from 1730–36 and again from 1739–47; he eventually served on the provincial council from 1755 to 1773. Edgar and Bailey, eds., *Biographical Directory of the South Carolina House of Representatives*, s.v. "Othniel Beale"; Sirmans, "South Carolina Royal Council," 392.

53. Henry Laurens to Thomas Shute the younger, "Passenger in the Sloop *Susannah & Francis*, Thos. Beezely master, for Phila.," 26 Sept. 1747, Laurens, *Papers of Henry Laurens*, 1:58–59. Joseph Shute paid export duties of sixteen pounds, eighteen shillings, on sole leather sent to Philadelphia on this voyage. Journal A, 1735–1748, 352, Records of the Public Treasurer of South Carolina, 1725–1776, SCDAH. After the younger Thomas Shute reached Philadelphia, he advertised the sole leather as "JUST imported from South Carolina, in the sloop Susannah and Frances, Thomas Beazely Commander," and requested that prospective passengers for the return trip consult him or the sloop's master. He did not advertise Laurens's saddlery ware, suggesting that he immediately found a buyer for those goods. *Pennsylvania Gazette*, 5 Nov. 1747, 2.

54. For clearance from Philadelphia, see ibid., 11 March 1735/6, 4. For the announcement of the loss, see *South Carolina Gazette*, 15 May 1736, 2.

55. Shute and partners Anthony Morris of Philadelphia and Joseph Wragg of Charleston registered the new fifty-ton snow at Philadelphia on 4 July 1736. "Ship Registers for the Port of Philadelphia," 381.

56. Probably *Anna* was lost to a late-season hurricane. *Anna* cleared Kingston, Ja-

maica, for New York on 12 Oct. 1742, conned by master Alexander Tisdale and loaded with cocoa, fourteen hogsheads of sugar, and forty-seven tons of lignum vitae. List of Vessels Cleared Out, 29 Sept.–25 Dec. 1742, Kingston, Jamaica, Shipping Returns, CO 142/15, BNA. *Anna*'s arrival was not reported in the *New York Weekly Journal* from October 1742 to April 1743. Another vessel bound from Jamaica to New York at almost the same time nearly sank in a violent storm described by the master, Alexander Forbes, in a letter dated 31 Dec. 1742 and published in the *American Weekly Mercury,* 1 March 1742/3, 3.

57. From the fall of 1739 through the summer of 1745, Shute imported goods as small portions of much more valuable cargoes on the following vessels: *Prince* (entered 19 Jan. 1739/40), *Two Sisters* (9 Oct. 1740), *Charming Sally* (15 Aug. 1741), *Agnes and Betty* (24 March 1741/2), [unknown] (12 Dec. 1743), *Postillion* (27 Aug. 1744), *Aurora* (28 Jan. 1744/5), *Friendship* (same day), *Mary Anne* (25 Feb. 1744/5), and *Musley Galley* (18 March 1744/5). In only a single instance (the *Prosperity,* entering 17 Dec. 1744 from Surinam) did Shute pay duties for an entire cargo during this period. Journal A, 1735–1748, Records of the Public Treasurer of South Carolina, 1725–1776, SCDAH.

58. The *Industry* appears in no newspaper list of entries or clearances before the capture, so this may have been its first voyage after construction. *South Carolina Gazette,* 19 Aug. 1745, 2. The date of capture is given as 6 Aug. 1745 in ibid., 24 Oct. 1745, 2. The ten-ton *Industry,* master Thomas L. Brumley, was built in South Carolina in 1744; Brumley and Shute were partners in the vessel. Entry dated 17 July 1745, South Carolina Secretary of State, Ship Registers, 1734–1783, 1:329, SCDAH. A Spanish vessel under flag of truce repatriated Brumley and fifty-one other English prisoners taken from eight vessels several months later. *South Carolina Gazette,* 24 Oct. 1745, 2.

59. Entry dated 1 July 1746, South Carolina Secretary of State, Ship Registers, 1:3, SCDAH; *South Carolina Gazette,* 28 July 1746, 2.

60. Ibid., 15 Dec. 1746, 2.

61. Entries dated 13 Feb. 1746/7, 24 April 1747, 30 June 1747, Bahamas Shipping Returns, CO 27/12, BNA; *South Carolina Gazette,* 12 Jan. 1746/7, 3; 4 May 1747, 3; 20 July 1747, 3; 23 Nov. 1747, 3; 11 Jan. 1747/8, 2; 1 June 1748, 2; 8 June 1748, 2.

62. The *Victory*'s master and crew rowed ashore when Spanish boarders approached and traveled overland to Philadelphia, arriving on 17 June. *Pennsylvania Journal,* 23 June 1748, 2–3.

63. Merchants initially welcomed the war but collectively suffered more than they benefited. Stumpf, "Implications of King George's War."

64. Judgment Rolls (CCP), Box 29A, items 4A, 14A, SCDAH. Crokatt served on the South Carolina Council from 1738 to 1741. Sirmans, "South Carolina Royal Council," 392. For a social analysis of indebtedness during this period, see Woods, "Culture of Credit in Colonial Charleston."

65. Easterby, ed., *Journal of the Commons House of Assembly, 1745–1746,* 289, 316, 353–54, 527. Stumpf describes details of the South Carolina problem in "Implications of King George's War," 167–68. For the same problem in Pennsylvania during the next war, see Johnson, "Fair Traders and Smugglers in Philadelphia, 1754–1763."

66. In the governor's absence, the colonial lieutenant governor received one third of the forfeited goods. See, for example, South Carolina Court of Vice Admiralty Records, vol. C, part 2, 20–29, SCDAH.

67. Results of the 20 March 1744/5 grand jury were reported in the *South Carolina Gazette,* 15 April 1745, 1.

68. Ibid., 18 May 1745, 3; 25 May 1745, 2.

69. In South Carolina, smuggling apparently was relatively rare and generally limited to abuses of the flag-of-truce system. Stumpf, "Implications of King George's War," 167–68.

70. *South Carolina Gazette,* 4 April 1748, 2.

71. Shute's original petition of 14 June 1748 was read by the council two days later. Entry dated 16 June 1748, "Journal of the Proceedings of the Upper House of Assembly," Records of the States of the United States, LOC; Easterby and Green, eds., *Journal of the Commons House of Assembly, 1748,* 323–24. The contraband was packed in twenty-four tierces, each estimated to hold forty-three and one-third gallons.

72. Deeds of lease and release, 7, 8 June 1748, Conveyance Book, DD:281–87, SCDAH.

73. On 25 Feb. 1747/8, Shute filed a claim for £133:10:6, "being for Sundries supplied the Public for the Use of Indians, the Galley, and the two Sloops that were hired to guard the Coast." When the annual appropriations act finally passed, Shute received £32:10:0. Easterby and Green, eds., *Journal of the Commons House of Assembly, 1748,* 68, 384. On 12 July 1748, Shute gave Morton and Samuel Brailsford his note of hand for £340 plus interest payable in one month. Judgment Rolls (CCP), Box 32A, item 62A, SCDAH.

74. Partners Thomas Shute the younger and Frederick Merkley posted their first advertisement for "their store on the Bay lately possessed by Joseph Shute" in early December. *South Carolina Gazette,* 3 Dec. 1748, 3 (repeated twice).

75. For dissolution of the Shute and Merkley partnership and young Thomas Shute's return to Pennsylvania, see ibid., 4 Sept. 1749, 3. Shute paid duties for cargoes on *Virgin* (entered Charleston from New Providence, 19 Jan. 1748/9) and *Happy-Go-Lucky* (from New York, 24 March 1748/9). Journal B, 1748–1765, Records of the Public Treasurer of South Carolina, 1725–1776, SCDAH.

76. Thomas Shute will, Philadelphia County WB, I:5, HSP.

77. *South Carolina Gazette,* 19 Dec. 1748, 2–3.

78. Anna Shute died on 26 June 1749. Hinshaw, *Encyclopedia of American Quaker Genealogy,* 1:1075; *South Carolina Gazette,* 24 July 1749, 3.

79. Ibid.

80. Ibid. As a creditor, Shute had already been on the opposite end of this process: his debt suit against shipwright John Jelsey forced exactly the same process in early 1748. Ibid., 1 Nov. 1748, 3.

81. Alternatively, creditors could decline to accept the partial settlement and sue independently for the entire debt and damages. Governor James Glen signed the bill on 25 May 1745. "An Additional and Explanatory Act to an Act of the General Assembly of This Province Entitled 'An Act for the More Effectual Relief of Insolvent Debtors,'" Cooper and McCord, eds., *Statutes at Large of South Carolina,* 3:662–65.

82. *South Carolina Gazette,* 1 July 1745–24 July 1749. Before Shute's financial failure, one merchant in Beaufort declared insolvency, and a second bankrupt debtor was identified as a femme sole trader. Subsequently, a broad sample of colonial-era Court of Common Pleas litigation indicates that merchants appeared as defendants in over 11 percent of all debt litigation. Woods, "Culture of Credit in Colonial Charleston," 361.

83. *South Carolina Gazette,* 31 July 1749, 3; repeated the following week. No other bankruptcy advertised in the *South Carolina Gazette* from 1745 to this date includes a comparable proposition.

84. Thomas Shute the younger received a license to marry Philadelphian Rebecca Coates on 1 May 1749. "Pennsylvania Marriage Licenses," 478. In August, he arranged freight and passage for a sloop at Philadelphia's Market Street Wharf, and by early September, his partner, Frederick Merkley, acknowledged that "The Copartnership of Merckley and Shute is now broke up, by reason of Thomas Shute being settled in Philadelphia." *Pennsylvania Gazette,* 31 Aug. 1749, 2; *South Carolina Gazette,* 4 Sept. 1749, 3.

85. Ibid., 23 April 1750, 3; repeated with minor variations on 7, 14, 21 May, and 4 June 1750.

86. Ibid., 11 June 1750, 3, and inserted postscript page, 2; both advertisements repeated the following week.

87. The earliest documented reference to Shute's Folly was the provost marshal's advertisement for the sale at public auction of "*Shute's Delight* (otherwise called *Shute's Folly*) . . . seized on execution." Ibid., 11 June 1750, 3.

88. Coldham, ed., *American Wills Proved in London, 1611–1775,* 196. Historian Michael Woods finds that in a comparable case a few years later, Shute's former peer, merchant Dougal Campbell, not only retained his community standing after bankruptcy but eventually recovered his fortunes. "Culture of Credit in Colonial Charleston," 369–72. Shute's experience demonstrates that while such recoveries were possible, the culture of credit in Charleston did not automatically guarantee security.

89. For Shute's summer departure from Charleston, see his description as "being now in Town" at Philadelphia on 30 Aug. 1751. Philadelphia Monthly Meeting (Arch Street) Minutes, 1745–1755, 190, FHL. Shute's final defense by attorney in South Carolina was in October 1760; he last appeared by attorney as plaintiff three months later. Judgment Rolls (CCP), Box 51A, item 212A; Box 53A, item 155A, SCDAH.

90. Thomas Shute will, Philadelphia County WB, I:5, HSP.

91. *Pennsylvania Gazette,* 14 May 1752, 3.

92. Only part of Thomas Shute's estate accounts survive; that portion includes an entry for £120:8:11 due the Philadelphia County sheriff for "several executions in his hands." "Settlement on the Estate of Thomas Shute, 1787," Philadelphia County WB, I:5, HSP.

93. Ibid., entries dated 12 Nov. 1754.

94. Edward Warner, James Fox, and William Davis, executors of Thomas Shute, grantors to Abel James, grantee, deed, 2 Nov. 1754, Philadelphia County DB, H-10:399–402, PMHC.

95. Thomas Shute's home tract is described in the *Pennsylvania Gazette,* 14 May 1752, 3. For modern photographs of neighboring stylish houses Belmont (built 1742–45), Woodford (1756), and Mount Pleasant (1763), see Moss, *Historic Houses of Philadelphia,* 62–65. Another of Shute's contemporaries developed a country house about three miles from the Shute home. Reinberger and McLean, "Isaac Norris's Fairhill."

96. Abel James and wife Rebecca to Joseph Shute, 29 June 1756, Philadelphia County DB, H-10:396–99, PMHC.

97. "Settlement on the Estate of Thomas Shute, 1787," Philadelphia County WB, I:5,

HSP. Of this second £1,000, over £419 came back immediately to Joseph Shute: £150 for his own legacy; £100 for his brother Isaac's legacy, which now fell to Joseph as administrator of Isaac's estate; £100 loaned by him to his brother Jacob on his father's order; £10 for a legacy to his minor son John; £5 for a legacy paid to one of Thomas Shute's granddaughters; £50 bequeathed to William Davis but assigned by him to Joseph Shute; and £4:7:0 in Thomas Shute's debts previously paid by Joseph Shute.

98. Entries dated 19, 26 June; 2, 12, 22 July; 3, 14 Aug. 1756, Stephen Paschall Account Book, 1735–1756, Paschall Family Papers, HSP.

99. Joseph Shute to Joseph Galloway, mortgage, 12 July 1756, Philadelphia County Mortgage Book, X2:902–3, PCA.

100. Joseph Shute to Joseph Galloway, mortgage, 24 Nov. 1757, ibid., X3:416–18.

101. *Pennsylvania Gazette*, 24 May 1759, 3; 15 May 1760, 3; Samuel Morris to Benjamin Mifflin, 17 Feb. 1760, Philadelphia County Sheriffs DB, A1:274–75, PCA; Morris to Joshua Howell, ibid., A1:277; Morris to Joseph Galloway, ibid., A1:282.

102. On 13 Nov. 1759, Shute won a lawsuit in the South Carolina Court of Common Pleas to recover a sixteen-year-old debt of £88:8:9 plus damages of £61:14:9. *Joseph Shute v. Stephen Dubose*, Judgment Rolls (CCP), Box 47B, item 37A, SCDAH. He sold two tracts of land in November and December for a total of £850. Shute to Jonathan Witter, 12 Nov. 1759, Conveyance Book, WW:35–40, SCDAH; Shute to Thomas Wright, 29 Dec. 1759, ibid., WW:238–40.

103. Ibid., PP:309–14.

104. Charleston MM Minutes, 24, 31, 36.

105. South Carolina Miscellaneous Records, HH:413–14, SCDAH.

106. Accounts dated 14 Oct., 14 Dec. 1748, *Alexander McCauley v. Joseph Shute*, Judgment Rolls (CCP), Box 32B, item 18A, SCDAH. For son John Shute's 12 April 1739 birthday, see Hinshaw, *Encyclopedia of American Quaker Genealogy*, 1:1075.

107. Salley, *Register of St. Philip's Parish*, 149. Elizabeth Shute's new husband, John Bringhurst, Jr., also was a Quaker, so the couple probably married either against a parent's wishes or to conceal Elizabeth's pregnancy from the Quaker women required to discuss her fitness for marriage. Hinshaw, *Encyclopedia of American Quaker Genealogy*, 2:340, 472.

108. For the ban on smuggling, see Thayer, *Israel Pemberton*, 14. For Shute's second marriage, see Hinshaw, *Encyclopedia of American Quaker Genealogy*, 1:1076.

109. Inventory in Isaac Shute Estate Administration, 1755, no. 70, PRWA. The month of January is named for pagan deity Janus; Quakers referred to it instead as the eleventh month.

110. The committee consisted of Anthony Morris (a former business partner of Joseph Shute), Israel Pemberton, John Kinsey, and John Bringhurst (the future father-in-law of Joseph Shute's daughter Elizabeth). Entry dated 25 Nov. 1748, Philadelphia Monthly Meeting (Arch Street) Minutes, 1745–1755, 70, FHL. For Morris's 1736 partnership with Joseph Shute in the snow *Endeavour*, see table 8. "Journal of the Proceedings of His Majesty's Honourable Council," Records of the States of the United States, LOC; James Glen Papers, 1738–1777, South Caroliniana Library.

111. Entry dated 25 Nov. 1748, Philadelphia Monthly Meeting (Arch Street) Minutes, 1745–1755, 70, FHL.

112. Entry dated 30 Aug. 1751, ibid., 190.

113. For the report of the committee's 1751 success, see ibid., 194; for the document itself (which only reached Charleston in August 1754), see Charleston MM Minutes, 42–43.

114. Conveyance Book, PP:309–14, SCDAH. When he signed over the tract to the new trustees, Shute also delivered the lot's original patent, its annexed plat, and the deeds of lease and release appointing Joseph Shute as one of the Quaker trustees. Charleston MM Minutes, 44.

115. Ibid., 41, 45. Shute's creditors could not claim the meetinghouse tract because title to the property was held by a set of trustees, of whom Shute was only one.

116. Ibid., 40. For Shute's Philadelphia residence and implicit comfort level, see *Pennsylvania Gazette*, 7 June 1753, 2. In this source, Shute invited gentlemen seeking information about South Carolina land investments to "apply to the subscriber at the house of Rebecca Steel," implying that gentlemen investors would find their surroundings reassuringly appropriate and conducive to an investment with Shute. For his relationship to Steel, see his reference to her father James as uncle; see also Shute's half-brother William's marriage to James and Rebecca Steel's daughter Elizabeth, cited above. Rebecca Steel was named as a Philadelphia shopkeeper as late as 1769, per Philadelphia County DB, EF-10:9, PMHC.

117. Entry dated 29 Oct. 1755, Philadelphia Monthly Meeting (Arch Street) Minutes, 1745–1755, 340, FHL.

118. Entries dated 29 Oct., 3 Dec. 1755, ibid., 340, 341; entries dated 31 Dec. 1755, 28 Jan., 26 Feb. 1756, Philadelphia Monthly Meeting (Arch Street) Minutes, 1751–1756, 188, 191, 195, FHL.

119. Entries dated 27 April, 30 June, 27 Oct. 1756, ibid., 206, 221, 242. No further appeal was recorded in the Philadelphia Yearly Meeting Minutes, 1747–1779, FHL.

120. *South Carolina Gazette*, 8 Nov. 1735, 2; entry dated 16 Dec. 1735, List of Vessels Entered Inward, SC Shipping Returns, CO 5/510, BNA.

121. *Anna* carried no guns in 1738, the year she was built. List of Vessels Entered In, 25 June–29 Sept. 1738, SC Shipping Returns, CO 5/510, BNA. When Shute had her re-registered in Jamaica on 9 Nov. 1741, the sole change in *Anna*'s description was her armament. List of Vessels Cleared Out, 29 Sept.–25 Dec. 1742, Kingston, Jamaica, Shipping Returns, CO 142/15, BNA.

122. Compared to his peers, Shute ranked as only a minor importer of slaves into colonial Charleston: between 1735 and 1774, 209 Charlestonians paid more total duties for slaves imported than he did. Higgins, "Charles Town Merchants and Factors Dealing in the External Negro Trade, 1735–1775."

123. Shute's location is uncertain in 1761. His Charleston attorney filed suit in the Court of Common Pleas against an old debtor's estate on 20 Jan. 1761. *Joseph Shute v. William Lewis executors,* Judgment Rolls (CCP), Box 53A, item 155A, SCDAH. Shute sued by attorney and so could have been elsewhere when the suit was initiated in Charleston.

3. THE SKINNER

1. William Davis's birth was not recorded in the Abington Monthly Minutes. Given the routine approval of his parents' marriage by the male and female leadership of Arch Street Monthly Meeting, it seems likely he was born after their 1717 marriage.

2. Entries dated 23 Sept.–26 Dec. 1736, Pine Forge Ledger, 1732–1740, 105; entries dated 3 Oct. 1738–6 Aug. 1739, Coventry Forge Ledger F, 1736–1741, 165, 277, both Potts Mss., HSP.

3. Entries dated 28 July, 6 Aug. 1739, William Davis account, Coventry Forge Ledger F, 1736–1741, 165, Potts Mss., HSP; entry dated 5 July 1741, Bartholomew Penrose account, Mount Pleasant Furnace Ledger, 1737–1739, 75, Potts Mss., HSP; entry dated 15 July 1741, Thomas Potts, Sr., account, ibid., 57.

4. Davis was identified as subclerk at Warwick Furnace in Coventry Forge records beginning on 28 May 1743 and continuing through 9 Sept. 1745. Coventry Forge Ledger, 1742–1748, 167, Potts Mss., HSP. He was identified explicitly as manager in the records of Warwick Furnace on 9 Oct. 1749. Warwick Furnace Ledger D, 1748–1749, 183, Potts Mss., HSP.

5. In 1745, for example, ironmaster John Potts recorded paying a total of £99:5:7 in cash to William Davis on fifteen occasions. Warwick Company debit accounts, Warwick Furnace Ledger, 1744–1751, 4, Potts Mss., HSP.

6. Warwick Furnace Ledger C, 1745–1748, 24, 54, 65, 84, 99, 117, Potts Mss., HSP. Davis's cash debit account in this source opens with a £278:11:3 balance carried forward from the previous ledger on 23 May 1745; when Davis and his employers examined this account on 12 May 1746, the debit balance was £436:19:11, reflecting the £158:8:8 Davis paid over the period. Davis's cash contra account opens with £289:2:11 brought forward on 23 May 1745; when examined on 15 April 1746, the contra balance was £427:10:5, indicating Davis received £137:7:6 over the period. Because he had expended £9:9:6 more than his employers had compensated, Davis carried that amount forward to his personal account with Grace and Potts as a credit to him.

7. For Philadelphia and Lancaster County, see William Davis accounts, entries dated 8, 15, 22 June 1745, Warwick Furnace Account Book, Ledger C, 1745–1748, 24, Potts Mss., HSP. For Chester County, see William Davis, manager, accounts, entry dated 15 Aug. 1749, Warwick Furnace Ledger D, 1748–1749, 183, Potts Mss., HSP.

8. Entry dated 3 May 1746, William Davis personal account, Warwick Furnace Account Book, Ledger C, 1745–1748, 44, Potts Mss., HSP. For characterization of salary, compare to the Middle Octorara congregation's subscription of over seventy-seven pounds for support of Rev. Alexander Craighead in 1735. Entry dated 4 April 1735, Donegal Presbytery Minutes, 1:58, UPS.

9. William Davis accounts, entry dated 3 Nov. 1744, Mount Pleasant Furnace Ledger, 1740–1744, 231, Potts Mss., HSP.

10. Edward Warner, James Fox, and William Davis, executors of Thomas Shute, grantors, to Abel James, grantee, deed, 2 Nov. 1754, Philadelphia County DB, H-10:399–402, PHMC.

11. The last dated entry for "William Davis manager" is 9 Oct. 1749, Warwick Furnace Ledger D, 1748–1749, 183, Potts Mss., HSP; this account is noted as carried forward to folio 229, which has been cut from the ledger. The last entry for Davis's personal account with Warwick Furnace is dated 24 Jan. 1749/50. Warwick Furnace Account Book, Ledger C, 1745–1748, 203, Potts Mss., HSP. Davis was employed on a year-to-year contract beginning on 3 May. Entry dated 3 May 1746, ibid., 44.

12. For details of Joseph Shute's activities in Philadelphia in the 1750s, see chapter

2. For Tarr's statement to the Moravians and payment to Davis, see the introduction. Davis was identified as "William Davis of Lancaster County yeoman" in a complaint dated 2 April 1752, *Isaac Davis v. William Davis,* Lancaster County Court of Common Pleas, Narrative Files, Feb. 1752, case no. 190, LCHS. Two land deeds identify Davis as a resident of Lancaster Borough in 1754 and 1755. Edward Warner, James Fox, "and William Davis of the Borough of Lancaster in the County of Lancaster," executors of Thomas Shute, grantors, to Abel James, grantee, deed, 2 Nov. 1754, Philadelphia County DB, H-10:399–402; William Davis, grantor, to Benjamin Koster, grantee, deed, 6 April 1755, Lancaster County DB, II:652–54, both PHMC. Davis acknowledged the latter deed before Lancaster County magistrate William Jevon on the same day as the date of the deed.

13. For advertisement of a town lot the sheriff previously offered unsuccessfully at public vendue, see *Pennsylvania Gazette,* 7 Nov. 1751, 2. For advertisement of Shute's two-hundred-acre home place, see ibid., 14 May 1752, 3. For repeated advertisements of twelve acres, see ibid., 22 Jan. 1756, 3; 29 April 1756, 3.

14. Ibid., 15 July 1756, 3.

15. Entries dated 3 Dec. 1757–26 April 1760, Pine Forge Receipt Book, 1752–1760, Potts Mss., HSP. Numerous carting entries throughout ironworks ledgers indicate that a standard wagon load for bar and pig iron was one ton.

16. *Pennsylvania Gazette,* 31 July 1760, 1.

17. The distinctive letter D in Davis's signature on this agreement matches the 1757–60 Davis signatures in the Pine Forge Receipt Book, 1752–1760, Potts Mss., HSP. William Preston of Augusta County and William Davis of Philadelphia City, memorandum of agreement, 19 Aug. 1760, William and John Preston Papers, Perkins Library.

18. Ibid.; John Hunter and James Moore appraisal, 23 Sept. 1760, William and John Preston Papers, Perkins Library.

19. Alden, *John Stuart and the Southern Colonial Frontier;* Corkran, *The Cherokee Frontier;* Hatley, *Dividing Paths;* Oliphant, *Peace and War on the Anglo-Cherokee Frontier.*

20. "An Act . . . for the Relief of the Garrison of Fort Loudon," Hening, ed., *Statutes,* 7:358.

21. For example, see the service of "Colo William Prestons wagan & James Robinson Driver" to support Colonel Byrd in the New River Valley during the summer of 1760. Alexander Sayers to James Robinson, 30 Aug. 1760, Draper Mss., 2QQ 30. By the end of the war the following year, the most distant post (Great Island) had a store of 15,000-weight of flour, or 8.4 modern short tons. Another 3.5 short tons of flour were at Stalnaker's on the upper Holston River, and 10 more tons were positioned at the lead mines on New River. The same posts also stocked beef in the quantity of 30 hundredweight, 54 hundredweight, and 3 hundredweight, respectively. Adam Stephen to Francis Fauquier, Returns of Supplies, ca. Dec. 1761, Fauquier, *Official Papers of Francis Fauquier,* 2:653. For liquor, see Fauquier's report that volunteers fortified Great Island in exchange for a gill (4 fluid ounces) of rum a day. Fauquier to Jeffrey Amherst, 11 Dec. 1761, ibid., 2:614. For the bullock drovers, see Adam Hoops to Henry Bouquet, 20 July 1761, Bouquet, *Papers of Henry Bouquet,* 5:641. Regarding profiteering, Fauquier commented as early as 24 June 1760 that Augusta County residents "have long enjoyed the Sweets" of militia postings on the frontier. Fauquier, *Official Papers of Francis Fauquier,* 1:382.

22. William Davis to Fields the wagoner, 20 June 1761, Walker Papers, LOC. By "Gears," Davis meant harness. Davis's signature matches his agreement with William Preston and his Pine Forge receipts noted above. John Paxton resided near the southern edge of Borden's Grant. Augusta DB, 2:849, 10 July 1750.

23. For Christian's service as a commissary to the Byrd expedition, see Kneebone et al., eds., *Dictionary of Virginia Biography*, s.v. "Israel Christian."

24. For Fauquier's opinion that "The Money granted [for the expedition] last Year was entirely thrown away, and things have not a much better prospect" this year, see Fauquier to Jeffery Amherst, 15 Aug. 1761, Fauquier, *Official Papers of Francis Fauquier*, 2:558. For Cherokee negotiations, see Alden, *John Stuart and the Southern Colonial Frontier*, 126–32. For tithables, see Augusta OB, 6:429, 19 Nov. 1760; Augusta Parish VB, 351, 20 Nov. 1761. No systematic census was created for Augusta County in the colonial period, but expansion and contraction of the population can be discerned in the annual tally of tithables, as taxable persons were called. For purposes of capitation (taxes on a per capita basis), Virginia law as of 1705 defined tithables as "all male persons, of the age of sixteen years, and upwards, and all negro, mulatto, and Indian women of the age of sixteen years, and upwards, not being free." Hening, ed., *Statutes*, 3:258. From 1723 to 1769, free females of color aged sixteen years and older also were tithables. Ibid., 4:133, 8:393. Heads of household owed capitation taxes for each tithable in the household.

25. "An Act for Further Continuing the Regiment in the Service of This Colony," Nov. 1761, Hening, ed., *Statutes*, 7:464. Moravians in North Carolina recorded that "The first week of December was much disturbed by the soldiers returning from Holston's River." *Records of the Moravians in North Carolina*, 1:238.

26. "Division of Horses," 29 Nov. 1761, Preston Memorandum Book, William and John Preston Papers, Perkins Library.

27. James Adams, "Receipt of Wm Preston," 9 April 1761, Preston Family Papers, 1727–1896, VHS; James Adams, "Fragmentary Letter to Wm Preston," 11 Feb. 1762, ibid.

28. For example, two other Augusta County residents of relatively low status helped Preston transact business with Delaware printer James Adams. David Scott paid Adams for blank land deeds on behalf of Preston on 6 April 1763. "Receipt for Wm Preston," ibid. Scott purchased two hundred acres in Borden's Land in 1765 and held no offices in Augusta County through 1769. Augusta DB, 12:100. Yeoman and Roanoke River Valley resident David Cloyd delivered a letter and payment from Preston to Adams in 1766. James Adams to William Preston, 13 Aug. 1766, Preston Family Papers, 1727–1896, VHS. For Cloyd's identity as a yeoman and his emigration from Newcastle County, Delaware, to the James River Valley, see Orange County DB, 10:33, 22 May 1745, LOV. In a 20 Sept. 1754 survey, Cloyd was noted as living in the Roanoke River Valley. Augusta County Surveyor Book, 1:76, LOV. Cloyd served as road overseer in 1755 and constable through the following year but never attained higher office. Augusta OB, 4:439, 5:110.

29. For "four Dollars," see Preston Memorandum Book, William and John Preston Papers, Perkins Library. For the lottery quotations, see *Pennsylvania Gazette*, 10 Dec. 1761, 4. Davis attended Augusta County court on 17 Aug. 1762. Augusta OB, 7:282.

30. Ibid., 1:1, 7:1, 8:113; Augusta County Court Martial Records, 1756–1796, 7, 20, LOV; Draper Mss., 1QQ 137. Per Chalkley, *Chronicles*, 1:324, the *Thomas Bowyer v. Wil-*

liam Cabeen incident occurred on 10 Sept. 1757. For Bowyer's office, see Augusta OB, 3:436, 16 May 1753.

31. Sturtz, "The Ladies and the Lottery"; Breen, "Horses and Gentlemen."

32. Preston paid Davis £84:9:6 "at Different Payments in full of all accounts before this 7th Day of July 1766." William Preston, "Receipt," Preston Family Papers, 1727–1896, VHS; Augusta OB, 8:225. For particular friends, see Terry, "Family Empires," 50–51. Robinson witnessed a power of attorney by Philadelphia County resident William Young on 15 Feb. 1764; the document facilitated Young's sale of four hundred acres of New River Valley land to Davis. As described below, Davis made a profit of almost 100 percent.

33. Davis's trips to Augusta County are calculated based on records of his physical presence there. Sometimes these events were associated with activities that did not necessarily require physical presence; for example, twenty-four days before Davis appeared in court during trip 1, the Augusta County surveyor filed a land entry for William Davis of Philadelphia, per Augusta County Entry Book, 1:49, LOV. For trip 1, see acknowledged deeds of lease and release, 17 Aug. 1762, Augusta OB, 7:282. For trip 2, he stood ready to serve as a witness in *Charles Lewis and David Robinson v. Martha Galbreath* and acknowledged deeds of lease and release, 21 Sept. 1763, ibid., 8:225, 229, 315. For trip 3, he settled accounts with and signed a receipt for William Preston, 7 July 1766, William Preston Receipt, Preston Family Papers, 1727–1896, VHS. For trip 4, possibly two trips, including treatment by Dr. William Fleming, see entries dated 5 April, 14 July 1768, William Fleming Ledger, 26, Special Collections, Leyburn Library. For trip 5, further treatment by Fleming, see entries dated 14, 15, 18 Feb. 1769, ibid. For trip 6, see William Davis deed to William Christian, witnessed by William Fleming, David May, and Stephen Trigg, 4 Oct. 1770, Botetourt County DB, 1:188–89, LOV.

34. William Young, power of attorney to convey land to William Davis, 15 Feb. 1763, Augusta DB, 11:400–401; William Davis, power of attorney and will, 1 March 1764, Philadelphia County WB, P:115, HSP; Cornelius Brown's attorney, deed to William Davis, 17 Nov. 1767, Augusta DB, 14:34.

35. Appraisals of estates of John Peter Salley (Salling), Joseph Long, Nicholas Nutt, and James Buchanan, 26 July 1755, 6 March 1758, 12 Dec. 1756, 22 Sept. 1759, Augusta WB, 2:124, 228, 249, 333. For Indians trading with settlers, see chapter 6.

36. In his essential study of the Valley of Virginia, historical geographer Robert D. Mitchell assessed fur trading overall as "not important in the region" but noted that in the upper valley, "there is ample evidence that small-scale hunting and trapping was commercially important." Mitchell thought commercial deer hunting in the valley insignificant but I disagree. Augusta County settlers waged an ongoing war against wolves that by Mitchell's tally claimed between 100 and 250 wolves annually between 1750 and 1769. *Commercialism and Frontier*, 134–35. Vigorous destruction of predators and creation of new edge-forest habitat would have encouraged explosive deer herd growth. Ironically, by eradicating wolves, farmers created conditions that helped draw Indian hunters to white settlement areas.

37. Entry dated 7 March 1759, *JHB, 1758–1761*, 81. Previous Frederick County complaints against peddlers included four separate grievances filed at the 10 Feb. 1752 court of propositions, claims, and grievances. Frederick County OB, 4:101–3, LOV.

38. Entry dated 14 March 1759, *JHB, 1758–1761*, 92.

39. *South Carolina Gazette*, 11 Dec. 1749, 1.

40. *JHB, 1758–1761*, 81. Virginia burgesses found the Winchester petition reasonable and rejected the Augusta County petition. Entry dated 14 March 1759, ibid., 92. For resulting regulation, see "An Act for Reducing the Several Acts for Licensing Pedlars, and Preventing Frauds in the Duties upon Skins and Furs, into One Act," Hening, ed., *Statutes*, 7:283–88.

41. For diversity of skin trade, see an account by Davis's partner Matthew Reid, a Staunton merchant with whom Edward Tarr had current accounts between 1765 and 1770; as of 9 Sept. 1769, Reid inventoried fox, raccoon, wolf, otter, fisher, mink, muskrat, and cat skins at his store. Reed (*sic*) Financial Papers, 1764–1776, no. 228, Stuart-Baldwin Papers, 1742–1832, Alderman Library.

42. Entries dated 17 May, 27 July 1762, 12 May 1767, Augusta County Entry Book, 1:49, 79, LOV.

43. For the definitive scholarly analysis of colonial Virginia land law and practices, see Hughes, *Surveyors and Statesmen*.

44. Survey by assistant surveyor James Trimble for William Davis of Pennsylvania, 18 Feb. 1767, Augusta County Surveyor Book, 2:66, LOV.

45. Thomas Ruckman, grantor, to William Davis, grantee, deeds of lease and release, 28, 29 June 1762, Augusta DB, 10:408–12; William Davis, grantor, to John Wiley, Jr., grantee, deeds of lease and release, 16, 17 Aug. 1762, ibid., 10:412–16.

46. William Young, by his attorney, grantor, to William Davis, grantee, deeds of lease and release, 20, 21 Sept. 1763, ibid., 11:401–4; William Davis, grantor, to John Wiley, Jr., grantee, deeds of lease and release, 21, 22 Sept. 1763, ibid., 11:409–12. The dates of Young's deeds of lease and release to Davis mask the actual timing of the transaction; Young's power of attorney authorizing Augusta County clerk John Madison to make a deed to William Davis is dated 15 Feb. 1763, per ibid., 11:400–401.

47. Samuel Ekerling, grantor, to William Davis, grantee, deed of bargain and sale, 16 Oct. 1767, ibid., 14:210–12; William Davis, grantor, to William Christian, grantee, deed of bargain and sale, 4 Oct. 1770, Botetourt County DB, 1:188–89, LOV. Ekerling was himself a skinner who in 1748 had exported from Augusta County three elk skins, twenty-six undressed deerskins, and fifty-two dressed deerskins. Entry dated 7 May 1748, James Patton, "A Register Book of the De[u]ty of Skins for Augusta Countey," Preston Family Papers, 1727–1896, VHS.

48. For complications arising from military campaigns, death, and theft, see the accounts of Davis's widow Christiana Davis, March 1787, Philadelphia County Orphans Court Record Book, 14:271, HSP.

49. There were two original Lot Nines because Staunton had two ordinal sets of numbered tracts. Lots west of Augusta Street were sold directly by William Beverley, and those east of Augusta Street were sold by county commissioners after Beverley gave twenty-five acres to Augusta County to ensure the seating of the courthouse in what became Staunton. Beverley deed to Augusta County magistrates, 21 April 1749, Augusta DB, 2:246. Only the eastern lots are shown in the plat Beverley provided to the county. "A Plan of the Town of Staunton, in Augusta County," ibid., 2:410.

50. Robert McClenachan deed to George Wilson, 21 Aug. 1766, ibid., 13:64. For Wil-

son's one-year ordinary license during the Cherokee expedition, see Augusta OB, 6:400, 21 Aug. 1760.

51. For Reid's participation, see Archibald Stuart's 21 May 1791 note to pay George Wilson's heir John Wilson twenty-seven pounds, ten pence, on account of William Davis's heir George Davis. This note is endorsed "the above appears to us to be the balance of the money now due Geo: Wilsons Estate for Mathew Reid for a Lott purch[ase]d of him [i.e., Wilson] in Staunton for which the above ment[ione]d Wilsons heir is now about to Execute a conveyance to Geo Davies." Stuart Family Papers, 1791–1958, VHS.

52. Benjamin Loxley to Colonel William Preston and Captain William Christian, 11 May 1789, Preston Family Papers, 1727–1896, VHS.

53. Reid resided on the lot as of 1 Sept. 1773 and possessed "a bond from George Wilson to make a Conveyance" of the lot. On that date, Reid conveyed his claim and Wilson's bond to George Davis of Philadelphia. Augusta DB, 20:216–18. Wilson's executor John Wilson conveyed the quarter-acre portion of Lot Nine to George Davis, by then a resident of Trenton, New Jersey. Ibid., 27:147, 21 May 1791.

54. Reid and Johnston Ledger, 1761–1770, Special Collections, Swem Library.

55. On 23 July 1748, William Davis agreed to sell "his negro andrew that now workes at worwick" for seventy pounds; the transaction was completed on 5 Feb. 1749/50. Colebrookdale Furnace Account Book, 1744–1751, 116, 166, Potts Mss., HSP. Davis's estate sold slave Tom for eighty pounds Pennsylvania currency on 7 March 1772. Davis inventory, Philadelphia County WB, P:115, HSP.

56. "William Davies of the City of Philadelphia," deed to William Christian, 4 Oct. 1770, witnessed by William Fleming, David May, and Stephen Trigg, and proved by the witnesses in court on 14 Nov. 1770, Botetourt County DB, 1:188–89, LOV.

57. William Davis will, proved 24 July 1771, Philadelphia County WB, P:115, HSP. For his age, see note 1, above.

58. "William Davis of Philadelphia" accounts, 5 April, 4 July 1768, 14, 15, 18 Feb. 1769, William Fleming Ledger, 26, Special Collections, Leyburn Library.

59. William Davis inventory and executor accounts, Philadelphia County WB, P:115, HSP.

60. Benjamin Loxley to Colonel William Preston and Captain William Christian, 11 May 1789, Preston Family Papers, 1727–1896, VHS.

61. Munger, *Pennsylvania Land Records*, 5–7.

62. Comparable hard choices long have been documented in New England openfield villages; c.f., Greven, "Family Structure in Seventeenth-Century Andover, Massachusetts."

63. For recent scholarship exploring the hazards of popular demand for real estate on Pennsylvania frontiers, see Spero, "The Conojocular War," and Gallo, "'Fair Play Has Entirely Ceased, and Law Has Taken Its Place.'"

64. Thomas Shute and wife Elizabeth to their eldest son William Shute, his wife Elizabeth, and their children Rebecca, Martha, and Elizabeth, 10 June 1739, Philadelphia County DB, H-1:280, PHMC; the price was recorded as natural love and affection plus five shillings. William's marriage to Elizabeth Steel was reported on 30 June 1721. Philadelphia Monthly Meeting (Arch Street) Women's Minutes, 1:127, FHL.

65. For details, see chapter 1.

66. Thomas Shute will, Philadelphia County WB, I:5, HSP.

67. William Shute's recalcitrance was first noted on 25 Oct. 1751; he finally condemned his actions in a written statement by August 1752. Philadelphia Monthly Meeting (Arch Street) Minutes, 1745–1755, 198, 201, 205, 210, 213, 217, 219, 222, 224, FHL.

68. Pine Forge Ledger, 1735–1742, 30, 142, 174, Potts Mss., HSP. Plaintiffs against Isaac Shute included Ralph Lees, Leonard Milburn, William Corker's executors, Samuel Taylor, Edward Dougharty, and Thomas York. Entries dated 1 May, 7 Aug., 6 Nov. 1733, 5 Feb. 1733/4, 6 Aug. 1734, 5 Aug. 1735, 2 Aug. 1737, Lancaster County Court of Common Pleas, Appearance Dockets, 1731–1732, 1733–1734, 1737–1738, LCHS. William Shute remarked on 21 July 1755 that "my Brother Isaac Somtime Since dyed Intestate having Right to a Small personal Estate and I am not Inclinable to take the Berthen of the administration on my self." Isaac Shute Estate Administration, 1755, no. 70, PRWA.

69. Philadelphia Monthly Meeting (Arch Street) Minutes, 1715–1744, 161, 300, FHL. In May 1739, a Philadelphia chair maker credited Jacob Shute for two loads of stones almost certainly taken from his father's quarries. Solomon Fussell Account Book, 84, LOC. On 29 July 1755, Joseph Shute bound himself in the penal amount of three hundred pounds to administer Jacob Shute's estate, indicating an estate worth no more than half that amount. Jacob Shute Estate Administration, 1756, no. 69, PRWA.

70. Entries dated 31 Oct., 28 Nov. 1740, 30 Jan., 27 Feb. 1740/1, Philadelphia Monthly Meeting (Arch Street) Minutes, 1715–1744, 321–24, FHL.

71. Henretta recognized that "The gains of one generation, the slow accumulation of capital resources through savings and invested labor, had been dispersed among many heirs," but did not pursue the rivalries that such dispersals inevitably generated. "Families and Farms," 22. Allan Kulikoff explicitly recognizes and scrutinizes economic tensions within families but focuses on rivalries of gender rather than generation. "Transition to Capitalism in Rural America," 133, 138–40. Comparable issues are better documented in New England town studies, but these tend to focus on the portion of the population remaining in place, not the emigrants.

72. Henretta, "Families and Farms," 30–32.

4. The Slave

1. *Virginia Gazette* (Pinckney), 9 Feb. 1775, 3.

2. *American Weekly Mercury*, 6–13 July 1732, 4.

3. Andrew Robeson will, proved 27 Feb. 1719/20, Philadelphia County WB, D:145–46, HSP. A beating mill, also known as a fulling mill, mechanically finished textiles.

4. Historian Gary B. Nash found that only 6 percent of Philadelphia slave owners held four or more slaves. "Slaves and Slaveowners in Colonial Philadelphia," 244.

5. *Pennsylvania Gazette*, 15 March 1738/9, 3.

6. Examples of runaway ironworkers clad in leather include *American Weekly Mercury*, 1 March 1719/20, 2; 8 June 1721, 2; 23 Sept. 1725, 4; 2 Dec. 1725 2; 14 March 1727/8, 2; 22 Aug. 1728, 3; *Pennsylvania Gazette*, 21 May 1747, 3. For an ironworks providing leather breeches to slaves, see entries dated 28 Dec. 1742, 10 Jan. 1745/6, 25 Jan. 1745/6, Coventry Forge Ledger, 1742–1748, 106, 287, 301, Potts Mss., HSP.

7. *Pennsylvania Gazette,* 15 March 1738/9, 3. Tarr's association with Mulatto Will, also known as William MacBean, is discussed below.

8. Fries, transl. and ed., "Diary of a Journey of Moravians," 338–39. For a slightly different translation from the original German, see Hinke and Kemper, eds., "Moravian Diaries of Travels through Virginia," 147–49.

9. The tally omits subsequent publications of the same advertisements. *American Weekly Mercury,* 21 July 1720, 3; 27 Oct. 1720, 4; 21 June 1722, 4; 15 Nov. 1722, 2; 18 April 1723, 4; 25 April 1723, 2; 20 June 1723, 2; 22 Aug. 1723, 4; 7 Nov. 1723, 4; 17 June 1725, 2; 8 June 1727, 4; 27 Nov. 1729, 4; 4 June 1730, 4; 13 Aug. 1730, 4; 3 June 1731, 4; 2 Sept. 1731, 4; 11 Jan. 1732/3, 2; 6 June 1734, 5; 20 June 1734, 4; 24 Oct. 1734, 4; 7 Nov. 1734, 3; 24 June 1736, 3; 16 Dec. 1736, 4; 28 Dec. 1736, 3; 9 June 1737, 3; 28 July 1737, 3; 10 Nov. 1737, 3; 8 Dec. 1737, 4; 28 Feb. 1737/8, 3; 19 Dec. 1738, 4; 21 April 1739, 3; *Pennsylvania Gazette,* 10 Sept. 1730, 4; 1 Oct. 1730, 4; 11 March 1730/1, 4; 11 Oct. 1733, 4; 27 June 1734, 4; 20 April 1738, 4; 25 May 1738, 3; 29 June 1738, 3; 6 July 1738, 3; 3 Aug. 1738, 3; 19 Oct. 1738, 4.

10. *American Weekly Mercury,* 18–25 April 1734, 4.

11. Andrew Robeson Estate Administration, 20 May 1740, no. 127, PRWA.

12. Ibid.

13. Entry dated 21 Jan. 1746/7, Coventry Forge Ledger, 1742–1748, 330, Potts Mss., HSP. Caesar's assignments as a hammer-man bracketed his 1747 stint as a smith. For a 1745 example of Caesar's labor making anchonies, see Coventry Forge Ledger, 1745–1748, 262, Potts Mss., HSP; for a 1748 example of Caesar's production of bar iron, see ibid., 357.

14. Gordon, *American Iron,* 14.

15. According to the records of one Pennsylvania forge, a single bushel of charcoal required over half a cord of wood, a full cord being a stack four feet wide and tall, and eight feet long. A 120-bushel cartload of charcoal required seventy cords of wood. Pool Forge Journal, 1749–1759, 2, 124, Potts Mss., HSP. An acre of land could produce twenty to twenty-five cords of wood. Bining, *Pennsylvania Iron Manufacture,* 63; Gordon, *American Iron,* 40.

16. Ibid., 33–36; Bezís-Selfa, *Forging America,* 27–31.

17. The descriptions of ironmaking in this and the following two paragraphs rely on Gordon, *American Iron,* 7–124, an essential introduction to iron processes; thanks to Lee Sauder for this reference. Bezís-Selfa describes and discusses iron processes vividly, albeit more briefly, in *Forging America,* 27–38.

18. For personnel estimates, see Henry Drinker to Richard Blackledge, 4 Dec. 1786, Drinker Letterbook, 1786–1790, 83, cited in Bining, *Pennsylvania Iron Manufacture,* 62–63.

19. Dew, *Bond of Iron,* 10–11; Bezís-Selfa, *Forging America,* 36–37.

20. John Hansen and helper Thomas Minion hammered out a ton and a half of anchonies in 1736, the same year Minion was burned. Entries dated 10 March 1735/6, 2 Aug. 1736, Coventry Forge Ledger, 1734–1740, 213, 285, Potts Mss., HSP. See also John Hanson accounts, Coventry Forge Ledger, 1732–1733, 277, and Coventry Forge Ledger, 1734–1740, 258, both Potts Mss., HSP. For other examples of finer injuries, see Bezís-Selfa, *Forging America,* 37–38.

21. William Bird Ledger, 1741–1747, 177, 287, Potts Mss., HSP.

22. William Bird Ledger, 1744–1761, 19, Potts Mss., HSP.

23. Ibid.

24. Robert Grace pig metal account, Warwick Furnace Account Book, Ledger C, 1745–1748, 3, Potts Mss., HSP.

25. Ibid. Ned hauled three hundredweight of iron bars from William Bird's forge to one John Martain Frittes on 11 [month uncertain] 1746/7. William Bird Ledger, 1744–1761, 1, Potts Mss., HSP.

26. Michael V. Kennedy argues convincingly that the hiring and moving of slaves for industrial labor produced significant undercounting of the enslaved labor force in the mid-Atlantic region. "The Hidden Economy of Slavery."

27. Isaac Shute's earliest identification as a blacksmith was in a 1728 bill for smith's work he performed for one Richard Hill's estate. Logan Papers, 1664–1871, 18:89, HSP. He also was identified as a Philadelphia blacksmith in an administrator's bond by his brother Joseph dated 29 July 1755. Isaac Shute Estate Administration, 1755, no. 70, PRWA. Anthony Nicholas married Rebecca, daughter of Thomas Shute, on 16 Nov. 1734, in Philadelphia. Hinshaw, *Encyclopedia of American Quaker Genealogy*, 2:651. Shute was charged for a total of 2.5 long tons of pig iron delivered to Nicholas in 1742/3 and on 12 Aug. 1745. Pine Forge Ledger, 1735–1742, 174, Potts Mss., HSP.

28. *Pennsylvania Gazette*, 9 July 1767, 3 (repeated twice); William Davis, grantor, to Benjamin Koster, grantee, 6 April 1755, Lancaster County DB, II:652–54, PHMC; William Shute, grantor, to Benjamin Koster, grantee, 10 May 1755, ibid., II:654–56.

29. For an example of harsher Pennsylvania slave laws, see the discussion of Tarr's marriage in chapter 5.

30. Fries, transl. and ed., "Diary of a Journey of Moravians," 339.

31. Zinzendorf, *Sixteen Discourses*.

32. Documents surviving in Tarr's hand were preserved in the course of lawsuits discussed in subsequent chapters and summarized in appendix 4.

33. *American Weekly Mercury*, 5–12 Feb. 1722/3, 4. The following week the would-be tutor extended the offer to both males and females. Ibid., 12–19 Feb. 1722/3, 2.

34. William Bird Ledger, 1744–1761, 19, 23, Potts Mss., HSP. See also Elizabeth Smith, entries dated 30 June–27 Aug. 1750, Coventry Forge Account Book, 1746–1754, 136, Potts Mss., HSP. Accounts at Coventry Forge in 1732 show that board for laborers was billed at five shillings per week. In the absence of a recorded period for the board account, it is impossible to estimate how many additional subscribers were enrolled for the schoolmaster's support. Coventry Forge Ledger, 1730–1732, 16, Potts Mss., HSP.

35. Frederick Douglass, *Narrative of the Life of Frederick Douglass, an American Slave*, in *Autobiographies* (1845; repr., New York: Library of America, 1994), 44–45.

36. For examples, see receipts marked by "Mallatoe James" and "Jacob Negro" in Warwick Furnace, Receipt Book for Pigg Mettle, 133, 151, 152, Potts Mss., HSP. See also receipts marked by "Molattoe Joseph" and "Molata James," 4 May 1754, 22 March 1757, Pine Forge Receipt Book, 1752–1760, Potts Mss., HSP.

37. Entries dated 19 Oct., 20 Dec. 1745, Warwick Furnace Ledger C, 1745–1748, 84, 99, Potts Mss., HSP. For additional details of accounts in stores at ironworks, see Bezís-Selfa, *Forging America*, 126–28.

38. Entry dated 8 Sept. 1732, Colebrookdale Ledger C, 1730–1733, 186, Potts Mss., HSP.

39. Warwick Furnace Ledger, 1750–1760, 345, Potts Mss., HSP.

40. William Bird Ledger, 1741–1747, 287, endpapers; William Bird Ledger, 1744–1761, endpapers, both Potts Mss., HSP.

41. Complainant's account, *Edward Tarr v. George Stevenson,* Judgment Files, Augusta CCC. 42. Penal bond of Edward Tarr and Joseph Kennedy, *William Todd, assignee of Jacob Gray, v. Edward Tarr and Joseph Kennedy,* ibid.

42. For example, on 6 April 1733, Thomas Potts assigned two shillings of credit to Patrick Clerk "By Nigroe Mingoe's Order on me." Thomas Potts's Ledger C, 242, 244, Potts Mss., HSP. Potts "paid Bittle" £2:11:9 for Black Mingo on 23 June 1732, and "paid in Town for you [i.e., Mingo] 40/ to James Steele's Son in Law" on 2 Oct. 1732. Ibid., 186.

43. For details of William MacBean's carting in 1728 to 1730, see Coventry Forge Ledger B, 1727–1730, passim, Potts Mss., HSP. MacBean's association with Tarr is discussed later in this chapter.

44. Coventry Forge Ledger, 1730–1732, 114, Potts Mss., HSP. Herculus was still "Driveing team" for Coventry Forge as late as the summer of 1739 for the increased wages of two pounds per month; he also continued driving hard bargains, receiving a bonus beyond his wages of eighteen shillings, nine pence, for "hauling a Hogshead of Salt from Town" on 8 Jan. 1738/9. Coventry Forge Ledger F, 1736–1741, 327, Potts Mss., HSP.

45. For risk of charcoal ignition and the necessity of prompt delivery, see Bezís-Selfa, *Forging America,* 29–31.

46. *Pennsylvania Gazette,* 15 March 1738/9, 3. For MacBean's identity as "Mulatto Will," see Coventry Forge Ledger B, 1727–1730, 51, Potts Mss., HSP.

47. "An Act for the Better Regulating of Negroes in This Province," 5 March 1725/6, *Statutes at Large of Pennsylvania,* 4:63–64.

48. Franklin, *Papers of Benjamin Franklin,* 1:211–12.

49. Hazard, ed., *Minutes of the Provincial Council of Pennsylvania,* 4:244, 3 Sept. 1737.

50. *Statutes at Large of Pennsylvania,* 4:61.

51. Ibid., 4:64.

52. Entry dated 17 April 1734, Colebrookdale Ledger C, 1730–1733, 77; entries dated 29 Dec. 1735, 15 Jan., 20 Feb. 1735/6, 18 Jan., 16 March 1736/7, Pine Forge Ledger, 1735–1742, 54, 204, both Potts Mss., HSP.

53. Hansen was credited for 2,212 pounds of anchonies made with Coventry Forge slave Ben on 28 Feb. 1736. Coventry Forge Ledger, 1734–1740, 258, Potts Mss., HSP. Other examples of refiners' working with slaves include "John Mills Hammerman" and "Negroe Lambeth" drawing bar iron, entries dated 1 Jan. 1742/3, 25 March 1744, Coventry Forge Ledger, 1742–1748, 138, 215, Potts Mss., HSP; "Henry Doile, finer" and "Old Cesar" making anchonies, entries dated 19 April, 5 June 1745, ibid., 262; George Thomas and Caesar making anchonies, entry dated 6 Dec. 1745, ibid., 287; Henry Goucher and Lambo [Lambeth] making anchonies, entry dated 9 April 1747, ibid., 334; Russell Moore "Drawing Anchonys with Lambo & Cudge," entry dated 17 May 1747, ibid., 347; Richard Goucher and Lambo making anchonies, entry dated 15 May 1747, ibid., 351; and Samuel Tamplin making anchonies with Lambo, Cudjo, and Caesar, entry dated 9 April 1748, ibid., 357.

54. Franklin, *Papers of Benjamin Franklin*, 1:212; Nash, *Forging Freedom*, 34–36.

55. For a discussion of overwork that alludes to customary slave time off, see Bezís-Selfa, *Forging America*, 92–93.

56. Fries, transl. and ed., "Diary of a Journey of Moravians," 339.

57. Fogleman, *Jesus Is Female*, 192–209; "Memoir of George Nixdorf"; Nyberg, "The *Irene* in Peril at Sea."

58. Fogleman, *Jesus Is Female*, 192–209.

59. Moravians famously extended their message to members of all denominations. For Indians, blacks, and other non-Germans ministered to by Moravians from Pennsylvania, see Fogleman, "Religious Conflict and Violence," 188. For black Moravians in North Carolina, see Sensbach, *A Separate Canaan*. For the diverse religious context Ned found in Lancaster County, see Wood, *Conestoga Crossroads*, 181–94.

60. In 1727, Moravians began conducting love-feasts, song services during which the congregation ate bread or sweetened buns and drank beverages such as tea or coffee. The service was and is conducted on a variety of festivals and whenever members wish to mark "the headship of the Lord and the oneness and brotherhood of His followers." Fries, *Customs and Practices of the Moravian Church*, 66–68. Thanks to Sylvia Pulliam Lackey of Staunton, Virginia, for calling my attention to this source and for suggesting the love-feast interpretation for the breakfast prepared by Tarr's wife. Tarr's membership in the Presbyterian congregation at Timber Ridge is further discussed in chapter 5.

61. Rev. Samuel Davies was an early proselytizer among slaves in Hanover County, Virginia, in the 1750s. Morgan, "Slave Life in Piedmont Virginia," 472–73.

62. Entries dated 14d 12m 1744, 22d 5m 1745, 6d 9m, 18d 9m 1746, First Presbyterian Church, "Register of Marriages and Baptisms," PHS.

63. Craighead was present in Augusta County by at least the beginning of June 1752. *EJC*, 5:399. Tarr's earliest documented presence in Augusta County was 4 April 1752. *Edward Tarr v. George Stevenson*, Judgment Files, Augusta CCC.

64. Indenture of bargain and sale, Benjamin Borden's heir Benjamin, Jr., to Craighead, 8 March 1753, Augusta DB, 5:257–59.

65. Entry dated 4 April 1735, Donegal Presbytery Minutes, 1:58, UPS; Timber Ridge and Providence Congregations, "Call from Timber Ridge and Providence, Virginia," PHS.

66. Augusta DB, 2:849.

67. Thomas Shute will, Philadelphia County WB, I:5, HSP. Shute's executors presented his will to Philadelphia County's Register General on 10 December 1748.

68. Ibid. The "Negro Woman of mine" Shute mentioned as mother of "a Molatto Girl" either no longer belonged to Shute or was not included in his dispensations; Shute's probate accounts do not include a complete inventory of his personal property. Facts and the quotation in the following paragraph also come from this source.

69. Ibid.

70. At the time of Shute's death, contemporary Quaker opinions about slavery remained divided. Germantown Quakers famously renounced slavery in 1688. Other Quakers like Shute accepted slavery, however, and it expanded in Pennsylvania through the Seven Years' War. Germantown Quakers' Renunciation of Slavery, 1688; Nash, "Slaves and Slaveowners in Colonial Philadelphia."

71. The price of ironworking slaves appears to have risen about the time of Shute's death, so it is possible that his figure reflected traditional prices. William Branson, a partner in Coventry Forge, bought a slave man on 14 June 1736 for thirty-five pounds. Coventry Forge Ledger F, 1736–1741, 155, Potts Mss., HSP. Bartholomew Penrose sold a slave man for five and a half tons of pig iron on 5 July 1741, valued at thirty-eight pounds, ten shillings. Mount Pleasant Furnace Ledger, 1737–1739, 75, Potts Mss., HSP. John Potts purchased a slave man on 3 August 1744 for thirty-five pounds. Germantown/Philadelphia Day Book, 1742–1754, Potts Mss., HSP. Shortly before and also not long after Shute's death, Potts paid more: fifty pounds for one man on 15 September 1748 and sixty-one pounds for another on 2 November 1749. Ibid., 97, 144.

72. *Pennsylvania Gazette,* 24 July 1755, 3.

73. Augusta WB, 3:227, 6 Oct. 1761.

5. The Freeholder

1. For facts and quotations in this and the following paragraph, see Fries, transl. and ed., "Diary of a Journey of Moravians," 330–32, 335, 338, 339.

2. Moravian problems with Presbyterians had a wider context of conflict among Moravians and other German-speaking colonists. Fogleman, "Religious Conflict and Violence."

3. Jacob Gray, grantor, to Edward Tarr, grantee, 15 May 1754, Augusta DB, 6:212–14. Free blacks acquired real estate elsewhere in Virginia throughout the history of slavery. Breen and Innes, *"Myne Owne Ground";* Ely, *Israel on the Appomattox,* 95–100, 362–64.

4. Benjamin Borden, Jr., executors, to James McClung, Augusta DB, 6:398–99. Deeds for one adjoining tract mention "Edward Tarrs line"; like the McClung transaction, this tract was conveyed from Borden's executors after Tarr's purchase. Deeds, 14 Oct. 1765, 18 March 1772, ibid., 12:336, 18:130. Deeds for other neighboring tracts such as one belonging to Rev. William Dean (conveyed from Benjamin Borden before Tarr's purchase) used original metes and bounds if the property changed hands without changing shape; this was normal. Tarr therefore was not named in other transfers of adjoining tracts.

5. For example, the boundary between tax parcels 50–A–101A and 50–2–1 traces the first two courses of Tarr's 1754 deed. Rockbridge County, Virginia, Geographic Information System, http://arcgis.webgis.net/va/rockbridge/.

6. Robert Huston, deed to Samuel McDowell, John McClung, John Lyle, William Alexander, and John Thompson, trustees, 21 Nov. 1759, Augusta DB, 8:212–13.

7. Augusta OB, 4:411, 24 March 1755; 424, 21 May 1755.

8. Greenlee deposition, Couper, *History of the Shenandoah Valley,* 1:274–75. Mary Greenlee's account of the family's arrival was confirmed by a deposition of her younger brother, Samuel McDowell, dated 17 Nov. 1806, in Chalkley, *Chronicles,* 2:273. Greenlee's claim to have arrived in Virginia in 1737 also was confirmed by her older brother John McDowell, who swore on 28 Feb. 1739/40 that he imported himself, his son, his wife, and a servant "in the year 1737 to dwell in this Colony." Orange County OB, 2:110, LOV. For Borden's grant, see Virginia Land Office Patents and Grants, 18:360, LOV. The Borden grant had not yet been surveyed and patented when the McDowells ar-

rived; John McDowell served as Borden's agent in the grant until McDowell's death in 1742. McCleskey, "Rich Land, Poor Prospects," 472–74.

9. Although title for the 1,359-acre McDowell home place was not conveyed until 1755, John McDowell lived there and was buried there considerably earlier in what became a private family cemetery. The transfer of title was delayed first by McDowell's death in late 1742, then by the death of Benjamin Borden the following year. Borden's heir, Benjamin Borden, Jr., moved to Timber Ridge and married Magdalene, John McDowell's widow. He delayed conveying the land while Magdalene's son Samuel McDowell was a minor. Benjamin, Jr., died in 1753 without conveying the property. Eventually his executors (including his and McDowell's remarried widow, Magdalene McDowell Borden Bowyer) conveyed the tract to Samuel McDowell in 1755, minus four hundred acres covenanted for sale by John McDowell. Augusta DB, 7:102.

10. Salley, "Brief Account of the Travels of John Peter Salley," 211.

11. For McCown's oath (a step toward claiming land via head-rights), see Orange County OB, 2:207, 24 July 1740, LOV.

12. John Craig, List of Baptisms, 1740–1749, UPS; for a more accessible alphabetized transcription, see Wilson, *Tinkling Spring*, 470–84. For fifty-three men in McDowell's vicinity, see "Petition of Frontiersmen," 10 July 1742, Virginia (Colony), Colonial Papers, 1630–1778, LOV. The number is almost the same as the fifty men listed in McDowell's militia company in an undated roster, the context of which is a 14 September general muster conducted before Captain McDowell's death in mid-December 1742. Draper Mss., 1QQ 18. The first mention of a general muster for "that Part of Orange County, called Augusta" was dated 10 June 1742. *JHB, 1742–1747, 1748–1749,* 56.

13. My interpretation of broad support for hierarchical authority in colonial Augusta County differs from the contested authority described by Albert H. Tillson, Jr., in *Gentry and Common Folk.* Tillson's interpretation is consistent with Beeman, *Evolution of the Southern Backcountry,* which offers a case study of Lunenburg County, Virginia. A fresh quantitative study of Lunenburg might produce a different result; until then, qualitative differences between contemporary new settlements in Southside Virginia and the valley may be reconciled by reference to Hofstra, *Planting of New Virginia,* ch. 2. Hofstra demonstrates that Virginia's colonial leadership perceived settlements west of the Blue Ridge as strategically critical; given this official attention as well as a somewhat different immigrant stream, it is unsurprising that societies evolved differently in the two regions.

14. *EJC,* 5:3, 1 Nov. 1739.

15. "An Act for Dividing Spotsylvania County," Aug. 1734, Hening, ed., *Statutes,* 4:450–51.

16. For the definitive narrative of the imperial context and consequences of Virginia's settlements west of the Blue Ridge, see Hofstra, *Planting of New Virginia.*

17. County grand inquests in Pennsylvania were the equivalent of county grand juries in Virginia. For Woods's service on the 6 Nov. 1733 grand inquest, see Hawbaker, ed., *Lancaster County, Pennsylvania, Quarter Sessions Abstracts,* 23. For John McDowell's petit jury service on 6 Aug. 1734, 6 May, 4 Nov. 1735, and 3 Aug. 1736, see ibid., 31, 36, 42, 51. County sheriffs in Virginia typically impaneled petit jurors opportunistically from

among the day's bystanders as apparently happened at least once to John McDowell in Pennsylvania. He and his father, Ephraim McDowell, were litigants in Lancaster County the same day as John's initial jury service on 6 Aug. 1734. Lancaster County Court of Common Pleas, Appearance Docket, 1733–1734, LCHS. Ephraim McDowell also served as a grand inquest member once in Lancaster County on 4 Feb. 1734/5. Hawbaker, ed., *Lancaster County, Pennsylvania, Quarter Sessions Abstracts*, 33.

18. Roeber, *Faithful Magistrates and Republican Lawyers*, esp. chs. 2, 3; Isaac, *Transformation of Virginia*, 88–94; Lounsbury, *Courthouses of Early Virginia*.

19. "Petition of Frontiersmen," 10 July 1742, Virginia (Colony), Colonial Papers, 1630–1778, LOV.

20. Bushman, "Farmers in Court," 389–90. Frontier residents expected order; when the symbiosis of local residents and local authorities was neglected, as in North Carolina in the 1760s, yeoman frustration led to violence. Whittenburg, "Planters, Merchants, and Lawyers."

21. In the 1970s and 1980s, historian Richard Beeman assessed Lunenburg County as only feebly duplicating Tidewater Virginia's secular and religious institutions. "Social Change and Cultural Conflict"; *Evolution of the Southern Backcountry*.

22. McDowell was added to the 1 Nov. 1739 Orange County commission of the peace. *EJC*, 5:2. He attended regularly scheduled Orange County court sessions in February, May, and November 1740, and February and August 1741. Orange County OB, 2:106, 107, 114, 155, 278, 283, 305, 313, 460, 472; 3:197, LOV. He missed courts in March, June, July, August, September, and October 1740, and a very brief but routine session in January 1741; he also missed March, May, June, July, September, and October sessions in 1741. Orange County conducted no courts in April and December 1740 nor in April 1741. A new commission omitting McDowell was presented at the November 1741 court. From February 1739/40 through October 1741, court met for eighteen sessions of up to three days each. Ibid., 2:132–54, 186–276, 305, 322–459; 3:5–51. McDowell's removal appears to have been engineered by James Patton in an example of in-fighting among frontier elite factions. McCleskey, "Across the First Divide," 222–35. McDowell's oath as militia captain was in preparation for the Augusta County militia's first general muster in mid-September 1742. "Proceedings of Militia Court Martial," 15 Sept. [1742], Draper Mss., 1QQ 18.

23. Augusta County was authorized by "An Act, for Erecting Two New Counties, and Parishes," Hening, ed., *Statutes*, 5:78–80. The act provided for the creation of Frederick and Augusta counties at the discretion of the governor and council, which in Augusta County's case the council authorized on 29 October 1745. *EJC*, 5:191.

24. John McDowell was killed by Indians in 1742 and so was omitted from later commissions of the peace. His widow's subsequent husbands Benjamin Borden, Jr., and John Bowyer served as magistrates for the upper James River Valley. In Augusta County's initial commission of the peace, the magistrates from the James and Roanoke River valleys were, in order of seniority, George Robinson (Roanoke River) and Richard Woods (Maury River). Augusta OB, 1:1, 9 Dec. 1745. From 13 August 1753 to 20 March 1755, Augusta County magistrates operated under a commission of the peace that included, in order of seniority, George Robinson (Roanoke River), Richard Woods (Maury River), and John Mathews (Forks of James River). Ibid., 4:1, 382. In addition

to three 1753 magistrates in the upper James and Roanoke valleys, a fourth, John Buchanan, had by then established residence in the New River Valley; Buchanan was a member of the 1745 commission of the peace but at that time resided in Beverley Manor.

25. Woods was included in all but one of the first eight Augusta County commissions of the peace, effective December 1746 through March 1755. Ibid., 1:1; 2:127, 149, 287; 3:176, 242; 4:1; *EJC*, 5:289–91, 303, 389. The governor and council omitted him from the second commission, which covered the sessions from June 1746 through March 1749. Augusta OB, 1:68; *EJC*, 5:214. For the first day of Woods's attendance at ten sessions, see Augusta OB, 1:1, 17, 19, 21; 2:287, 380, 433, 500, 561; 3:209.

26. This range in size is computed from twelve of thirteen grand juries impaneled from 1746 through 1753; the grand jury of 1752 was not named in court orders.

27. For the presentment of Eleanor Dryden and her father's landholding, see ibid., 2:119, 17 May 1749; Augusta DB, 1:53, 21 May 1747. David Dryden was named as Eleanor's father during his attempt to have her fined for bearing an illegitimate child; see Augusta OB, 2:429, 29 Aug. 1750.

28. Augusta Parish churchwardens—vestry members who reported offenses against good social order in the parish—presented none of the thirty-six cases in or proximal to Tarr's neighborhood before the Moravian passage (see table 15). John K. Nelson argues convincingly in *A Blessed Company* for the essential role of Virginia's parishes in county governance. After Augusta Parish was established in 1747, it too performed numerous important social functions, but churchwardens and Edward Tarr never interacted in a way that generated a surviving document.

29. For sources, see table 15.

30. Augusta OB, 4:64, 76, 77, 81; Augusta DB, 1:463, 505; 2:442; 4:256, 729; 5:161.

31. Couper, *History of the Shenandoah Valley*, 1:278.

32. Tarr and David Dryden signed the call for Rev. John Brown, a document discussed in more detail below.

33. On 24 March 1755, the county court ordered three Timber Ridge residents to "view & marke the nearest and best way from Isaac Taylor to Tarrs Shop and report their proceedings to the next Court." On 21 May 1755, the road viewers "appointed to view a Road from Isaac Taylors to Tarrs Shop reported ma[d]e return that the new Road is the nearest & best way," and the court accordingly "ordered that Robert Huston and Moses McClures be surveyors thereof." Augusta OB, 4:41, 424. Huston's land lay north of this road segment.

34. "An Act Concerning Servants and Slaves," Oct. 1705, Hening, ed., *Statutes*, 3:453–54. The ban and punishment were renewed without modification shortly after Tarr arrived in Virginia. "An Act for the Better Government of Servants and Slaves," Nov. 1753, ibid., 6:361–62.

35. Ibid.

36. "An Act for the Better Regulating of Negroes in This Province," 5 March 1725/6, *Statutes at Large of Pennsylvania*, 4:62–63.

37. Augusta DB, 2:223; Augusta OB, 6:211; Hildebrand, "Map Showing 92,100 Acre Grant for Benjamin Borden," LOV.

38. See chapter 8 for slavery's origins in the upper Valley of Virginia.

39. Fries, transl. and ed., "Diary of a Journey of Moravians," 339.

40. For this process in the Valley of Virginia during the earliest years of settlement, see Wilson, *Tinkling Spring*, 36–63.

41. Entry dated 15 June 1742, Donegal Presbytery Minutes, 1:242, UPS.

42. Ibid., 1:243, 16 June 1742; 1:242.2, 21 Sept. 1742; Virginia Land Office Patents and Grants, 23:945, LOV. For a minister ordained to an Augusta County congregation in 1745 but then refusing to come, see Rev. Samuel Black's case in Wilson, *Tinkling Spring*, 80.

43. The call "from the congregations of Timber Ridge and forks of James's River" was presented directly to the Synod of New York on 18 May 1748; "Synod refer[ed] the consideration thereof to the Presbytery of New Castle, to which Mr. Dean doth belong, and do recommend it to said Presbytery to meet at Mr. Dean's meeting-house on Wednesday next upon said affair, and that Mr. Dean and his people be speedily apprized of it." New York Synod Minutes, *Records of the Presbyterian Church*, 236; Benjamin Borden, Jr., deed to Rev. William Dean, Augusta DB, 1:461–62.

44. Augusta OB, 2:20, 20 May 1748; Robert Huston, deed to Samuel McDowell, John McClung, John Lyle, William Alexander, and John Thompson, trustees, Augusta DB, 8:212–13, 21 Nov. 1759.

45. Dean's will was dated 7 July 1748 according to the deed from Rev. William Dean's heirs to Hugh Kelso, ibid., 18:278–81, 21 May 1772. Dean was first listed as a member of the New York Synod in 1746 and as a deceased member in 1749; he attended the 1747 synod meeting but was absent in 1746 and 1748. New York Synod Minutes, 9 Oct. 1746, 20 May 1747, 18 May 1748, 17 May 1749, Klett, ed., *Minutes of the Presbyterian Church in America*, 234, 235, 237.

46. New Castle Presbytery minutes do not survive to describe supply ministries at Timber Ridge, but a comparison is possible with the vacant North Mountain Meetinghouse a decade later. Three supply ministers preached a total of just five times at North Mountain during the year from April 1758 to April 1759. Entries dated 26 April, 28 Sept. 1758, 25 April 1759, Hanover Presbytery Minutes, 1755–1785, 1:26; 2:13, 20, UPS. Like Timber Ridge, North Mountain Meetinghouse was located in a well-populated portion of Augusta County that was not directly attacked in the Seven Years' War. The two congregations thus appear demographically comparable.

47. Augusta OB, 2:570, 582, 28, 29 May 1751. Fulling mills mechanically finished woven cloth.

48. Timber Ridge and Providence Congregations, "Call from Timber Ridge and Providence, Virginia," PHS.

49. Ibid.

50. Ibid.

51. Ibid.

52. See, for example, Augusta OB, 1:1.

53. Timber Ridge Congregation subscription list, 22 July 1753, Preston Family Papers, 1727–1896, VHS. Augusta and Orange County land records confirm that the people named on the call's second page were all from New Providence, and the people on the third page were all from Timber Ridge. The subscription list is a typescript copy of the now-lost original document; Edward Tarr's surname was erroneously typed as "Garr."

54. Augusta DB, 8:212.

55. Augusta OB, 3:440–41; Augusta Parish VB, 4.

56. For a 1748 example of demissions in Augusta County, see Tinkling Springs Commissioner Book, 1741–1767, 29b, UPS.

57. These baptisms were performed by Rev. John Craig, pastor of the Tinkling Spring and Augusta Stone congregations near Staunton. John Craig, List of Baptisms, 1740–1749, UPS.

58. Augusta WB, 3:227.

59. Augusta OB, 3:198; 4:64, 169.

60. "An Act for Settling the Titles and Bounds of Lands, and for Preventing Unlawful Hunting and Ranging," Oct. 1748, Hening, ed., *Statutes*, 5:408–31 ("three witnesses," 409; "dower," 410; "four years . . . renewed," 426). For English antecedents to Virginia practice, see Nelson, *A Blessed Company*, 15–16.

61. Augusta OB, 4:482; Augusta Parish VB, 139, 151–52, 267, 385, 428.

62. Contemporary Augusta County wages ranged from one to three shillings per day. William Preston paid millwright John Robinson a shilling per day "for building a grannery at Evans mill." William Preston Account Book, Draper Mss., 6QQ 159, 25 July 1759. Charles Donnelly credited James Hartgrove in 1761 for five shillings "By 2 Days Work," or 2/6 per day. *Charles Donnelly v. James Hartgrove*, Aug. 1762, Judgment Files, Augusta CCC. Nathaniel Lyon credited Simon Dehart "By three Days work at s2 6p" in 1761. *Nathaniel Lyon v. Simon Dehart*, Aug. 1762, ibid. William Thompson credited George Scott in 1763 or 1764 for laboring at fodder and mowing at one shilling a day; Thompson also provided cooking, washing, and lodging. George Scott Account, Preston Family Papers, 1727–1896, VHS. Millwright James Oliver charged three shillings a day for skilled work building John McCoy's mill from December 1760 to February 1761. *James Oliver v. John McCoy*, Nov. 1762, Judgment Files, Augusta CCC.

63. For Preston's oath of office as sheriff, see Augusta OB, 6:316. For his replacement by John Buchanan, see ibid., 7:107.

64. Preston Quitrent Roll, 1760–1761, Preston Family Papers, 1727–1896, VHS. One so-called insolvent in the Borden's Land portion of Preston's quitrent roll was William Russell, an Orange County magistrate who exemplifies the leniency extended by some Augusta County sheriffs to eastern Virginians who owned frontier land. Russell's tracts in Borden's Land totaled seven thousand acres.

65. "An Act Prescribing the Method of Appointing Sheriffs, and for Limitting the Time of Their Continuance in Office, and Directing Their Duty Therein," Oct. 1748, Hening, ed., *Statutes*, 5:518–19; "An Act for Settling the Titles and Bounds of Lands, and for Preventing Unlawful Hunting and Ranging," Oct. 1748, ibid., 5:418–19.

66. In addition to William Russell, noted above, the leading tax delinquents in Preston's quitrent roll were Colonel James Wood and the heirs of Robert Green, from whom Preston finally extracted overdue quitrents for as much as seven years dating back to 1753. The Green and Wood delinquent accounts are recorded near the end of Preston's unpaginated book.

67. For tithables, see chapter 3n24.

68. Complainant's account, *Edward Tarr v. George Stevenson*, June 1757, Judgments, Augusta CCC.

69. Ibid. Tarr billed Stevenson for £2:3:8½ for the three years 1753–55, for an annual average of approximately 14/7.

70. For details of Tarr's credit arrangements and litigation flowing from them, see appendix 4.

71. Rutman and Rutman, *Place in Time*, 205–11.

72. Complainant's account, *Edward Tarr v. George Stevenson*, June 1757, Judgment Files, Augusta CCC.

6. The Warriors

1. Hofstra, *Planting of New Virginia*, 17–49.

2. Autobiography of John Craig, 25, UPS. Craig first began preaching as a supply minister in Augusta County in the winter of 1739–40. Wilson, *Tinkling Spring*, 69.

3. Petition of German settlers, 1733, Palmer, ed., *Calendar of Virginia State Papers*, 1:220.

4. *EJC*, 4:414, 22 April 1738. In response to this petition, the council organized and armed Beverley Manor residents as a militia company captained by John Lewis.

5. Samuel McDowell to Arthur Campbell, 27 July 1808, Draper Mss., 4ZZ 4. For a detailed account of this party and its clash with settlers in the Forks of James River, see McCleskey, "Across the First Divide," 249–52. Warren R. Hofstra puts the episode in an intercolonial perspective in *Planting New Virginia*, ch. 1 and passim.

6. Augusta OB, 1:17, 19 Feb. 1746.

7. Journal of Thomas Walker, 8 April 1750, Walker Papers.

8. Ludovic Grant to Governor James Glen, 22 July 1754, McDowell, ed., *Colonial Records of South Carolina: Documents Relating to Indian Affairs, 1754–1765*, 15–16.

9. Augusta County Surveyor's Book, 1:52, 22 March 1750/1, LOV; William Thompson bill to Alexander Boyd, 1762, Preston Family Papers, 1727–1896, VHS. The same merchant rated deerskins at seventeen pence per pound. For the Harman robberies, see Deposition of Henry Leonard, 18 May 1750, Palmer, ed., *Calendar of Virginia State Papers*, 1:243.

10. For example, the Augusta County court paid bounties on 256 wolves killed in 1750, 261 in 1754, and 251 in 1767. Augusta OB, 2:486, 4:321–22, 11:484.

11. Autobiography of John Craig, 29, 31, UPS; entry dated 21 Sept. 1757, Smith Creek/ Linville Creek Meeting Minutes, 12, BHS.

12. DeHaas, *History of the Early Settlement;* Waddell, *Annals of Augusta County;* Withers, *Chronicles of Border Warfare.*

13. For an early example, see Merrell, "Cultural Continuity among the Piscataway Indians." Richard H. White's *Middle Ground* underpins a scholarly reimagining of intercultural accommodation in the eastern woodlands. For my own work on how nonviolent Indian-white relations in colonial Augusta County were revealed by accounts of violence, see "Across the First Divide," 249–334.

14. Entries dated 27, 29, 31 Oct. 1753, *EJC*, 5:444–45; Washington, *Diaries of George Washington*, 1:130–60; Ward, *Breaking the Backcountry*, 30–32. For the French commander's reply and translation, see *EJC*, 5:458–60, 21 Jan. 1754.

15. James Patton to Lt. Gov. Robert Dinwiddie, 2 July 1754, Preston Family Papers,

1727–1896, VHS. Patton was sworn in as county lieutenant—the senior colonel—on 19 Aug. 1752. Augusta OB, 3:310.

16. Ward, *Breaking the Backcountry,* 33–35.

17. Patton to Dinwiddie, 2 July 1754, Preston Family Papers, 1727–1896, VHS.

18. Entry dated 3 Sept. 1754, *JHB, 1752–1758,* 202.

19. Preston Register, Draper Mss., 1QQ 83.

20. Ward, *Breaking the Backcountry,* 37–42.

21. Preston Register, 18 June 1755, Draper Mss., 1QQ 83; Bethabara Diary, *Records of the Moravians in North Carolina,* 1:133, 19 July 1755; Captain Raymond Demeré to Governor Lyttelton, 7 July 1756, McDowell, ed., *Colonial Records of South Carolina: Documents Relating to Indian Affairs, 1754–1765,* 133.

22. *EJC,* 5:351, 9 Aug. 1751.

23. According to Doctor Thomas Walker, a peripatetic Virginian with an abiding interest in Virginia's frontier, "In April 1744 I met the above mentioned Stalnaker between the Reedy Creek Settlement [in the New River Valley], and Holstons River, on his way to the Cherokee Indians." Walker again encountered Stalnaker encamped on the Holston River in March 1749/50 and "helped him to raise his house." Journal of Thomas Walker, 23, 24 March 1749/50, Walker Papers. James Patton reported in 1753 that "by what I can understand he [Stalnaker] is in great Esteem with the greatest Part of the Cherrokee Nation." James Patton to [Robert Dinwiddie], n.d. but estimated as Jan. 1753, Draper Mss., 1QQ 73.

24. Ludovic Grant to Governor James Glen, 22 July 1754, McDowell, ed., *Colonial Records of South Carolina: Documents Relating to Indian Affairs, 1754–1765,* 15.

25. Jennings, *Empire of Fortune,* 189–92; Ward, *Breaking the Backcountry,* 49–50.

26. Ibid., 60–61; McConnell, *A Country in Between,* 48–50; White, *Middle Ground,* 240–45. For the largely frustrated diplomatic efforts to win hearty Cherokee support, see Alden, *John Stuart and the Southern Colonial Frontier,* 38–56; Dowd, "'Insidious Friends.'"

27. "Diary of the Rev. Hugh McAden," Foote, *Sketches of North Carolina,* 160–62.

28. Ibid., 162.

29. Preston Register, 3 July 1755, Draper Mss., 1QQ 83.

30. "Diary of the Rev. Hugh McAden," Foote, *Sketches of North Carolina,* 162.

31. Ibid., 162–63.

32. Landsman, "Religion, Expansion, and Migration," 115.

33. "Diary of the Rev. Hugh McAden," Foote, *Sketches of North Carolina,* 163.

34. Ibid., 163–64.

35. Preston Register, 30 July 1755, Draper Mss., 1QQ 83.

36. Ibid.

37. Deliberations by a Virginia council of war in Winchester on 14 May 1756 make explicit the depth of colonial misunderstanding: when George Washington asked his officers "whether it was advisable to send part of the Militia now here, to Guard and cover our Southern Frontiers?," they declined because of "The Southern Frontiers lying at a greater distance from, and less exposed to, the Enemy, than these northern frontiers; and being more difficult to come at: It is believed they can not suffer much, before

the Draughts for completing the Regiment, may be sent thither." Washington, *Papers of George Washington, Colonial Series*, 3:129, 14 May 1756.

38. John Buchanan, Account of Travel, ca. June 1756, Preston Family Papers, 1727–1896, VHS. Vause's Fort was located in the vicinity of modern Shawsville, Virginia.

39. [Andrew Lewis?] to [Lt. Gov. Robert Dinwiddie], ca. late June 1756, Draper Mss., 1QQ 132.

40. Crawford, "Frontier of Fear"; Ward, *Breaking the Backcountry*, 7–8.

41. Augusta OB, 4:495. Dinwiddie estimated that white tithables in Virginia represented 25 percent of the colony's total white population, and the overwhelming majority of Augusta County's population was white at this time. Dinwiddie, *Official Records of Robert Dinwiddie*, 2:345.

42. For refugees from southwest Virginia to North Carolina, see Bethabara Diary, 19 July 1755, *Records of the Moravians in North Carolina*, 1:133.

43. William Bird Ledger, 1744–1761, 245, Potts Mss., HSP.

44. The October 1758 Treaty of Easton guaranteed western Indian lands against English encroachment, and the November 1758 seizure of Fort Duquesne neutralized an important French base. Most western tribes accepted the treaty and stopped raiding frontier settlements, though Augusta County was hit once more in the fall of 1759. Jennings, *Empire of Fortune*, 396–403; Ward, *Breaking the Backcountry*, 178–82, 187–89.

45. Grand jury presentment, [16] May 1759, Criminal Causes, Box 1, Augusta CCC. The sheriff's grand jury pool is listed on the back of the presentment; for the list of jurors who served, see Augusta OB, 6:257, 16 May 1759. The order book entry noted that the grand jury made several presentments and recorded the order for process to issue but did not name the persons presented.

46. *Oxford English Dictionary*, online edition, s.v. "harbor."

47. For sexual improprieties presented by grand juries through 21 November 1753, see table 15. Thereafter to May 1759, see Augusta OB, 4:254, 316; 6:139, 206.

48. Summons, May Court 1759, *Grand Jury v. Ann Moore*, 1765, Criminal Causes, Box 1, Augusta CCC.

49. James Montgomery was alive as late as 12 March 1756, when he and his wife Ann signed a petition complaining that a neighbor was a common liar and disturber of the neighborhood. Chalkley, *Chronicles*, 1:315. Ann Montgomery made a bond to inventory her husband's estate in court on 19 Nov. 1756. Augusta WB, 2:176.

50. Augusta OB, 6:199, 19 Aug. 1758; Augusta County MB, 15 March–22 Nov. 1758, n.p., LOV.

51. As is explained below, the same grand jury presented Edward Tarr for a crime. His offense was listed immediately before Ann's.

52. For an example of a Timber Ridge man's campaigning against Indian raiders, see Archibald Alexander, a militia captain during the Sandy Creek expedition, in Dinwiddie, *Official Records of Robert Dinwiddie*, 1:xii, n.

53. For an essential analysis of colonial American women's striking back with words, see Norton, "Gender and Defamation in Seventeenth-Century Maryland." See also Walsh, "Community Networks in the Early Chesapeake," 236–38.

54. Grand jury presentment, [16] May 1759, Criminal Causes, Box 1, Augusta CCC.

55. [James Patton] to [Zachary Lewis or Thomas Walker?], [1750], Draper Mss.,

1QQ 61; "An Act for Regulating Ordinaries, and Restraint of Tipling Houses," Hening, ed., *Statutes*, 6:71–76.

56. Augusta OB, 6:296, 17 Aug. 1759. The churchwardens bound Vance to John Bowen, Jr., on 24 Aug. 1759. Augusta Parish VB, 247.

57. Grand jury presentment, May 1759, Criminal Causes, Box 1, Augusta CCC.

58. Woods's enemies thought him unfit for the office of sheriff; when the new county of Botetourt was subdivided from Augusta County, Israel Christian objected so strenuously to Woods's appointment as to draw the governor's and council's censure of Christian's behavior. *EJC*, 6:371, 23 Oct. 1770. For Christian's request that the Botetourt County clerk of court document Woods's inattention, see "Deposition of John May," 16 Oct. 1770, Virginia (Colony) Colonial Papers, 1630–1778, LOV.

59. Augusta OB, 6:459, 24 Nov. 1760. Tarr's deferral could have been ordered by the magistrates but more likely came from county clerk John Madison; clerks set the docket and could continue cases in order to ensure that the court dealt with the most pressing business during a given session.

60. Ibid., 7:102, 24 Aug. 1761.

61. The resolution of Moore's presentment for disturbing the peace is described in chapter 9.

62. Charles Donnelly petition, n.d., *Charles Donnelly v. Edward Tarr,* Judgment Files, Augusta CCC. The hamlet surrounding the Augusta County Courthouse officially became the town of Staunton with the November 1761 "Act for Establishing the Towns of Staunton, in the County of Augusta," Hening, ed., *Statutes,* 7:473–76. Town lot deeds first referred to Staunton in 1752. Augusta DB, 4:315. The initial attempt to establish Staunton was disallowed in England for unknown reasons in 1751. "An Act for Establishing a Town in Augusta County and Allowing Fairs to Be Kept Therein," May 1749, Winfree, comp., *Laws of Virginia,* 431–32, 460n173.

63. Augusta Parish VB, 318, 20 May 1760.

64. According to introductory notes in the microfilm edition of the *Virginia Gazette,* no issues of that paper survive for 1760. Fortunately, John Randolph of Roanoke abstracted items from colonial Virginia newspapers, and these abstracts were published by the Virginia Historical Society. "Historical and Genealogical Notes and Queries," *Virginia Magazine of History and Biography* 16 (Oct. 1908): 207. Randolph's abstracted account is corroborated by more general reports in the *Pennsylvania Gazette,* 17 April 1760, 3, and *Maryland Gazette,* 24 April 1760, 2. On 10 May 1760, Colonel William Byrd deplored conditions on "the South West Frontier, where the Cherokees continue to make horrid Devestation, & I dare say whole Countys will very soon be abandon'd." Byrd to Henry Bouquet, Bouquet, *Papers of Henry Bouquet,* 4:555.

65. Virginia Land Office Patents and Grants, 31:507; 32:706, 711, LOV; Augusta DB, 2:599, 8:238, 10:34; Kegley, *Kegley's Virginia Frontier,* 86.

66. For campaign details, see chapter 3.

67. "An Act for Raising the Sum of Thirty-Two Thousand Pounds, for the Relief of the Garrison of Fort Loudoun in the Cherokee Country," May 1760, Hening, ed., *Statutes,* 7:358.

68. *EJC,* 6:166, 23 July 1760.

69. *Pennsylvania Gazette,* 14 Aug. 1760, 2.

70. *EJC,* 6:169, 16 Sept. 1760. Sayers patented 536 acres on Reed Creek on 20 June 1753. Virginia Land Office Patents and Grants, 32:158, LOV. His mill is mentioned as a terminus for a 25 March 1754 road order to Holston River. Augusta OB, 4:142.

71. For reconnaissance, see Andrew Lewis to William Byrd, 9 Sept. 1760, Fauquier, *Official Papers of Francis Fauquier,* 1:409. Henry Timberlake accurately estimated that Great Island was "about 140 miles from the enemy's settlements." Williams, ed., *Timberlake's Memoirs,* 38.

72. For Byrd's continued presence at Sayer's mill as late as 19 Sept. 1760, see entry dated 6 Oct. 1760, *EJC,* 6:171. For the order to disband, see "An Act . . . for the Relief of the Garrison of Fort Loudon," Hening, ed., *Statutes,* 7:358.

73. For the troops' arrival in Staunton "on Wednesday" and food shortages, see Byrd to Fauquier, 29 May 1761, Fauquier, *Official Papers of Francis Fauquier,* 2:532.

74. A small portion of Byrd's command was assigned elsewhere. He reported a total strength of 39 officers; 6 staff; 67 sergeants, fifers, and drummers; and 688 effectives, plus a total of 87 noneffectives: 53 additional men sick and 34 deserted. "Return of the Virginia Reg't, 6th June 1761, Enclosed in Col Byrd's of the 7th Ditto," War Office, Series 34, Baron Jeffrey Amherst, Commander in Chief, Papers, 47:267, BNA. For Byrd's report from Fort Chiswell in the New River Valley at the end of the month, see "Return of the Virginia Reg't, 30th June 1761, Enclosed in Col Byrd's of 1st July," ibid., 270. See also "A General Return of the Virginia Regiment of Foot Comanded by the Hono'ble Colo Wm Byrd Encamp[ed] at Stalnakers July 31 1761," ibid., 274.

75. Petition, n.d., and summons, 10 Oct. 1761, *John Lewis v. Edward Tarr,* Judgment Files, Augusta CCC.

76. Augusta OB, 7:149, 21 Nov. 1761. If Tarr had been absent, judgment on the petition automatically would have been recorded for the plaintiff. Ibid., 7:198, 22 Feb. 1762.

77. Charles Donnelly petition, n.d., *Charles Donnelly v. Edward Tarr,* Judgment Files, Augusta CCC.

78. Augusta WB, 3:227.

7. The Anomalies

1. Bishop Roberts and George Hunter, "The Ichnography of Charles-Town. At High Water," New York Public Library.

2. The following plaintiffs in the Carolinas initiated lawsuits in Augusta County before the onset of the Seven Years' War. Charles Beatty: Augusta OB, 1:355; 2:25, 40; Chalkley, *Chronicles,* 2:413. Morgan Bryan: Augusta OB, 3:54; Augusta DB, 2:271, 731. John Carmichael: Augusta OB, 1:232; Linn, comp., *Abstracts of the Minutes of the Court of Pleas and Quarter Sessions,* 6. James Goodfellow: Augusta OB, 3:352, 369, 468; Chalkley, *Chronicles,* 2:399–400. Samuel Hairstone: Augusta OB, 4:25; Chalkley, *Chronicles,* 1:340. James Hemphill: Augusta OB, 4:214; *Richard Borden v. James Hemphill,* Judgment Files, Augusta CCC. John Hopes: Augusta OB, 3:127, 172; Chalkley, *Chronicles,* 1:491, 2:439. Edward Hughes: Augusta OB, 2:92; Linn, comp., *Abstracts of the Minutes of the Court of Pleas and Quarter Sessions,* 5. Andrew Johnston: Augusta OB, 2:589; 3:136, 152, 159, 194; 4:57, 89, 125, 137, 209, 210, 223, 225, 295, 311; Chalkley, *Chronicles,* 1:368. Alexander Moore: Augusta OB, 1:78; Chalkley, *Chronicles,* 1:342. John Neglee: Augusta OB, 3:273; Augusta DB, 2:793. Samuel Wilkins: Augusta OB, 2:551; 3:304–5, 349; Augusta

DB, 3:118. William Williams: Augusta OB, 3:151, 4:217. Bryan, Hopes, Hughs, Johnston, Wilkins, and Williams resided in Augusta County before moving to the Carolinas. Beatty, Carmichael, Goodfellow, Hairstone, Hemphill, Moore, and Neglee were not named in Augusta County road orders, militia rosters, or office appointments; this is strong circumstantial evidence that they either never resided in the county or lingered there only briefly.

3. Edward Tarr certificate, 6 Oct. 1761, Augusta WB, 3:227.

4. *James Young v. Hugh Montgomery*, petition, Judgment Files, Augusta CCC. Young requested a summons on 28 November 1753. Young lived on modern Whistle Creek, a tributary of the Maury River that was a few miles from Edward Tarr's Mill Creek land. Benjamin Borden deed to James Young, 18 June 1742, Orange County DB, 8:170, LOV.

5. The summons was returned not executed at court sessions on 26 March 1754 and 17 May 1754. Augusta OB, 4:176, 209.

6. Linn, comp., *Abstracts of the Minutes of the Court of Pleas and Quarter Sessions*, 74. Thanks to Joanna Miller Lewis for this reference.

7. The debt was for £475:13:4 North Carolina currency. "Public Debts Due in This Province for the Years Undermentioned [1758]," Saunders, ed., *Colonial Records of North Carolina*, 8:280–81.

8. *John Gordon v. Hugh Montgomery*, Judgment Rolls (CCP), Box 54A, item 196A, SCDAH.

9. McCusker, "How Much Is That in Real Money?" 333.

10. Hugh Montgomery receipt to Thomas Walker, 1 Feb. 1762, Walker Papers, LOC.

11. Augusta WB, 3:227.

12. Hening, ed., *Statutes*, 5:552–53.

13. Augusta WB, 3:227.

14. Preston loaned Davis six pounds on 28 November 1761, and the two divided their horses, wagons and equipment on the following day. Entries dated 28, 29 Nov. 1761, William Preston Memorandum Book, William and John Preston Papers, Perkins Library.

15. For Davis's association with Christian, a commissary for the Byrd expedition, see chapter 3.

16. Tarr certificate, Augusta WB, 3:227.

17. Augusta OB, 7:152 (receiving stolen goods, £500); 9:252 (counterfeiting, £1,000), 429 (spouse abuse, £500); 11:209 (attempted rape, £500).

18. Ibid., 7:104, 107, 111, 118, 125.

19. Ibid., 7:145, 125; Augusta WB, 3:227.

20. Augusta OB, 7:149; petition, 1761, *John Lewis v. Edward Tarr*, Judgment Files, Augusta CCC. For details of Lewis's suit, see chapter 6.

21. John McFarland deed to Hugh Montgomery, 4 May 1763, Augusta DB, 11:329; Patrick Calhoun, Jr., to Hugh Montgomery, 17 Oct. 1765, Augusta DB, 14:2. Montgomery identified the former tract in his will as "being on New river . . . which I heretofore purchased from Widow Nobles' son"; the discrepancy in grantors is explained in John Noble, estate appraisal, 16 Jan. 1753, Augusta WB, 1:483, which noted that Noble had bargained for the 106-acre tract, but McFarland had not made over title before Noble died. Hugh Montgomery will, 16 Dec. 1779, Hugh Montgomery Papers, 1779–

1830, Campbell Family Papers, Perkins Library. Thanks to Johanna Miller Lewis for advice regarding Montgomery's career.

22. Hugh Montgomery deed of gift, 13 Dec. 1779, ibid.

23. Virginia law stipulated that blacks could not "be sworn as a witness, or give evidence in any cause whatsoever, except upon the trial of a slave for a capital offense." "An Act Directing the Trial of Slaves Committing Capital Crimes; and for the More Effectual Punishing Conspiracies and Insurrections of Them; and for the Better Government of Negroes, Mulattoes, and Indians, Bond or Free," Oct. 1748, Hening, ed., *Statutes*, 6:107.

24. Augusta WB, 3:227.

25. Redd, "Reminiscences of Western Virginia," 339–40. As transcribed in the *Virginia Magazine of History and Biography* version of his "Reminiscences," Redd's letter discretely cites this mulatto as "Wm. ____," but the original 1842 manuscript in the Virginia Historical Society names the hunter as "Wm. Carr." Redd stated he met Carr in Powell's Valley about 1775; the Powell River is a tributary to the Holston River in today's Wise County, Virginia. Redd's account is supported by a 1771 tithable list from Botetourt County that names a William Carr as a head of household; Botetourt County at that time included Powell's Valley. This tithable list does not indicate race for any enumerated heads of household. "List of Tithables in my Company," [1771], Botetourt County Tithables, 1770–1782, 21, LOV.

26. Appraisal of Joseph Bell, ordered 26 March 1760, presented 23 Aug. 1760, Augusta WB, 2:414–15.

27. Account of "The astate of Joseph Bell (milato)," *George Wilson v. Joseph Bell's administrator [William Wilson]*, Judgment Files, March 1759, Augusta CCC.

28. George Wilson's militia roster, Augusta County Court Martial Records, 1756–1796, 3, LOV. For examples of landowning privates on Cowpasture River, see Augusta DB, 6:181, 300; Virginia Land Office Patents and Grants, 30:372, 378; 34:132, LOV.

29. Account of "The astate of Joseph Bell (milato)," *George Wilson v. Joseph Bell's administrator [William Wilson]*, Judgment Files, March 1759, Augusta CCC.

30. Augusta OB, 3:328, 22 Aug. 1752.

31. "An Act for the Better Securing the Payment of Levies, and Restraint of Vagrants and for Making Provision for the Poor," Oct. 1748, Hening, ed., *Statutes*, 6:32; "An Act for the Better Management and Security of Orphans, and Their Estates," Oct. 1748, ibid., 5:452.

32. Augusta Parish VB, 112, 22 Nov. 1752; 104, 22 Aug. 1752; 103, 22 Nov. 1752; Augusta OB, 4:249, 20 May 1754. Only three churchwarden contracts for Smith children were recorded in the Augusta Parish vestry book.

33. Augusta OB, 4:249, 20 May 1754; 4:244.

34. Ibid., 4:252–53, 21 May 1754.

35. Ibid., 4:290, 24 Aug. 1754. Smith's attorney was mentioned but not named in this entry; Gabriel Jones was identified as serving the plaintiff during the following court session. Ibid., 4:363.

36. Augusta WB, 2:131; Augusta OB, 6:276.

37. The magistrates listed were James Patton, David Stewart, Robert McClenachan,

James Lockhart, John Mathews, and George Robinson. Eventual slave owners included Stewart and McClenachan, but McClenachan recused himself. Ibid., 4:340, 14:269, 7:71.

38. Ibid., 4:340, 363. Although McClenachan was named twice as one of the defendants against Smith's petition, his name was omitted from the defendants on 25 November. I speculate this omission is a clerical error, a conclusion supported by the timing of McClenachan's departure from the bench and by the fact that two defendants, Robert Breckinridge and Elijah McClenachan, possessed between them the components of Robert McClenachan's name, which might have confused a hastily writing clerk. The clerk noted that defendants Robert Breckinridge, Elijah McClenachan, William Preston, and George Wilson appeared "in their proper persons," meaning that they were not represented by attorneys.

39. William Preston, "List of Militia Company," 29 Nov. 1757, Preston Family Papers, 1727–1896, VHS; Augusta Parish VB, 104.

40. Free blacks could only serve legally as noncombatants. "An Act for . . . the Protection of His Majesty's Subjects on the Frontiers of This Colony," Hening, ed., *Statutes*, 6:533. For problems of recruitment and desertion, see Ward, *Breaking the Backcountry*, 62–63, 107–10.

41. William Preston, "An acount of Pay Due the Company of Rangers in Augusta raised by Act of Assembly, from their Inlisting untill ye first of Feb[ruar]y 1756" and "A list of the Company of Rangers Commanded by Capt Wm Preston Lieutenants Audley Paul and David Robinson of Augusta County," n.d. [earliest enlistment was 16 July 1755 and latest desertion date was 25 April 1756], Draper Mss., 1QQ 91, 92.

42. William Preston, "List of Militia Company," 29 Nov. 1757, Preston Family Papers, 1727–1896, VHS.

43. William Preston, "Indian Campaigns," 1758–1759, Preston Family Papers, 1727–1896, VHS. Smith's presence on militia pay rolls is indicated by his promissory notes dated 4 August and 2 October 1758 for "money Colo John Buchanan is to Stop out of the first of the said Smiths Peay." Nicholas Smith, "Order to John Buchanan to pay Alex Buchanan," and Alexander Buchanan, "2 Orders to John Buchanan," both Preston Family Papers, 1727–1896, VHS. For Bell's death, see Augusta WB, 2:414–15.

44. Augusta OB, 6:317, 21 Nov. 1759; 461, 24 Nov. 1760.

45. Ibid., 10:213, 20 Aug. 1766. Smith's summer of 1766 departure is confirmed by his inclusion as a "runaway" in a 1767 list of delinquent tithables in William Preston's precinct; such lists referred to residents for years ending 10 June, so Smith departed between 10 June and 20 August 1766. Chalkley, *Chronicles*, 2:420. Preston was appointed as a tithable taker for the south side of the James River in May 1766. Augusta OB, 10:152.

46. "A list of the Tithables in the Lower District of New river," [1771], Botetourt County Tithables, 1770–1782, 23, LOV; "A List of Tithables Taken by Geo Skillern on the Big Levels of Greenbrier, Antonys Creek, Sincking Creek & muddy Creek and the Head of the Sink Hole Land," 8 June 1774, ibid., 141.

47. "A List of Tithables in Green Briar including the little & Great Levels, Spring Creek, the two Sinking Creeks, Anthony's Creek, Howards D[itt]o, & Muddy Creek; Returned according to Order of Court By Andrew Donnally," 7 March 1775, ibid., 154;

"A List of Tithables in Green Briar, extending from the little Levels downwards, including the two sinking Creeks, & Muddy Creek, also Anthony's Creek & Howards Creek on the East side of the River, Taken by Andrew Donnally," 1 Aug. 1775, ibid., 193.

48. Indenture, John Smiley and Elizabeth Joseph, 2 Feb. 1760, Judgment Files, Augusta CCC; Augusta OB, 6:346, 19 March 1760; "An Act for the Better Government of Servants and Slaves," Nov. 1753, Hening, ed., *Statutes*, 6:359.

49. Augusta Parish VB, 104, 22 Aug. 1752; 112, 22 Nov. 1752; 103, 22 Nov. 1752.

50. Alexander Stuart advertisement, *Virginia Gazette* (Pinckney), 9 Feb. 1775, 3, emphasis in original.

51. "All children shall be bond or free, according to the condition of their mothers." "An Act for the Better Government of Servants and Slaves," Nov. 1753, Hening, ed., *Statutes*, 6:357.

52. "An Act for Suppressing Outlying Slaves," April 1691, ibid., 3:86–88; "An Act Concerning Servants and Slaves," Oct. 1705, ibid., 3:447–62.

53. Augusta OB, 1:288, 16 Sept. 1747; Augusta Parish VB, 49, 16 Feb. 1747/8.

54. Augusta OB, 2:7, 20 May 1748; 2:112, 17 May 1749.

55. Ibid., 6:177, 20 May 1758; 6:221, 17 Nov. 1758; 6:285, 19 May 1759; 7:101, 24 Aug. 1761; Summonses, Nov. 1758, May 1759, Judgment Files, Augusta CCC. Jane Knox received as a minimal legacy from her father a single shilling sterling; it is impossible to tell whether her father previously provided Jane's inheritance or whether the shilling represented his sole bequest to her. James Knox will, 11 April 1769, Augusta WB, 4:510–11. For James Knox's Cowpasture freehold, see Virginia Land Office Patents and Grants, 34:736–37, LOV.

56. Augusta OB, vols. 1–14, passim; Augusta Parish VB, passim. Like their sisters east of the Blue Ridge, Augusta County white indentured servant women rarely bore mixed race illegitimate children. In an extensive review of piedmont Virginia court records, Philip D. Morgan found "only 9 white servant women cited by grand juries for having a 'mulatto bastard' before 1755. After this date the number drops to 2." "Slave Life in Piedmont Virginia," 471n68.

57. Seven contracts survive binding mulatto minors (legitimate or otherwise) to white adults. Augusta Parish VB, 49, 103, 104, 112, 118, 509; Sarah Joseph's indenture, 2 Feb. 1760, Judgment Files, Augusta CCC. Only the earliest, drawn for Christopher Roarrey on 16 February 1748/9, includes no mention of schooling. Augusta Parish VB, 49.

58. *Edward Tarr v. George Stevenson*, Judgment Files, Augusta CCC. For details of the suit, see appendix 4.

59. Augusta OB, 7:9, 20 May 1761.

60. Ibid., 7:462, 17 Feb. 1763; 8:122, 22 June 1763.

61. *JHB, 1766–1769*, 198.

62. "An Act for Exempting Free Negro, Mulatto, and Indian Women, from the Payment of Levies," Nov. 1769, Hening, ed., *Statutes*, 8:393.

8. The Rebels

1. By the early 1780s, "ironmasters owned almost one-quarter of the 824 slaves" in York, Chester, and Lancaster Counties. Bezís-Selfa, "Slavery and the Disciplining of Free Labor in the Colonial Mid-Atlantic Iron Industry," 278, citing Carl D. Oblinger,

"New Freedoms, Old Miseries: The Emergence and Disruption of Black Communities in Southeastern Pennsylvania, 1780–1860" (Ph.D. diss., Lehigh University, 1988), 31–32.

2. Dinwiddie, *Official Records of Robert Dinwiddie*, 2:352. See appendix 3n1 for my argument that this list reflects reports that were effective as of 10 June 1755. Tithables are defined in chapter 3n24.

3. For biographical notes on Augusta County's enslaved pioneers, see appendix 3.

4. Schwarz, *Twice Condemned*, 62.

5. For individual colonial-era patents of Augusta County land, see "Grants by the Proprietor of the Northern Neck in Augusta County, 1747/8–1756," and Land Office Patents and Grants, vols. 16–42, LOV.

6. These figures include the counties of Rockingham, Augusta, and Rockbridge. Mitchell, *Commercialism and Frontier*, 86, 100.

7. Simmons and Sorrells, "Slave Hire and the Development of Slavery in Augusta County," 169.

8. As of June 1755, blacks comprised 56.5 percent of the 3,091 total tithables in Albemarle County. Dinwiddie, *Official Records of Robert Dinwiddie*, 2:352.

9. Morgan and Nicholls, "Slaves in Piedmont Virginia, 1720–1790"; Kulikoff, *Tobacco and Slaves*, 396–401.

10. Beverley Manor's tithable taker erroneously charged King for the added tithable, but King successfully petitioned the Orange County court to deduct his slave from the 1742 list on the grounds that the slave was not yet in the county on 10 June, the annual accounting date. Orange County OB, 3:237, 28 Aug. 1742, LOV. McDowell's appraisers valued the slave boy and girl at twenty pounds each in an appraisal dated 20 April 1743. Orange County WB, 1:271, 23 June 1743, LOV. McDowell's executors subsequently sold the boy for £34:9:2. Augusta OB, 2:157, 24 Aug. 1749.

11. In the three counties west of the Blue Ridge, the white/black tithable ratio was Augusta 2,273/40, Frederick 2,173/340, and Hampshire 558/12. Dinwiddie reported 43,329 white and 60,078 black tithables for Virginia. He estimated the total white population to be four times the tithable count, and the total black population to be twice the tithable count. "A List of Tithables Sent the Lords of Trade," 23 Feb. 1756, Dinwiddie, *Official Records of Robert Dinwiddie*, 2:352–53. Virginia statute defined tithables as males aged sixteen years and older, and enslaved, free black, and Indian females aged sixteen or older. "An Act Concerning Tithables," Oct. 1748, Hening, ed., *Statutes*, 6:40–41.

12. See, for example, Morgan, "Task and Gang Systems" and Walsh, "Slave Life, Slave Society, and Tobacco Production in the Tidewater Chesapeake, 1620–1820."

13. Axtell, *The European and the Indian*, 6.

14. William Preston receipt, 28 Aug. 1759, Preston Family Papers, 1727–1896, VHS.

15. At the court immediately following Preston's purchase in August, four Augusta County masters produced five slave children for certification of the newcomers' ages. Entries dated 21 Nov. 1759, Augusta OB, 6:314, 316. For two slaves Preston assigned to work on a tract rented by white tenants, see William Preston's Memorandum of Agreement with George Patterson and John Rork, 23 Jan. 1761, Breckinridge Collection, HMWV.

16. Augusta DB, 5:33, 6:477, 7:514, 7:520, 8:90, 8:176, 10:146. Preston purchased all but the last of these tracts, which he inherited from his father, John Preston (who died by

19 Feb. 1747/8). Augusta WB, 1:72. For Preston's surveys, see Augusta County Surveyor Book, 1:77, 87, 88, LOV.

17. Terry, "Family Empires," 151.

18. Louis Ourry to Henry Bouquet, 29 Nov. 1761, Henry Bouquet Manuscript, LOC. This document was not published in Bouquet, *Papers of Henry Bouquet*, but is calendared in ibid., 6:805.

19. Three other potential transactions of ten or more slaves can be documented in early Augusta County. Staunton merchant Felix Gilbert purchased twenty-one slaves in 1761; as discussed below, he sold almost all of these shortly thereafter. Felix Gilbert to Thomas Walker, 16 July 1761, Walker Papers, LOC. John Sutton advertised fifteen slaves for sale at the Augusta County courthouse in 1770. *Virginia Gazette* (Rind), 31 May 1770, 4. See also the McRedie quarter discussed below.

20. For Tidewater planters Carter and Nathaniel Burwell's Shenandoah Valley quarters north of Augusta County, see Hofstra, *Planting of New Virginia*, 221–22, 279–80.

21. No record survives of the slaves' fate; the land was not sold until 1768. *Virginia Gazette*, 28 Feb. 1755, 4; Augusta DB, 17:278.

22. Adams resided in New Kent County when he bought his first Calfpasture River land in 1766 and still lived there as late as 19 March 1772. Ibid., 13:54, 18:171. Adams appears to have moved some slaves to the frontier by the 1770s; an estate appraisal drawn for deceased Calfpasture River landowner Robert Graham, dated 30 April 1774, mentions "William Anderson Overseer for Mr Thomas Adams." Augusta WB, 5:241. By the time he wrote his will in 1785, Adams had moved to the Calfpasture Valley. Thomas Adams will, 14 Oct. 1785, Adams Family Papers, 1672–1792, VHS. At his death in 1788, Adams had slaveholdings in three counties. Augusta WB, 7:99.

23. In 1753, McCune owned two tracts totaling 406 acres in Beverley Manor. Orange County DB, 5:99, LOV; Augusta DB, 2:421–22. Approximately one quarter of Augusta County's patented acreage was owned that year by residents holding four hundred acres or less. McCleskey, "Rich Land, Poor Prospects," 471.

24. Gloster's story was narrated as part of the jury's special verdict in *Samuel McCune v. Joseph Teas*, 25 March 1754, Augusta OB, 4:139–41. Unless otherwise annotated, all quotations regarding the episode are drawn from this source. Joseph Teas was identified as a farmer in a 1739 land deed. Orange County DB, 3:271, LOV.

25. In 1769, an Augusta County slave owner paid 9/4 for a slave shirt, the same price for a pair of slave shoes, and £1:0:8 for a slave coat and pair of breeches, making a total of £1:19:4. John Buchanan, "Notebook of Accounts," entry dated 3 Feb. 1769, Preston Family Papers, 1727–1896, VHS. Thanks to Frances Pollard for assistance locating this source.

26. Hannah Herndon's account versus Hugh Donegho, 1 Jan. 1770, Judgment Files, Augusta CCC; "Diary of Thomas Lewis," entry dated 12 Nov. 1774, Lewis Family Papers, 1749–1920, VHS. Adjusted for inflation, the £6 that Teas projected in 1754 would have been worth £6.9 in 1769 (vice £10 for Herndon) and £7.2 in 1774 (vice £18 for Lewis). Inflation adjustments employ a composite consumer price index of 81 in 1754, 93 in 1769, and 97 in 1774. For example, 93 ÷ 81 × £6 = £6.9. McCusker, "How Much Is That in Real Money?" 324–25.

27. "An Act to Restrain the Taking of Excessive Usury," Hening, ed., *Statutes*, 6:101–4.

28. In Beverley Manor, where Joseph Teas and Samuel McCune both lived, the average resale price for land between 1745 and 1754 was £21:5:0 per 100 acres (N = 102). Mitchell, *Commercialism and Frontier,* 77.

29. "An Act Concerning Tithables," Oct. 1705, Hening, ed., *Statutes,* 3:258–61; "An Act Concerning Tithables," Oct. 1748, ibid., 6:40–44; Morgan and Nicholls, "Slaves in Piedmont Virginia, 1720–1790," 217–23, 247–51.

30. Holton, *Forced Founders,* 66–71.

31. Felix Gilbert to Thomas Walker, 16 July 1761, Walker Papers, LOC.

32. Augusta OB, 7:50–71, 18–22 Aug. 1761. New owners registered twenty-three children during this period, but two of these slaves were certified by masters living in the north end of the county. Almost all of the remaining masters owned property in Staunton, in the surrounding Beverley Manor, or on the nearby Middle Shenandoah River. Augusta DB, vols. 1–10; Orange County DB, vols. 3–9, LOV; Virginia Land Office Patents and Grants, vols. 16–34, LOV. Three masters—John Anderson, Jr., John Hinds, and James Gamble—owned no land in August 1761 but presumably were Gilbert's neighbors because they were listed the previous year as heads of household within the bounds of his militia company. "Wm Preston Tax Rolls, Augusta Settlement," 1760, Preston Family Papers, 1727–1896, VHS.

33. Preston Agreement with Patterson and Rork, Breckinridge Collection, HMWV.

34. William Carvin appraisal, 28 May 1751, Executive Papers, 336, Augusta CCC.

35. Augusta DB, 11:783. His will, drawn 20 October 1767 and proved 16 March 1768, referred to this 150-acre Mill Creek tract as where "I now live on." Augusta WB, 4:84–85. He also owned an adjoining two-hundred-acre tract. Augusta DB, 10:342. The slave Lue, anonymously identified as a "Negro Wench" in Taylor's estate inventory, was valued at forty pounds by Taylor's appraisers. Augusta WB, 4:126, 14 May 1768. In an eighteenth-century context, "to raise bread" meant to grow edible crops; c.f. Joseph Wolgamote to George Washington, 20 June 1758, Washington, *Papers of George Washington, Colonial Series,* 5:232–33.

36. For hemp production in western Virginia, see Mitchell, *Commercialism and Frontier,* 163–66, and especially Herndon, "The Story of Hemp in Colonial Virginia." For the Winchester ropewalk, see Mitchell, *Commercialism and Frontier,* 166. For Virginia hemp bounties, see "An Act for Encouraging the Making of Tar, and Hemp," Oct. 1748, Hening, ed., *Statutes,* 6:144–46, and "An Act for Encouraging the Making Hemp," Nov. 1769, ibid., 8:363–64.

37. Augusta OB, 10:151, 153, 191, 193–96, 198, 200–204, 206, 212–13, 232, 236, 294, 317, 334–35, 337–42, 345–46, 349, 351, 358, 364, 423, 459, 463, 465–70, 473, 481–82, 486–87, 489, 498; 11:59–63, 67–69, 83–85, 90, 98–99, 202, 211–14, 222–23, 232–33, 238–39, 248, 312–13, 337–38, 342–43, 346–47, 350–51, 366, 374.

38. Sources for slaveholders are given in table 22.

39. A total of 2,460 resident men held freehold titles to land in Augusta County between 1738 and the end of 1770. Of these, 281 (11.4%) can be identified as German. McCleskey, "Across the First Divide," table following p. 174. I counted as German all known Dunkers and members of Lutheran or German Reformed congregations, persons with the same surname as members of those denominations, persons with Anglicized phonetic spellings of Germanic surnames such as Caspar Brenner, Hans Bum-

gardner, or Mathias Gabhard, and valley persons identified as Germanic in Wust, *Virginia Germans.*

40. Twenty-six resident Anglican male landowners can be identified in Augusta County by the end of 1770. These men, who constituted 1.1 percent of the resident male landowners, did not necessarily all come from eastern Virginia. I counted as Anglicans those men who hosted an itinerant Anglican service, sponsored construction of Anglican chapels, held office in the Church of England or American Episcopal Church, or were immediately related to such persons (father, brother, son) if no other family member was positively identified in affiliation with any denomination except Anglican. For an essential introduction to religion and ethnicity in the colonial Valley of Virginia, see Mitchell, *Commercialism and Frontier,* 104–9.

41. Apparently the colonial tithable lists were gone by the time Lyman C. Chalkley began his prodigious albeit badly flawed abstraction project, *Chronicles of the Scotch-Irish Settlement in Virginia.* Only a few colonial fragments survive, most notably the lists of tithables within the bounds of two militia companies headed by Captains Felix Gilbert and Patrick Martin, circa 1760, and a short list of supplemental levies for the same year."Wm Preston Tax Rolls, Augusta Settlement," Preston Family Papers, 1727–1896, VHS. Even these lists do not differentiate between servant, slave, and family tithables.

42. The four German slaveholders include George Bowman, John Spear, Ephraim Vause, and Jacbor Lorton. Entry dated 16 Aug. 1749, Executive Papers, 384, Augusta CCC; Augusta OB, 6:210, 15 Nov. 1758; [Andrew Lewis] to [Lt. Gov. Robert Dinwiddie], June 1756, Draper Mss., 1QQ_133; Augusta DB, 15:481), 21 June 1769 By contrast, in the Maryland piedmont, Germans constituted a higher proportion of landowners and also seem to have participated much more actively in slavery. Five out of forty-seven German estates (10.6%) appraised in Frederick County, Maryland, from 1749 to 1775 included at least one slave. Kessel, "Germans in the Making of Frederick County, Maryland," 97.

43. Madison was clerk of court from 1745 through the colonial period. Jones was licensed as an attorney in Augusta County in 1745 and appointed as king's attorney on 15 April 1746. Augusta OB, 1:2, 24. Beyond their close professional connection, the two men were married to sisters.

44. William Preston receipt to John Champe and Company for sum paid for 16 slaves, 28 Aug. 1759; Thomas Lewis to William Preston, 4 Sept. 1760, both Preston Family Papers, 1727–1896, VHS. The *Marques of Rockingham* delivered two hundred slaves from Sierra Leone in the Rappahannock Naval District on 18 Aug. 1760. Voyage 90338, Trans-Atlantic Slave Trade Database. Preston's purchase from Champe was part of a cargo of 350 slaves brought from the Gold Coast to Maryland by the *True Blue,* which landed on 16 Aug. 1759. Voyage 90763, ibid.

45. Morgan and Nicholls, "Slaves in Piedmont Virginia, 1720–1790," 250–51.

46. Waddell, *Annals of Augusta County,* 197.

47. *Virginia Gazette* (Dixon and Hunter), 4 Dec. 1778, 4.

48. Ross witnessed Alexander Boyd's mortgage of real estate and slaves on 28 Nov. 1764. Augusta WB, 12:40. After Boyd's death, Ross supervised the sale of Boyd's slaves at Boyd's store in what by then had become Botetourt County. *Virginia Gazette* (Pur-

die and Dixon), 31 Jan. 1771, 3. Ross sold two slaves to Major Robert Breckenridge on 16 Aug. 1771. David Ross receipt to Breckinridge, Breckinridge Collection, HMWV.

49. Colonel John McNeill estate accounts, 6 June 1765, Augusta WB, 4:40.

50. Joseph Steps deed to Daniel Smith, 5 Sept. 1764, Augusta DB, 12:181.

51. John Buchanan, "Notebook of Accounts," Preston Family Papers, 1727–1896, VHS.

52. "An Act to Authorize the Citizens of South Carolina and Georgia to Remove Their Slaves into This State," May 1780, Hening, ed., *Statutes*, 10:307–8.

53. Davis (10 Nov. 1781) and Twig (17 Jan. 1782) lists, Augusta County List of Slaves Removed to Virginia from Georgia, 1781, LOV.

54. Patrick Lockhart's list of taxable property in Captain Smith's, Robinson's, and Holston's companies, 10 April 1782, Botetourt County Tithables, 1770–1782, 265, LOV.

55. Augusta DB, vols. 1–16.

56. Will of William Skillern, 16 Jan. 1744/5, Orange County WB, 2:63 (second page of this number), LOV; Orange County DB, 6:267, LOV.

57. Bill of sale, 7 Nov. 1766, Stuart-Baldwin Papers, 1742–1832, Alderman Library.

58. Augusta OB, 7:109, 18 Nov. 1761; 8:245, 23 Sept. 1763; John Craig estate appraisal, 24 June 1774, Augusta WB, 6:505.

59. "Charles Cummings and Sinking Springs Church 1772–1789," Campbell Family Papers, Perkins Library; Augusta OB, 11:64.

60. Ibid., 6:143, 7:208, 10:225.

61. Todd to Preston, William and John Preston Papers, Perkins Library.

62. Augusta OB, 4:140.

63. Hildebrand, "The Beverley Patent, 1736."

64. Petition, *James Given v. John Stewart*, May 1749, Judgment Files, Augusta CCC.

65. McCleskey, "Across the First Divide," 141.

66. These cases were identified in petitions presented at special court sessions for certifying propositions, claims, and grievances to the General Assembly. The petitioners sought rewards or restitution of expenses that had not already been remitted by eastern slaveholders. The actual number of apprehended fugitives therefore was almost certainly much higher. For sources, see map 4.

67. Augusta OB, 4:501, 20 Nov. 1755.

68. *Virginia Gazette* (Purdie and Dixon), 2 May 1766, 3; 23 May 1766, 3. From a historiographic perspective, it is important to note that Augusta County slaves seized in Hanover, New Kent, and Richmond counties were not thwarted maroons, fugitives attempting to establish independent communities in the continental interior beyond the reach of Anglo-American authority. Indeed, no conclusive evidence has yet come to light that colonial Virginia slaves ever attempted a maroon settlement west of the Blue Ridge in the eighteenth century, notwithstanding the claim by Gerald W. Mullin that in the 1720s a group of slaves briefly set up a maroon community "near the present site of Lexington, Virginia"; the location Mullin projected is on the southwestern edge of what became the Timber Ridge Presbyterian congregation. The primary source Mullin cites does not indicate this attempt was located west of the Blue Ridge. *Flight and Rebellion*, 43, citing Sir (*sic*) William Gooch to Board of Trade, 29 June 1729, CO 5/1322, 19, BNA.

69. William Dudley receipt to William Preston, 26 July 1761, Preston Family Papers, 1727–1896, VHS. Preston paid Dudley three pounds, nine shillings, "on Acct of three runaway negroes . . . for the takeing them up & the sherif fees."

70. Claim of Griffin Garland, 1 Nov. 1762, Richmond County OB, 15:27, LOV. Thanks to Camille Wells for this information. Doggett purchased two tracts totaling 535 acres on Reed Creek on 19 May 1761. Augusta DB, 9:379, 382.

71. Dunn, "Servants and Slaves," 177.

72. Norton, "Gender and Defamation in Seventeenth-Century Maryland"; Morgan, "Slave Life in Piedmont Virginia," 443–44.

73. For three of many examples, see Augusta OB, 2:425; 4:6, 330.

74. Ibid., 4:140.

75. William Taylor will, 20 Oct. 1767, Augusta WB, 4:85; Augusta DB, 10:342, 11:783.

76. Whitley certified Jack's age on 21 May 1755. Augusta OB, 4:424; Virginia Land Office Patents and Grants, 24:365, LOV.

77. Paul Whitley will, 2 Dec. 1771, Botetourt County WB, 1:13–14, LOV.

78. Augusta OB, 8:325, 9 Nov. 1763.

79. Ibid., 14:59, 13 Nov. 1769.

80. Ibid., 11:488, 15 Feb. 1768; 12:134, 17 May 1768.

81. Through 1772, twenty-two out of forty-three Augusta County estate inventories (51.2%) including slaves also included a musket, pistol, or rifle.

82. Magistrates could license slaves to carry firearms. "An Act . . . for the Better Government of Negros, Mulattos, and Indians, Bond or Free," May 1723, Hening, ed., *Statutes*, 4:126–34. Virginia renewed this section of the law almost verbatim in 1748. "An Act Directing the Trial of Slaves Committing Capital Crimes," ibid., 6:110.

83. Courts of oyer and terminer handed down six convictions. Augusta OB, 6:35, 3 Oct. 1757; 8:325, 9 Nov. 1763; 11:488, 15 Feb. 1768; 12:133–34, 17 May 1768; 13:72–73, 29 Nov. 1768. The last case was a simultaneous trial of two slaves. A called court ordered that a slave receive a lashing and lose an ear. Ibid., 14:59, 13 Nov. 1769. A regularly scheduled court ordered the castration of a slave. Ibid., 5:125, 21 May 1756.

84. Hoffer and Scott, eds., *Criminal Proceedings in Colonial Virginia*, 133–34, 180–81, 181–82, 187–88, 213–14, 222–23, 225–26, 227–28, 232–33, 236–38, 239–42, 244–46. Because the Richmond County records end in 1754, I was obliged to compare nonconcurrent time periods. I counted as a conviction the 1730 death while in prison of slave James, because the court ordered the sheriff to quarter James's body and impale the head on a pole. Ibid., 133–34. I also counted the 1745 trial of Scipio as a conviction because, though acquitted of the charge of store-breaking, Scipio received thirty-nine lashes for escaping from jail and refusing to reveal the name of the person who assisted him. Ibid., 225–26.

85. For 1755 slave and white tithable figures, see "A List of Tithables Sent the Lords of Trade," 23 Feb. 1756, Dinwiddie, *Official Records of Robert Dinwiddie*, 2:352–53.

86. Philip J. Schwarz estimates that "between 1740 and 1785, at least twenty-four white people died violently at the hands of a slave or a group of slaves." *Twice Condemned*, 144. Augusta County slaves murdered two of these victims, one in 1763, the second in 1772. Augusta OB, 8:325–26, 9 Nov. 1763; 14:362, 11 April 1772.

87. By contrast, tithable blacks in Richmond County outnumbered tithable whites almost two to one. Dinwiddie, *Official Records of Robert Dinwiddie*, 2:352–53.

88. Augusta OB, 5:125. For punitive and legal contexts of castration, see Schwarz, *Twice Condemned*, 22, 156, 162–63.

89. Augusta OB, 6:35–36, 3 Oct. 1757. For statutory authorization to pay masters for their losses by the execution of a slave, see "An Act Directing the Trial of Slaves Committing Capital Crimes," Oct. 1748, Hening, ed., *Statutes*, 6:107. For practice and implications of compensation in Virginia, see Schwarz, *Twice Condemned*, 11, 20, 40, 52–53, 73. For analysis of compensation in North Carolina, see Kay, "'The Planters Suffer Little or Nothing.'"

90. Patterson, *Sociology of Slavery*, 275–76.

91. For example, servant William Bishop complained in 1750 that his master Charles Campbell "had stolen his money and [was] abusing him," but the court judged Bishop's complaint "to be groundless" and so ordered "that he receive on his bare back at the Public Whiping post Ten lashes well laid on." Five years later, another of Campbell's servants complained of abuse and met an identical fate. Augusta OB, 2:362, 4:471. Servant women who charged their masters ran the same risk; Margaret Farrell "Complained of the Ill Usage of her Master" in 1762, but the county magistrates ruled "that she was in fault" and sentenced Farrell to "Twentyfive Lashes on her back well Laid on." Ibid., 7:297.

92. Ibid., 2:65, 3:184. In the latter example, dated 28 Aug. 1751, white servant boy Henry Wetherington "had an Iron lock round his neck with a gag in his mouth."

93. The Augusta County court found six white servants guilty of violence directed against masters in the quarter century from 1745 through 1769. These episodes included threatening the wife of a master, murder of a master, violent resistance, abuse, stabbing a freeholder, and beating and abuse. Ibid., 2:425; 3:198; 4:289, 325; 9:247, 258.

94. In Augusta County through 1769, 69 named and 24 anonymous teenaged or adult males can be identified; thus, the known adult males numbered between 69 and 93 individuals. For male slaves not accounted for in slave sources cited in table 22, see Executive Papers, 384, Augusta CCC; Augusta DB, 3:60; 5:445; 7:450; 10:405; 11:232, 564, 656; 12:41, 181; Augusta MB, 17 Feb.–19 Dec. 1761, entry dated December 1761, LOV; Augusta OB, 2:65, 157, 353, 356, 370, 500; 3:444; 4:70, 109, 139, 262, 424; 5:125, 187, 193, 248, 379; 6:36, 143, 210, 295, 316, 387; 7:50, 52 (second page of this number), 54–56, 64, 69, 71, 105, 109, 163, 173, 209, 212, 219, 295, 463 (second page of this number); 8:34, 120, 245, 326, 386, 424, 469, 489, 497; 9:72, 162–63, 231, 239, 323, 341, 438, 446; Augusta WB, 1:140, 166, 362, 385; 2:23, 131, 312, 388, 406, 418; 3:24, 46, 119, 123, 163, 271, 289, 318, 328, 352, 359, 373, 389, 392; 4:471; *JHB, 1766–1769*, 66; Orange County OB, 3:349, LOV; Orange County WB, 1:271, 2:63, LOV; Richmond County OB, 15:27, LOV; Spotsylvania County WB, B:264, LOV; *Virginia Gazette*, 28 Feb. 1755, 4; *Virginia Gazette* (Purdie and Dixon), 2 May 1766, 3.

95. Thornton, "African Dimensions of the Stono Rebellion."

96. For African martial experience with firearms, see ibid., 1108–13; petition, *James Given v. John Stewart*, May 1749, Judgment Files, Augusta CCC.

97. John Harrison registered Farmer as nine years old on 19 May 1762. Augusta OB, 7:219. Gabriel Jones, the king's attorney, accused Farmer at a called court on 2 January 1764. Ibid., 8:386.

98. For a rare mention of a local master's quarter, see "the Negro Quarter of John

Madison" broken into by the marauding Hampton in 1757. Ibid., 6:35. Madison's assignment of slaves to a quarter may reflect the fact that, unlike most Augusta County masters, he grew up in eastern Virginia. For Madison's origins, see Kegley, *Kegley's Virginia Frontier*, 604.

99. Augusta OB, 4:289–90, 24 Aug. 1754.

100. For comparable eastern Virginia perceptions, see Holton, *Forced Founders*, 137–39.

101. "Diary of the Rev. Hugh McAden," Foote, *Sketches of North Carolina*, 163.

102. Robert Dinwiddie to John and Capel Hanbury, 23 July 1754, Dinwiddie, *Dinwiddie: Correspondence Illustrative of His Career*, 584.

103. William Fleming to Francis Fauquier, 26 July 1763, Draper Mss., 3ZZ 50.

104. Four were slaves of David Cloyd; see *Pennsylvania Gazette*, 3 May 1764, 2; *David Cloyd v. James Montgomery*, Augusta OB, 10:237, 23 Aug. 1766. A fifth captured slave, Adam, belonged to John Trimble. Waddell, *Annals of Augusta County*, 197; Augusta OB, 7:56.

105. See the episode involving Harrison's servant John Stagg above.

106. Harrison, *Settlers by the Long Grey Trail*, 181. County magistrates convened a called court on 9 Nov. 1763 in accordance with a commission of oyer and terminer dated 22 Oct. 1763. Augusta OB, 8:324–26.

107. *Pennsylvania Gazette*, 20 Oct. 1763, 2; John Blair to Thomas Gage, 22 Oct. 1763, Thomas Gage Papers, Clements Library, University of Michigan.

108. According to family tradition well supported by contemporary land records, Harrison lived at Lacey Spring, eight miles north of modern Harrisonburg. Harrison, *Settlers by the Long Grey Trail*, 160.

109. As eighteenth-century legal scholar William Blackstone described it, the court of oyer and terminer was convened "to hear and determine all treasons, felonies, and misdemesnors." *Commentaries*, 4:266–67. See Schwarz, *Twice Condemned*, 16–22, on the colonial evolution of Virginia's courts of oyer and terminer for slaves.

110. "An Act Directing the Trial of Slaves Committing Capital Crimes," Oct. 1748, Hening, ed., *Statutes*, 6:105–6; Augusta OB, 8:324–26.

111. In descending seniority, the six magistrates were James Lockhart, Patrick Martin, Israel Christian, John Poage, Abraham Smith, Andrew Bird. Ibid.

112. Hening, ed., *Statutes*, 6:105–6; Augusta OB, 8:324–26.

113. Augusta OB, 8:386, 2 Jan. 1764. Virginia law required a unanimous vote to convict slaves of capital crimes, so Farmer's denial may have convinced as few as one magistrate. Hening, ed., *Statutes*, 6:106. Conviction of slaves accused of murdering whites was likely but not automatic: "In sixty-six prosecutions of slaves for murdering whites between 1706 and 1785, about 81 percent of the slaves received guilty verdicts and 4.6 percent had the charge reduced to a misdemeanor." Schwarz, *Twice Condemned*, 46.

114. "Pre-1790s [Virginia] minute and order books contained indictments and verdicts, but rarely included testimony." Ibid., 51.

115. Augusta OB, 8:326.

116. By law, Staunton's fairs were held on the second Tuesday in June and November, "to continue for the space of two days." "An Act for Establishing the Towns of

Staunton, in the County of Augusta," Nov. 1761, Hening, ed., *Statutes*, 7:473–76. Tom's trial was on the second day of the November fair.

117. Ibid., 6:106.

118. David Robinson to William Preston, 21 March 1763, Draper Mss., 2QQ 39. For characterization of court days in colonial Virginia as popular events, see Isaac, *Transformation of Virginia*, 90.

119. Schwarz, *Twice Condemned*, 81–82; Blackstone *Commentaries*, 4:92.

120. Augusta OB, 8:326.

9. The Concubine

1. Augusta OB, 8:326.

2. Schwarz, *Twice Condemned*, 72, 82, 92.

3. Tarr's precise location now is unknown because, although "Edward Tarrs old Shop" was still a road landmark at Timber Ridge as late as 22 November 1764, officials never mentioned the site of his new shop. Augusta OB, 9:172. Staunton in 1763 was surrounded by large tracts owned by William Preston, Felix Gilbert, William Beverley's heir, and John Lewis's heirs.

4. Ibid., 14:362.

5. J. R. Hildebrand, "The Beverley Patent, 1736, including original grantees, 1738–1815, in Orange & Augusta Counties, Va.," in Wilson, *Tinkling Spring*, endpapers; Augusta DB, 2:659, 5:238, 20:78.

6. Alias summons, *Grand Jury v. Ann Moore*, May 1765, Criminal Causes, Box 1, Augusta CCC. In English common law, an alias summons was issued on the plaintiff's request after the sheriff failed to serve the initial summons. Blackstone, *Commentaries*, 3:283.

7. Other jokes by John Madison included describing the lawsuit *Edward Beard v. John Flood* as "Square and Compass vs. Pill and Bolus" and calling plaintiff Andrew McCool "Priest of the World." Chalkley, *Chronicles*, 1:308; *Andrew McCool v. James Stewart*, August 1747, Judgment Files, Augusta CCC.

8. Augusta OB, 7:355; summons, Nov. 1762, *Grand Jury v. Ann Moore*, May 1765 [date of judgment], Criminal Causes, Box 1, Augusta CCC.

9. Augusta OB, 1:134, 199, 331; 2:118, 362, 568; 3:437; 4:64, 254; 6:139, 285; 8:321; 9:64; Grand Jury Presentments, May 1759, Criminal Causes, Box 1, Augusta CCC.

10. Ibid. (two folders of same label); Augusta OB, 9:64, 431, 432. For the earliest example of the fine, see ibid., 1:234.

11. Webb, *Office and Authority of a Justice of Peace*, 5; Augusta OB, 10:143, 22 Oct. 1765; 425, 24 Nov. 1766.

12. Ibid., 1:336, 21 Nov. 1747. In a related issue, magistrates repeatedly ordered the whipping of poor white women who could not pay fines for bearing illegitimate children. Ibid., 1:358, 16 March 1747/8; 2:313, 27 Feb. 1749/50; 3:247, 20 May 1752; 3:264, 17 June 1752; 13:322, 16 Aug. 1769.

13. Ibid., 11:334.

14. Capias, *Andrew Greer v. Edward Tarr*, Judgment Files, Augusta CCC; Augusta OB, 7:439. For Greer's license to keep "Ordinary at his house," see ibid., 6:431, 19 Nov.

1760. Insufficient documentation regarding this suit survives to know why Greer sued on a writ of trespass on the case; in Augusta County practice, such writs were applied to a wide range of issues, including overdue unsecured store accounts.

15. Capias, *John Bowyer v. Edward Tarr*, March 1767, Judgment Files, Augusta CCC.

16. Augusta OB, 10:478.

17. Ibid., 10:482.

18. Ibid., 11:25.

19. Reid and Johnston Ledger, 74, Special Collections, Swem Library. The check cloth purchase was dated 7 June [probably 1768]. For Smiley's occupation, see *Smiley v. Thompson,* cited in Chalkley, *Chronicles,* 1:356.

20. Undersheriff Michael Bowyer's 1768 accounts, Executive Papers, 164, Augusta CCC.

21. Israel Christian's account, 29 April 1768, William Fleming Ledger, 3, Special Collections, Leyburn Library. Christian's account with Fleming named an enslaved patient on this folio in a way that supports the identification of "Negro Ned" as Edward Tarr. Fleming bled and wormed a patient identified only as "Isaac" with no racial identifier. Isaac was inventoried in 1785 as a slave in the deceased Israel Christian's estate in Montgomery County, Virginia, where Christian moved shortly before his death. Thus Fleming distinguished in his account book between "Negro Ned" and his father-in-law's slave "Isaac," a distinction that I interpret as indicating Ned's free status. Montgomery County Deeds and Wills, B:67–68, LOV. For Fleming's residence, see Augusta County Trustees grantors to Fleming, 10 March 1765, Augusta DB, 11:829. Fleming charged patients for house calls involving a journey but did not levy this charge on those who consulted him in Staunton; the entry for "Blooding Negro Ned" does not include Fleming's journey charge, indicating Tarr was treated by Fleming in Staunton.

22. William Davis of Philadelphia account, 5 April 1768, William Fleming Ledger, 26, Special Collections, Leyburn Library.

23. For Tarr's purchase, see Reid and Johnston Ledger, 74, Special Collections, Swem Library. For Davis's lot, see chapter 3.

24. "Fragment of Account," Pendleton, *Letters and Papers of Edmund Pendleton,* 1:79.

25. "An Act, to Prevent Lawyers Exacting or Receiving Exorbitant Fees," May 1742, Hening, ed., *Statutes,* 5:181.

26. For details of this complex scheme, see Dewey, "The Waterson-Madison Episode." Dewey noted that "By April 1770 the company [i.e., the persons suing to seize tax-delinquent land] had over 450 caveats and petitions pending" before the General Court. In the May 1770 General Assembly, burgess Edmund Pendleton was ordered to draft a bill to inhibit those cases. Ibid., 173–74. Pendleton named Byers and Cook, two of the fourteen other surnames listed with Tarr in the April 1770 account fragment, in a 29 April 1771 letter to magistrate William Preston regarding frontier land caveats. Pendleton, *Letters and Papers of Edmund Pendleton,* 1:64. The surnames of Byers, Cook, and nine more persons plus Tarr were names of Augusta County landowners; the additional Augusta County landowners on Pendleton's April 1770 account were Nealy, Scott, Hollis, McSherry, Brenegar, Loy, Adams, Kindar, and C. Kindar. The latter probably was Conrad Kinder. As sheriff of Augusta County in 1760 and 1761, William Pres-

ton listed Conrad Kinder as owning land "sold by Col Patton on the Waters of Mississipia" but did not mark Kinder as having paid his quitrents. Preston annotated one James Scott as insolvent in his quitrent roll; the other surnames either are not represented in Preston's roll or appear to have paid their quitrents for 1760 and 1761. Quitrent Roll, Preston Family Papers, 1727–1896, VHS.

27. Benjamin Borden's executors, deed to Isaac Gray, 30 May 1751, Augusta DB, 3:365; Borden's executors, deed to William Lusk, 14 Oct. 1765, ibid., 12:336; Lusk's executors, deed to Thomas Stuart, 18 March 1772, ibid., 18:130. Stuart is identified as a merchant in the latter document.

28. Lusk signed his will on 2 May 1771. His executors proved the document at the August 1771 court, seven months before selling Lusk's Mill Creek land to Thomas Stuart. Augusta WB, 4:423.

29. Christian's contract generated extensive correspondence; see Bouquet, *Papers of Henry Bouquet*, 4:504, 508; 5:263, 299, 337, 352, 353.

30. The earliest reference to this Mill Creek is in Benjamin Borden's deed to John Patterson dated 26 Nov. 1741, Orange County DB, 6:321–22, LOV. For colonial wheat production, see Klingaman, *Colonial Virginia's Coastwise and Grain Trade*. Historical geographer Robert D. Mitchell noted how the colonial wars created a local market for wheat produced in the Valley of Virginia. *Commercialism and Frontier*, 144–46. For the nineteenth-century culmination of wheat production, see Koons, "'The Staple of Our Country'".

31. Alexander Stuart advertisement dated 17 Jan. 1775, *Virginia Gazette* (Pinckney), 9 Feb. 1775, 3, emphasis in original. McChesney is identified as a horse trader in Washington, *Diaries of George Washington*, 2:255.

32. Jacob Gray, grantor, to Edward Tarr, grantee, 15 May 1754, Augusta DB, 6:212–14; Edward Tarr, grantor, to Samuel McChesney, grantee, 19 Aug. 1772, ibid., 18:493–96.

33. Given a Composite Consumer Price Index of 81 in 1754 and 109 in 1772, £45 in 1772 would have equaled 81 ÷ 109 × £45 = £33.4 in 1754, or 55.7 percent of Tarr's original £60 purchase price. Table A-2, "Consumer Price Indexes, United States, 1700–1991," McCusker, "How Much Is That in Real Money?" 324–25.

34. Average real estate resale prices in Borden's Land between Tarr's purchase in 1754 and sale in 1772 rose 86.4 percent before adjusting for inflation, as calculated with average resale prices in Borden's Land per 100 acres of £18:6:6 (£18.3250) from 1745 to 1754 and of £34:3:4 (£34.1667) from 1765 to 1774. For price data, see table 7, "Average Resale Prices in the Upper Shenandoah Valley, 1745–74," Mitchell, *Commercialism and Frontier*, 77.

35. Augusta OB, 14:408.

36. The four justices were Daniel Smith, Abraham Smith, Michael Bowyer, and John Gratton. Augusta OB, 14:403.

37. Daniel Smith purchased twenty-two-year-old slave Tom from Joseph Steps for forty-five pounds in 1765. Joseph Steps, deed to Daniel Smith, 5 Sept. 1764, Augusta DB, 12:181; Augusta OB, 14:362.

38. Deputy Sheriff Michael Bowyer endorsed as executed the capias dated 4 Feb. 1767, *John Bowyer v. Edward Tarr*, March 1767, Judgment Files, Augusta CCC.

39. Given that McChesney wanted to retain Tarr's tract, he was unlikely to renege on both the agreements with Stuart and Tarr.

40. Andrew Hays and wife Margaret, grantors, to Alexander Stuart, grantee, 16 Aug. 1773, Augusta DB, 19:426–28.

41. Stuart's public notice in the *Virginia Gazette* (Pinckney), 9 February 1775, 3, claimed that he had initiated legal action, but the earliest extant official record of his suit is a 20 September 1775 summons to McChesney for an action in chancery. The deputy sheriff endorsed the original summons "not found." An alias summons dated 21 October 1775 was executed. The suit's later progress is undocumented: chancery suits typically dragged on for years, and this was no exception. The quality of entries in Augusta County court orders deteriorated significantly during this period, so details of legal sparring went unrecorded. In May 1779, the case was marked as discontinued by parties' agreement. *Alexander Stuart v. Samuel McChesney*, in chancery, May 1779, Judgment Files, Augusta CCC; Augusta OB, 16:583, 20 May 1779. For summonses, see Augusta County Chancery Causes, Case 1775–001, Local Government Records Collection, LOV. McChesney deeded the land to Stuart on 8 May 1776; the deed was partially proved by two witnesses on 18 March 1777, but the third witness did not acknowledge his signature until 18 October 1787. Augusta DB, 26:64–66.

42. William M. Dabney, "Convention Army," in Blanco and Sanborn, eds., *American Revolution*, 381–83.

43. Ibid.

44. Anburey, *Travels*, 2:316–18, 20 Jan. 1779.

45. Ibid., 150. The reference to Nineveh is ambiguous, but given the context, the writer most likely metaphorically invoked a flourishing city. The Jungfernsteig in Hamburg, Brunswick, was a sophisticated urban promenade. "History of Jungfernstieg."

46. Anburey, *Travels*, 2:451–52, 18 April 1780.

47. Ibid., 2:467.

48. Subsequently the governor and council authorized one man "who is now Confined in Staunton Jail as a Prisoner of War, to go at large in the said Town taking his Parol not to depart therefrom till further Orders." *JCV*, 2:14, 21 Oct. 1777; 23, 5 Nov. 1777. This was a newer jail than the one repaired by Edward Tarr in 1767 and 1768. The court ordered a replacement for Tarr's jail on 23 May 1772. Augusta County MB, 1772, 65, LOV.

49. Specht came to America as a regimental commander in General Friederich Adolphus von Riedesel's Brunswick Corps, and the anonymous German author sent his letter to the principality of Brunswick. Specht was a prolific writer; the diary he maintained through the Saratoga campaign is comparable in style to this letter. Specht, *Specht Journal*. The anonymous letter had a Staunton dateline, and Specht was billeted in Staunton: he signed a receipt for "one Load of fire Wood for my use" in Staunton on 21 Oct. 1779. Auditor of Public Accounts, State Government Records Collection, LOV. After Riedesel's release and transfer to New York City, he wrote to Thomas Jefferson on 10 February 1780 asking Jefferson to forward an enclosed letter "to Brigr. General Specht at Stantown, as no other safe opportunity presents itself to convey a Letter to Him." Jefferson, *Papers of Thomas Jefferson*, 3:291. The last circumstantial evi-

dence suggesting Specht's authorship is that the anonymous author's descriptions of the Albemarle County barracks reflected a more Olympian perspective than those of the much-junior Lieutenant Anburey; the anonymous German author described gamecocks outside huts, not ravening rats inside.

50. Jefferson to James Wood, 3 March 1780, Jefferson, *Papers of Thomas Jefferson*, 3:308.

51. Jefferson to James Wood, 17 May 1780, ibid., 3:377.

52. For six jailed prisoners of war, see Alexander Kilpatrick's accounts as jailer, 1781, Chalkley, *Chronicles*, 1:528. In 1780, the Virginia council took alarm at the progress of the British Army in South Carolina, and Gov. Thomas Jefferson ordered preparations for moving the Convention Army. Jefferson specified that "This order is not meant to be intended to those beyond the blue ridge, as they are already where they should be. It may perhaps be proper, if they are scattered, to collect them at Staunton." Jefferson to James Wood, 9 June 1780, Jefferson, *Papers of Thomas Jefferson*, 3:428. According to Lieutenant Anburey, as of 12 Dec. 1779, "the Americans shew more indulgence to the Germans, permitting them to go round the country to labor." Anburey, *Travels*, 2:440–41.

53. *William Kyle v. James Call and Susanah Call*, Augusta OB, 20:138, 22 Aug. 1786. The jury found that Chapman resided in Augusta County "with the permission . . . of the British officers" when he was married.

54. James Culbertson will, 17 April 1788, recorded 17 June 1788, Augusta WB, 7:70.

55. Augusta OB, 17:301, 9 Sept. 1780.

56. *Commonwealth v. Joseph Thompson and Peter Blake*, March 1786, Criminal Cases, Box 2, Augusta CCC.

57. James Wood to Officer Commanding at Barracks, 17 April 1780, Colonel James Wood, Jr., Letterbook, Glass-Glen Burnie Foundation, Winchester, Virginia. Thanks to Warren R. Hofstra for calling this document to my attention.

58. Numerous British soldiers escaped from Albemarle County barracks. As of 12 December 1779, Lieutenant Anburey reported that "Near an hundred have reached New-York, and about sixty or seventy have been taken up, brought back and confined in a picketed prison near the barracks." *Travels*, 2:439. On 20 October 1779, there were 1,495 British Convention Army internees of all ranks. "State of the British & German Troops Charlotte Ville Barracks," War Office, 30/11/1, 27, BNA. By the time they were posted to York, Pennsylvania, in 1782, only 470 British personnel remained in American custody, less than one third of the October 1779 muster. Sampson, *Escape in America*, 184.

59. Wood to Officer Commanding at Barracks, 17 April 1780, Colonel James Wood, Jr., Letterbook, Glass-Glen Burnie Foundation, Winchester, Virginia.

60. Letter of 18 April 1780, dateline "Barracks, Charlottesville, in Virginia," Anburey, *Travels*, 2:448–63.

61. For drummer Richard Richardson, see Captain John Carter's Company, Muster Roll and Pay List, Jan. 1779, War Office, 10/159, BNA; for matross (i.e., the lowest ranking artilleryman) Thomas Richardson, see Captain Ellis Walker's Company, Muster Roll, Dec. 1779, War Office 10/162, BNA. No "Richardson" of a Royal Artillery unit was included in a tally of British and German soldiers who remained in America after the war. Smith, *British and German Deserters, Dischargees, and Prisoners of War*.

10. The Travelers

1. Jacob Peck, "A Map of Ninety two thousand one hundred Acres of Land Granted to Benjamin Borden by Patent The Sixth of November 1739, Exhibiting in their respective situations all the lands sold by B Borden the elder by B. Borden the younger and those under him as also the land Remaining unsold," *Jacob Peck heirs v. Robert Harvey and wife*, Augusta County Chancery Causes, 1850–027, 427, Local Government Records Collection, LOV. Thanks to Joshua Anderson for calling this document to my attention. Thanks especially to John Davis, clerk of Circuit Court, Augusta County, for permission to publish.

2. The court assigned administration of the estate to William Wilson, to whom Bell's minor son was bound. Augusta OB, 6:276, 18 May 1759. Bell's goods were sold at vendue on 23 Aug. 1760. Augusta WB, 2:414–15.

3. Cooper voluminously described pursuits, journeys, and migrations across frontier landscapes. *Leatherstocking Tales*. Tocqueville observed, "These men [emigrating from Ohio to Illinois around 1830] have left their first native country to be well-off; they leave their second to be still better-off: almost everywhere they encounter fortune, but not happiness.... For them, emigration began by being a need; today, it has become in their eyes a sort of game of chance, in which they love the sensation as much as the gain." *Democracy in America*, 270–71. Turner famously attributed immigration to a desire for cheap farmland but acknowledged "the pioneer farmers who move from the love of adventure." "Significance of the Frontier in American History," 21.

4. "The astonishing mobility—running both in and out of [Lunenburg C]ounty— nearly eliminated the hope of creating a stable and all-encompassing locally based community life." Beeman, *Evolution of the Southern Backcountry*, 30. "The high geographic mobility of backcountry settlers impeded the development of social and kinship ties that could have drawn [frontier] communities together." Ward, *Breaking the Backcountry*, 16.

5. "Perhaps most important among the things these groups ["Irish," "Scots," and "Ulster Scots"] shared was a history of movement—back and forth across the Irish Sea, across the Atlantic to Pennsylvania, and to various places within the colony [Pennsylvania]." Landsman, "Religion, Expansion, and Migration," 107. Landsman's summation of scholarship regarding Scottish and Irish mobility is especially valuable. Ibid., 107–9.

6. The historian James G. Leyburn identified five colonial-era surges of what he called Scotch-Irish immigration: 1717–18, 1725–29, 1740–41, 1754–55, and 1771–75. *The Scotch-Irish*, 169–73. For the Revolutionary-era culmination of this multi-ethnic process, see Joseph S. Tiedemann, "Interconnected Communities: The Middle Colonies on the Eve of the American Revolution."

7. A. G. Roeber notes that "the majority of Lutheran and Reformed Germans came from inland territories, settled in places far from the sea (with two exceptions: Philadelphia and Charleston), and wasted no time ruminating about the passage or the ocean." *Palatines, Liberty, and Property*, 97.

8. McCleskey and Squire, "Pennsylvania Credit in the Virginia Backcountry."

9. McCleskey, "Price of Conformity."

10. For examples of side saddles or women's saddles mentioned in civil litigation, see *William Mitchell and wife Margaret v. Andrew Evans*, Augusta OB, 2:493, 28 Nov. 1750;

John Lewis v. James Wood, ibid., 3:271, 18 June 1752; *Robert Breckenridge v. John Nealy,* ibid., 3:393, 20 Nov. 1752; *George Parks v. Samuel Harrison,* ibid., 4:431, 22 May 1755; *John Bowyer v. Samuel Crawford,* ibid., 5:37, 18 March 1756; *Felix Gilbert v. Philip Halverson,* ibid., 7:459, 16 Feb. 1763; *James Craig v. Thomas Stevenson,* ibid., 7:465, 17 Feb. 1763. The earliest side saddle in an Augusta County estate inventory was on 12 June 1746, six months after the county court opened for business. Inventory, John Dobkins, Sr., deceased, Augusta WB, 1:32.

11. William Young, power of attorney to John Madison, 15 Feb. 1763, Augusta DB, 11:400–401.

12. Complaint, [ca. Nov. 1755], *Joshua Mathews, assignee of Jacob Gray, v. Edward Tarr and Joseph Kennedy,* March 1756, Judgment Files, Augusta CCC.

13. Salley, "Brief Account of the Travels of John Peter Salley," 203–22.

14. "Memorandum Book of John Buchanan," Draper Mss., 1QQ 39.

15. Harrison, "Virginians on the Ohio and Mississippi," 206; Fry and Jefferson, "A Map of the Most Inhabited Part of Virginia." Fry and Jefferson located Salley (Salling) at the confluence of the North (now Maury) and Fluvanna (now James) rivers.

16. Rose, *Diary of Robert Rose,* 31 May 1751, 105.

17. Fleming to Preston, 17 Dec. 1756, Draper Mss., 1QQ 140–41.

18. Redd, "Reminiscences of Western Virginia," 339–40.

19. *JHB, 1758–1761,* 239, 30 March 1761.

20. Augusta Parish VB, 420, [no day] Oct. 1766.

21. *JHB, 1758–1761,* 221, 20 March 1761.

22. The historical literature on the origins of southern identity is vast. For a detailed synopsis focusing on the emergence of the American backcountry as southern cultural hearth, see Fischer, *Albion's Seed,* 633–782.

23. The centrality of those concerns is closely analyzed in Roeber, *Palatines, Liberty, and Property.*

24. Beeman, *Evolution of the Southern Backcountry,* 22–24, 64, 66; Mitchell, *Commercialism and Frontier,* 77.

25. Historian Richard Lyman Bushman's metaphor captures this process of building farms ahead of market connections: "the market can be envisioned as a rising tide that gradually inundated more and more regions, not as a switch turned at some moment for the entire continent." "Markets and Composite Farms," 361. Colonial-era land deeds described a tract's boundaries, not its buildings, so it is impossible to calculate the extent to which price increases reflected grantor improvements.

26. McCleskey, "Shadow Land."

27. Bushman, "Farmers in Court."

28. This conclusion differs from that of Richard R. Beeman, who interpreted high turnover among land owners in the colonial period as *a priori* evidence of social instability in Lunenburg County. *Evolution of the Southern Backcountry,* 30.

29. On 15 February 1763, Robinson witnessed William Young's power of attorney in Pennsylvania as is discussed above and cited in note 11. On 21 September 1763, the day that Davis completed proof of Young's land deed, Davis also served as a witness in *Charles Lewis and David Robinson v. Martha Galbreath,* Augusta OB, 8:225. Robinson too was a wide-ranging Augusta County resident: by the time he witnessed the 1763

document in Pennsylvania, Robinson already had journeyed to South Carolina (1759) and Boston (1761). Robinson to Preston, 22 Aug. 1759, Draper Mss., 2QQ 24; Robinson to Preston, 5 Nov. 1761, ibid., 2QQ 34.

30. An extensive literature examines the social web and colonial politics. For a Virginia summary, see Isaac, *Transformation of Virginia*, 110–13; Billings et al., *Colonial Virginia*, 71–73; and Evans, *"Topping People,"* 23–89. For social networks in a geospatial context, see Rutman and Rutman, *Place in Time*, 27–30.

31. Morgan and Nicholls, "Slaves in Piedmont Virginia, 1720–1790."

32. "An Act to Prevent the Practice of Selling Persons as Slaves That Are Not So, and for Other Purposes Therein Mentioned," Oct. 1765, Hening, ed., *Statutes*, 8:133–35.

33. "An Act for Exempting Free Negro, Mulatto, and Indian Women, from the Payment of Levies," Nov. 1769, ibid., 8:393.

34. *JHB, 1761–1765*, 262, 16 Nov. 1764; ibid., 359–60.

35. Hening, ed., *Statutes*, 8:393.

36. *JHB, 1766–1769*, 198, 10 May 1769.

37. Ibid., 198–99, 203, 218.

38. Ibid., 246, 251, 267, 275, 295, 304; *LJC*, 3:1397, 1400, 1401; Hening, ed., *Statutes*, 8:393.

39. Ira Berlin remarked that some blacks on the eve of the American Revolution listened to the discussion of natural rights and considered how to "turn it to their advantage," but in general Berlin characterized free blacks in colonial America as oppressed. *Slaves without Masters*, ch. 1; 11 (quotation). In a widely cited study of gender and race relations in colonial Virginia, Kathleen M. Brown passed lightly over the 1769 levy revision and did not mention the 1765 alignment of servitude terms for mixed-race illegitimate children of white mothers with those for illegitimate white children. *Good Wives, Nasty Wenches, and Anxious Patriarchs*, 222.

40. Nicholls, "Passing through This Troublesome World." Nicholls's insights are especially important as they are based on records of eight counties within a region; as noted below, this regional approach is essential for fully comprehending the historical significance of widely dispersed but mobile free black populations.

41. Deal, "Race and Class in Colonial Virginia," 241–471.

42. Dinwiddie, *Official Records of Robert Dinwiddie*, 2:352–53.

43. Richter, "A Community and Its Neighborhoods"; Brown, *Good Wives, Nasty Wenches, and Anxious Patriarchs*, ch. 7. For Revolutionary and early national restrictions and an overview of other changes concerning Virginia slaves and free blacks, see Dunn, "Black Society in the Chesapeake."

44. Nicholls, "Passing through This Troublesome World," 56–59.

45. Berlin, "From Creole to African."

46. Redd, "Reminiscences of Western Virginia," 339–40.

47. James Wood to Officer Commanding at Barracks, 17 April 1780, Colonel James Wood, Jr., Letterbook, Glass-Glen Burnie Foundation, Winchester, Virginia.

48. Jordan, *White over Black*, ch. 4; Morgan, *American Slavery, American Freedom*, 333–37; Brown, *Good Wives, Nasty Wenches, and Anxious Patriarchs*, ch. 6.

49. Jordan, "American Chiaroscuro," 189–90.

50. For example, free blacks in early Augusta County and its offshoots (as elsewhere in Virginia) eventually were required to register in the county court. Bushman, *Registers*

of Free Blacks; Boyd-Rush, *Free Negroes Registered in the Clerk's Office, Botetourt County.* For a broad regional analysis of free blacks in the antebellum era, see Berlin, *Slaves without Masters.*

51. Wood to Officer Commanding at Barracks, 17 April 1780, Colonel James Wood, Jr., Letterbook, Glass-Glen Burnie Foundation, Winchester, Virginia.

APPENDIX 2

1. Thanks to Lucinda Stanton and the Central Virginia History Researchers for assistance searching for frontier connections with free blacks in Piedmont Virginia.

2. Augusta OB, 17:138, 21 Sept. 1779.

3. Augusta County Personal Property Tax Records, 1782–1795, LOV.

4. Augusta OB, 7:462, 17 Feb. 1763; 8:122, 22 June 1763.

5. Ibid., 2:63, 20 Aug. 1748.

6. Ibid., 10:240, 23 Aug. 1766.

7. Ibid., 6:276, 18 May 1759; Augusta WB, 2:414–15, 23 Aug. 1760.

8. Augusta OB, 6:276, 18 May 1759.

9. Augusta WB, 6:298, appraised 16 May 1782, recorded 20 May 1783; list for Dickey's and Campbell's Companies, 9 April 1782, Augusta County Personal Property Tax List, 1782, LOV.

10. Augusta OB, 20:608, 16 Sept. 1788.

11. "84 [tithables] not listed [in Botetourt County lists]," 1772, Botetourt County Tithables, 1770–1782, 73, LOV. Woods patented ninety-four acres on the South Fork of Roanoke River in 1767; see Virginia Land Office Patents and Grants, 37:128, LOV.

12. Redd, "Reminiscences of Western Virginia," 339–40; for surname, omitted in the published transcription, see John Redd, Reminiscences, 1770–1800, VHS.

13. "List of Tithables in my Company," 1771, Botetourt County Tithables, 1770–1782, 21, LOV.

14. Botetourt County OB, 1771[–1772], 69, 12 Feb. 1772, LOV.

15. Augusta Parish VB, 506.

16. Augusta OB, 12:143; Augusta Parish VB, 452.

17. Augusta OB, 14:365; Augusta Parish VB, 509, 19 Sept. 1772; Augusta WB, 5:481, 18 March 1777.

18. Botetourt County OB, 1772–1776, 633, 14 Nov. 1775, LOV.

19. Augusta Parish VB, 118, 23 March 1753; Charles Campbell's list of tithables, n.d. [context is 1777], "Augusta County Tithables, Undated," *Magazine of Virginia Genealogy* 43 (May 2005): 173.

20. Smith Creek/Linville Creek Meeting Minutes, 18, BHS.

21. Indenture, John Smiley and Elizabeth Joseph, 2 Feb. 1760, Judgment Files, Augusta CCC.

22. Ibid.; Augusta OB, 6:346, 19 March 1760.

23. Ibid., 6:177, 20 May 1758; 6:221, 17 Nov. 1758; 6:285, 19 May 1759; 7:101, 24 Aug. 1761; Summonses, Nov. 1758, May 1759, Criminal Causes, Box 1, Augusta CCC; James Knox will, drawn 11 April 1769, Augusta WB, 4:510–11.

24. Augusta OB, 16:92, 22 Nov. 1775. For the mother, see Augusta County MB, 7:35, LOV.

25. Administrator's accounts of the estate of Robert Andrews, 26 Oct. 1766, Augusta WB, 4:71. For the slave boys named Moses, see estate appraisal of Daniel Harrison, 21 Aug. 1771, ibid., 4:440, and appraisal of estate of John Gay, 19 Aug. 1777, ibid., 5:518. The latter boy was described as mulatto.

26. Ibid., 3:289, 16 April 1763.

27. Augusta OB, 16:230, 17 Sept. 1777.

28. Ibid., 16:302, 20 May 1778.

29. Ibid., 4:192, 15 May 1754; Archibald Stuart will, drawn 5 Sept. 1759, proved 17 Nov. 1761, Augusta WB, 3:87–88; Archibald Stuart appraisal, recorded 21 June 1763, ibid., 3:260; Bushman, *Registers of Free Blacks,* iv.

30. Augusta OB, 14:62, 22 Nov. 1769.

31. Ibid., 1:288, 16 Sept. 1747; Augusta Parish VB, 49, 16 Feb. 1749; Augusta WB, 2:368–70, will drawn 30 Oct. 1760, proved 20 May 1760; appraisal in ibid., 2:428–29, 7 June 1760.

32. Administrator's accounts, recorded 21 Nov. 1766, ibid., 3:485–86.

33. York County Judgments and Orders, 1:451, LOV.

34. Augusta OB, 7:9, 20 May 1761.

35. Ibid., 2:7, 20 May 1748; 2:112, 17 May 1749.

36. Ibid., 14:331, 18 March 1772.

37. Ibid., 10:213, 20 Aug. 1766.

38. Ibid., 4:252–53, 21 May 1754.

39. Ibid., 10:213, 20 Aug. 1766; "A list of the Tithables in the Lower District of New river," 1771, Botetourt County Tithables, 1770–1782, 23, LOV.

40. Augusta OB, 3:328, 22 Aug. 1752; 4:249, 20 May 1754; 4:252–53, 21 May 1754; 4:290, 24 Aug. 1754; 4:363, 25 Nov. 1754; 6:317, 21 Nov. 1759; 6:461, 24 Nov. 1760; 10:213, 20 Aug. 1766; Augusta Parish VB, 104, 22 Aug. 1752; 103, 112, both dated 22 Nov. 1752; Chalkley, *Chronicles,* 1:346, 30 Dec. 1762; 2:420, 1767. For the militia service, see William Preston, "List of Militia Company," 29 Nov. 1757, and William Preston, Indian Campaigns, 1758–1759, Preston Family Papers, 1727–1896, VHS.

41. Augusta Parish VB, 104, 22 Aug. 1752; Augusta OB, 10:213, 20 Aug. 1766.

42. Augusta Parish VB, 112, 22 Nov. 1752.

43. "A List of Tithables Taken by Geo Skillern on the Big Levels of Greenbrier, Antonys Creek, Sincking Creek & muddy Creek and the Head of the Sink Hole Land," 8 June 1774, Botetourt County Tithables, 1770–1782, 141, LOV.

44. "A List of Tithables in Green Briar including the little & Great Levels, Spring Creek, the two Sinking Creeks, Anthony's Creek, Howards Do, & Muddy Creek; Returned according to Order of Court By Andrew Donnally," 7 March 1775, ibid., 154; "A List of Tithables in Green Briar, extending from the little Levels downwards, including the two sinking creeks, & Muddy Creek, also Anthony's Creek & Howards Creek on the East side of the River, Taken by Andrew Donnally," 1 Aug. 1775, ibid., 193.

45. Augusta Parish VB, 103, 22 Nov. 1752.

46. Augusta OB, 15:469, 18 May 1774.

47. Ibid., 5:248, 17 Aug. 1757.

48. *Virginia Gazette* (Rind), 31 May 1770, 4. Thanks to Michael L. Nicholls for identifying John Sutton's role as an active slave trader in eastern Virginia.

APPENDIX 3

1. Dinwiddie, *Official Records of Robert Dinwiddie*, 2:352; "An Act Concerning Tithables," Hening, ed., *Statutes*, 6:40–41. Dinwiddie enumerated tithables in each Virginia county in a dispatch to the Lords of Trade dated 23 February 1756, noting that Augusta County held 2,273 whites and 40 blacks. Dinwiddie's list apparently drew on annual tithable reports that local tithable takers compiled as of 10 June 1755 and that county courts employed in their late autumn sessions to calculate the annual county levy. In Augusta County's 19 November 1755 court session, the clerk of court reported 2,272 tithables for purposes of apportioning the county levy. The clerk's figure at the 19 November court was forty-one tithables fewer than Dinwiddie's. Most if not all of the difference appears to have been accounted for by statutory exemptions: constables and beneficed ministers were exempt from levy payments. At least thirty-four Augusta County constables were in service as of 10 June 1755, and Augusta Parish was tended by an Anglican minister. The difference of six unaccounted-for tithables probably was drawn from the thirteen constables known to have been appointed in 1754, but with no subsequent removal recorded in the court order books. In the absence of any contemporary explanation for the difference between Dinwiddie's report and the county levy tithable count, it seems most likely that Dinwiddie included statutory levy exemptions in an attempt to present a more accurate tally of Virginia's actual population.

2. Augusta OB, 2:137 (sheriff's first return of capias), 3:12, 3:34, 3:46, 2:370 (trial), 2:482, 3:96, 3:114, 3:235, 3:359 (judgment confirmed).

3. Spotsylvania County WB, B:264, recorded 5 Sept. 1755, LOV.

4. Ibid.

5. Augusta WB, 2:23.

6. Augusta OB, 2:65.

7. Spotsylvania County WB, B:264, recorded 5 Sept. 1755, LOV.

8. Augusta OB, 2:356, 3:242.

9. Captain Buchanan's and Captain Long's companies, 10 April 1782, Augusta County Personal Property Tax Records, 1782–1795, LOV.

10. Augusta OB, 1:113.

11. Augusta WB, 2:1–2, 22–26.

12. Ibid., 2:131.

13. Augusta DB, 3:060.

14. Ibid., 5:445.

15. Augusta WB, 1:292, 340.

16. Augusta OB, 2:356.

17. Augusta WB, 1:166.

18. Ibid., 2:1–2, 23.

19. Augusta OB, 2:500.

20. Augusta WB, 2:131.

21. Augusta OB, 353–54.

22. Augusta WB, 2:23.

23. Augusta DB, 5:445; Augusta OB, 7:173–74.

24. Ibid., 2:364. Craig was identified in the source as a yeoman to differentiate him from Reverend John Craig, a Presbyterian minister who also became a slave owner.

25. Spotsylvania County WB, B:264, recorded 5 Sept. 1755, LOV.

26. Augusta OB, 5:428.

27. Augusta WB, 1:362.

28. Orange County WB, 1:315, LOV.

29. William Carvin's evaluation, Executive Papers, 336, Augusta CCC.

30. Augusta WB, 1:166.

31. Petition in chancery, *James Given v. John Stewart and Thomas Fulton,* May 1749, Chancery Causes, Augusta County, Case 1749–003, Local Government Records Collection, LOV; Augusta OB, 8:11, 170, 259 (dismissed).

32. Augusta WB, 1:292

33. Executive Papers, 386, Augusta CCC.

34. *John Mills v. Joseph Love,* 17 May 1754, Augusta OB, 4:203.

35. Orange County WB, 1:271, LOV.

36. Ibid.

37. Orphan court accounts of Benjamin Borden and Magdalene McDowell Borden, 24 Aug. 1749, Augusta OB, 2:157.

38. *Virginia Gazette,* 28 Feb. 1755, 4; Augusta DB, 17:278.

39. Augusta WB, 2:131.

40. Ibid., 1:259; Samuel Scott will, ibid., 1:140.

41. Ibid., 2:143, 148–49; *Samuel McCune v. Joseph Teas,* Augusta OB, 4:139.

42. Chalkley, *Chronicles,* 2:414.

43. Augusta OB, 4:317.

APPENDIX 4

1. The bond does not survive; it was described as a "writing obligatory sealed with the seal of the defendts" in Joshua Mathews's undated complaint, *Joshua Mathews, assignee of Jacob Gray, v. Edward Tarr and Joseph Kennedy,* Judgment Files, Augusta CCC. (Quotations in the following two paragraphs are from this source.) Sealed obligations, known as penal bonds, promised to pay a loan's principle plus interest under penalty of forfeiting an amount of double the principle. Mathews's complaint stated that the bond's amount was thirty pounds, so the actual debt secured was half that amount. For the Virginia practice of discharging judgment on penal bonds by payment of the principle plus interest and court costs, see "An Act to Prevent Frivolous and Vexatious Suits: And to Regulate Attorneys Practising in the County Courts," May 1732, Hening, ed., *Statutes,* 4:359. Augusta County judgments on penal bonds uniformly reflected the actual principle, not the doubled amount, as directed by statute. For Tarr's purchase, see Jacob Gray deed of bargain and sale to Edward Tarr, 15 May 1754, Augusta DB, 6:212–14.

2. Mathews was appointed constable in the Forks of the James on 16 May 1754. Augusta OB, 4:194. In 1756, Joshua Mathews belonged to a militia company composed of men living in the Forks of the James. Augusta County Court Martial Records, 1756–1796, 3, LOV.

3. Blackstone, *Commentaries,* 3:290.

4. Bails for Tarr and Kennedy were annotated on the reverse of the capias. Gray owned two tracts of land at Timber Ridge totaling 241 acres. Augusta County DB, 1:436, 6:394; Timber Ridge congregation subscription list, 22 July 1753, Preston Family

Papers, 1727–1896, VHS. The average pledge was 14.7 shillings with a standard deviation of 6.0 (see table 16).

5. Augusta OB, 2:127, 4:465; Augusta Parish VB, 157; Augusta County Court Martial Records, 1756–1796, 7, LOV; Augusta DB, 4:183, 5:228, 6:518. Some of Buchanan's extensive involvement in land speculation is described in McCleskey, "Rich Land, Poor Prospects," 478–82.

6. Sheriff James Lockhart endorsed the reverse of the capias as executed. For Lockhart's oath as sheriff on 19 November 1755, see Augusta OB, 4:493. Kennedy previously had abused Lockhart and other sitting magistrates in the aftermath of Kennedy's removal from the commission of the peace. EJC, 5:389, 30 April 1752; Augusta OB, 3:242–43, 249, 20 May 1752. Kennedy abused the court again on 19 August 1762, drawing a twenty-shilling fine with costs and additional jail time "during the pleasure of the Court." Ibid., 7:293.

7. Ibid., 5:87. The March 1756 session was the next regular court in course after the November 1755 session. For details of Augusta County's unique court calendar, see McCleskey, "Quarterly Courts in Backcountry Counties of Colonial Virginia."

8. The suits on a writ of debt described here are found in Augusta OB, 1:9–4:462.

9. Penal bond, *Reed assignee v. Edward Tarr*, Judgment Files, Augusta CCC. Like Tarr, Fitzpatrick (also rendered Fichpatrick) joined the 1753 Timber Ridge congregation's call for Rev. John Brown and committed to pay the same annual amount as Tarr, ten shillings, for support of the minister. Fitzpatrick was not a landowner when he witnessed Tarr's penal bond; Fitzpatrick first became a landowner in 1765 when he purchased 150 acres at Timber Ridge. Borden's executors, deed to Fitzpatrick, 30 May 1765, Augusta DB, 12:330.

10. Thomas Paxton, Jr., grantor, to John Robson, grantee, 29 May 1751, ibid., 3:233.

11. William Thompson's bond to administer estate of William Reed, 21 May 1760, Augusta WB, 2:387.

12. Reed certified on 22 November 1753 that one Henry Fuller was indebted to him for £2:9:8, having previously obtained a summons returned not executed on 26 November 1753. At court on 26 March 1754, Reed's summons again was returned as not executed. Process was served during the summer of 1754; on 26 August 1754, Reed received judgment by default. Augusta OB, 4:71, 80, 180, 307. For Reed's jury service on 23 November 1754, 21 August 1755, and 22 November 1755, see ibid., 4:336, 469, 509.

13. Complaint, n.d., and capias, 20 May 1756, *William Reed, assignee of John Robinson, v. Edward Tarr*, Judgment Files, Augusta CCC. As of May 1756, five attorneys practiced in Augusta County court. Augusta OB, 3:347; 4:10, 256, 377.

14. Capias, 20 May 1756, *William Reed, assignee of John Robinson, v. Edward Tarr*, Judgment Files, Augusta CCC; the deputy sheriff endorsed Baptist McNabb as Tarr's bail on the reverse of the capias. For the court's appointment of McNabb as a militia ensign, see Augusta OB, 1:153, 19 Feb. 1746/7. McNabb purchased 218 acres on Mill Creek near Tarr in 1750 but occupied the tract as early as 1747, when the tract was named as his in a deed for an adjoining plot. John McNabb, grantor, to Baptist McNabb, grantee, 29 Aug. 1750, Augusta DB, 2:842; Benjamin Borden's executors, grantors, to John McKay, grantee, 21 May 1747, ibid., 1:267. By 1756, McNabb owned an additional two tracts totaling 308 acres in the Roanoke River Valley. Ibid., 2:842, 3:425. Like Tarr,

McNabb signed the 1753 Timber Ridge congregation's call for Rev. John Brown, and in the same year McNabb subscribed to pay fifteen shillings annually to support Brown. For McNabb's service as road overseer from Borden's place north of Timber Ridge Meetinghouse to the North (now Maury) River, see Augusta OB, 4:192, 15 May 1754; 5:124, 21 May 1756.

15. Ibid., 5:195. For special bail, see § XVII, "An Act for Establishing County Courts, and for Regulating and Settling the Proceedings Therein," Oct. 1748, Hening, ed., *Statutes,* 5:496–97.

16. Augusta County documents do not systematically record the identities of lawyers in suits, or even whether a lawyer was employed, but in at least seventeen cases during the court's first decade of civil litigation, Gabriel Jones served as plaintiff's attorney and requested special bail. Augusta OB, 1:263, 284, 333, 362, 364; 2:20, 91, 123, 124, 125, 153, 300, 453, 594. The complaint in this case was endorsed "Jones for Plt" and Gabriel Jones was the sole person with that surname licensed as an attorney in Augusta County.

17. As of 1753, Mathew Patton owned two tracts on the South Branch of the Potomac River totaling 347 acres, plus a 266-acre tract on Craig Creek, a tributary of the James River. Augusta DB, 1:408, 3:155, 6:152. His location on the former river is indicated by his 1755 service as a parish land processioner examining boundaries of tracts located on the Potomac. For the centrality of credit to social order, see Breen, *Tobacco Culture,* 91–106.

18. Augusta OB, 6:221, 17 Nov. 1758.

19. Ibid., 5:195. For the statute, see note 1, above.

20. Bond, 26 April 1754, *William Todd, assignee of Jacob Gray, v. Edward Tarr and Joseph Kennedy,* Judgment Files, Augusta CCC.

21. For Todd's land ownership on Buffalo Creek adjoining Borden's Land, see Robert Young, deed to William Todd, 31 March 1750, Augusta DB, 2:749. For Todd's residence on that land, see his enumeration in a 21 March 1753 road assignment, Augusta OB, 3:415. Todd subsequently moved east across the Blue Ridge to Bedford County, Virginia, per his deed to Samuel Todd, 20 Nov. 1761, Augusta DB, 10:107. Todd returned to Augusta County by 1770. William Todd, grantor, to Charles Cobb, grantee, 29 Oct. 1770, Bedford County DB, 3:501–2, LOV.

22. Capias, 1 June 1756, and complaint, n.d., *William Todd, assignee of Jacob Gray, v. Edward Tarr and Joseph Kennedy,* Judgment Files, Augusta CCC.

23. Augusta OB, 4:126; Augusta DB, 9:197.

24. Semple was named as Reed's lawyer in the complaint; for his swearing of an attorney's "usual oaths" in order to practice in Augusta County, see Augusta OB, 4:377, 19 March 1755.

25. Augusta DB, 6:256, 15 May 1754. Processioners Joshua Mathews and John Armstrong reported reviewing Porter's property lines in Captain John Maxwell's company. Normally processioners required landowners to show their deeds and walk their borders, but Porter received neither patent nor deed in Augusta County as of 1770, after the Forks of the James became part of Botetourt County. Possibly Porter married a freeholder's widow; alternatively, the processioners found Porter on land to which he did not hold clear title and erroneously recorded him as a freeholder. Augusta Parish VB, 460. For Moore's jury appearance, see Augusta OB, 4:469, 21 Aug. 1755.

26. *William Todd, assignee of Jacob Gray, v. Edward Tarr and Joseph Kennedy,* debt, ibid., 5:218.

27. Ibid., 5:288, 24 Nov. 1756; 5:304, 18 March 1757.

28. *William Todd, assignee of Jacob Gray, v. Edward Tarr and Joseph Kennedy,* debt, ibid., 5:405.

29. In English common law, losers paid all court costs and were responsible for all attorney fees.

30. Petition, *Edward Tarr v. George Stevenson,* Judgment Files, Augusta CCC.

31. "An Act for Establishing County Courts, and for Regulating and Settling the Proceedings Therein," Oct. 1748, Hening, ed., *Statutes,* 5:498–99.

32. Ibid. For prohibition against blacks "to be sworn as a witness, or give evidence in any cause whatsoever" against a white person, see "An Act . . . to Disable Certain Persons, Therein Mentioned, to Be Witnesses," May 1732, Hening, ed., *Statutes,* 4:327.

33. Summons, *Edward Tarr v. George Stevenson,* Judgment Files, Augusta CCC. In his discussion of legal process, Blackstone stated that a summons "is a warning to appear in court . . . given to the defendant . . . either in person or left at his house or land." *Commentaries,* 3:279. Virginia law refined the process: the summons "together with a copy of the petition, and of the account, where the demand is upon an account, shall be delivered to the defendant or left at his or her usual place of abode, ten days at least before the next succeeding court." Hening, ed., *Statutes,* 5:498.

34. Augusta OB, 5:416.

35. Petition data includes all petitions with original filing dates from the first one in Augusta County (10 Feb. 1745/6, ibid., 1:6) through the last one filed in the May 1755 court (26 May 1755, resolved 22 Aug. 1755, ibid., 4:478).

36. Hening, ed., *Statutes,* 5:499.

37. Tarr's petition suggests that the Stevensons had fallen on hard times since George Stevenson's 1753 pledge for an above-average twenty shillings to support Rev. John Brown at Timber Ridge. Timber Ridge Congregation Subscription List, Preston Family Papers, 1727–1896, VHS. By decade's end, Stevenson and his son Andrew were listed as insolvents on the sheriff's quitrent roll, possibly indicating that they had departed Timber Ridge. Preston, "Quitrent Roll," Preston Family Papers, 1727–1896, VHS. Preston served as Augusta County's sheriff for two years beginning in November 1759. When George Stevenson sold his two-hundred-acre Timber Ridge tract in 1762, he was identified as residing in Louisa County, east of the Blue Ridge. Augusta DB, 10:205. Andrew Stevenson served a one-year stint as constable, replacing another Timber Ridge resident in that rotating duty on 21 March 1764. Augusta OB, 8:394, 9:231.

38. Ibid., 6:188–89, 217.

39. Petition, n.d., and summons, 10 Oct. 1761, *John Lewis v. Edward Tarr,* Judgment Files, Augusta CCC; Augusta OB, 7:149, 198.

40. Account, 2 Sept. 1761; petition, n.d.; summons [day illegible] July 1762, *Charles Donnelly v. Edward Tarr,* Aug. 1762, Judgment Files, Augusta CCC; Augusta OB, 7:349.

41. Capias, 9 Nov. 1762, *Andrew Greer v. Edward Tarr,* Judgment Files, Augusta CCC; Augusta OB, 7:439.

42. Capias, 4 Feb. 1767, *John Bowyer v. Edward Tarr,* Judgment Files, Augusta CCC; Augusta OB, 11:025.

Bibliography

Manuscript Sources

American Philosophical Society, Philadelphia, Pennsylvania
Israel Pemberton Letterbook D
John Reynell Daybook, 1 July 1731–19 Dec. 1732
Joseph Shippen Waste Book, 1749–1750

Augusta County Clerk of Circuit Court, Staunton, Virginia
Chancery Causes
Criminal Causes
Executive Papers
Judgment Files

British National Archives, Kew (formerly British Public Record Office)
Colonial Office
Series 5/509, 510, South Carolina Shipping Returns
Series 27/12, Bahamas Shipping Returns
Series 142/15, 16, Kingston, Jamaica, Shipping Returns
War Office
Series 10, Commissary General of Musters Office and Successors: Artillery Muster
  Books and Pay Lists
Series 30/11/1, "State of the British & German Troops Charlotte Ville Barracks."
Series 34, Baron Jeffrey Amherst, Commander in Chief, Papers

William L. Clements Library, University of Michigan, Ann Arbor
Thomas Gage Papers

Colonial Williamsburg Foundation, Williamsburg, Virginia
Bishop Roberts, *View of Charleston, South Carolina,* ca. 1735–1739

Friends Historical Library, Swarthmore College, Swarthmore, Pennsylvania
Abington Monthly Meeting Minutes, 1682–1746 (microfilm)
Charleston, South Carolina, Monthly Meeting Minutes and Records, 1718–1786 (microfilm)
Philadelphia Monthly Meeting (Arch Street) Minutes, 1715–1744 (microfilm)
Philadelphia Monthly Meeting (Arch Street) Minutes, 1745–1755 (microfilm)
Philadelphia Monthly Meeting (Arch Street) Minutes, 1751–1756 (microfilm)
Philadelphia Monthly Meeting (Arch Street) Women's Minutes, vol. 1 (microfilm)
Philadelphia Yearly Meeting Minutes, 1747–1779 (microfilm)

Glass-Glen Burnie Foundation, Winchester, Virginia
Colonel James Wood, Jr., Letterbook

Historical Society of Pennsylvania, Philadelphia
Leonard T. Beale Collection, Lewis Family Papers, Thomas Wharton Ledger
Chalkley Family Papers, New Bristol Hope Account Book, 1729–1732
Chester County Will Book C (microfilm)
George M. Conarroe Papers, vol. 1
Collections of the Genealogical Society of Pennsylvania
Logan Papers, 1664–1871, vol. 18
Paschall Family Papers, Stephen Paschall Account Book, 1735–1756
Penn Manuscript, Papers Relating to Iron, Peltries Trade, etc., 1812–1817
Pennsylvania Provincial Council Records
Philadelphia County Orphans Court Record Books 3, 14 (microfilm)
Philadelphia County Will Books (microfilm)

Potts Manuscripts
William Bird Ledger, 1741–1747 (Amity Township Store/Pine Forge)
William Bird Ledger, 1744–1761 (New Pine/Hopewell Forge)
Colebrookdale Furnace Account Book, 1744–1751
Colebrookdale Ledger C, 1730–1733
Colebrookdale Ledger, 1740–1750
Coventry Forge Account Book, 1727–1733
Coventry Forge Account Book, 1746–1754
Coventry Forge Ledger B, 1727–1730
Coventry Forge Ledger, 1730–1732
Coventry Forge Ledger, 1732–1733
Coventry Forge Ledger, 1734–1740
Coventry Forge Ledger F, 1736–1741
Coventry Forge Ledger, 1742–1748
Coventry Forge Ledger, 1745–1748
Germantown/Philadelphia Day Book, 1742–1754, Potts Philadelphia Account Books
Mount Pleasant Furnace Ledger, 1737–1739
Mount Pleasant Furnace Ledger, 1740–1744
Pine Forge Ledger, 1732–1740
Pine Forge Ledger, 1735–1742

Pine Forge Receipt Book, 1752–1760
Pool Forge Journal, 1749–1759
Warwick Furnace Account Book, Ledger C, 1745–1748
Warwick Furnace Ledger (John Potts), 1744–1751
Warwick Furnace Ledger C (Grace and Potts), 1745–1748
Warwick Furnace Ledger D, 1748–1749
Warwick Furnace Ledger, 1750–1760
Warwick Furnace, Receipt Book for Pigg Mettle, 1752, 1753, 1754
Wharton Family Papers, 1679–1891, Thomas Wharton Daybook E, 1762–1780

History Museum of Western Virginia, Roanoke
Breckinridge Collection

Lancaster County Historical Society, Lancaster, Pennsylvania
Lancaster County Court of Common Pleas, Appearance Dockets, 1731–1732, 1733–1734, 1737–1738
Lancaster County Court of Common Pleas, Narrative Files

James Graham Leyburn Library, Washington and Lee University, Lexington, Virginia
William Fleming Medical Journal, 1765

Library of Congress, Washington, D.C.
Henry Bouquet Manuscript (photostats; originals held by the British Museum)
Solomon Fussell Account Book
Thomas Walker Papers, 1744–1835

Records of the States of the United States
"Journal of the Proceedings of His Majesty's Honourable Council [South Carolina]"
"Journal of the Proceedings of the [South Carolina] Upper House of Assembly"

Library of Virginia, Richmond
Auditor of Public Accounts, State Government Records Collection
Chancery Causes, Local Government Records Collection
Virginia (Colony), Colonial Papers, 1630–1778
Virginia Land Office Patents and Grants, vols. 16–42

County Records (microfilm)
Augusta County, Virginia, Court Martial Records, 1756–1796
Augusta County, Virginia, Deed Books 1–20
Augusta County, Virginia, Entry Book 1
Augusta County, Virginia, List of Slaves Removed to Virginia from Georgia, 1781
Augusta County, Virginia, Minute Books 1–7
Augusta County, Virginia, Order Books 1–20
Augusta County, Virginia, Personal Property Tax Records, 1782–1795
Augusta County, Virginia, Surveyor Books 1–2

Augusta County, Virginia, Will Books 1–4
Bedford County, Virginia, Deed Book 3
Botetourt County, Virginia, Deed Book 1
Botetourt County, Virginia, Order Book, 1770–1771
Botetourt County, Virginia, Order Book, 1771[–1772]
Botetourt County, Virginia, Order Book, 1772–1776
Botetourt County, Virginia, Tithables, 1770–1782
Botetourt County, Virginia, Will Book A
Frederick County, Virginia, Order Book 4
Montgomery County, Virginia, Deeds and Wills Book B
Orange County, Virginia, Deed Books 3–10
Orange County, Virginia, Order Book 2–3
Orange County, Virginia, Will Book 1
Richmond County, Virginia, Order Book 15
Spotsylvania County, Virginia, Will Book B
York County, Virginia, Judgments and Orders 1–2

Maps
J. R. Hildebrand, "Map Showing 92,100 Acre Grant for Benjamin Borden, Lying and Being on the West Side of the Blue Ridge in the County of Augusta," 1964

Carol M. Newman Library, Virginia Polytechnic and State University
Preston Family Papers, 1747–1897, Charles Peale Didier Collection

New York Public Library
Bishop Roberts and George Hunter, "The Ichnography of Charles-town. At High Water. A Sketch of the Harbor"

Pennsylvania Historical and Museum Commission Archives, Harrisburg
Peter Baynton Bills of Lading, 1730–1732 (microfilm)
Peter Baynton Journal, Ledger E, 1734–1743 (microfilm)
Peter Baynton Ledger C (microfilm)
Peter Baynton Letterbook, 3 April–10 Nov. 1729 (microfilm)
Bucks County Deed Books (microfilm)
Copied Surveys
Lancaster County Deed Books (microfilm)
Miscellaneous Papers of the Philadelphia Company
Original Purchases Register, 1682–1762
Patent Books A5, A6, A8, A11 (microfilm)
Patent Registers, 1701–1728 and 1732–1741
Philadelphia County Court of Quarter Sessions (microfilm)
Philadelphia County Deed Books (microfilm)
Philadelphia County Exemplification Book 7 (microfilm)
Survey Books B23, C182, D81, D88, D89 (microfilm)

William R. Perkins Library, Duke University, Durham, North Carolina
Campbell Family Papers
William and John Preston Papers

Philadelphia City Archive
Philadelphia County Mortgage Books
Philadelphia County Sheriffs Deed Books

Philadelphia Register of Wills Archive
Estate Administrations

Presbyterian Historical Society, Philadelphia
First Presbyterian Church, Philadelphia, "Register of Marriages and Baptisms"
Timber Ridge and Providence Congregations, "Call from Timber Ridge and Providence, Virginia," to New Castle Presbytery, 1753

South Carolina Department of Archives and History, Columbia
Charleston Will Book 4 (microfilm)
Colonial Land Grants (Copy Series), 1675–1788
Conveyance Books, 1719–1776
Judgment Rolls, Court of Common Pleas, 1703–1790
Records of the Public Treasurer of South Carolina, 1725–1776, Journal A, 1735–1748; Journal B, 1748–1765
South Carolina Court of Vice Admiralty Records
South Carolina Miscellaneous Records GG, HH, II
South Carolina Plat Book 3
South Carolina Secretary of State, Ship Registers, 1734–1783

South Caroliniana Library, University of South Carolina
James Glen Papers, 1738–1777

Earl G. Swem Library, College of William and Mary, Williamsburg, Virginia
Ledger of Matthew Reid and Hugh Johnston, merchants, Staunton, Virginia, 1761–1770

Union Presbyterian Seminary, Richmond, Virginia
Autobiography of John Craig (microfilm)
John Craig, List of Baptisms Performed by Rev. John Craig, 1740–1749 (microfilm)
Donegal Presbytery Minutes, vol. 1 (microfilm)
Hanover Presbytery Minutes, 1755–1785, vol. 1 (microfilm)
Tinkling Springs Commissioner Book, 1741–1767 (microfilm)

Albert and Shirley Small Special Collections, University of Virginia, Charlottesville
Augusta Parish Vestry Book (photocopy)
Stuart-Baldwin Papers, 1742–1832

Virginia Baptist Historical Society, Richmond
Smith Creek/Linville Creek Meeting Minutes

Virginia Historical Society, Richmond
Adams Family Papers, 1672–1792
Beverley Family Papers, 1654–1901
Lewis Family Papers, 1749–1920
Preston Family Papers, 1727–1896
John Redd, Reminiscences, 1770–1800, of Experiences in Henry County, Va., and Kentucky, Dictated to His Grandson, Mr. Fontaine, in 1842
Stuart Family Papers, 1791–1958

Winterthur Museum Library
Samuel Powel, Jr., Daybook, 1735–1739, Powel Family Business Papers, 1724–1778

Wisconsin Historical Society
Lyman Copeland Draper Manuscripts
Series QQ, William Preston Papers
Series ZZ, Virginia Papers

NEWSPAPERS
American Weekly Mercury (Philadelphia)
Daily Journal (London)
Maryland Gazette (Annapolis)
New York Weekly Journal
Pennsylvania Gazette (Philadelphia)
Pennsylvania Journal (Philadelphia)
South Carolina Gazette (Charleston)
Virginia Gazette (Williamsburg; editors are indicated in citations for years with multiple editions)

PUBLISHED SOURCES

"Account of Servants Bound and Assigned before James Hamilton, Mayor of Philadelphia." *Pennsylvania Magazine of History and Biography* 30 (1906): 348–52, 427–36; 31 (1907): 83–102, 195–206, 351–67, 461–73; 32 (1908): 88–103, 237–49, 351–70.

Alden, John Richard. *John Stuart and the Southern Colonial Frontier: A Study of Indian Relations, War, Trade, and Land Problems in the Southern Wilderness.* Ann Arbor, Mich.: Edward Brothers, 1944. Reprint New York: Gordian Press, 1966.

Anburey, Thomas. *Travels through the Interior Parts of America.* 2 vols. London: William Lane, 1789. Facsimile ed. New York: Arno Press, 1969.

"Articles of Agreement." *Pennsylvania Magazine of History and Biography* 33 (1903): 370–71.

"Augusta County Tithables, Undated." *Magazine of Virginia Genealogy* 43, no. 2 (May 2005): 169–73.

Axtell, James. *The European and the Indian: Essays in the Ethnohistory of Colonial North America.* New York: Oxford University Press, 1981.

Bates, Susan Baldwin, and Harriott Cheves Leland, eds. *Proprietary Records of South Carolina,* vol. 3, *Abstracts of the Records of the Surveyor General of the Province, Charles Towne 1678–1698.* Charleston: History Press, 2007.

Beeman, Richard R. *The Evolution of the Southern Backcountry: A Case Study of Lunenburg County, Virginia, 1746–1832.* Philadelphia: University of Pennsylvania Press, 1984.

———. "Social Change and Cultural Conflict in Virginia: Lunenburg County, 1746 to 1774." *William and Mary Quarterly,* 3d ser., 35 (1978): 455–76.

Berlin, Ira. "From Creole to African: Atlantic Creoles and the Origins of African-American Society in Mainland North America." *William and Mary Quarterly,* 3d ser., 53 (1996): 251–88.

———. *Slaves without Masters: The Free Negro in the Antebellum South.* New York: Pantheon Books, 1974.

Bezís-Selfa, John. *Forging America: Ironworkers, Adventurers, and the Industrious Revolution.* Ithaca, N.Y.: Cornell University Press, 2004.

———. "Slavery and the Disciplining of Free Labor in the Colonial Mid-Atlantic Iron Industry." *Pennsylvania History* 64 (special supplemental issue, summer 1997): 270–86.

Billings, Warren M., John E. Selby, and Thad W. Tate. *Colonial Virginia: A History.* White Plains, N.Y.: KTO Press, 1986.

Bining, Arthur Cecil. *Pennsylvania Iron Manufacture in the Eighteenth Century.* Rev. ed. Harrisburg: Pennsylvania Historical and Museum Commission, 1973.

Blanco, Richard L., and Paul J. Sanborn, eds. *The American Revolution, 1775–1783: An Encyclopedia.* New York: Garland, 1993.

Bodle, Wayne. "'Such a Noise in the World': Copper Mines and an American Colonial Echo to the South Sea Bubble." *Pennsylvania Magazine of History and Biography* 127 (April 2003): 131–65.

Blackstone, William. *Commentaries on the Laws of England.* 4 vols. Oxford: Clarendon Press, 1765–69. Facsimile ed. Chicago: University of Chicago Press, 1979.

Bond, Beverley W., Jr., ed. "The Captivity of Charles Stuart, 1755–1757." *Mississippi Valley Historical Review* 13 (1926): 58–81.

Bouquet, Henry. *The Papers of Henry Bouquet.* Edited by S. K. Stevens et al. 6 vols. Harrisburg, Penn.: Pennsylvania Historical and Museum Commission, 1951–94.

Boyd-Rush, Dorothy A. *Free Negroes Registered in the Clerk's Office, Botetourt County, Virginia, 1802–1836.* Athens, Ga.: Iberian Publishing Co., 1993.

Breen, T. H. "Horses and Gentlemen: The Cultural Significance of Gambling among the Gentry of Virginia." *William and Mary Quarterly,* 3d ser., 34 (1977): 239–57.

———. *Tobacco Culture: The Mentality of the Great Tidewater Planters on the Eve of Revolution.* Princeton, N.J.: Princeton University Press, 1985.

Breen, T. H., and Stephen Innes. *"Myne Owne Ground": Race and Freedom on Virginia's Eastern Shore, 1640–1676.* New York: Oxford University Press, 1980.

Brown, Kathleen M. *Good Wives, Nasty Wenches, and Anxious Patriarchs: Gender, Race, and Power in Colonial Virginia.* Chapel Hill: University of North Carolina Press, 1996.

Bushman, Katherine G. *The Registers of Free Blacks 1810–1864, Augusta County, Virginia and Staunton, Virginia.* Verona, Va.: Mid-Valley Press, 1989.

Bushman, Richard Lyman. "Farmers in Court: Orange County, North Carolina, 1750–1776." In *The Many Legalities of Early America,* edited by Christopher L. Tomlins and Bruce H. Mann, 388–413. Chapel Hill: University of North Carolina Press, 2001.

———. "Markets and Composite Farms in Early America." *William and Mary Quarterly,* 3d ser., 55 (1998): 351–74.

Calhoun, Jeanne A., Martha A. Zierden, and Elizabeth A. Paysinger. "The Geographic Spread of Charleston's Merchantile Community, 1732–1767." *South Carolina Historical Magazine* 86 (1985): 182–220.

Cayton, Andrew R. L., and Frederika J. Teute. *Contact Points: American Frontiers from the Mohawk Valley to the Mississippi, 1750–1830.* Chapel Hill: University of North Carolina Press, 1998.

Chalkley, Lyman C. *Chronicles of the Scotch-Irish Settlement in Virginia.* 3 vols. Rosslyn, Va.: Commonwealth Printing, 1912–13. Reprint Baltimore: Genealogical Publishing Co., 1980.

Clemens, Paul G. E., and Lucy Simler. "Rural Labor and the Farm Household in Chester County, Pennsylvania, 1750–1820." In *Work and Labor in Early America,* edited by Stephen Innes, 106–43. Chapel Hill: University of North Carolina Press, 1988.

Clinton, Henry. "Sir Henry Clinton's 'Journal of the Siege of Charleston, 1780.'" Edited by William T. Bulger. *South Carolina Historical Magazine* 66 (1965): 147–74.

Coclanis, Peter A. "Bitter Harvest: The South Carolina Low Country in Historical Perspective." *Journal of Economic History* 45 (1985): 251–59.

———. *The Shadow of a Dream: Economic Life and Death in the South Carolina Low Country, 1670–1720.* New York: Oxford University Press, 1989.

Colden, Cadwallader. *The Letters and Papers of Cadwallader Colden.* 9 vols. New York: New York Historical Society, 1918–37.

Coldham, Peter Wilson, ed. *American Wills Proved in London, 1611–1775.* Baltimore: Genealogical Publishing Co., 1992.

Cooper, James Fennimore. *The Leatherstocking Tales.* New York: Library of America, 1985.

Cooper, Thomas, and David J. McCord, eds. *The Statutes at Large of South Carolina.* 10 vols. Columbia, S.C.: A. S. Johnston, 1836–41.

Corkran, David H. *The Cherokee Frontier: Conflict and Survival, 1740–62.* Norman: University of Oklahoma Press, 1962.

Côté, Richard N., and Patricia H. Williams, eds. *Dictionary of South Carolina Biography,* vol. 1. Easley, S.C.: Southern Historical Press, 1985.

Couper, William B. *History of the Shenandoah Valley.* 3 vols. New York: Lewis Historical Publications, 1952.

Crawford, B. Scott. "A Frontier of Fear: Terrorism and Social Tension along Virginia's Western Waters, 1742–1775." *West Virginia History,* new series, 2 (2008): 1–29.

Deal, Douglas. "A Constricted World: Free Blacks on Virginia's Eastern Shore, 1680–1750." In *Colonial Chesapeake Society,* edited by Lois Green Carr, Philip D. Morgan, and Jean B. Russo, 276–305. Chapel Hill: University of North Carolina Press, 1988.

Deal, Joseph Douglas, III. "Race and Class in Colonial Virginia: Indians, Englishmen, and Africans on the Eastern Shore during the Seventeenth Century." Ph.D. diss., University of Rochester, 1981.

DeHaas, Wills. *History of the Early Settlement and Indian Wars of Western Virginia; Embracing an Account of the Various Expeditions in the West, previous to 1795.* Wheeling, W.Va.: H. Hoblitzell, and Philadelphia: King and Baird, 1851. Reprint Parsons, W.Va.: McClain Printing, 1960.

Dew, Charles B. *Bond of Iron: Master and Slave at Buffalo Forge.* New York: Norton, 1994.

Dewey, Frank L. "The Waterson-Madison Episode: An Episode in Thomas Jefferson's Law Practice." *Virginia Magazine of History and Biography* 90 (1982): 165–76.

Diderot, Denis, and Jean le Rond D'Alembert, eds. *Encyclopédie; ou, Dictionnaire raisonné des sciences, des arts et des métiers.* Edited by Robert Morrissey. Chicago: University of Chicago, ARTFL Encyclopédie Projet, 2010. http://encyclopedie.uchicago.edu/.

Dinwiddie, Robert. *The Official Records of Robert Dinwiddie, Lieutenant-Governor of the Colony of Virginia, 1751–1758.* Edited by R. A. Brock. 2 vols. Richmond: Virginia Historical Society, 1883–84.

———. *Robert Dinwiddie: Correspondence Illustrative of His Career in American Colonial Government and Westward Expansion.* Edited by Louis Knott Koontz. Berkeley and Los Angeles: University of California Press, 1951.

Doerflinger, Thomas M. *A Vigorous Spirit of Enterprise: Merchants and Economic Development in Revolutionary Philadelphia.* Chapel Hill: University of North Carolina Press, 1986.

Dowd, Gregory Evans. "'Insidious Friends': Gift Giving and the Cherokee-British Alliance in the Seven Years' War." In *Contact Points: American Frontiers from the Mohawk Valley to the Mississippi, 1750–1830,* edited by Andrew R. L. Cayton and Frederika J. Teute, 114–50. Chapel Hill: University of North Carolina Press, 1998.

Dunn, Richard S. "Black Society in the Chesapeake, 1776–1810." In *Slavery and Freedom in the Age of the American Revolution,* edited by Ira Berlin and Ronald Hoffman, 49–82. Charlottesville: University Press of Virginia, 1983.

———. "Servants and Slaves: The Recruitment and Employment of Labor." In *Colonial British America: Essays in the New History of the Early Modern Era,* edited by Jack P. Greene and J. R. Pole, 157–94. Baltimore: Johns Hopkins University Press, 1984.

Easterby, J. H., ed. *The Journal of the Commons House of Assembly, November 10, 1736–June 7, 1739.* Columbia: Historical Commission of South Carolina, 1951.

———, ed. *The Journal of the Commons House of Assembly, September 10, 1745–June 17, 1746.* Columbia: Historical Commission of South Carolina, 1956.

Easterby, J. H., and Ruth S. Green, eds. *Journal of the Commons House of Assembly, January 19, 1748–June 29, 1748.* Columbia: Historical Commission of South Carolina, 1961.

Edgar, Walter B., and N. Louise Bailey, eds. *Biographical Directory of the South Carolina House of Representatives,* vol. 2, *1719–1774.* Columbia: University of South Carolina Press, 1974.

Egnal, Marc. "The Changing Structure of Philadelphia's Trade with the British West Indies, 1750–1775." *Pennsylvania Magazine of History and Biography* 99 (1975): 156–79.

Ellefson, C. Ashley. *The County Courts and the Provincial Court in Maryland, 1733–1763.* New York: Garland, 1990.

Ely, Melvin Patrick. *Israel on the Appomattox: A Southern Experiment in Black Freedom from the 1790s through the Civil War.* New York: Knopf, 2004.

Evans, Emory G. *A "Topping People": The Rise and Decline of Virginia's Old Political Elite, 1680–1790.* Charlottesville: University Press of Virginia, 2009.

Fauquier, Francis. *The Official Papers of Francis Fauquier, Lieutenant Governor of Virginia, 1758–1768.* Edited by George Reese. 3 vols. Charlottesville: University Press of Virginia, 1980–83.

"First Tax List for Philadelphia County, The, A. D. 1693." *Pennsylvania Magazine of History and Biography* 8 (1884): 82–105.

Fischer, David Hackett. *Albion's Seed: Four British Folkways in America.* New York: Oxford University Press, 1989.

Fogleman, Aaron Spencer. *Jesus Is Female: Moravians and the Challenge of Radical Religion in Early America.* Philadelphia: University of Pennsylvania Press, 2007.

———. "Religious Conflict and Violence in German Communities during the Great Awakening." In *Backcountry Crucibles: The Lehigh Valley from Settlement to Steel,* edited by Jean R. Soderlund and Catherine S. Parzynski, 185–207. Bethlehem, Pa.: Lehigh University Press, 2008.

Foote, William Henry. *Sketches of North Carolina, Historical and Biographical, Illustrative of the Principles of a Portion of Her Early Settlers.* New York: Robert Carter, 1846.

Franklin, Benjamin. *The Papers of Benjamin Franklin.* Edited by Leonard W. Labaree et al. 40 vols. to date. New Haven, Conn.: Yale University Press, 1959–.

Fries, Adelaide L. *Customs and Practices of the Moravian Church.* Rev. ed. Winston-Salem, N.C.: Board of Christian Education and Evangelism, 1973.

———, transl. and ed. "Diary of a Journey of Moravians from Bethlehem, Pennsylvania, to Bethabara in Wachovia, North Carolina, 1753." In *Travels in the American Colonies,* edited by Newton D. Mereness, 327–56. New York: Macmillan, 1916.

Fry, Joshua, and Peter Jefferson. "A Map of the Most Inhabited Part of Virginia." London: Thomas Jefferys, 1755.

Gallo, Marcus. "'Fair Play Has Entirely Ceased, and Law Has Taken Its Place': The Rise and Fall of the Squatter Republic in the West Branch Valley of the Susquehanna River, 1768–1800." *Pennsylvania Magazine of History and Biography* 136 (2012): 405–34.

Germantown Quakers' Renunciation of Slavery, 1688. Quaker Heritage Press website, http://www.qhpress.org/texts/oldqwhp/as-1688.htm.

Gillingham, Harrold E., ed. "The Bridge over the Dock in Walnut Street." *Pennsylvania Magazine of History and Biography* 58 (1934): 260–69.

Gordon, Robert B. *American Iron, 1607–1900.* Baltimore: Johns Hopkins University Press, 1996.

Gregorie, Anne King, ed. *Records of the Court of Chancery of South Carolina, 1671–1779.* Washington, D.C.: American Historical Association, 1950.

Greven, Philip J., Jr. "Family Structure in Seventeenth-Century Andover, Massachusetts." *William and Mary Quarterly,* 3rd ser., 33 (April 1966): 234–56.

Griffin, Patrick. *The People with No Name: Ireland's Ulster Scots, America's Scots Irish, and the Creation of a British Atlantic World, 1689–1764.* Princeton, N.J.: Princeton University Press, 2001.

Harrison, Fairfax. "The Virginians on the Ohio and the Mississippi in 1742." *Virginia Magazine of History and Biography* 30 (1922): 203–22.

Harrison, J. Houston. *Settlers by the Long Grey Trail: Some Pioneers to Old Augusta County, Virginia, and Their Descendants, of the Family of Harrison and Allied Lines.* Dayton, Va.: J. K. Ruebush, 1935. Reprint Baltimore: Genealogical Publications, 1984.

Hatley, Tom. *The Dividing Paths: Cherokees and South Carolinians through the Revolutionary Era.* New York: Oxford University Press, 1995.

Hawbaker, Gary T., ed. *Lancaster County, Pennsylvania, Quarter Sessions Abstracts (1729–1742).* Hershey, Penn.: privately printed, 1986.

Hazard, Samuel, ed. *Minutes of the Provincial Council of Pennsylvania, from the Organization to the Termination of the Proprietary Government.* 16 vols. Philadelphia: Joseph Severns, 1852–53.

Hening, William Waller, ed. *The Statutes at Large: Being a Collection of All the Laws of Virginia.* 13 vols. Richmond: various publishers, 1819–23. Facsimile ed. Charlottesville: University Press of Virginia, 1969.

Henretta, James A. "Families and Farms: *Mentalité* in Pre-Industrial America." *William and Mary Quarterly,* 3d ser., 35 (1978): 3–32.

Herndon, George Melvin. "The Story of Hemp in Colonial Virginia." Ph.D. diss., University of Virginia, 1959.

Higgins, W. Robert. "Charles Town Merchants and Factors Dealing in the External Negro Trade, 1735–1775." *South Carolina Historical Magazine* 65 (1964): 205–17.

Hildebrand, J. R. "The Beverley Patent, 1736, Including Original Grantees, 1738–1815, in Orange & Augusta Counties, Va." In *The Tinkling Spring, Headwater of Freedom: A Study of the Church and Her People, 1732–1952,* edited by Howard McKnight Wilson, endpapers. Richmond, Va.: Garrett and Massie, 1954.

Hinke, William J., and Charles E. Kemper, eds. "Moravian Diaries of Travels through Virginia." *Virginia Magazine of History and Biography* 12 (1904): 134–53.

Hinshaw, William Wade. *Encyclopedia of American Quaker Genealogy.* 6 vols. Ann Arbor, Mich.: Edwards Bros., 1936–50.

"Historical and Genealogical Notes and Queries." *Virginia Magazine of History and Biography* 16 (1908): 199–210.

"History of Jungfernstieg" and "Redevelopment of Jungfernstieg." Hamburg International Competition for Ideas, 2002, http://www.lebendiger-jungfernstieg.de/history_20jungfernstieg2.pdf.

Hoffer, Peter Charles, and William B. Scott, eds. *Criminal Proceedings in Colonial Virginia: [Records of] Fines, Examination of Criminals, Trials of Slaves, etc., from March 1710 [1711] to [1754] [Richmond County, Virginia].* Athens, Ga.: American Historical Association, 1984.

Hofstra, Warren R. "Land, Ethnicity, and Community at the Opequon Settlement, Virginia, 1730–1800." *Virginia Magazine of History and Biography* 98 (1990): 423–48.

———. *The Planting of New Virginia: Settlement and Landscape in the Shenandoah Valley.* Baltimore: Johns Hopkins University Press, 2004.

Holton, Woody. *Forced Founders: Indians, Debtors, Slaves, and the Making of the American Revolution in Virginia.* Chapel Hill: University of North Carolina Press, 1999.

Hughes, Sarah S. *Surveyors and Statesmen: Land Measuring in Colonial Virginia.* Richmond: Virginia Surveyors Foundation and Virginia Association of Surveyors, 1979.

Isaac, Rhys. *The Transformation of Virginia, 1740–1790.* Chapel Hill: University of North Carolina Press, 1982.

Jefferson, Thomas. *Papers of Thomas Jefferson.* Edited by Julian P. Boyd et al. Princeton, N.J.: Princeton University Press, 1950–.

Jellison, Richard M. "Antecedents of the South Carolina Currency Acts of 1736 and 1746." *William and Mary Quarterly,* 3d ser., 16 (1959): 556–67.

———. "Paper Currency in Colonial South Carolina: A Reappraisal." *South Carolina Historical Magazine* 62 (1961): 134–47.

Jennings, Francis. *Empire of Fortune: Crowns, Colonies & Tribes in the Seven Years War in America.* New York: Norton, 1988.

Jensen, Arthur Louis. *The Maritime Commerce of Colonial Philadelphia.* Madison: State Historical Society of Wisconsin, 1963.

Johnson, Victor L. "Fair Traders and Smugglers in Philadelphia, 1754–1763." *Pennsylvania Magazine of History and Biography* 83 (1959): 125–49.

Jordan, Winthrop D. "American Chiaroscuro: The Status and Definition of Mulattoes in the British Colonies." *William and Mary Quarterly,* 3d ser., 19 (1962): 183–200.

———. *White over Black: American Attitudes toward the Negro, 1550–1812.* Chapel Hill: University of North Carolina Press, 1968.

Joyner, Peggy Shomo, comp. *Abstracts of Virginia's Northern Neck Warrants & Surveys, Orange & Augusta Counties, with Tithables, Delinquents, Petitioners, 1730–1754.* [Portsmouth, Va.?]: privately published, 1984.

Kay, Marvin L. Michael. "'The Planters Suffer Little or Nothing': North Carolina Compensations for Executed Slaves, 1748–1772." *Science and Society* 40 (1976): 288–306.

Kegley, F. B. *Kegley's Virginia Frontier.* Roanoke: Southwest Virginia Historical Society, 1938.

Kennedy, Michael V. "The Hidden Economy of Slavery: Commercial and Industrial Hiring in Pennsylvania, New Jersey, and Delaware, 1728–1800." *Essays in Economic and Business History* 21 (2003): 115–25.

Kessel, Elizabeth A. "Germans in the Making of Frederick County, Maryland." In *Appalachian Frontiers: Settlement, Society and Development in the Preindustrial Era,* edited by Robert D. Mitchell, 87–104. Lexington: University Press of Kentucky, 1991.

Klett, Guy S., ed. *Minutes of the Presbyterian Church in America, 1706–1788.* Philadelphia: Presbyterian Historical Society, 1976.

Klingaman, David C. *Colonial Virginia's Coastwise and Grain Trade.* New York: Arno Press, 1975.

Kneebone, John T., et al., eds. *Dictionary of Virginia Biography.* 3 vols. to date. Richmond: Library of Virginia, 1998–.

Koons, Kenneth E. "'The Staple of Our Country': Wheat in the Regional Farm Economy of the Nineteenth-Century Valley of Virginia." In *After the Backcountry: Rural Life in the Great Valley of Virginia, 1800–1900,* edited by Kenneth E. Koons and Warren R. Hofstra, 3–20. Knoxville: University of Tennessee Press, 2000.

Kulikoff, Allan. *Tobacco and Slaves: The Development of Southern Cultures in the Chesapeake, 1680–1800.* Chapel Hill: University of North Carolina Press, 1986.

———. "The Transition to Capitalism in Rural America." *William and Mary Quarterly,* 3d ser., 46 (1989): 120–44.

Lapp, Dorothy, ed. *Records of the Courts of Chester County, Pennsylvania,* vol. 2. Danboro, Penn.: Patterson and White, 1972.

Landsman, Ned C. "Religion, Expansion, and Migration: The Cultural Background to Scottish and Irish Settlement in the Lehigh Valley." In *Backcountry Crucibles: The Lehigh Valley from Settlement to Steel,* edited by Jean R. Soderlund and Catherine S. Parzynski, 104–24. Bethlehem, Pa.: Lehigh University Press, 2008.

———. *Scotland and Its First American Colony, 1683–1765.* Princeton, N.J.: Princeton University Press, 1985.

Laurens, Henry. *The Papers of Henry Laurens.* Edited by Philip M. Hamer et al. 16 vols. Columbia: University of South Carolina Press, 1968–2003.

Lemon, James T. *The Best Poor Man's Country: A Geographical Study of Early Southeastern Pennsylvania.* Baltimore: Johns Hopkins University Press, 1972. Reprint New York: Norton, 1976.

Leyburn, James G. *The Scotch-Irish: A Social History.* Chapel Hill: University of North Carolina Press, 1962.

Lounsbury, Carl R. *The Courthouses of Early Virginia: An Architectural History.* Charlottesville: University of Virginia Press, 2005.

Lydon, James G. "Philadelphia's Commercial Expansion, 1720–1739." *Pennsylvania Magazine of History and Biography* 91 (1967): 401–18.

Mayhill, R. Thomas, comp. *Lancaster County, Pennsylvania Deed Abstracts and Revolutionary War Oaths of Allegiance.* Rev. ed. Knightstown, Ind.: Bookmark, 1973.

McCleskey, Turk. "Across the First Divide: Frontiers of Settlement and Culture in Augusta County, Virginia, 1738–1770." Ph.D. diss., College of William and Mary, 1990.

———. "The Price of Conformity: Class, Ethnicity, and Local Authority on the Colonial Virginia Frontier." In *Diversity and Accommodation: Essays on the Cultural Composition of the Virginia Frontier,* edited by Michael J. Puglisi, 213–26. Knoxville: University of Tennessee Press, 1997.

———. "Quarterly Courts in Backcountry Counties of Colonial Virginia." *Journal of Backcountry Studies* 7, no. 2 (2012): 47–57. http://libjournal.uncg.edu/ojs/index.php /jbc/article/view/570/330.

———. "Rich Land, Poor Prospects: Real Estate and the Formation of a Social Elite in Augusta County, Virginia, 1738–1770." *Virginia Magazine of History and Biography* 98 (1990): 449–86.

———. "Shadow Land: Provisional Real Estate Claims and Anglo-American Settlement in Southwestern Virginia." In *The Southern Colonial Backcountry: Interdisciplinary Perspectives on Frontier Communities,* edited by David Colin Crass et al., 56–68. Knoxville: University of Tennessee Press, 1998.

McCleskey, Turk, and James C. Squire. "Pennsylvania Credit in the Virginia Backcountry, 1746–1755." *Pennsylvania History* (forthcoming 2014).

McConnell, Michael N. *A Country in Between: The Upper Ohio Valley and Its Peoples, 1724–1774.* Lincoln: University of Nebraska Press, 1992.

McCusker, John J. "Colonial Tonnage Measurement: Five Philadelphia Merchant Ships as a Sample." *Journal of Economic History* 27 (1967): 82–91.

——. "How Much Is That in Real Money? A Historical Price Index for Use as a Deflator of Money Values in the Economy of the United States." *Proceedings of the American Antiquarian Society* 101 (October 1991): 297–373.

——. *Money and Exchange Rates in Europe and America, 1600–1775: A Handbook.* Chapel Hill: University of North Carolina Press, 1978.

McCusker, John J., and Russell R. Menard. *The Economy of British America, 1607–1789.* Rev. ed. Chapel Hill: University of North Carolina Press, 1991.

McDowell, William L., Jr., ed. *Colonial Records of South Carolina: Documents Relating to Indian Affairs, 1754–1765.* Columbia: South Carolina Department of Archives and History, 1970.

McIlwaine, H. R., et al., eds. *Executive Journals of the Council of Colonial Virginia.* 6 vols. Richmond: Virginia State Library, 1925–67.

——, eds. *Journals of the Council of the State of Virginia.* 3 vols. Richmond: Virginia State Library, 1931–52.

——, eds. *Journals of the House of Burgesses of Virginia, 1619–[1776].* 12 vols. Richmond: Virginia State Library, 1905–15.

Menard, Russell R. "Financing the Lowcountry Export Boom: Capital and Growth in Early Carolina." *William and Mary Quarterly,* 3d ser., 51 (1994): 659–76.

Merrell, James H. "Cultural Continuity among the Piscataway Indians of Colonial Maryland." *William and Mary Quarterly,* 3d ser., 36 (1979): 548–70.

Miller, Kerby A. "'Scotch-Irish' Myths and 'Irish' Identities in Eighteenth- and Nineteenth-Century America." In *New Perspectives on the Irish Diaspora,* edited by Charles Fanning, 75–92. Carbondale and Edwardsville: Southern Illinois University Press, 2000.

——. "Ulster Presbyterians and the 'Two Traditions' in Ireland and America." In *Making the Irish American: History and Heritage of the Irish in the United States,* edited by J. J. Lee and Marion R. Casey, 255–70. New York: New York University Press, 2006.

Mitchell, Robert D. *Commercialism and Frontier: Perspectives on the Early Shenandoah Valley.* Charlottesville: University Press of Virginia, 1977.

Moore, W. O. "The Largest Exporters of Deerskins from Charles Town, 1735–1775." *South Carolina Historical Magazine* 74 (1973): 144–50.

Morgan, Edmund S. *American Slavery, American Freedom: The Ordeal of Colonial Virginia.* New York: Norton, 1975.

——. "Slavery and Freedom: The American Paradox." *Journal of American History* 59 (1972): 5–29.

Morgan, Philip D. "Slave Life in Piedmont Virginia, 1720–1800." In *Colonial Chesapeake Society,* edited by Lois Green Carr, Philip D. Morgan, and Jean B. Russo, 433–84. Chapel Hill: University of North Carolina Press, 1988.

——. "Task and Gang Systems: The Organization of Labor on New World Plantations." In *Work and Labor in Early America,* edited by Stephen Innes, 189–220. Chapel Hill: University of North Carolina Press, 1988.

Morgan, Philip D., and Michael L. Nicholls. "Slaves in Piedmont Virginia, 1720–1790." *William and Mary Quarterly,* 3d ser., 46 (1989): 211–51.

Moss, Roger W. *Historic Houses of Philadelphia: A Tour of the Region's Museum Homes.* Philadelphia: University of Pennsylvania Press, 1998.

Mulcahy, Matthew. "The 'Great Fire' of 1740 and the Politics of Disaster Relief in Colonial Charleston." *South Carolina Historical Magazine* 99 (1998): 135–57.

Mullin, Gerald W. *Flight and Rebellion: Slave Resistance in Eighteenth-Century Virginia.* Oxford: Oxford University Press, 1972.

Munger, Donna Bingham. *Pennsylvania Land Records: A History and Guide for Research.* Wilmington, Del.: Scholarly Resources, 1991.

Nash, Gary B. *Forging Freedom: The Formation of Philadelphia's Black Community, 1720–1840.* Cambridge, Mass.: Harvard University Press, 1988.

———. "Slaves and Slaveowners in Colonial Philadelphia." *William and Mary Quarterly,* 3d ser., 30 (1973): 223–56.

Nelson, John K. *A Blessed Company: Parishes, Parsons, and Parishioners in Anglican Virginia, 1690–1776.* Chapel Hill: University of North Carolina Press, 2001.

Nelson, Thomas Forsythe. *Report on the Chalkley Manuscripts.* Washington, D.C.: National Society, Daughters of the American Revolution, 1912.

Nicholls, Michael L. "Passing through This Troublesome World: Free Blacks in the Early Southside." *Virginia Magazine of History and Biography* 92 (1984): 50–70.

Norton, Mary Beth. "Gender and Defamation in Seventeenth-Century Maryland." *William and Mary Quarterly,* 3d ser., 44 (1987): 3–39.

Nixdorf, George. "Memoir of George Nixdorf" (1700–1785), http://bdhp.moravian.edu /personal_papers/memoirs/nixdorf/nixdorf.html.

[Nyberg, Laurentius.] "The *Irene* in Peril at Sea." *This Month in Moravian History* 43 (May 2009).

Oliphant, John. *Peace and War on the Anglo-Cherokee Frontier, 1756–63.* Baton Rouge: Louisiana State University Press, 2001.

Palmer, William P., et al., eds. *Calendar of Virginia State Papers and Other Manuscripts, 1652–1781, Preserved in the Capitol at Richmond.* 11 vols. Richmond: Virginia State Library, 1875–93. Reprint New York: Kraus, 1968.

Patterson, Orlando. *The Sociology of Slavery: An Analysis of the Origins, Development and Structure of Negro Slave Society in Jamaica.* Cranbury, N.J.: Fairleigh Dickinson University Press, 1967.

Pendleton, Edmund. *The Letters and Papers of Edmund Pendleton,* vol. 1. Edited by David John Mays. Charlottesville: University Press of Virginia, 1967.

Pennsylvania Archives. 9 series, 138 vols. Harrisburg and Philadelphia: various publishers, 1852–1949.

"Pennsylvania Marriage Licenses, Issued by Gov. James Hamilton, 1748–1752." *Pennsylvania Magazine of History and Biography* 32 (1908): 71–87, 233–36, 345–50, 471–86.

Pettengill, Ray Waldron, ed. *Letters from America, 1776–1779: Being Letters of Brunswick, Hessian, and Waldeck Officers with the British Armies during the Revolution.* Boston: Houghton Mifflin, 1924.

Price, Jacob M. "What Did Merchants Do? Reflections on British Overseas Trade, 1660–1790." *Journal of Economic History* 49 (1989): 267–84.

Rawle, William B. "Laurel Hill and Some Colonial Dames Who Once Lived There." *Pennsylvania Magazine of History and Biography* 35 (1911): 385–414.

Records of the Presbyterian Church in the United States of America. Philadelphia: Presbyterian Board of Publication, 1841.

Records of the Moravians in North Carolina, vol. 1, 1752–1771. Raleigh: North Carolina Historical Commission, 1922.

Redd, John. "Reminiscences of Western Virginia, 1770–1790." Virginia Magazine of History and Biography 6 (1899): 337–46; 7 (1899–1900):1–16, 113–28, 242–53.

Rediker, Marcus. Between the Devil and the Deep Blue Sea: Merchant Seamen, Pirates, and the Anglo-American Maritime World, 1700–1750. New York: Cambridge University Press, 1987.

——— "'Under the Banner of King Death': The Social World of Anglo-American Pirates, 1716 to 1726." William and Mary Quarterly, 3d ser., 38 (1981): 203–27.

Reinberger, Mark, and Elizabeth McLean. "Isaac Norris's Fairhill: Architecture, Landscape, and Quaker Ideals in a Philadelphia Colonial Country Seat." Winterthur Portfolio 32 (1997): 243–74.

Richter, Caroline Julie. "A Community and Its Neighborhoods: Charles Parish, York County, Virginia, 1630–1740." Ph.D. diss., College of William and Mary, 1992.

Riedesel, Friederike Charlotte Luise, Freifrau von. Letters and Memoirs Relating to the War of American Independence, and the Capture of the German Troops at Saratoga. New York: G. and C. Carvill, 1827.

Roeber, A. G. Faithful Magistrates and Republican Lawyers: Creators of Virginia Legal Culture, 1680–1810. Chapel Hill: University of North Carolina Press, 1981.

———. Palatines, Liberty, and Property: German Lutherans in Colonial British America. Baltimore: Johns Hopkins University Press, 1993.

Rose, Robert. The Diary of Robert Rose: A View of Virginia by a Scottish Colonial Parson, 1746–1751. Edited by Ralph Emmett Fall. Verona, Va.: McClure Press, 1977.

Rutman, Darrett B., and Anita H. Rutman. A Place in Time: Middlesex County, Virginia, 1650–1750. New York: Norton, 1984.

Salley, A. S., Jr., ed. Register of St. Philip's Parish, Charles Town, South Carolina, 1720–1758. Charleston: Walker, Evans, and Cogswell, 1904.

Salley, John Peter. "A Brief Account of the Travels of John Peter Salley, a German who Lives in the County of Augusta in Virginia." In Fairfax Harrison, "The Virginians on the Ohio and the Mississippi in 1742." Virginia Magazine of History and Biography 30 (1922): 203–22.

Sampson, Richard. Escape in America: The British Convention Prisoners 1777–1783. Chippenham, Wiltshire, U.K.: Picton, 1995.

Saunders, William L., ed. The Colonial Records of North Carolina, vol. 8. Raleigh: P. M. Hale, 1890.

Schwarz, Philip J. Twice Condemned: Slaves and the Criminal Laws of Virginia, 1705–1865. Baton Rouge: Louisiana State University Press, 1988.

Scott, Kenneth. "Sufferers in the Charleston Fire of 1740." South Carolina Historical Magazine 64 (1963): 203–11.

Sellers, Leila. Charleston Business on the Eve of the American Revolution. Chapel Hill: University of North Carolina Press, 1934.

Sensbach, Jon F. A Separate Canaan: The Making of an Afro-Moravian World in North Carolina, 1763–1840. Chapel Hill: University of North Carolina Press, 1998.

"Ship Registers for the Port of Philadelphia, 1726–1775." *Pennsylvania Magazine of History and Biography* 23 (1899): 254–64, 370–85, 498–515; 24 (1900): 108–15, 212–23, 348–66, 500–19; 25 (1901): 118–31, 266–81, 400–416, 560–74; 26 (1902): 126–43, 280–84, 390–400, 470–75; 27 (1903): 94–107, 238–47, 346–70, 482–98; 28 (1904): 84–100, 218–35, 346–74, 470–507.

Silver, Timothy. *A New Face on the Countryside: Indians, Colonists, and Slaves in the South Atlantic Forests, 1500–1800.* Cambridge: Cambridge University Press, 1990.

Simmons, J. Susanne, and Nancy T. Sorrels. "Slave Hire and the Development of Slavery in Augusta County, Virginia." In *After the Backcountry: Rural Life in the Great Valley of Virginia, 1800–1900,* edited by Kenneth E. Koons and Warren R. Hofstra, 169–84. Knoxville: University of Tennessee Press, 2000.

Sirmans, M. Eugene. "The South Carolina Royal Council, 1720–1763." *William and Mary Quarterly,* 3d ser., 18 (1961): 373–92.

Smith, Clifford Neal. *British and German Deserters, Dischargees, and Prisoners of War Who May Have Remained in Canada and the United States, 1774–1783: Part 1 and Part 2 [and] Deserters and Disbanded Soldiers from British, German, and Loyalist Military Units in the South, 1782.* Baltimore: Clearfield, 2004.

Soderlund, Jean R., ed. *William Penn and the Founding of Pennsylvania, 1680–1684: A Documentary History.* Philadelphia: University of Pennsylvania Press, 1983.

Specht, Johann Friederich. *The Specht Journal: A Military Journal of the Burgoyne Campaign.* Edited by Mary C. Lynn, translated by Helga Doblin. Westport, Conn.: Greenwood Press, 1995.

Spero, Patrick. "The Conojocular War: The Politics of Colonial Competition, 1732–1737." *Pennsylvania Magazine of History and Biography* 136 (2012): 365–403.

Statutes at Large of Pennsylvania from 1682 to 1801, The, vol. 4 (1724–1744). Harrisburg, Penn.: Clarence M. Busch, 1897.

Stumpf, Stuart O. "Implications of King George's War for the Charleston Mercantile Community." *South Carolina Historical Magazine* 77 (1976): 161–88.

Sturtz, Linda L. "The Ladies and the Lottery: Elite Women's Gambling in Eighteenth-Century Virginia." *Virginia Magazine of History and Biography* 104 (1996): 165–84.

Taylor, Alan. *The Civil War of 1812: American Citizens, British Subjects, Irish Rebels, and Indian Allies.* New York: Knopf, 2010.

Terry, Gail S. "Family Empires: A Frontier Elite in Virginia and Kentucky, 1740–1815." Ph.D. diss., College of William and Mary, 1992.

Thayer, Theodore. *Israel Pemberton, King of the Quakers.* Philadelphia: Historical Society of Pennsylvania, 1943.

Thornton, John K. "African Dimensions of the Stono Rebellion." *American Historical Review* 96 (1991): 1101–13.

Tiedemann, Joseph S. "Interconnected Communities: The Middle Colonies on the Eve of the American Revolution." *Pennsylvania History: A Journal of Mid-Atlantic Studies* 76 (Winter 2009): 1–41.

Tillson, Albert H., Jr. *Gentry and Common Folk: Political Culture on a Virginia Frontier.* Lexington: University Press of Kentucky, 1991.

Tocqueville, Alexis de. *Democracy in America.* Edited and translated by Harvey C. Mansfield and Delba Winthrop. Chicago: University of Chicago Press, 2000.

Tolles, Frederick B. *Meeting House and Counting House: The Quaker Merchants of Colonial Philadelphia, 1682–1763.* Chapel Hill: University of North Carolina Press, 1948. Reprint New York: Norton, 1963.

Tomlins, Christopher L., and Bruce H. Mann, eds. *The Many Legalities of Early America.* Chapel Hill: University of North Carolina Press, 2001.

Trans-Atlantic Slave Trade Database, The. http://www.slavevoyages.org/.

Turner, Frederick Jackson. "The Significance of the Frontier in American History." In *The Frontier in American History,* 1–38. New York: Holt, Rinehart, and Winston, 1920. Reprint Malabar, Fla.: Robert E. Krieger, 1985.

"Virginia Quitrent Roles, 1704 (Continued)." *Virginia Magazine of History and Biography* 32 (1924): 144–58.

Waddell, Joseph A. *Annals of Augusta County, Virginia, from 1726 to 1871,* 2nd ed. Staunton, Va.: C. Russell Caldwell, 1902.

Wainwright, Nicholas B. "Scull and Heap's Map of Philadelphia." *Pennsylvania Magazine of History and Biography* 81 (1957): 69–75.

Walsh, Lorena S. "Community Networks in the Early Chesapeake." In *Colonial Chesapeake Society,* edited by Lois Green Carr, Philip D. Morgan, and Jean B. Russo, 200–241. Chapel Hill: University of North Carolina Press, 1988.

———. "Slave Life, Slave Society, and Tobacco Production in the Tidewater Chesapeake, 1620–1820." In *Cultivation and Culture: Labor and the Shaping of Slave Life in the Americas,* edited by Ira Berlin and Philip D. Morgan, 170–99. Charlottesville: University Press of Virginia, 1993.

Ward, Matthew C. *Breaking the Backcountry: The Seven Years' War in Virginia and Pennsylvania, 1754–1765.* Pittsburgh: University of Pittsburgh Press, 2003.

Warren, Mary Bondurant, ed. *South Carolina Jury Lists, 1718 through 1783.* Danielsville, Ga.: Heritage Papers, 1977.

Washington, George. *The Diaries of George Washington.* Edited by Donald Jackson and Dorothy Twohig. 6 vols. Charlottesville: University Press of Virginia, 1976–79.

———. *The Papers of George Washington, Colonial Series.* Edited by W. W. Abbot et al. 10 vols. Charlottesville: University Press of Virginia, 1983–95.

Webb, George. *The Office and Authority of a Justice of Peace.* Williamsburg, Va.: William Parks, 1736. Facsimile ed. Holmes Beach, Fla.: William W. Gaunt and Sons, 1969.

White, Richard. *The Middle Ground: Indians, Empires, and Republics in the Great Lakes Region, 1650–1815.* Cambridge: Cambridge University Press, 1991.

Whittenburg, James P. "Planters, Merchants, and Lawyers: Social Change and the Origins of the North Carolina Regulation." *William and Mary Quarterly,* 3d ser., 34 (1977): 215–38.

Williams, Samuel Cole, ed. *Lieut. Henry Timberlake's Memoirs, 1756–1765.* Johnson City, Tenn.: Watauga Press, 1927.

Wilson, Howard McKnight. *The Tinkling Spring, Headwater of Freedom: A Study of the Church and Her People, 1732–1952.* Richmond, Va.: Garrett and Massie, 1954.

Winfree, Waverly K., comp. *The Laws of Virginia: Being a Supplement to Hening's The Statutes at Large, 1700–1750.* Richmond: Virginia State Library, 1971.

Withers, Alexander Scott. *Chronicles of Border Warfare; or, A History of the Settlement by* the Whites, of North-Western Virginia, and of the Indian Wars and Massacres in that section of the State. Clarksburg, Va.: J. Israel, 1831.

Wood, Jerome H., Jr. *Conestoga Crossroads: Lancaster, Pennsylvania 1730–1790.* Harrisburg: Pennsylvania Historical and Museum Commission, 1979.

Woods, Michael. "The Culture of Credit in Colonial Charleston." *South Carolina Historical Magazine* 99 (1998): 358–80.

Wright, Robert E. "Ground Rents against Populist Historiography: Mid-Atlantic Land Tenure, 1750–1882." *Journal of Interdisciplinary History* 29 (1998): 23–42.

Wust, Klaus. *The Virginia Germans.* Charlottesville: University Press of Virginia, 1969.

Zinzendorf, Count [*sic*]. *Sixteen Discourses On the Redemption of Man By the Death of Christ.* London: James Hutton, 1740.

———. *Sixteen Discourses on Jesus Christ Our Lord.* 2nd ed. London: William Bowyer, 1750.

Index

bonds for appearance, 112
Borden, Benjamin, Jr., 212
Borden's Land, 53, 81–83, 92, 102, 151, 157
Bowman, Ann, 212
Bowman, George, 212
Bowyer, John, 148, 225
Bowyer, Michael, 149, 152
Bowyer, Thomas, 54
Bowyer, William, 106
Boyd, Alexander, 131, 132
Braddock, Edward, 99, 102
Breckinridge, Robert, 115
Brewster, Samuel, 18
Bristol Township, Pennsylvania, 14
Brown, John, 54, 88–91, 93, 101, 132, 161, 193
Brunswick County, Virginia, 166
Buchanan, James, 92
Buchanan, John, 107, 131, 162
Burgoyne, John, 152
Butler (free black), 204
Byrd, William, III, 108, 111

Cabeen, William, 54
Caesar (slave), 67
Call, Susanna, 154
Campbell, Malcolm, 107
Carr, William, 114, 165, 167, 204
Carruthers, William, 85, 91
carters, 52, 73, 108–9, 161
Carvin, William, 128, 212, 214
Catawba (tribe), 96
Cather/Cauther, Betty, 205
Cather/Cauther, Rose, 205
Cather/Cauther, Sarah, 205
Champe, John, 125
Chapman, James, 154
charcoal use and production, 67–68
Charles (slave), 211
Charleston, South Carolina: fire disaster in, 33–34; Montgomery (Hugh) in, 111; as shipping port, 24–25; Shute (Joseph) as merchant in, 27–49, 177–83
Charlotte County, Virginia, 166
Cherokee (tribe), 52, 100–103, 160

Cherokee War (1760–1761), 92–93, 98
Christian, Israel: Davis's links to, 57; flour surplus exported by, 151; and Montgomery's suit against Tarr, 53, 109, 112–13; and Moore's presentment, 147; and Tom's murder trial, 142
Christian, William, 57
Church (slave), 211
Coburn, James, 214
Colebrookdale Furnace, 19, 74
colliers, 68
Conestoga Creek Bridge lottery, 53–54
Convention Army, 152–56
convicts. See indentured servants
Cooper, James Fenimore, 158
copper mining, 17–18, 60, 70
Cossens, Edmond, 39
Coventry Forge, 19, 51, 69, 73
Craig, John, 120, 132
Craighead, Alexander, 76, 132
credit risks, 37, 111–14
Crokatt, John, 39
Crow, William, 54
Cudjo (slave), 74
Cuffy (slave), 211
Cummings, Charles, 132

Daniel (slave), 135
Davis, Christiana, 58
Davis, Christian Shute, 17, 19, 22, 60
Davis, Edward, 131, 132
Davis, Samson, 17, 19, 22, 60, 160
Davis, William: in Augusta County, 149; as business manager, 19, 50–54, 60; career of, 3, 22, 50–62; carting business of, 52, 108–9, 161; copper mine inherited by, 60; as executor of Shute's estate, 3, 22, 44; mobility of, 160–61; real estate investments by, 55–56, 161–62; as skinner, 54–58; Tarr's payments for freedom received by, 51–52, 56–57, 78, 111
Dean, William, 88
Dinwiddie, Robert, 98, 124, 140
Doggett, Richard, 136
Dolphin (Shute vessel), 30, 38

Donegal Presbytery, 77, 87
Donnelly, Charles, 107, 224
Douglass, Frederick, 71
Dove (Shute vessel), 26, 31–32
Dover (slave), 211
Dowling, Timothy, 9
Drapers Meadow, 102
Drayton, Glen, 132
Dryden, David, 85

Edgerly Point, Pennsylvania, 14, 18
Elliott, Thomas, 26
Endeavour (Shute vessel), 30, 32, 38
European luxury items, 29
exchange rates, 35

Fairfax, Lord, 83
Farmer (slave), 142
Fauquier, Francis, 53
First Presbyterian Church, Philadelphia, 76
Fleming, Thomas, 26
Fleming, William, 141, 149, 163
Fort Necessity, 99
Fox, Joseph, 45
Franklin, Benjamin, 73, 75
Fredley, Edward/Edmund, 205
free blacks in Augusta County: lives of, 114–20, 203–9; and racial attitudes, 165–70; scrutiny of, 133–34. *See also specific individuals*
frontier land titles, 21
Fry, Joshua, 162
fugitive slaves, 74, 134, 136
Fulton, Thomas, 131
fur trade, 54–58, 190

Gadsden, Christopher, 32, 43
Galloway, Joseph, 45
Gap Mine, 17–18, 70, 76
Gay, Samuel, 210–11
George Town, South Carolina, 28, 33, 182
German-speaking colonists, 3, 5, 20, 66–67, 80, 129
Gilbert, Felix, 127, 132

Gilmore, William, 72
Givens, James, 214
Glegg, John, 32
Gloster (slave), 126, 127, 133–34, 136
Gottlob, Brother, 5
Grace, Robert, 51
grand juries, 85
Gray, Isaac, 157
Gray, Jacob, 80, 157, 220–22, 224
Greenlee, Mary McDowell, 81, 85
Greer, Andrew, 148, 225
Gregorian calendar, 7–8

Halifax County, Virginia, 166
Hall, Andrew, 92
Hall, Edward, 135
Hamilton, Andrew, 17
Hampton (slave), 138
Hannah (slave), 212
Hannibal (slave), 137
Hansen, John, 67, 68, 69, 71, 72, 74, 103
Harman, Adam, 96
Harrison, John, 139, 140–43
Harry (slave), 212
Hart, Silas, 213
Harvie, John, 153
Havana, Cuba, 39–40
Hays, Rebecca, 215
hemp production, 129, 199
Henning, Thomas, 29–30, 31, 38
Henretta, James A., 61
Herculus, John, 72–73
Hext, David, 38
Hopkins, John, 213
Hurley, Hannah, 205
Huston, Robert, 81, 90

indentured servants, 23, 48, 67, 73, 78, 118, 124, 134, 135, 138, 139, 147
Indian raids and wars, 95–109; and frontier competition, 98–99; refugees from, 99, 103–7; in Southwest Virginia, 99–100, 197, 202; Tarr affected by, 5, 100–103, 107–9, 140–41
Industry (Shute vessel), 38–39

of, 3; ironworking operations of, 18–20; Lancaster County interests of, 20–22; marriages of, 14–15; mining and quarrying businesses of, 17–18, 159; mobility of, 2–3, 159; Ned as slave of, 69–70, 72; real estate investments of, 14, 15–16, 172–74; shipping business of, 24–26; slaves' disposition in will of, 51–52, 77–78, 111

Shute, Thomas, Jr., 22, 160

Shute, Thomas (nephew to Joseph), 38, 41, 43

Shute, William (father of Thomas), 14

Shute, William (son of Thomas), 14, 22, 59–60, 160

Shute's Delight (Shute's Folly), 33, 43, 62

Shute's Plantation, 45

Shute's Wharf (Charleston), 32

Silvia (slave), 214

Simpson, Molly, 207

Skillern, William, 132

slavery: in Augusta County, 123–43, 198–201, 210–16; cultural origins of participants in, 129–33; economics of, 125–29; and mobility, 163–64; and racial attitudes, 165–70; and servile backlash, 133–40; Shute family's use of, 23–24, 48–49; and unsupervised slaves, 74, 134; violence against masters, 137–40

Smiley, John, 118, 149

Smith, Betty, 117, 207

Smith, Daniel, 131, 152

Smith, Esther, 117, 207

Smith, John, 117, 207–8

Smith, Nicholas, 115–18, 167, 169, 208

Smith, Nicholas, Jr., 115, 117, 208

Smith, Peter, 115, 117, 208

Smith, Sophia, 115, 117, 208

Smith, Thomas, 39

Smith, Tobias, 210–11

Smollett, Tobias, 2

smuggling, 39–40, 46

South Carolina Gazette: advertisements in, 29; bankruptcy advertisements in, 42–43; on gold and silver availability, 35

Spangenberg, August Gottlieb, 76

Specht, Johann Friederich, 153

speculators, 21–22

Stagg, John, 139

Stalnaker, Samuel, 99–100, 160

Staunton: and Montgomery's suit against Tarr, 1–2; real estate investments in, 56; Tarr moves to, 107–9

Steel, James, 17, 37

Steel, Rebecca, 48

Stevenson, Andrew, 72, 93

Stevenson, George, 72, 93, 196, 222–24

stone quarrying, 17–18, 45, 159

Strand (free black), 208

Stuart, Alexander, 151

Stuart, Thomas, 151, 152

Swift (slave), 128

Tarr, Edward: alcohol sold illegally by, 106; domestic arrangements of, 104–7, 145–47; freedom purchased by, 3–4, 6, 51–52, 56–57, 77–78, 111; as freeholder, 3–4, 6, 79–94; and Indian raids and wars, 5, 100–103, 107–9; land ownership by, 80, 91–93, 150–52, 194–95; lawsuits by and against, 217–25; marriage of, 6, 86–87, 168; Montgomery's suit against, 1–2, 110, 111–14; move to Staunton, 107–9; productivity of, 93–94, 196; and Timber Ridge Presbyterian Church, 89–91. *See also* Ned (slave)

Taylor, William, 128

Teas, Joseph, 126, 127, 133, 215–16

Thompson, Mary Patton, 213

Thompson, William, 213

Timber Ridge Presbyterian Church, 4, 80–81, 87–91, 193

Tocqueville, Alexis de, 158

Todd, John, 132

Todd, William, 220–22, 224

Tom (slave), 137, 141–45

transatlantic slave trade, 131

Trimble, James, 210–11

Trimble, John, 131

Turner, Frederick Jackson, 158

Twig, John, 131–32

Ulster Scots, 7

Vance, Joseph, 106
Vause's Fort, 103, 163
Victory (Shute vessel), 39

Warwick Furnace, 19, 51, 69, 71
Washington, George, 98, 99
Waters, Murty, 216
Whiteside, Moses, 132
Whitley, Paul, 136
Will (slave), 131, 214
Williams, William, 216
Wilpart, John David, 119
Wilson, George, 56, 112, 115

Wilson, William, 118
Winyah Bay, 33
Witter, John, 26
Woods, Richard, 83, 84, 106
Wragg, Samuel, 44

yeomen: affluence level of, 13; Davis
   identified as, 51; dilemma of, 58–62, 164;
   mobility of, 2–3, 164; Shute's (Thomas)
   career as, 13–26
Young, James, 209
Young, Ludwick, 214
Young, William, 161

Zinzendorf, Nicholas Ludwig von, 91

Early American Histories

A series of studies on early modern North America and the Caribbean from 1500 to 1815, Early American Histories promises innovative research and analysis of foundational questions central to the work of scholars and teachers of American, British, and Atlantic history—books that bring the early American world into focus.

Douglas Bradburn and John C. Coombs, editors
Early Modern Virginia: Reconsidering the Old Dominion

Denver Brunsman
The Evil Necessity: British Naval Impressment in the Eighteenth-Century Atlantic World

Jack P. Greene
Creating the British Atlantic: Essays on Transplantation, Adaptation, and Continuity

James Corbett David
Dunmore's New World: The Extraordinary Life of a Royal Governor in Revolutionary America—with Jacobites, Counterfeiters, Land Schemes, Shipwrecks, Scalping, Indian Politics, Runaway Slaves, and Two Illegal Royal Weddings

Turk McCleskey
The Road to Black Ned's Forge: A Story of Race, Sex, and Trade on the Colonial American Frontier